Translator : Jay Chung

Editors : Shawn Sanders / Kevin P. Croall

Production Artist : Chris Lee

US Cover Design : Hung-Ya Lin

Production Manager : Janice Chang

Art Director : Yuki Chung

Marketing : Nicole Curry

President : Robin Kuo

NOW Volume 4 © 2002 by Park Sung Woo
All rights reserved. This English Edition
published by arrangement with Seoul
Cultural Publishers Inc. through Shin Won
Agency Co.

English edition © 2004
by ComicsOne Corporation.
All rights reserved.

Publisher
ComicsOne Corporation
48531 Warm Springs Blvd., Suite 408
Fremont, CA 94539
www.ComicsOne.com

First Edition: June 2004
ISBN 1-58899-330-2

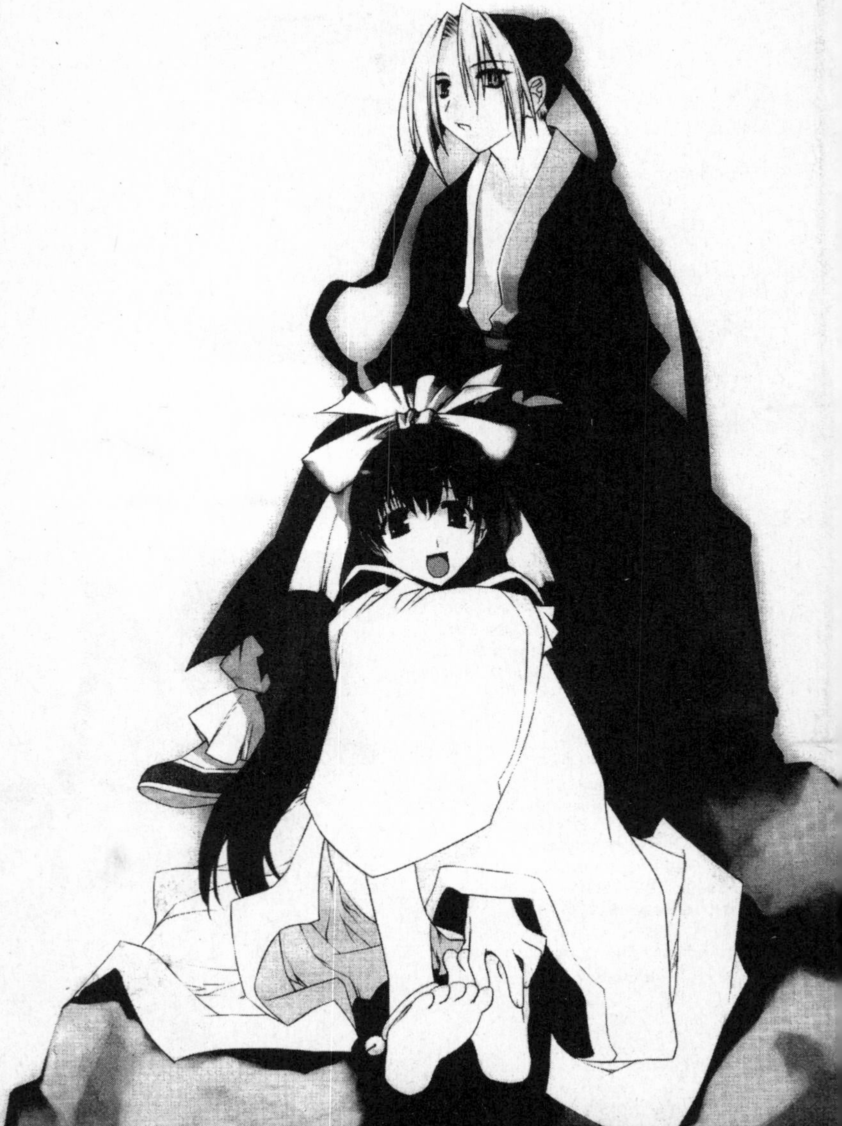

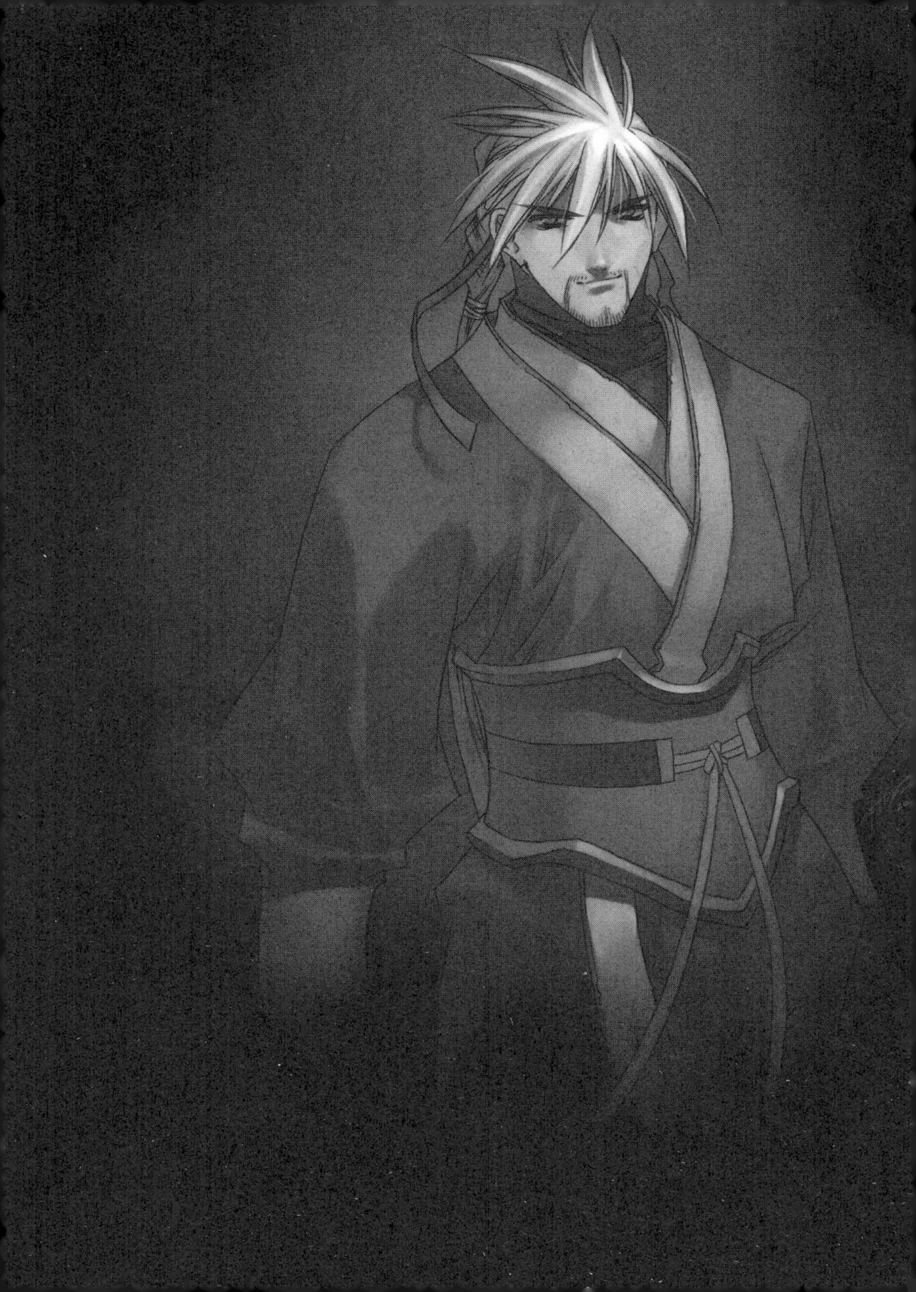

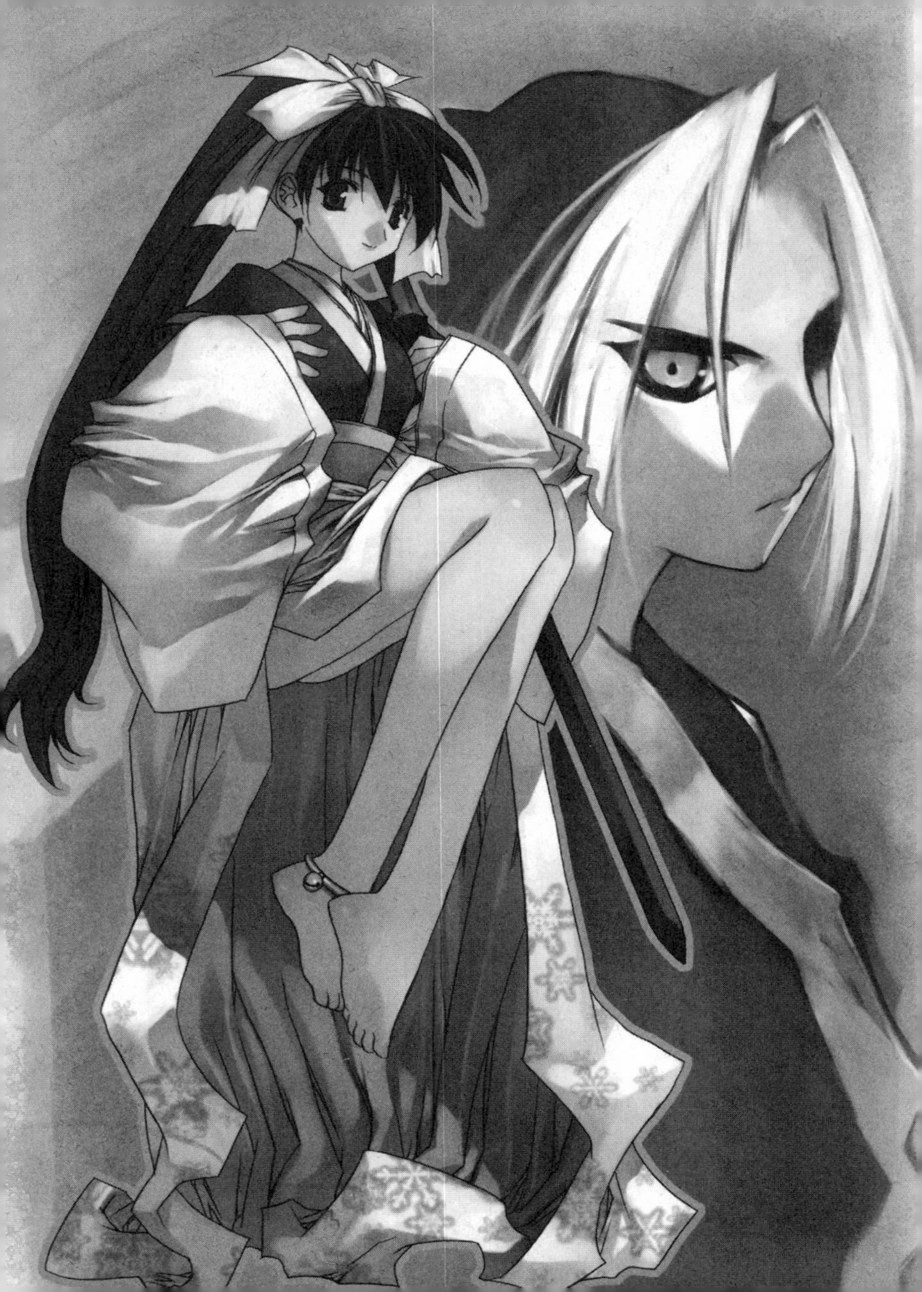

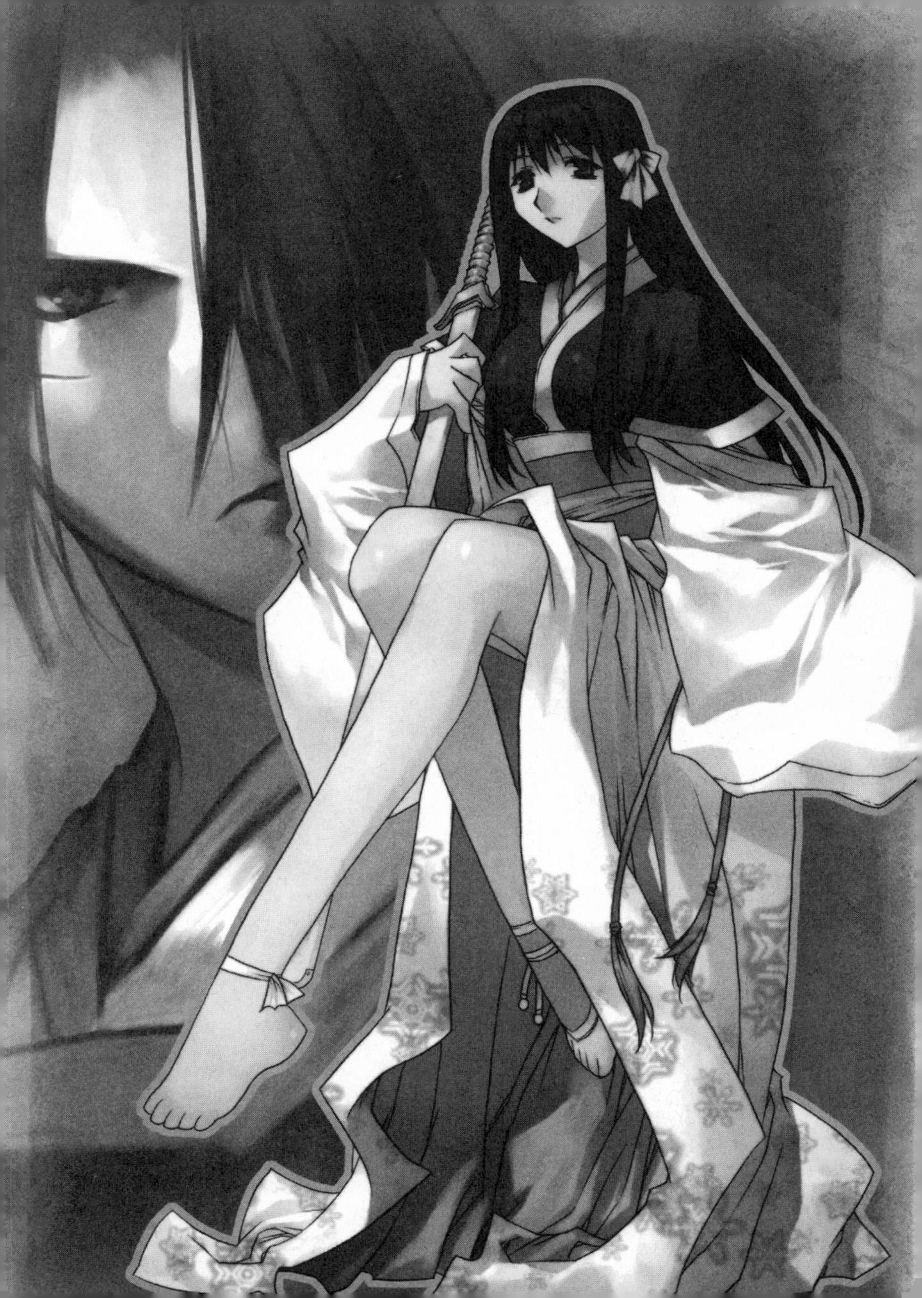

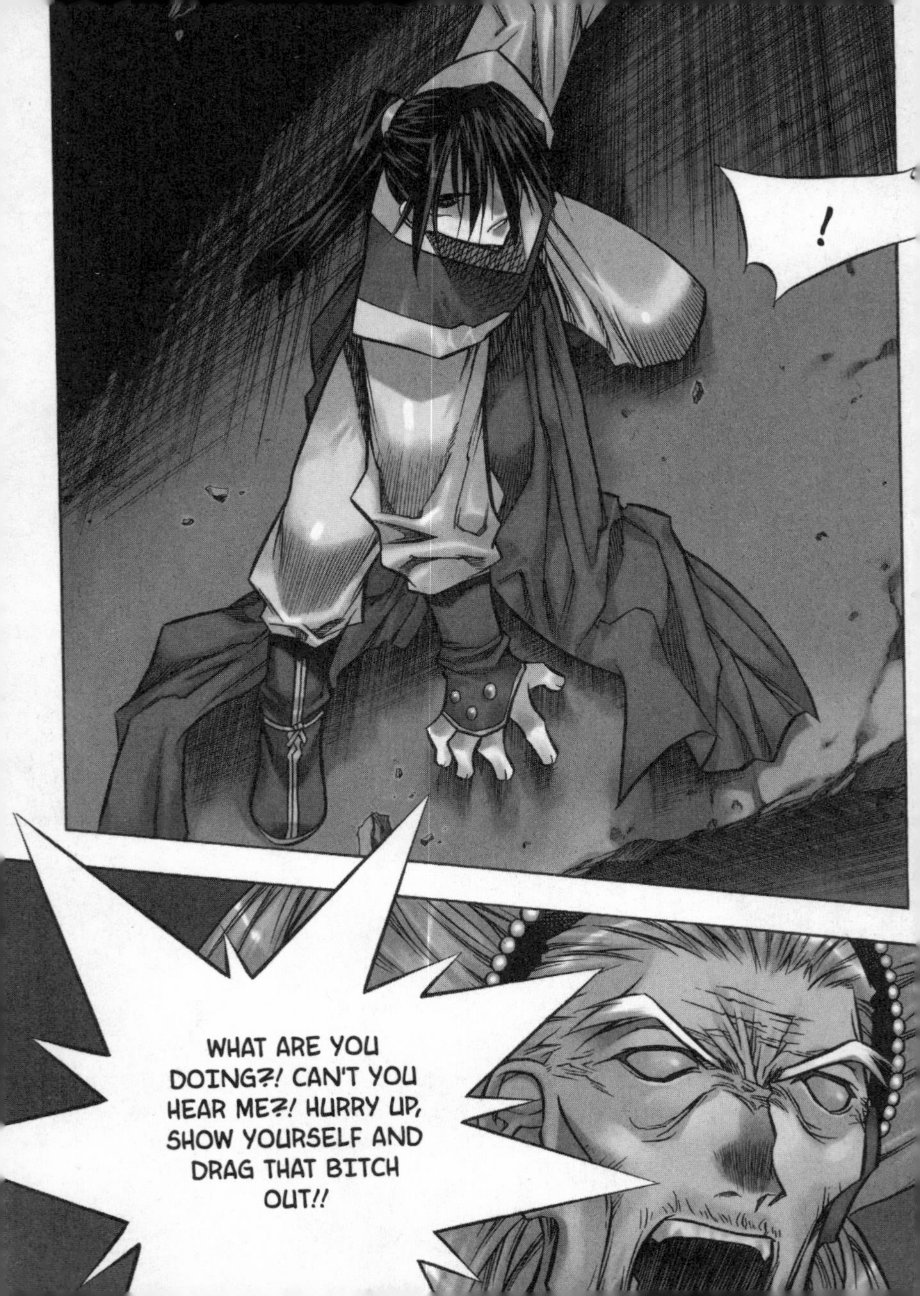
!
WHAT ARE YOU DOING?! CAN'T YOU HEAR ME?! HURRY UP, SHOW YOURSELF AND DRAG THAT BITCH OUT!!

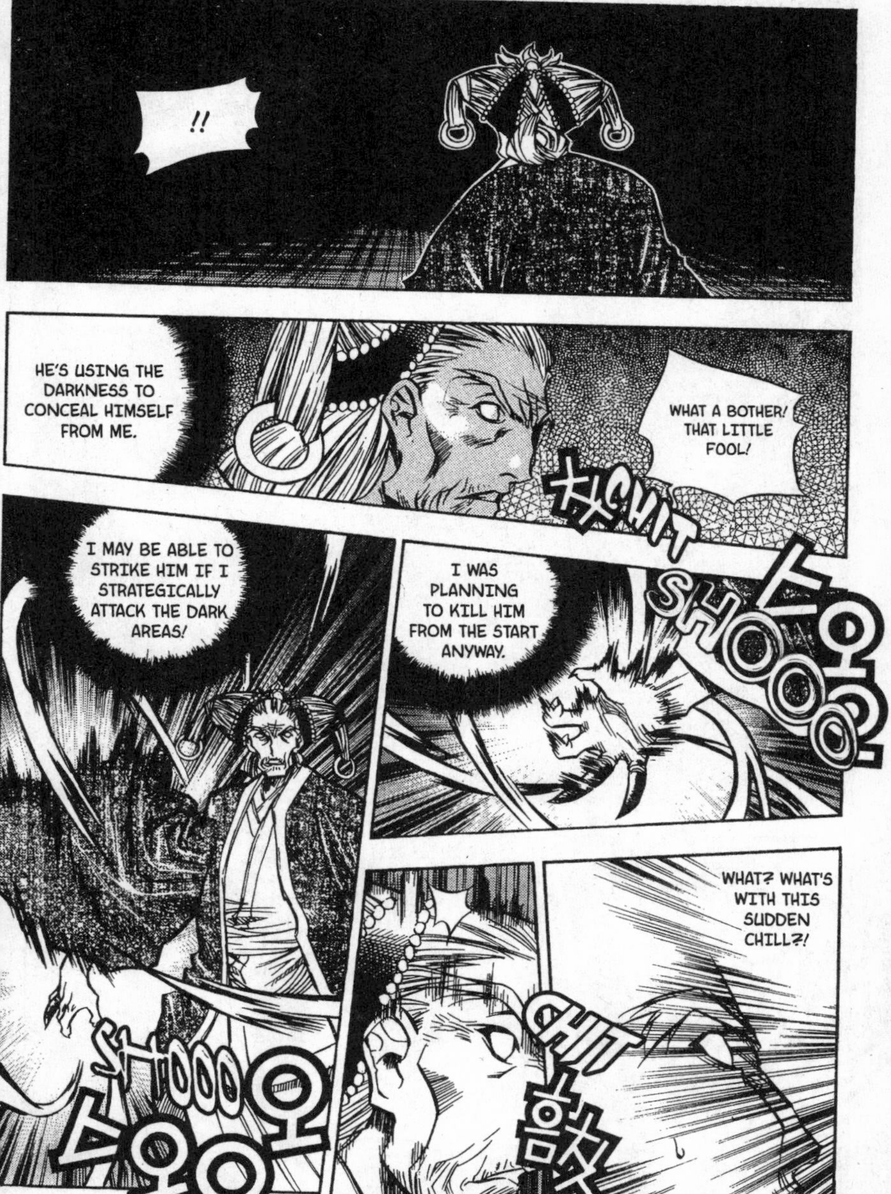
!!
HE'S USING THE DARKNESS TO CONCEAL HIMSELF FROM ME.
WHAT A BOTHER! THAT LITTLE FOOL!
CHIT
I MAY BE ABLE TO STRIKE HIM IF I STRATEGICALLY ATTACK THE DARK AREAS!
I WAS PLANNING TO KILL HIM FROM THE START ANYWAY.
SHOOOO!
SHOOOO!
WHAT? WHAT'S WITH THIS SUDDEN CHILL?!
CHIT

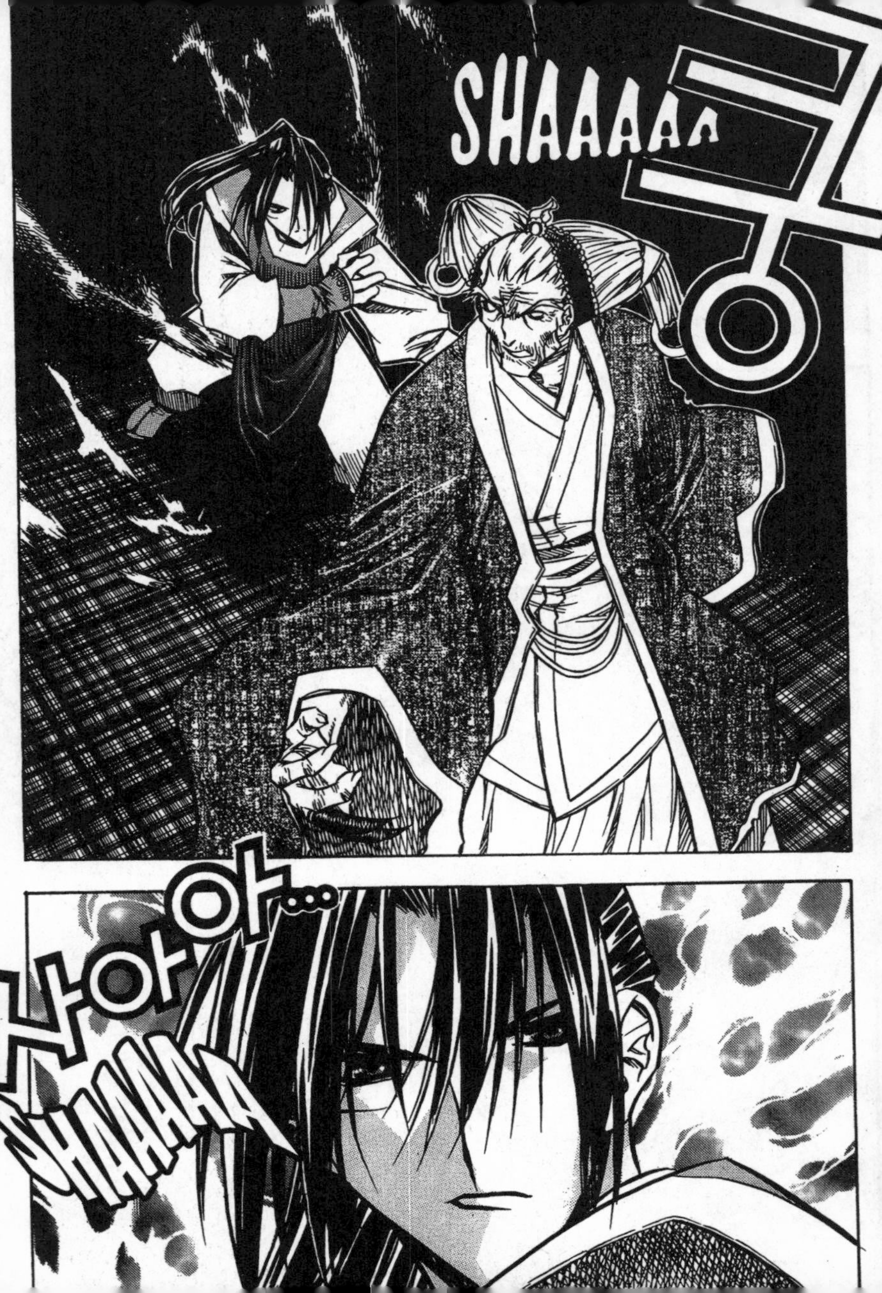
SHAAAAA
SHAAAAA

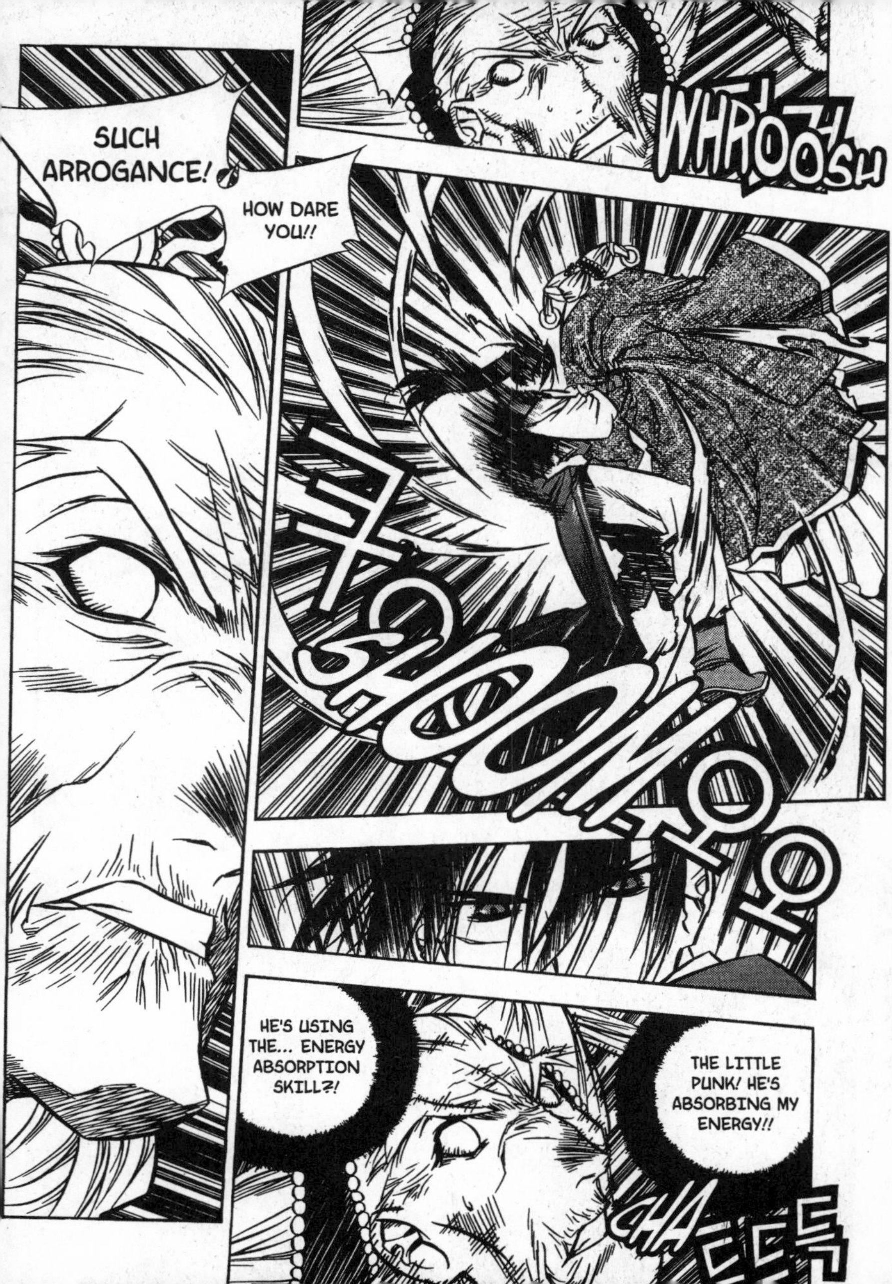
SUCH ARROGANCE!
HOW DARE YOU!!
WHROOSH
HE'S USING THE... ENERGY ABSORPTION SKILL?!
THE LITTLE PUNK! HE'S ABSORBING MY ENERGY!!
CHA

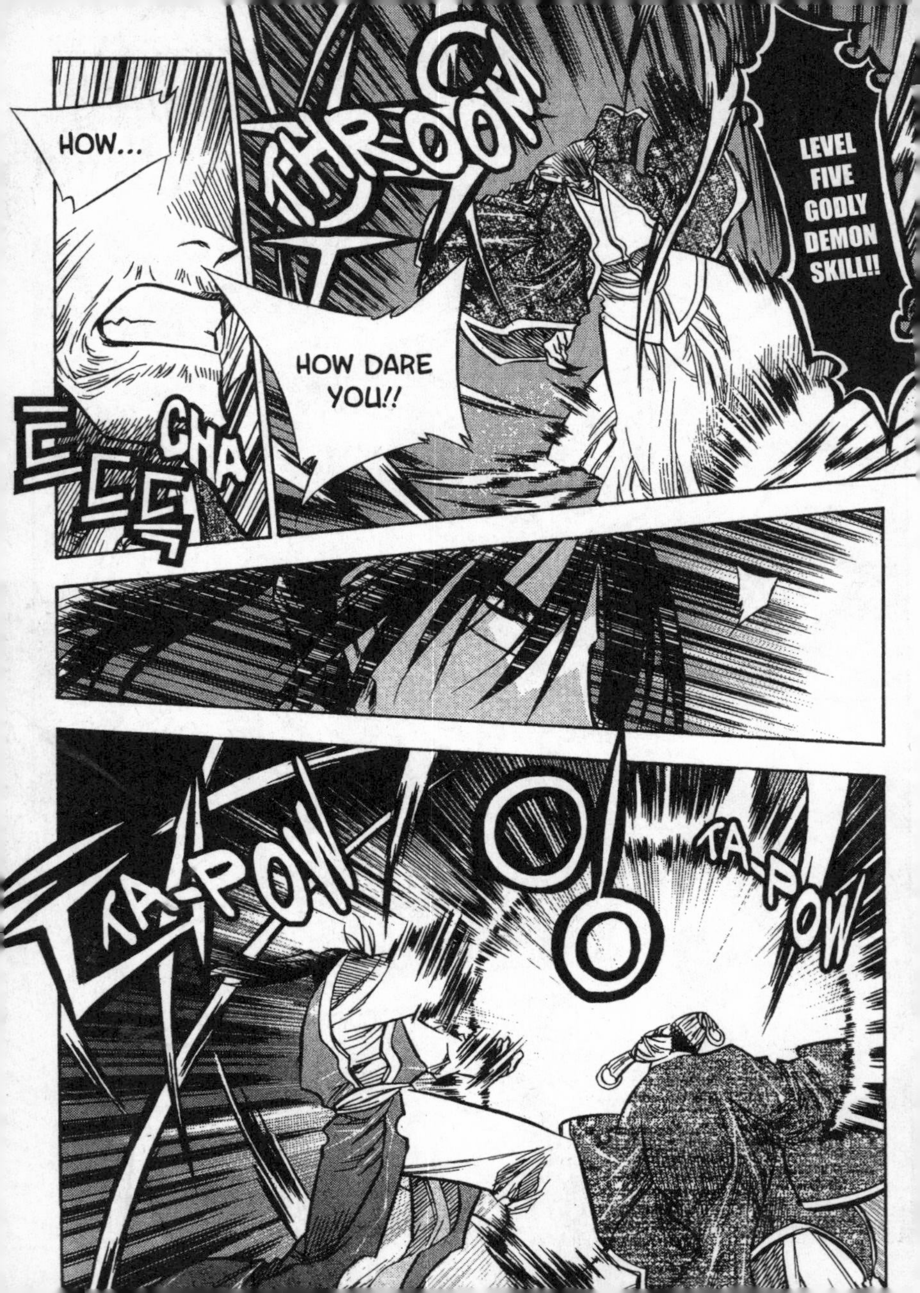
LEVEL FIVE GODLY DEMON SKILL!!
CA-THROOM
HOW...
HOW DARE YOU!!
CHA
TA-POW
TA-POW

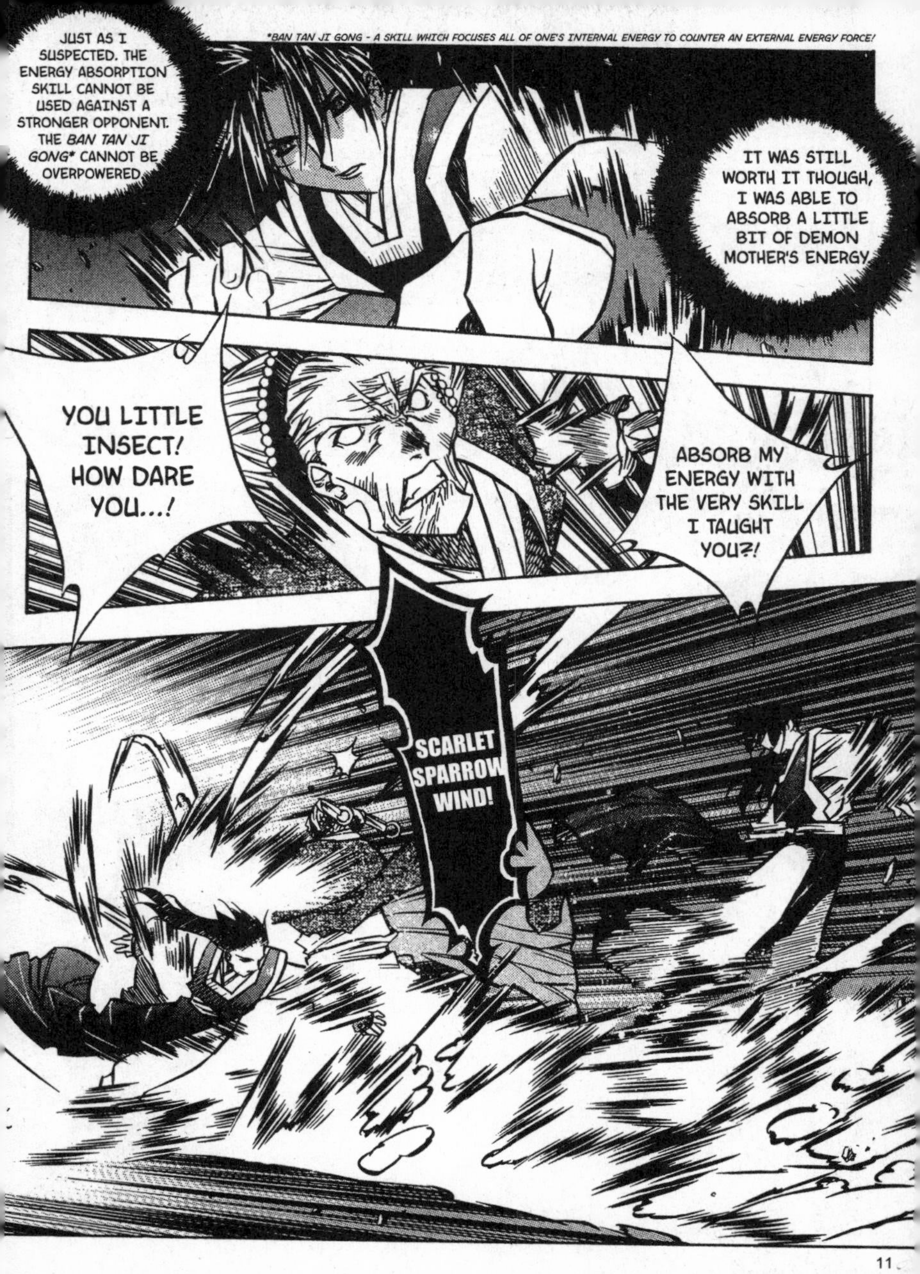
*BAN TAN JI GONG - A SKILL WHICH FOCUSES ALL OF ONE'S INTERNAL ENERGY TO COUNTER AN EXTERNAL ENERGY FORCE!
JUST AS I SUSPECTED. THE ENERGY ABSORPTION SKILL CANNOT BE USED AGAINST A STRONGER OPPONENT. THE BAN TAN JI GONG* CANNOT BE OVERPOWERED.
IT WAS STILL WORTH IT THOUGH, I WAS ABLE TO ABSORB A LITTLE BIT OF DEMON MOTHER'S ENERGY.
YOU LITTLE INSECT! HOW DARE YOU...!
ABSORB MY ENERGY WITH THE VERY SKILL I TAUGHT YOU?!
SCARLET SPARROW WIND!

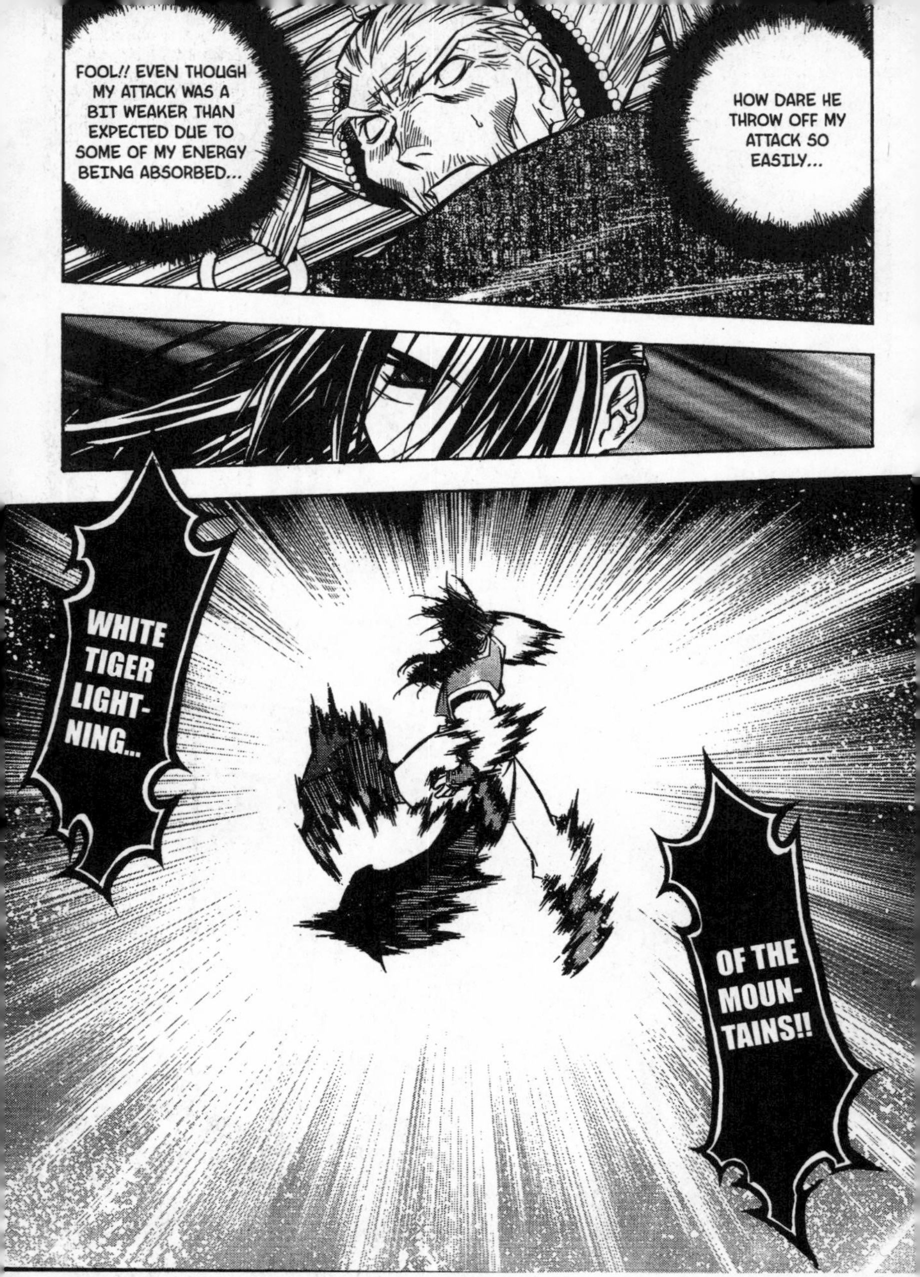

HOW DARE HE THROW OFF MY ATTACK SO EASILY...
FOOL!! EVEN THOUGH MY ATTACK WAS A BIT WEAKER THAN EXPECTED DUE TO SOME OF MY ENERGY BEING ABSORBED...
WHITE TIGER LIGHT-NING...
OF THE MOUN-TAINS!!

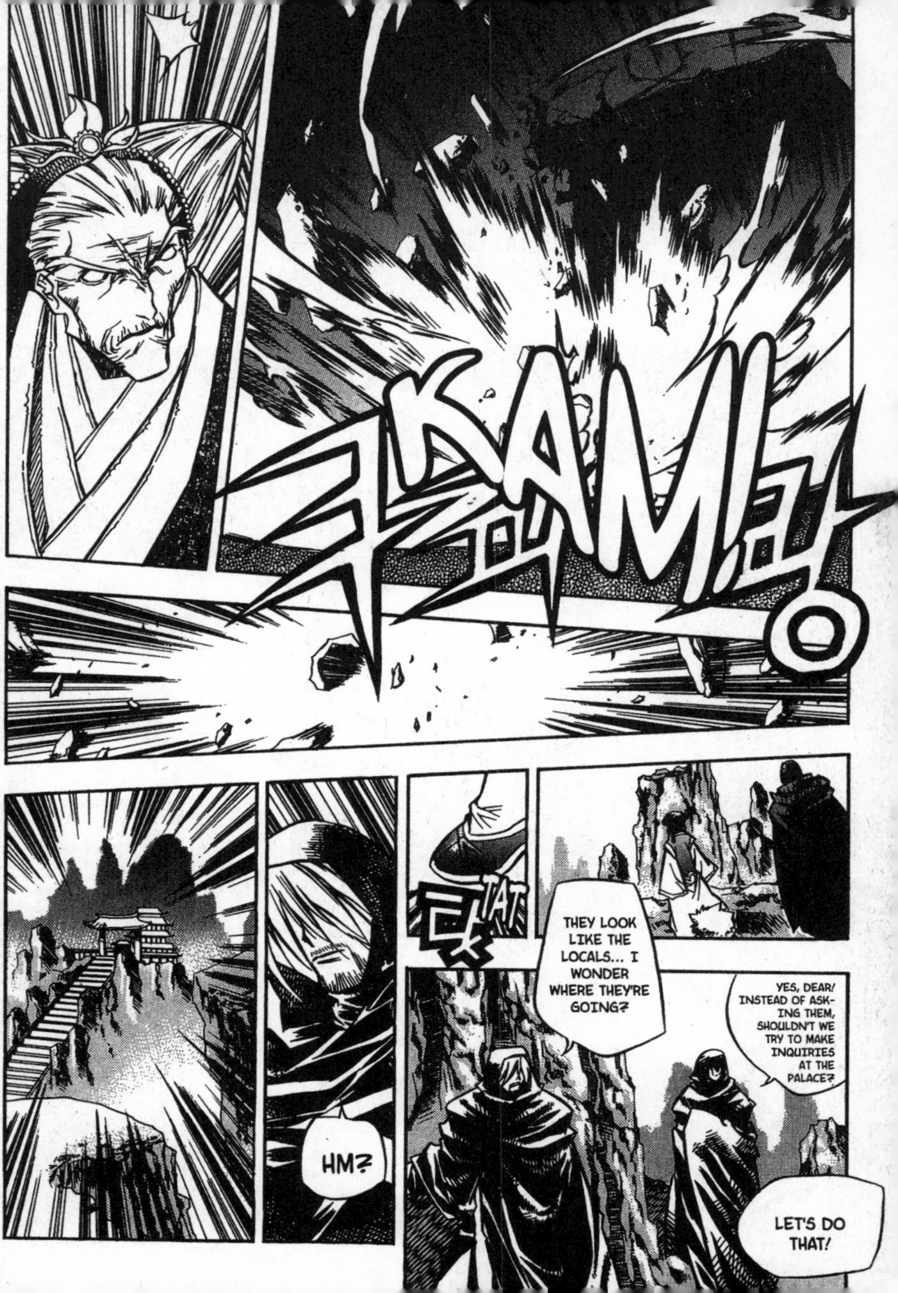

KAM!!
TAT
THEY LOOK LIKE THE LOCALS... I WONDER WHERE THEY'RE GOING?
YES, DEAR! INSTEAD OF ASKING THEM, SHOULDN'T WE TRY TO MAKE INQUIRIES AT THE PALACE?
HM?
LET'S DO THAT!

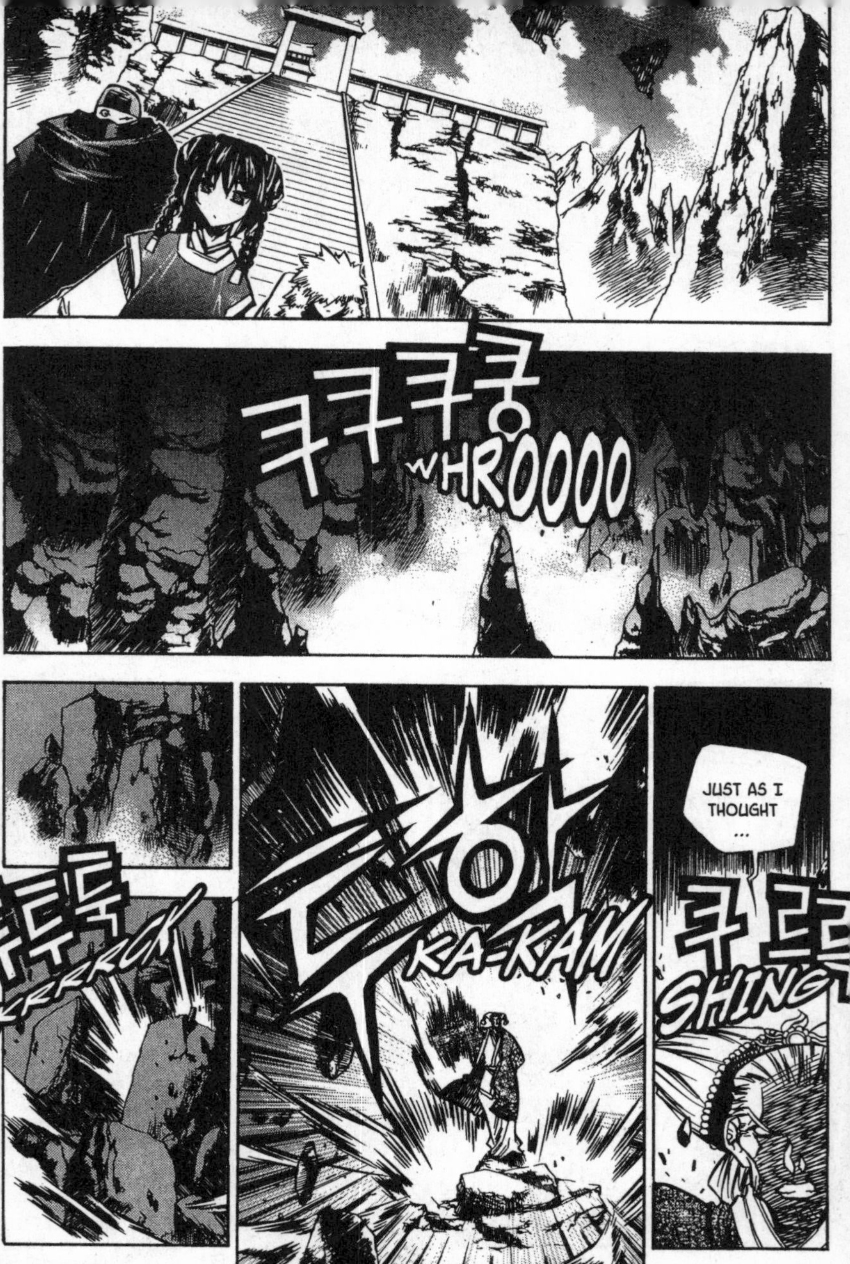
쿠쿠쿠쿵
WHROOOO
두두둑
KRRRCK
KA-KAM
JUST AS I THOUGHT ...
SHING

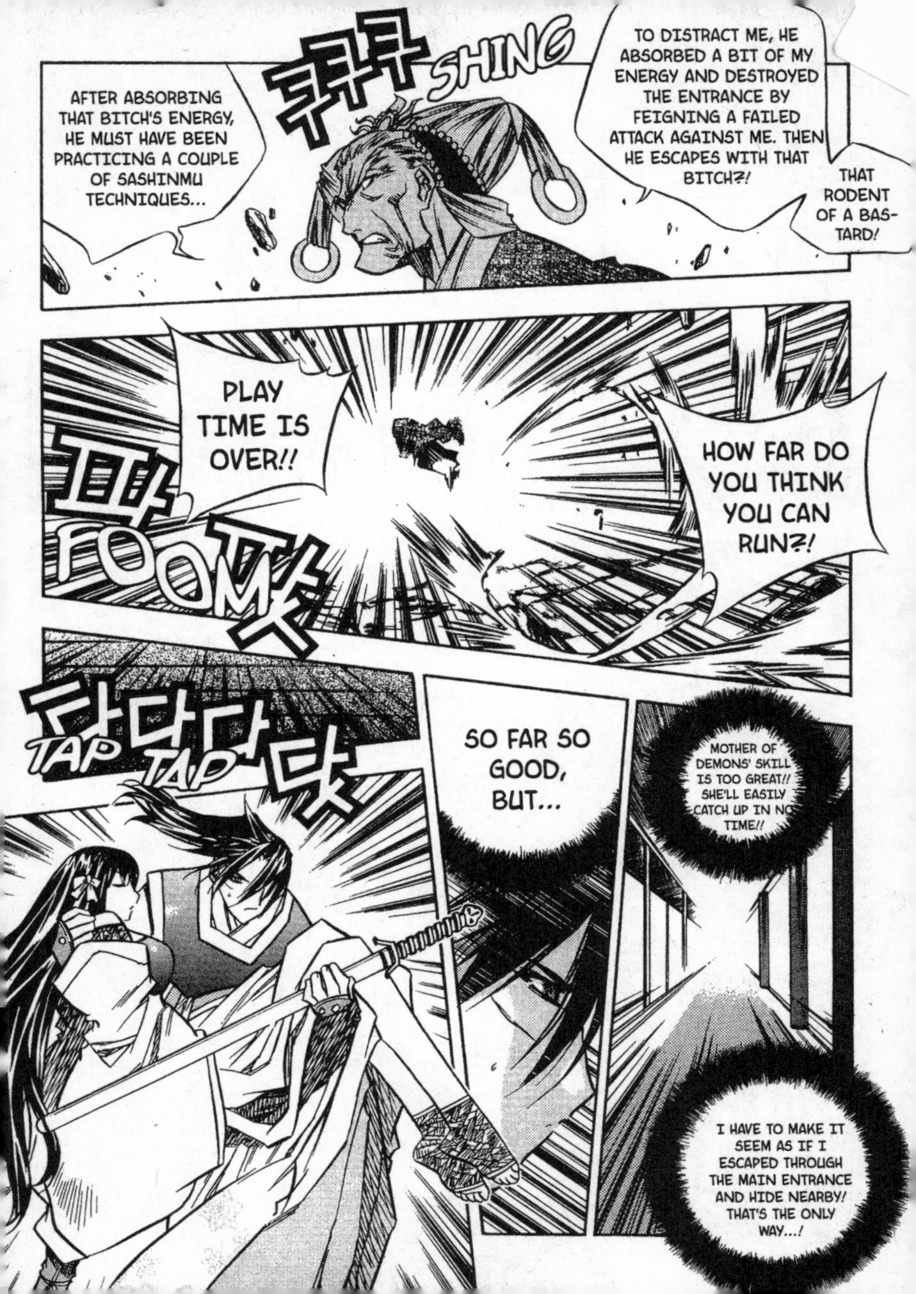

AFTER ABSORBING THAT BITCH'S ENERGY, HE MUST HAVE BEEN PRACTICING A COUPLE OF SASHINMU TECHNIQUES...
SHING
TO DISTRACT ME, HE ABSORBED A BIT OF MY ENERGY AND DESTROYED THE ENTRANCE BY FEIGNING A FAILED ATTACK AGAINST ME. THEN HE ESCAPES WITH THAT BITCH?!
THAT RODENT OF A BAS-TARD!
PLAY TIME IS OVER!!
FOOM
HOW FAR DO YOU THINK YOU CAN RUN?!
TAP TAP
SO FAR SO GOOD, BUT...
MOTHER OF DEMONS' SKILL IS TOO GREAT!! SHE'LL EASILY CATCH UP IN NO TIME!!
I HAVE TO MAKE IT SEEM AS IF I ESCAPED THROUGH THE MAIN ENTRANCE AND HIDE NEARBY! THAT'S THE ONLY WAY...!

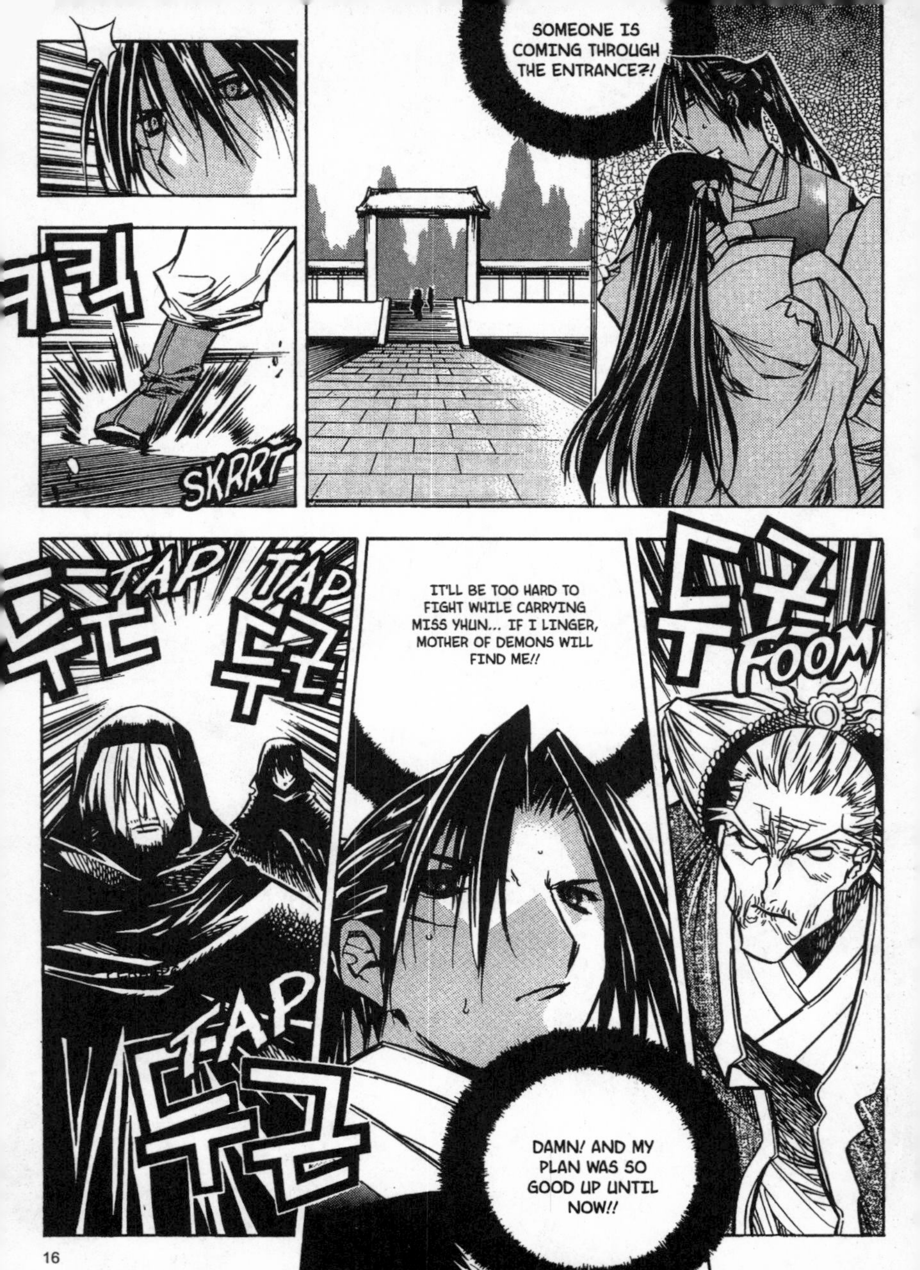
SOMEONE IS COMING THROUGH THE ENTRANCE?!
SKRRT
TAP TAP
IT'LL BE TOO HARD TO FIGHT WHILE CARRYING MISS YHUN... IF I LINGER, MOTHER OF DEMONS WILL FIND ME!!
FOOM
TAP
DAMN! AND MY PLAN WAS SO GOOD UP UNTIL NOW!!

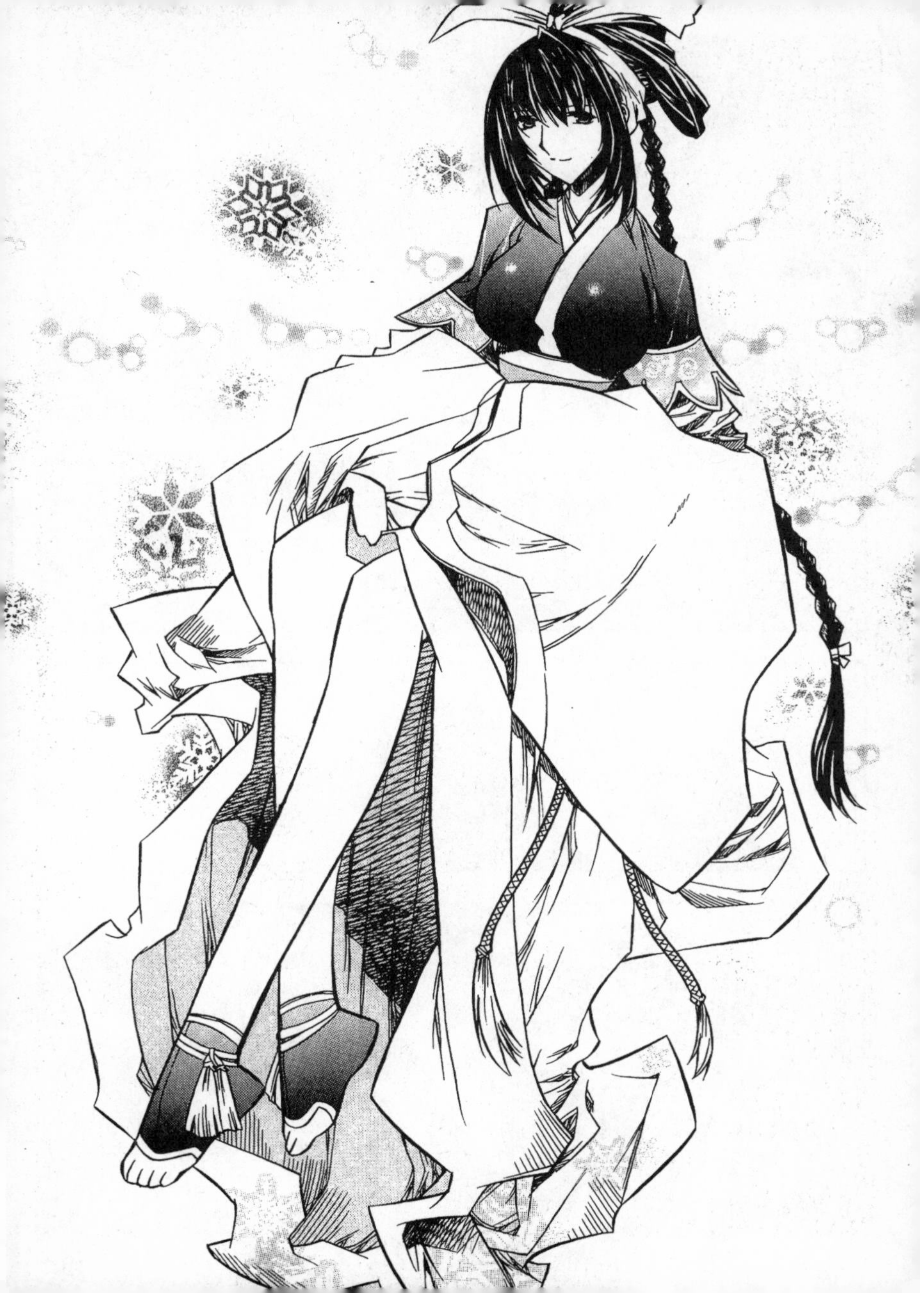

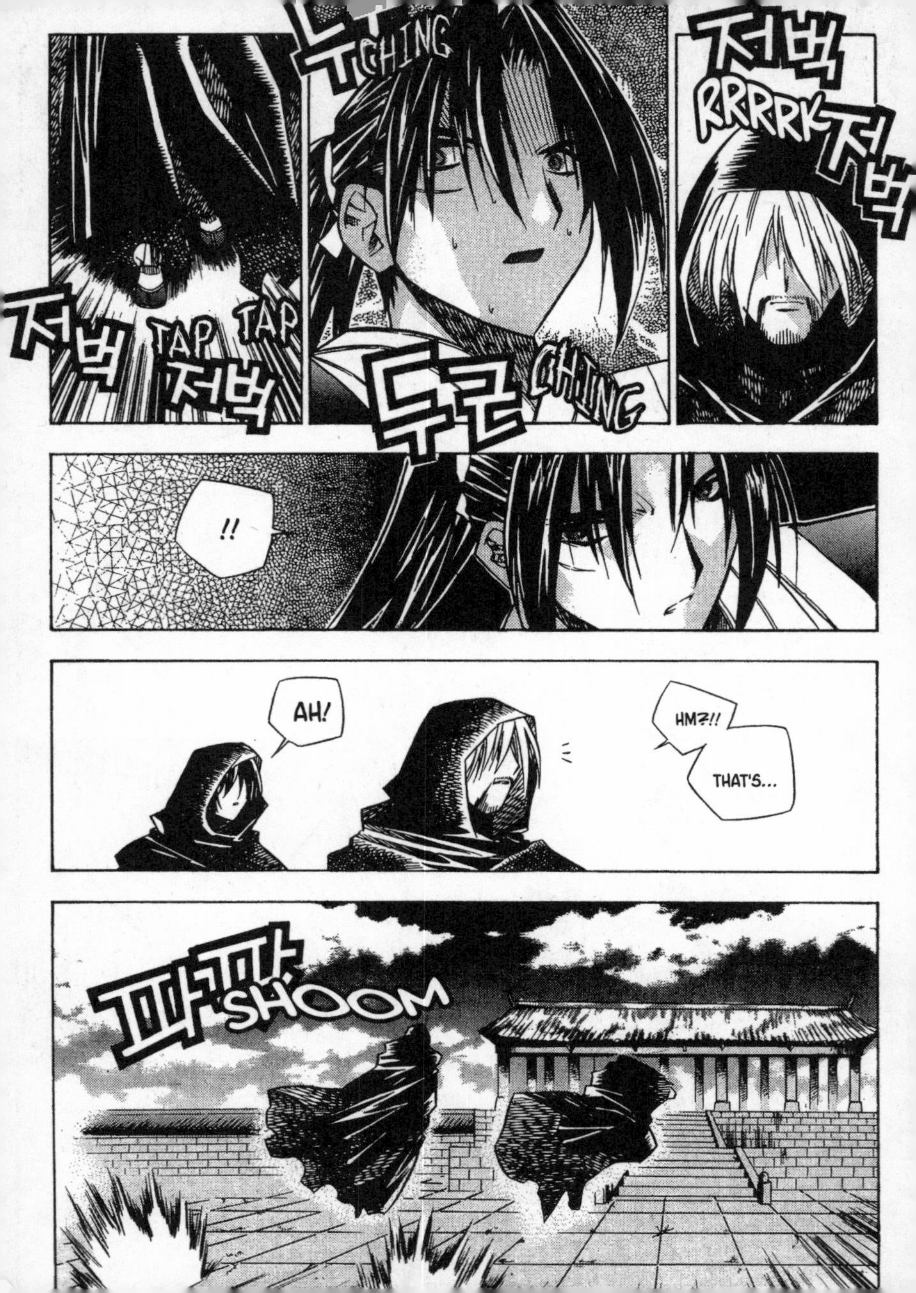

CHING
RRRRK
TAP TAP
CHING
!!
HM?!!
THAT'S...
AH!
SHOOM

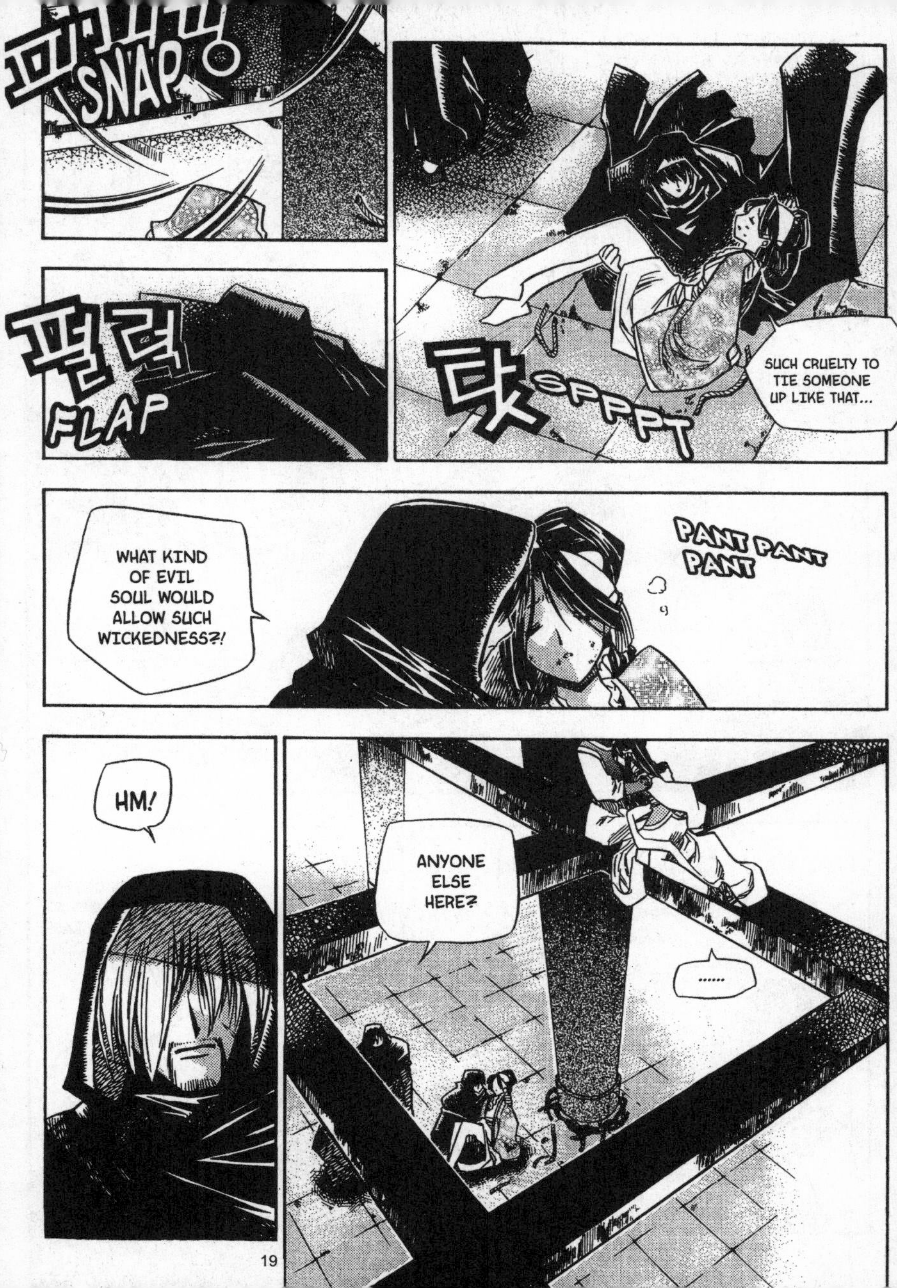
SNAP
FLAP
SPPPPT
SUCH CRUELTY TO TIE SOMEONE UP LIKE THAT...
PANT PANT PANT
WHAT KIND OF EVIL SOUL WOULD ALLOW SUCH WICKEDNESS?!
HM!
ANYONE ELSE HERE?
......

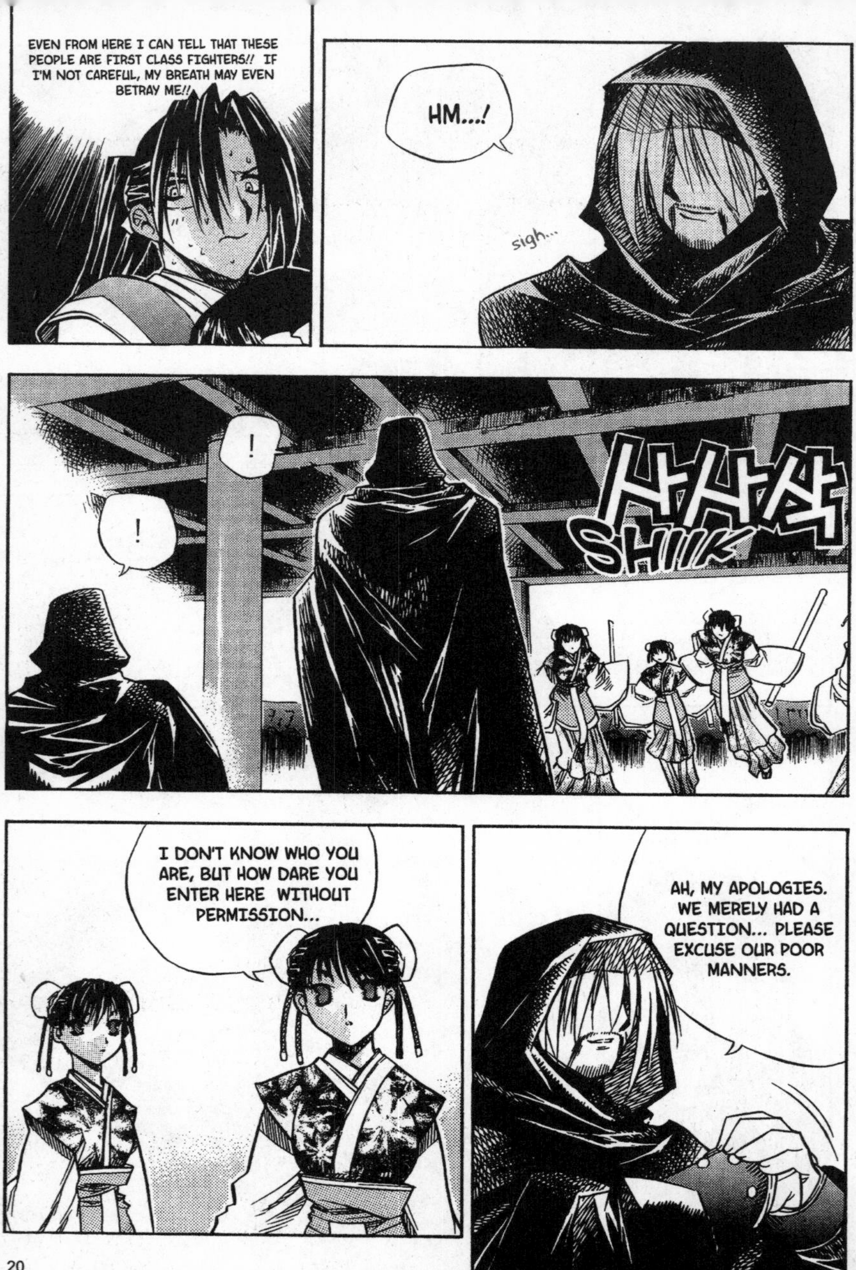
EVEN FROM HERE I CAN TELL THAT THESE PEOPLE ARE FIRST CLASS FIGHTERS!! IF I'M NOT CAREFUL, MY BREATH MAY EVEN BETRAY ME!!
HM...!
sigh...
!
!
SHIIK
I DON'T KNOW WHO YOU ARE, BUT HOW DARE YOU ENTER HERE WITHOUT PERMISSION...
AH, MY APOLOGIES. WE MERELY HAD A QUESTION... PLEASE EXCUSE OUR POOR MANNERS.

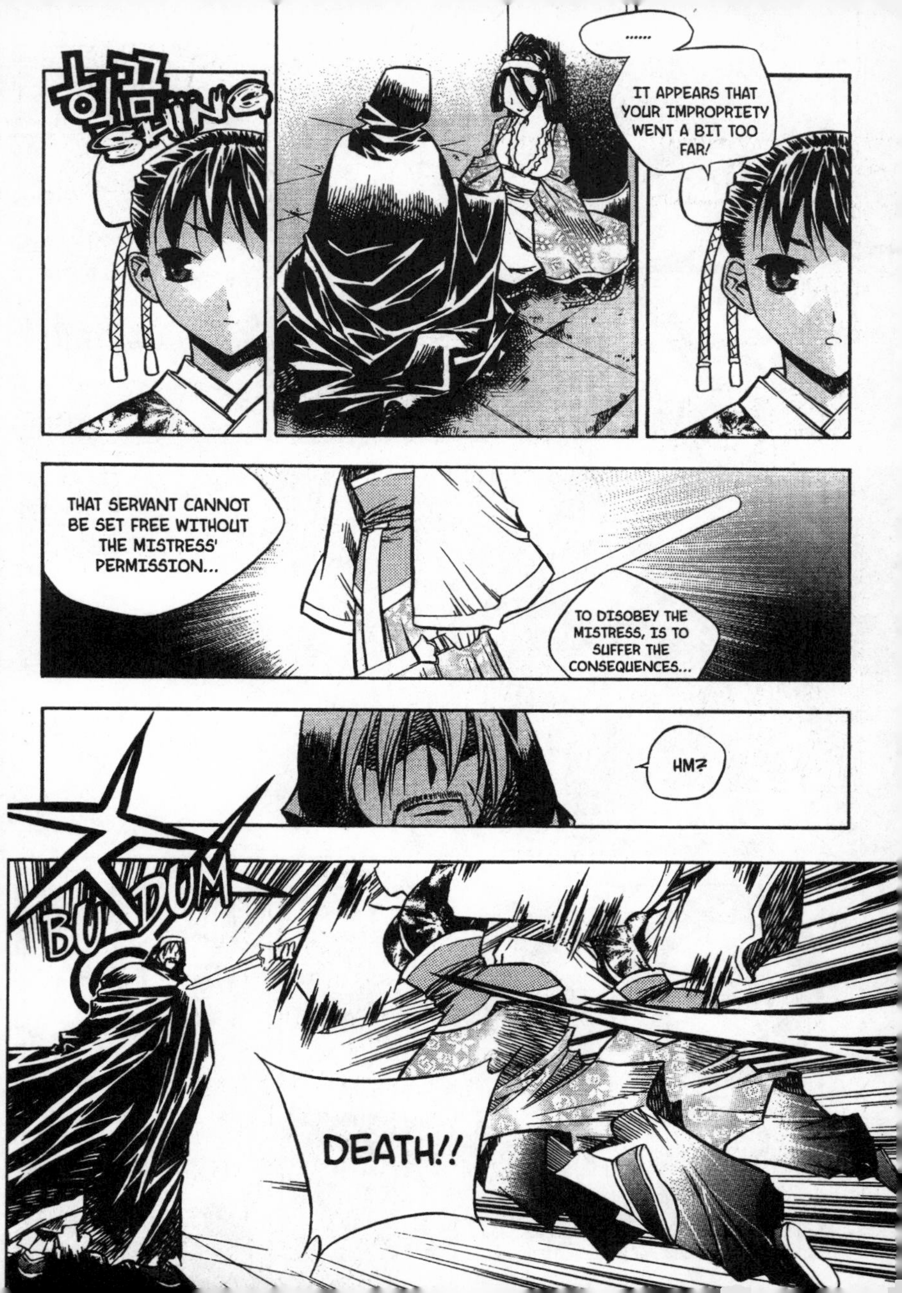

SHING
......
IT APPEARS THAT YOUR IMPROPRIETY WENT A BIT TOO FAR!
THAT SERVANT CANNOT BE SET FREE WITHOUT THE MISTRESS' PERMISSION...
TO DISOBEY THE MISTRESS, IS TO SUFFER THE CONSEQUENCES...
HM?
BU DUM
DEATH!!

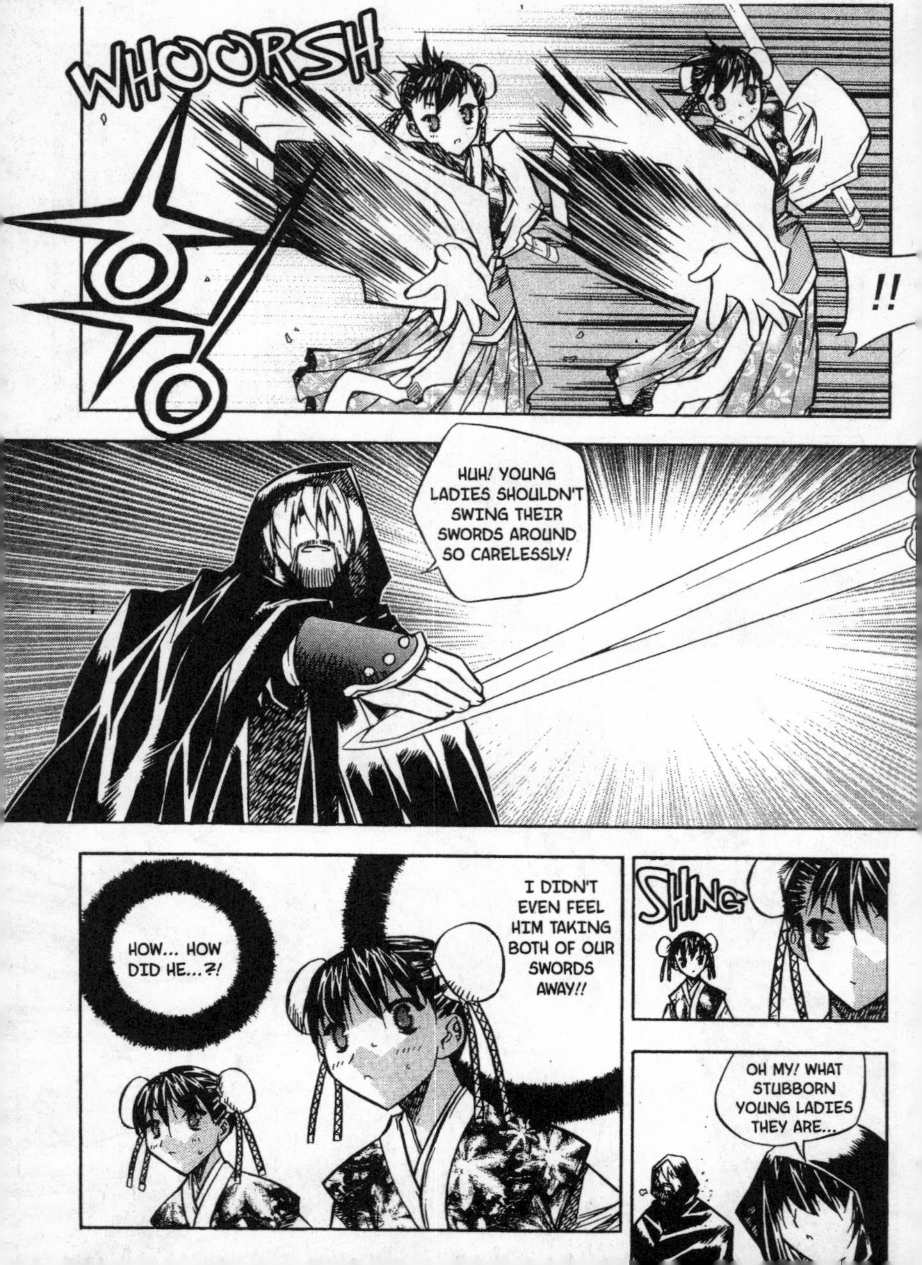

!!
WHOORSH
HUH! YOUNG LADIES SHOULDN'T SWING THEIR SWORDS AROUND SO CARELESSLY!
SHING
I DIDN'T EVEN FEEL HIM TAKING BOTH OF OUR SWORDS AWAY!!
HOW... HOW DID HE...?!
OH MY! WHAT STUBBORN YOUNG LADIES THEY ARE...

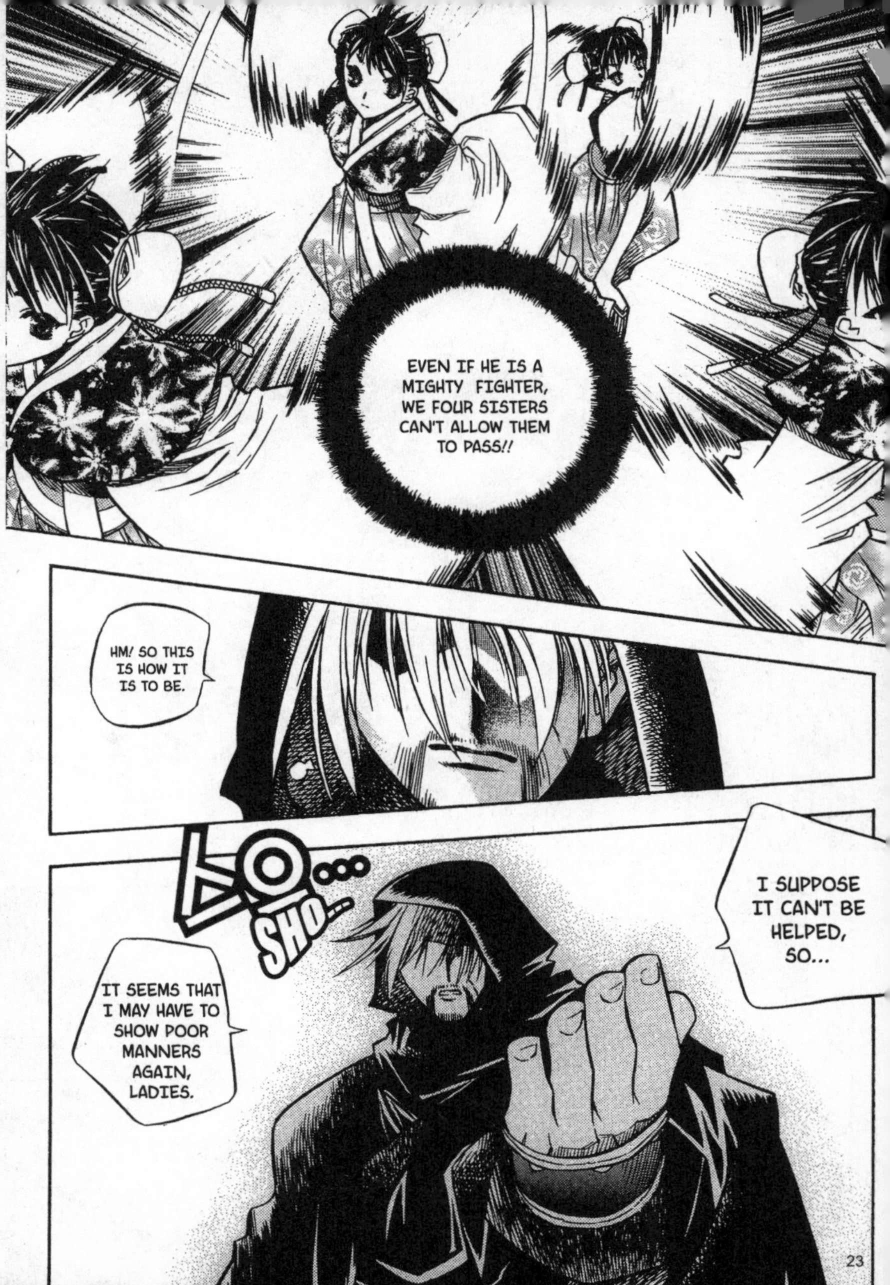
EVEN IF HE IS A MIGHTY FIGHTER, WE FOUR SISTERS CAN'T ALLOW THEM TO PASS!!
HM! SO THIS IS HOW IT IS TO BE.
SHO...
I SUPPOSE IT CAN'T BE HELPED, SO...
IT SEEMS THAT I MAY HAVE TO SHOW POOR MANNERS AGAIN, LADIES.

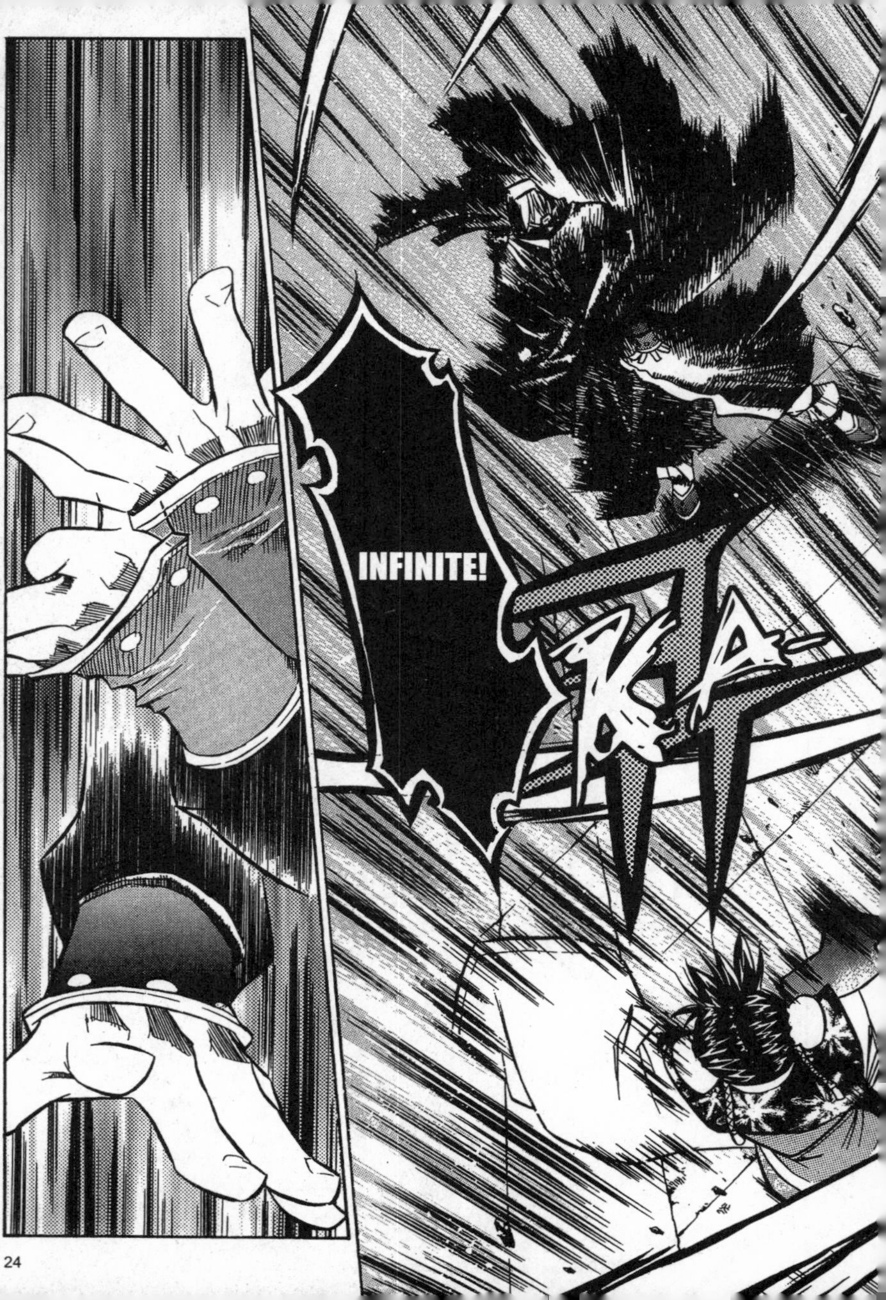
INFINITE!
KA-

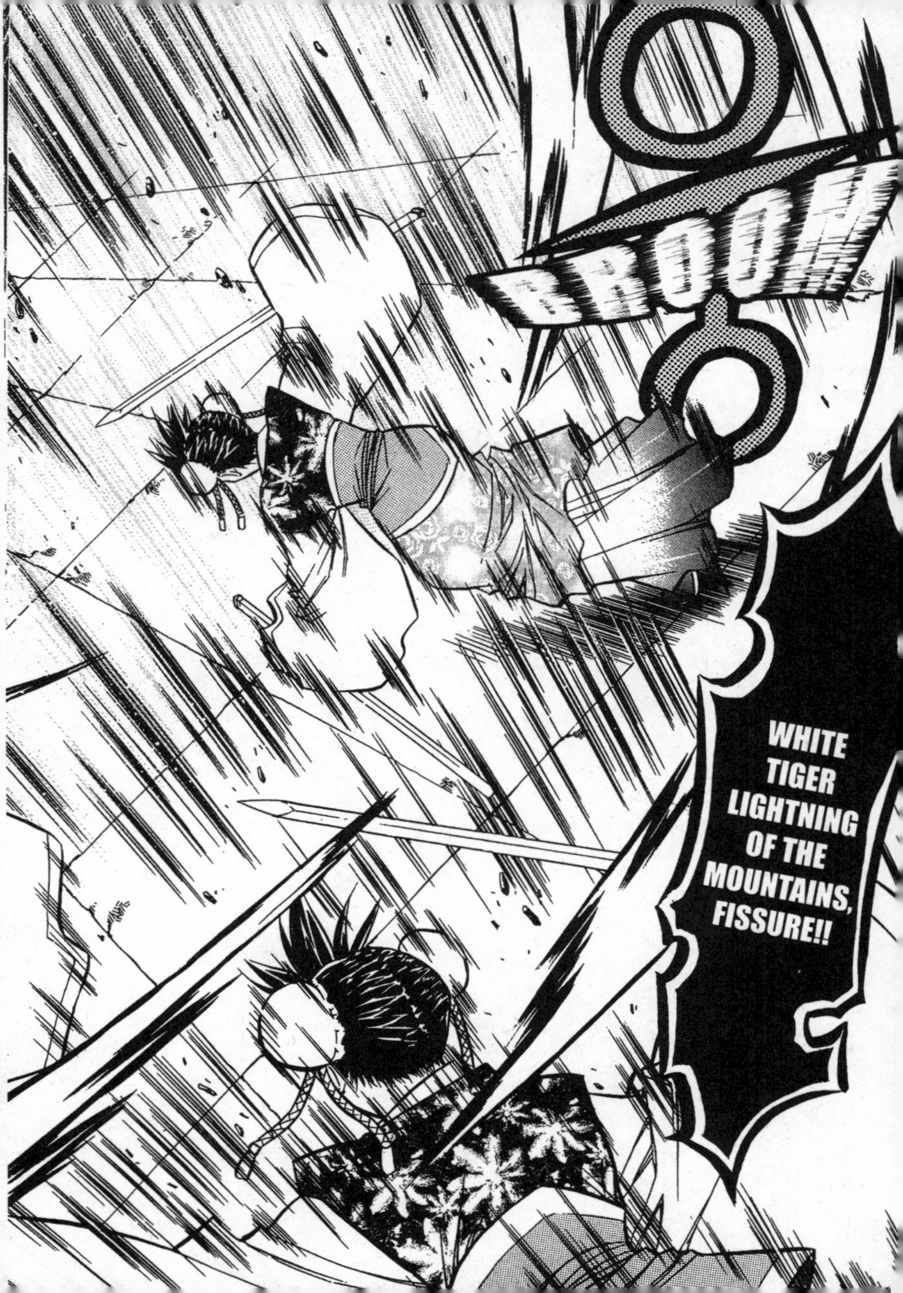
BROOM
WHITE TIGER LIGHTNING OF THE MOUNTAINS, FISSURE!!

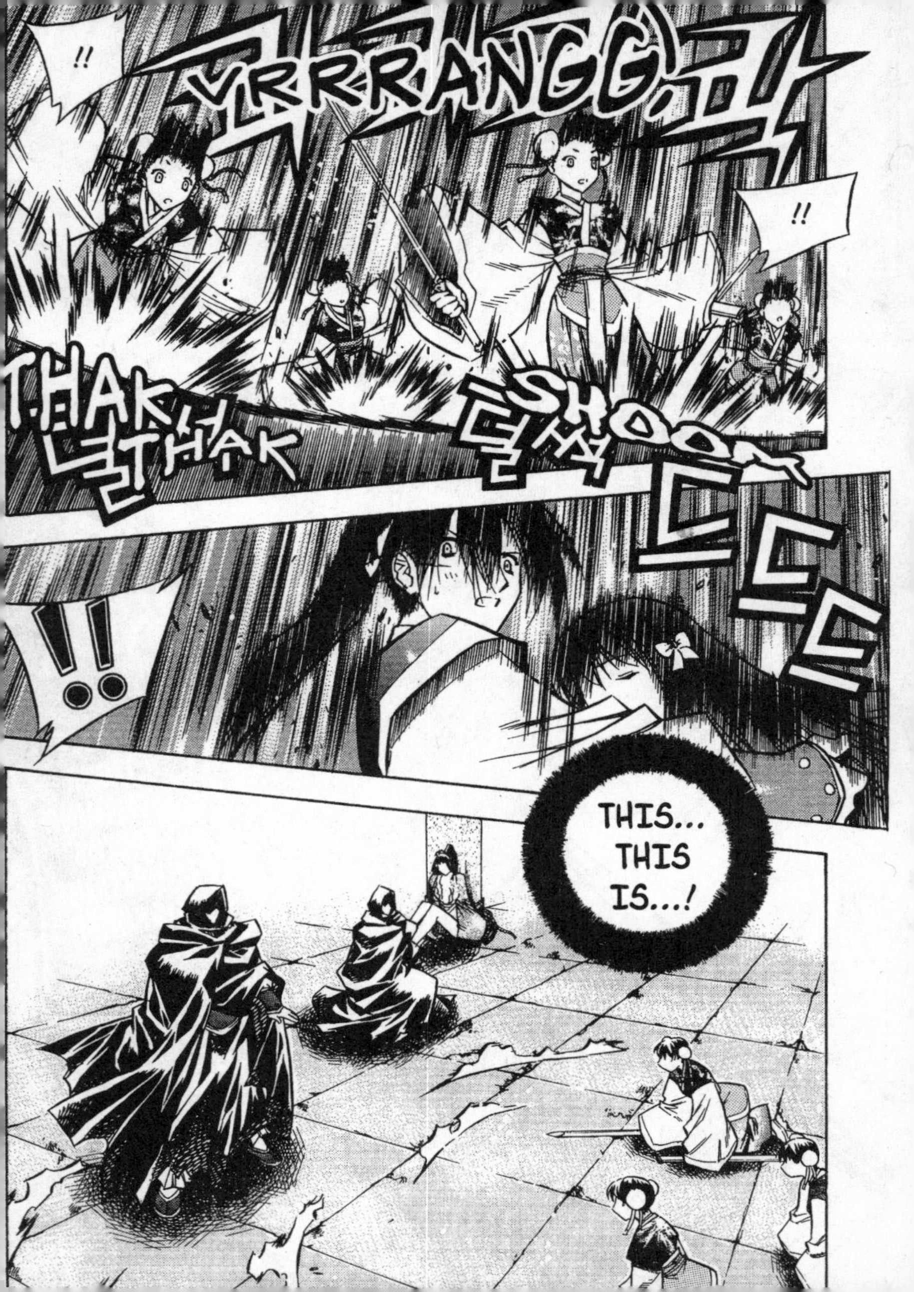
YRRRANGG!!
!!
!!
SHOOM
THAK THAK
!!
THIS... THIS IS...!

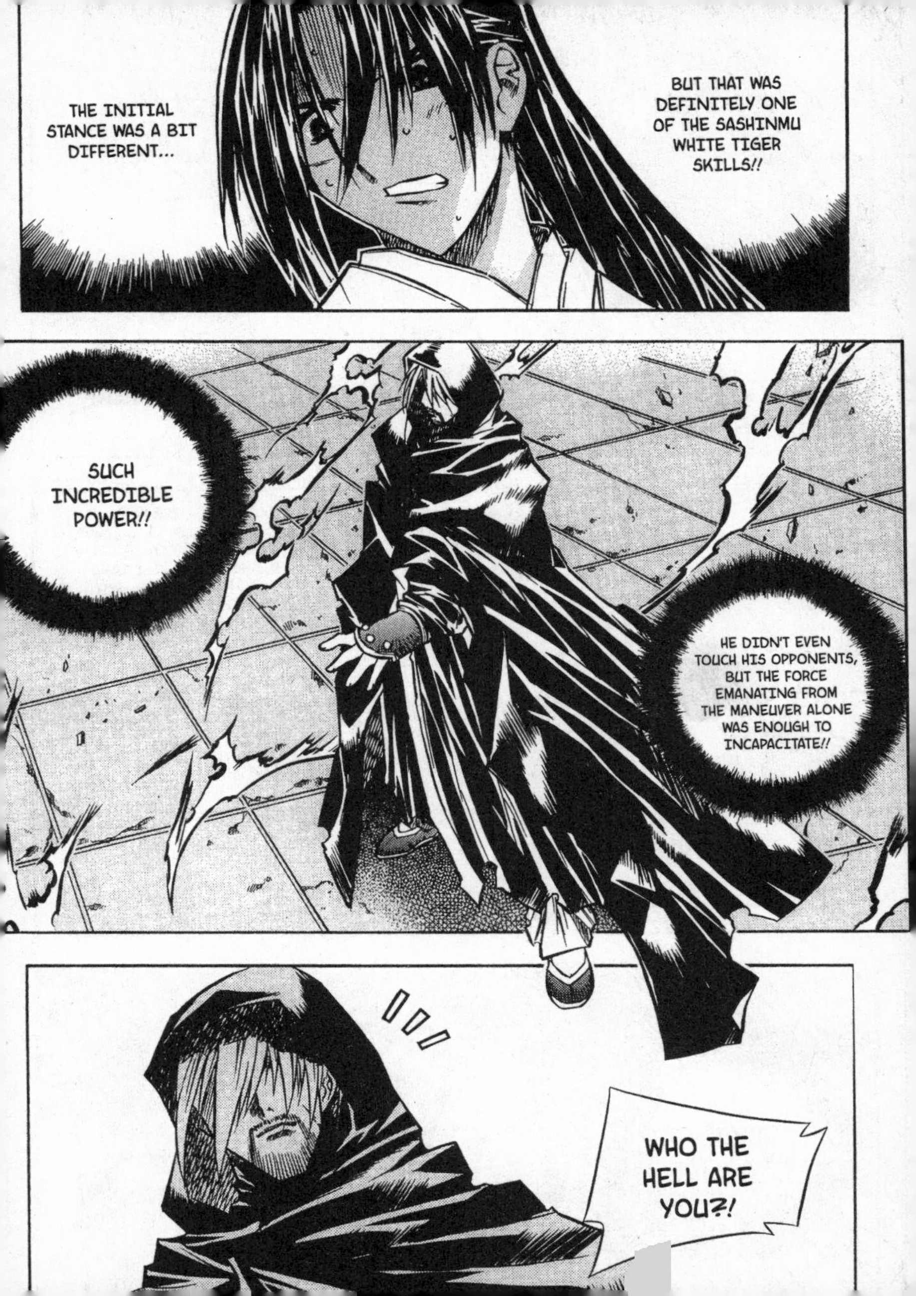
BUT THAT WAS DEFINITELY ONE OF THE SASHINMU WHITE TIGER SKILLS!!
THE INITIAL STANCE WAS A BIT DIFFERENT...
HE DIDN'T EVEN TOUCH HIS OPPONENTS, BUT THE FORCE EMANATING FROM THE MANEUVER ALONE WAS ENOUGH TO INCAPACITATE!!
SUCH INCREDIBLE POWER!!
WHO THE HELL ARE YOU?!

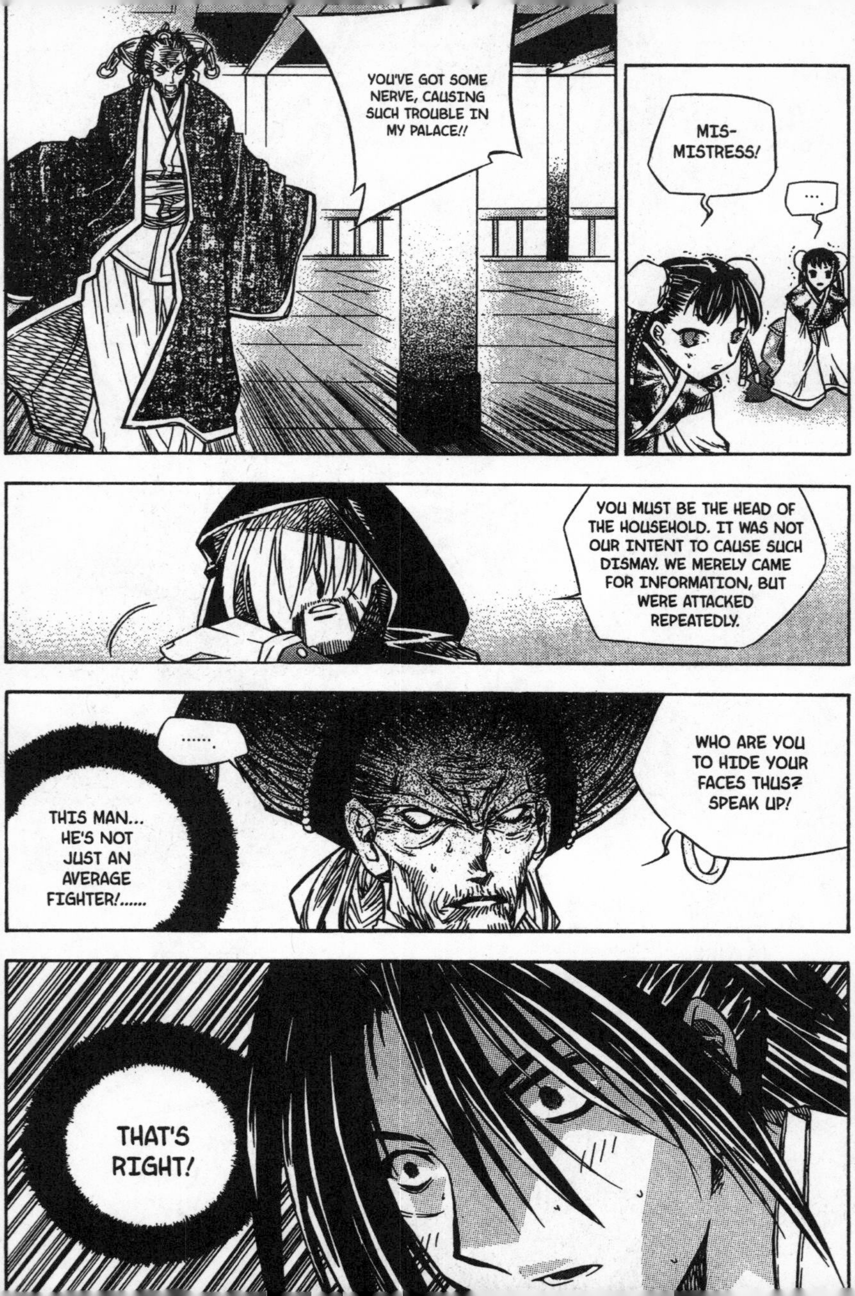
YOU'VE GOT SOME NERVE, CAUSING SUCH TROUBLE IN MY PALACE!!
MIS- MISTRESS!
...
YOU MUST BE THE HEAD OF THE HOUSEHOLD. IT WAS NOT OUR INTENT TO CAUSE SUCH DISMAY. WE MERELY CAME FOR INFORMATION, BUT WERE ATTACKED REPEATEDLY.
WHO ARE YOU TO HIDE YOUR FACES THUS? SPEAK UP!
.......
THIS MAN... HE'S NOT JUST AN AVERAGE FIGHTER!......
THAT'S RIGHT!

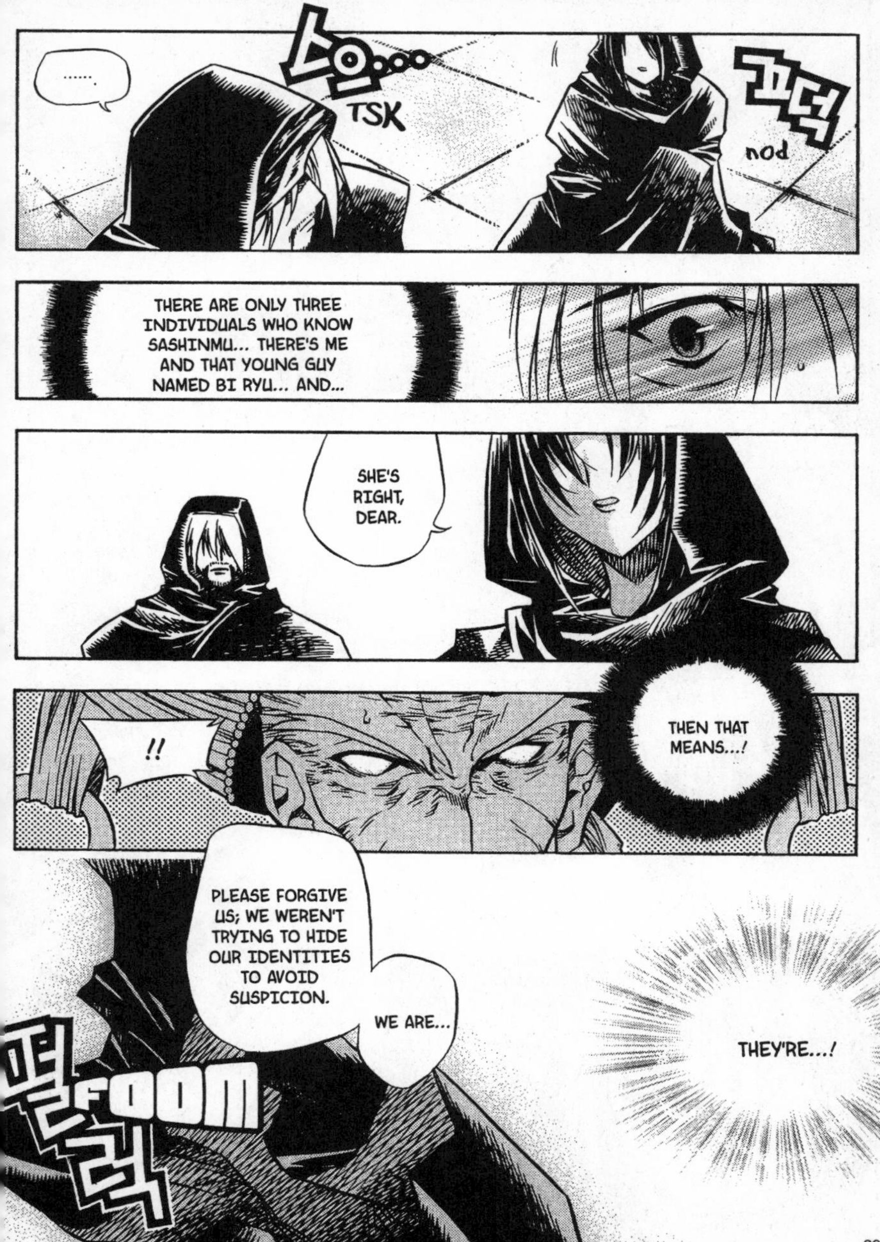
.......
TSK
nod
THERE ARE ONLY THREE INDIVIDUALS WHO KNOW SASHINMU... THERE'S ME AND THAT YOUNG GUY NAMED BI RYU... AND...
SHE'S RIGHT, DEAR.
!!
THEN THAT MEANS...!
PLEASE FORGIVE US; WE WEREN'T TRYING TO HIDE OUR IDENTITIES TO AVOID SUSPICION.
WE ARE...
FOOM
THEY'RE...!

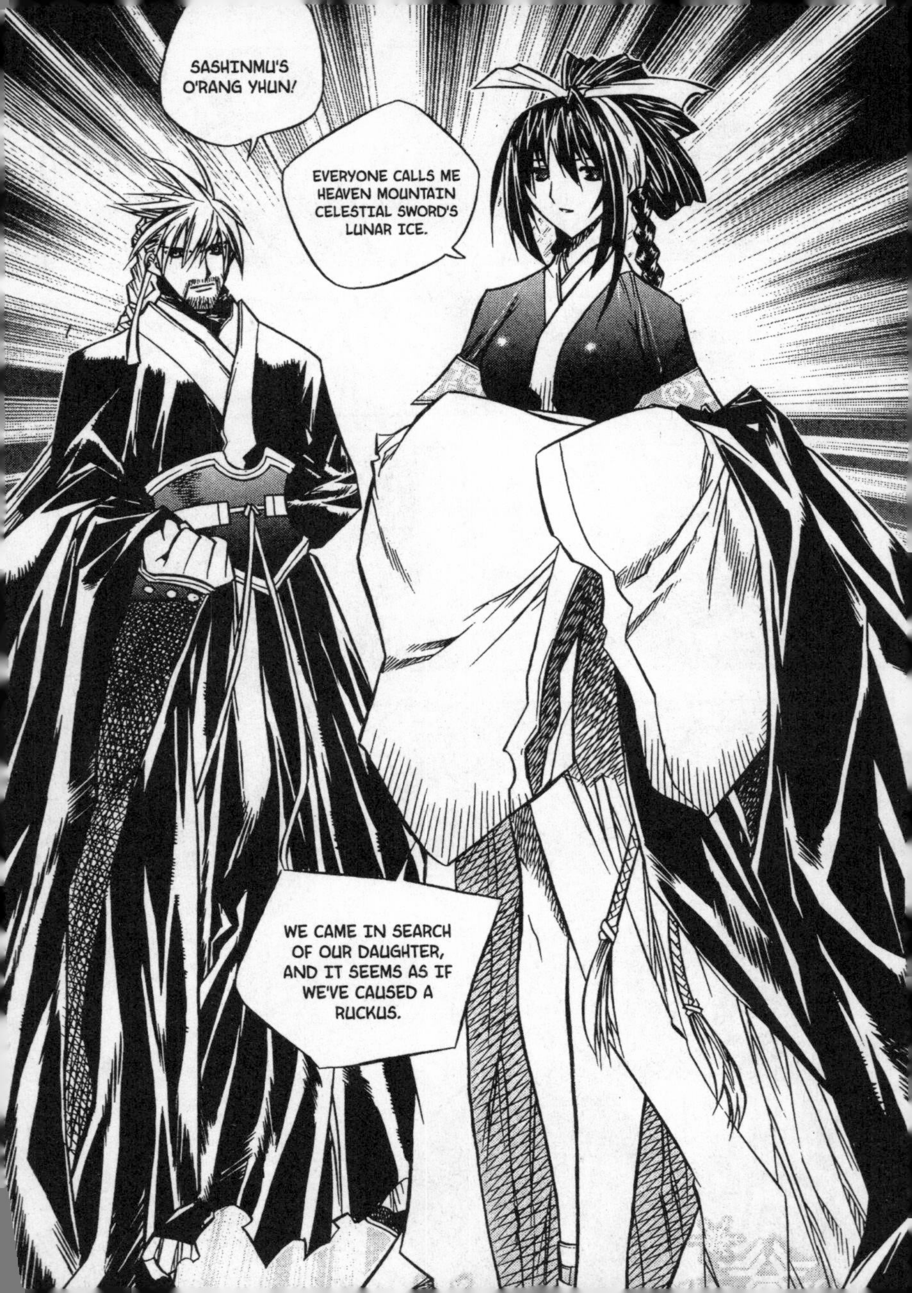
SASHINMU'S O'RANG YHUN!
EVERYONE CALLS ME HEAVEN MOUNTAIN CELESTIAL SWORD'S LUNAR ICE.
WE CAME IN SEARCH OF OUR DAUGHTER, AND IT SEEMS AS IF WE'VE CAUSED A RUCKUS.

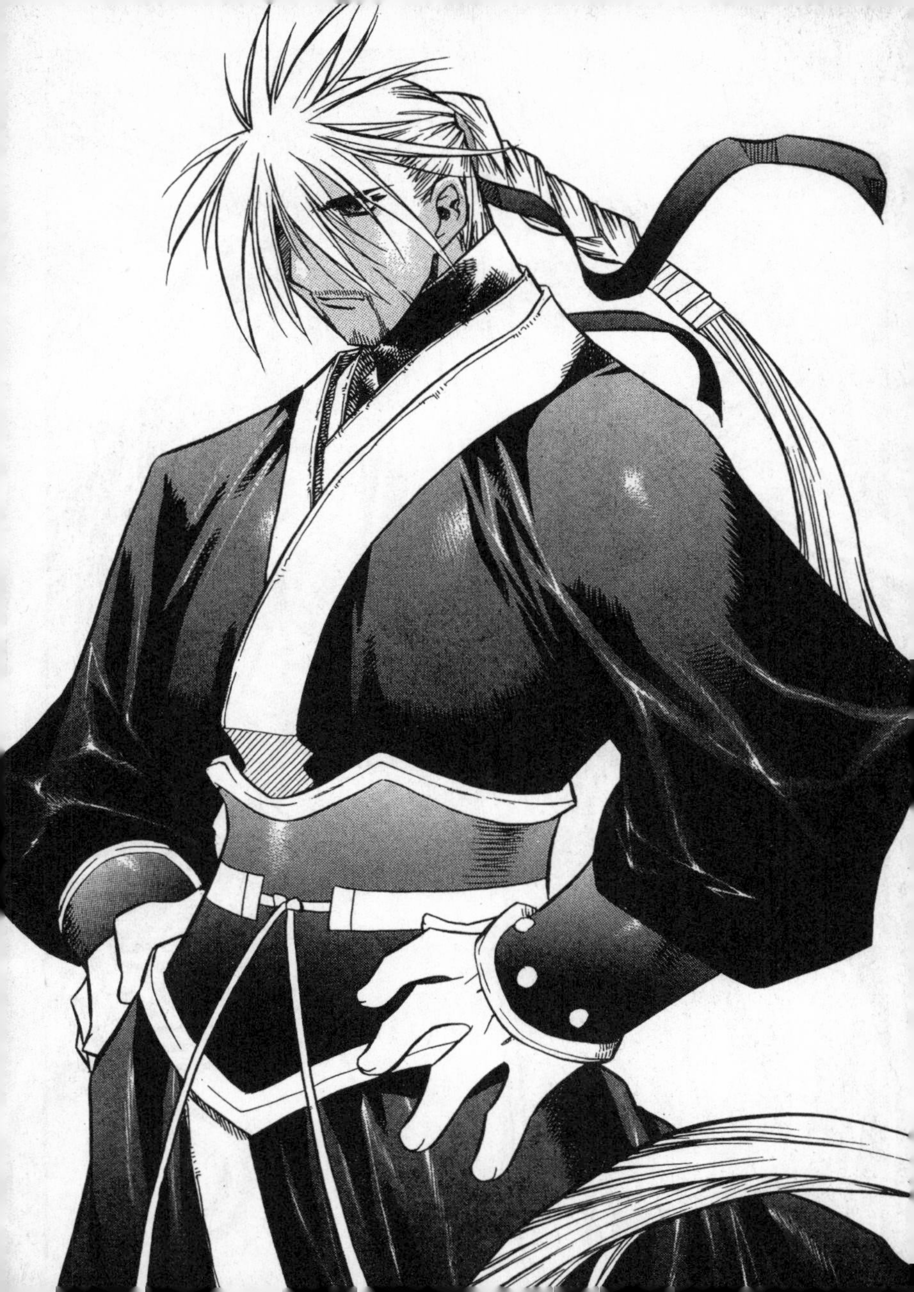

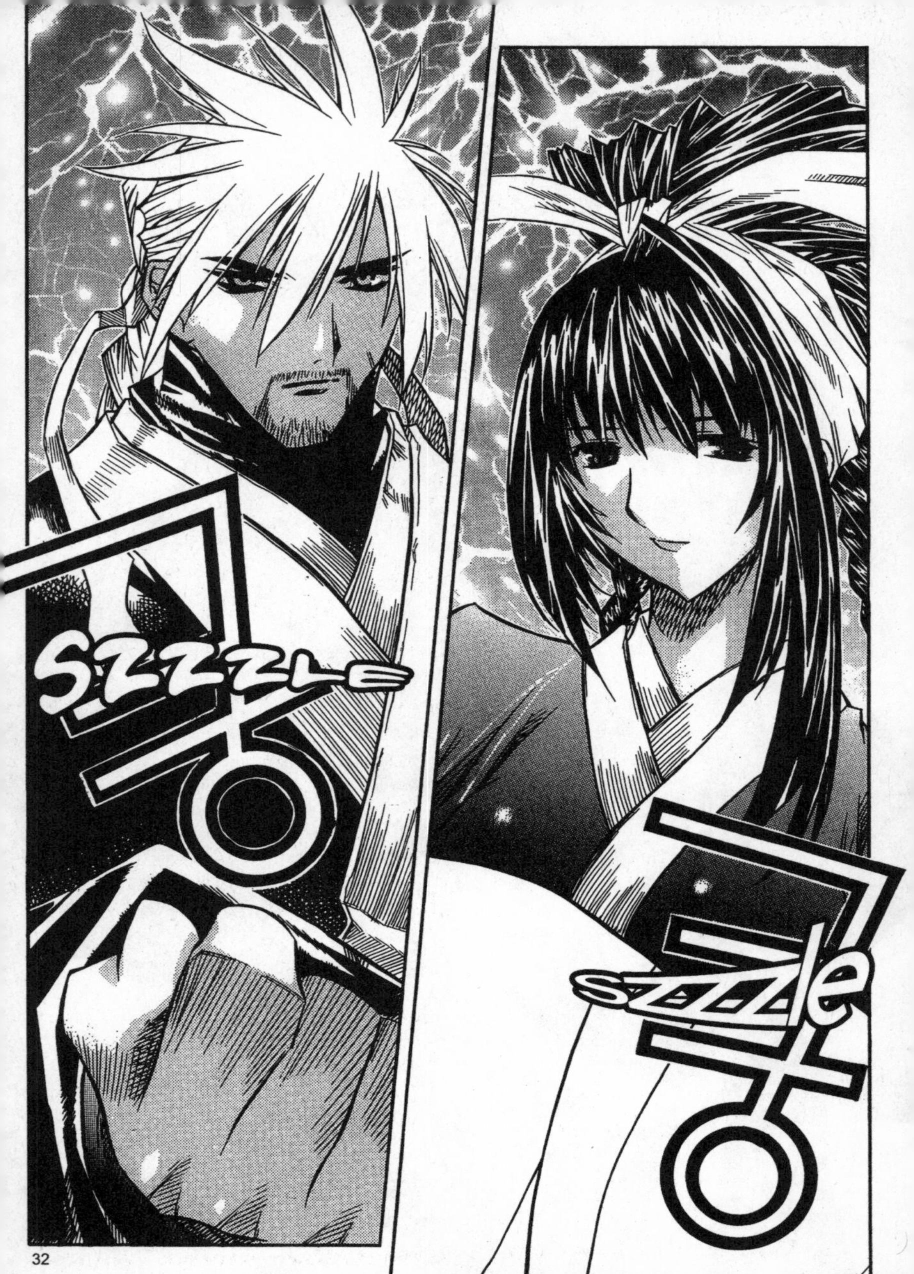
SZZZZLE
SZZZZLe

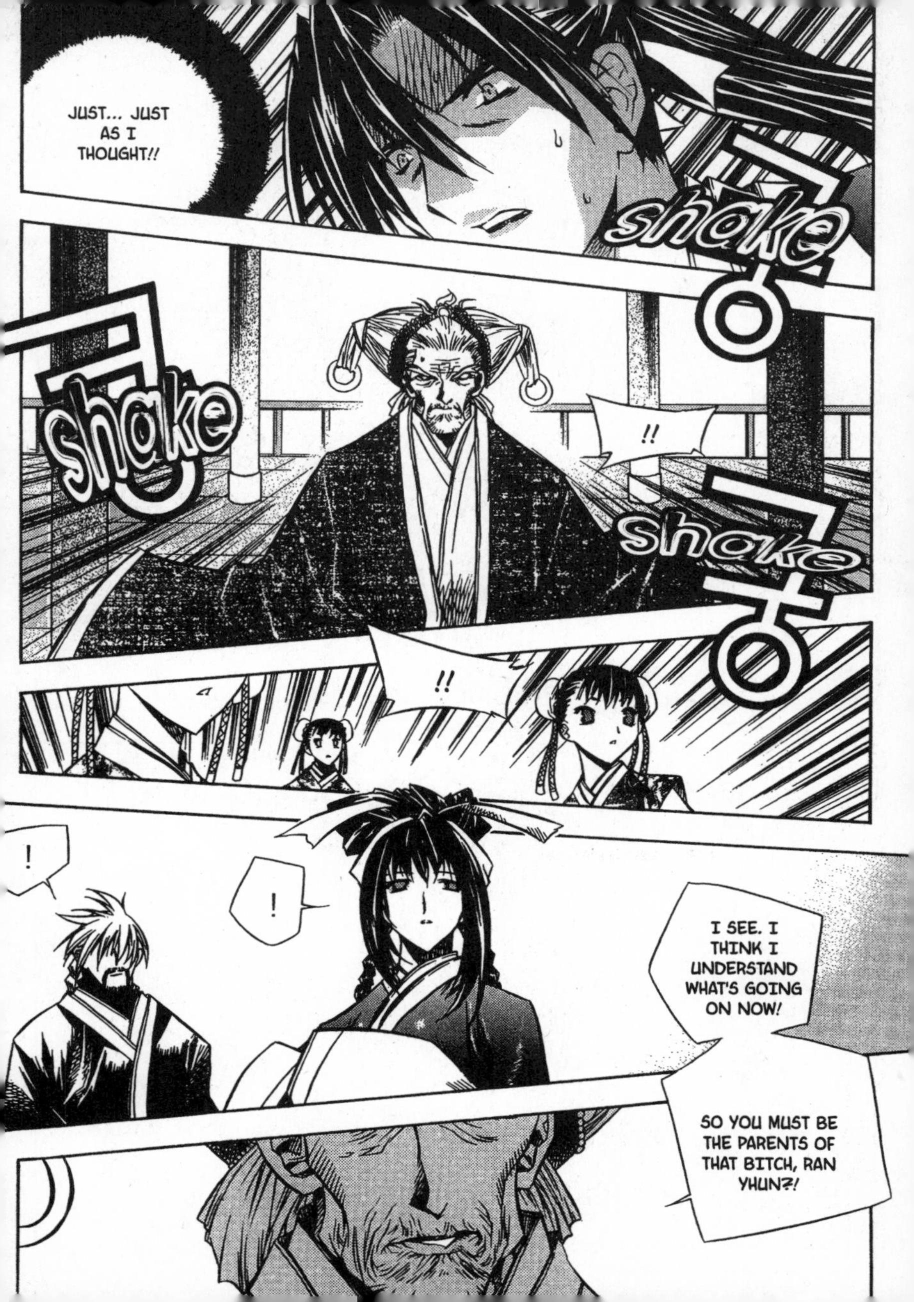

JUST... JUST AS I THOUGHT!!
shake
shake
!!
shake
!!
!
!
I SEE. I THINK I UNDERSTAND WHAT'S GOING ON NOW!
SO YOU MUST BE THE PARENTS OF THAT BITCH, RAN YHUN?!

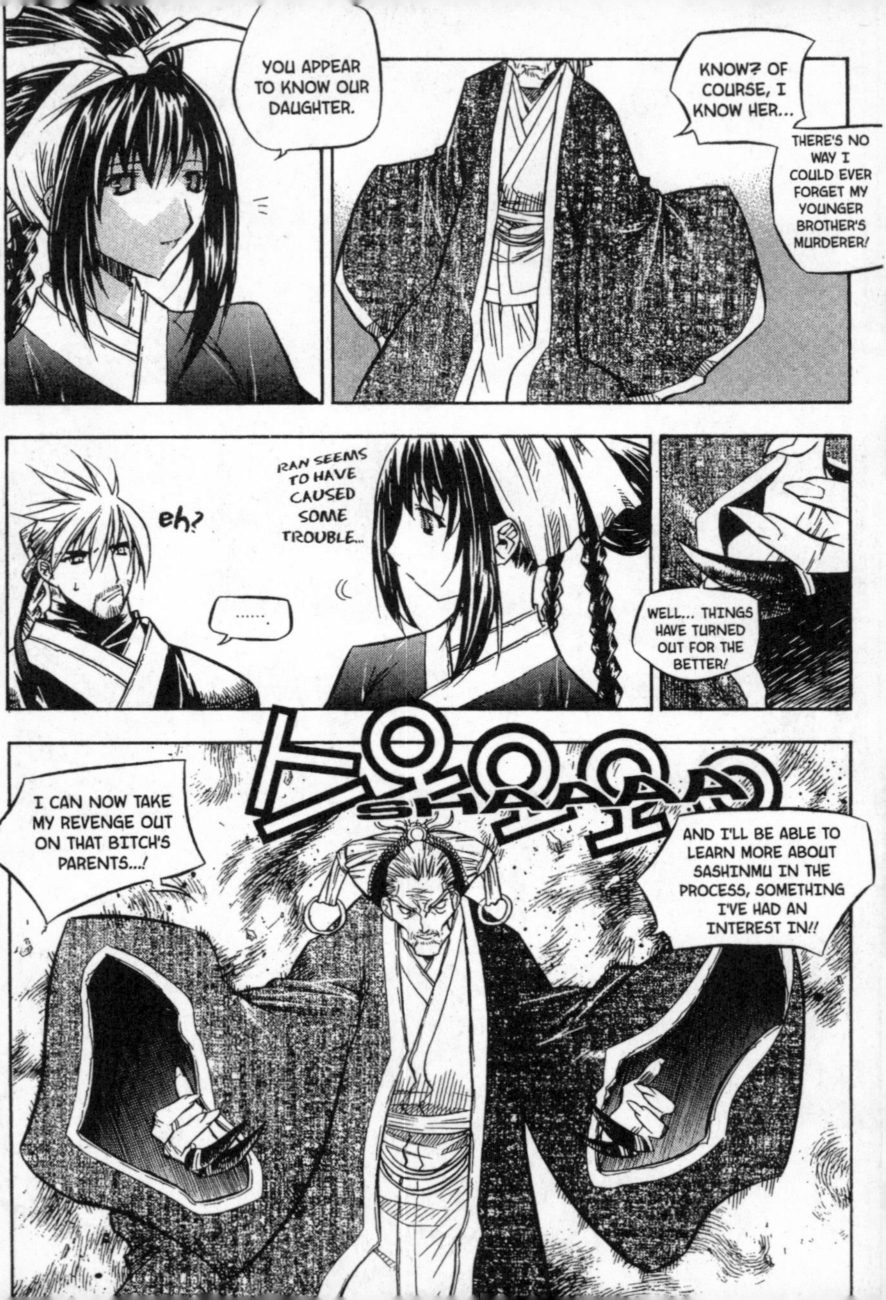
YOU APPEAR TO KNOW OUR DAUGHTER.
KNOW? OF COURSE, I KNOW HER...
THERE'S NO WAY I COULD EVER FORGET MY YOUNGER BROTHER'S MURDERER!
eh?
RAN SEEMS TO HAVE CAUSED SOME TROUBLE...
......
WELL... THINGS HAVE TURNED OUT FOR THE BETTER!
I CAN NOW TAKE MY REVENGE OUT ON THAT BITCH'S PARENTS...!
AND I'LL BE ABLE TO LEARN MORE ABOUT SASHINMU IN THE PROCESS, SOMETHING I'VE HAD AN INTEREST IN!!

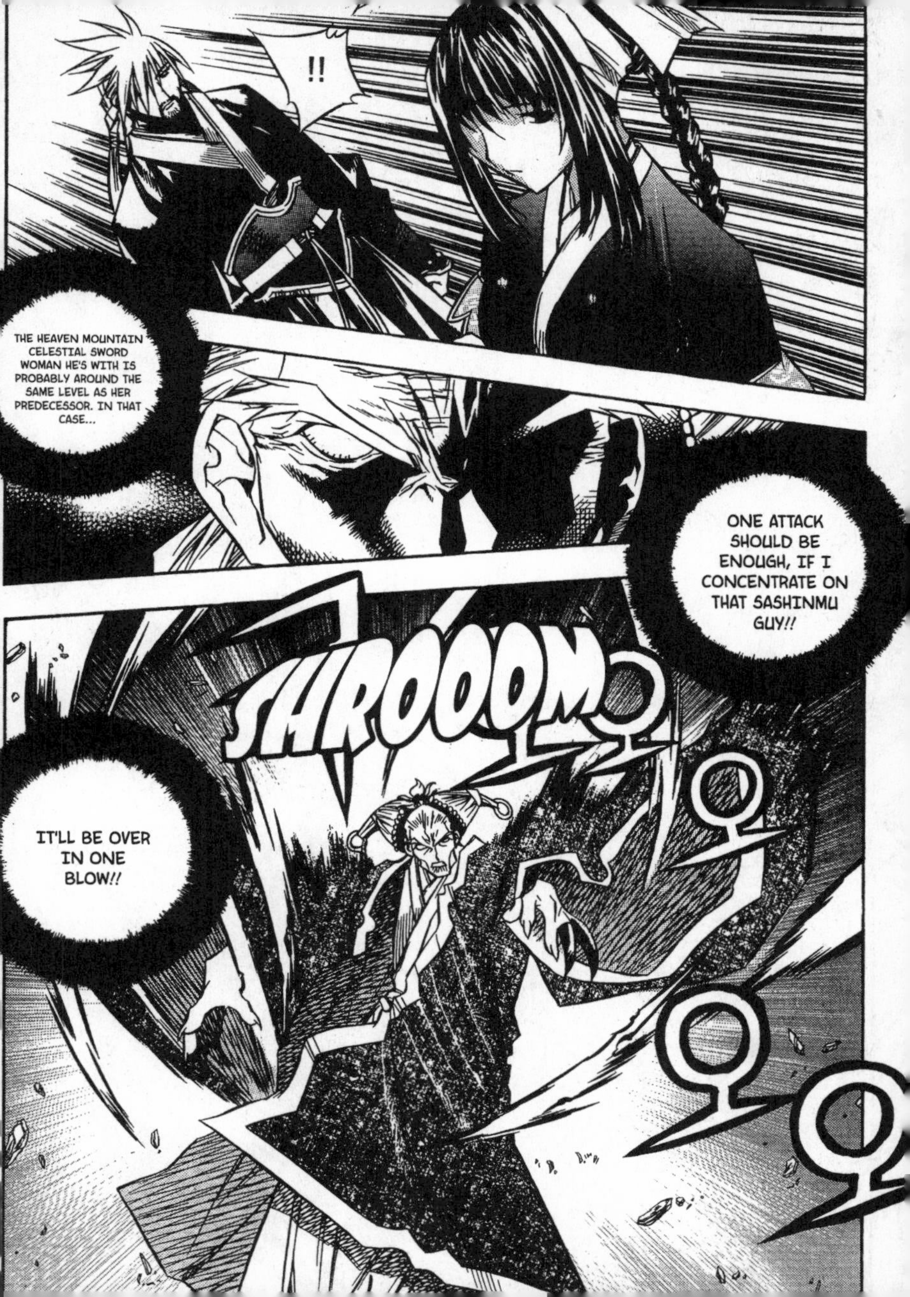
!!
THE HEAVEN MOUNTAIN CELESTIAL SWORD WOMAN HE'S WITH IS PROBABLY AROUND THE SAME LEVEL AS HER PREDECESSOR. IN THAT CASE...
ONE ATTACK SHOULD BE ENOUGH, IF I CONCENTRATE ON THAT SASHINMU GUY!!
SHROOOM
IT'LL BE OVER IN ONE BLOW!!

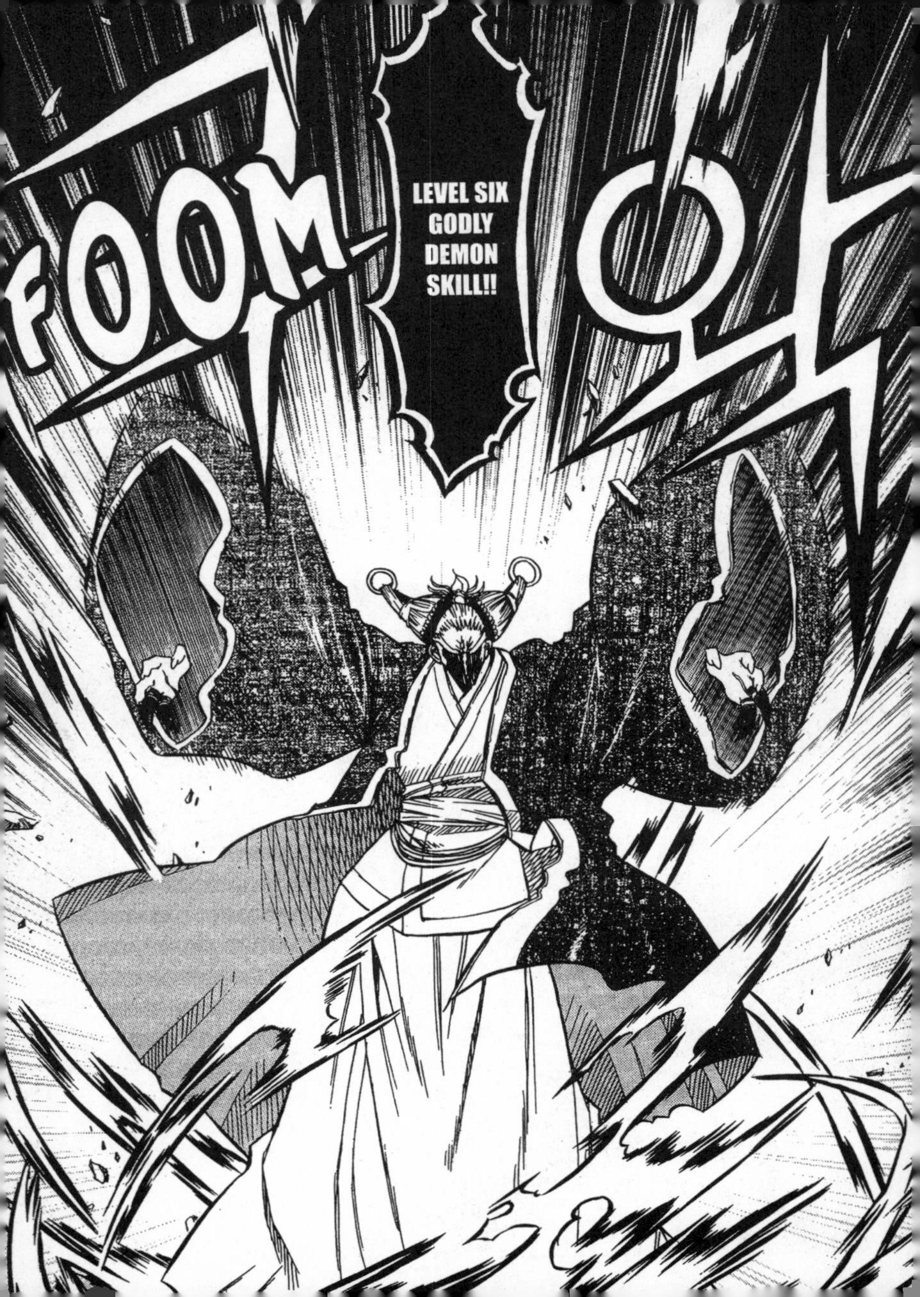
FOOM
LEVEL SIX GODLY DEMON SKILL!!

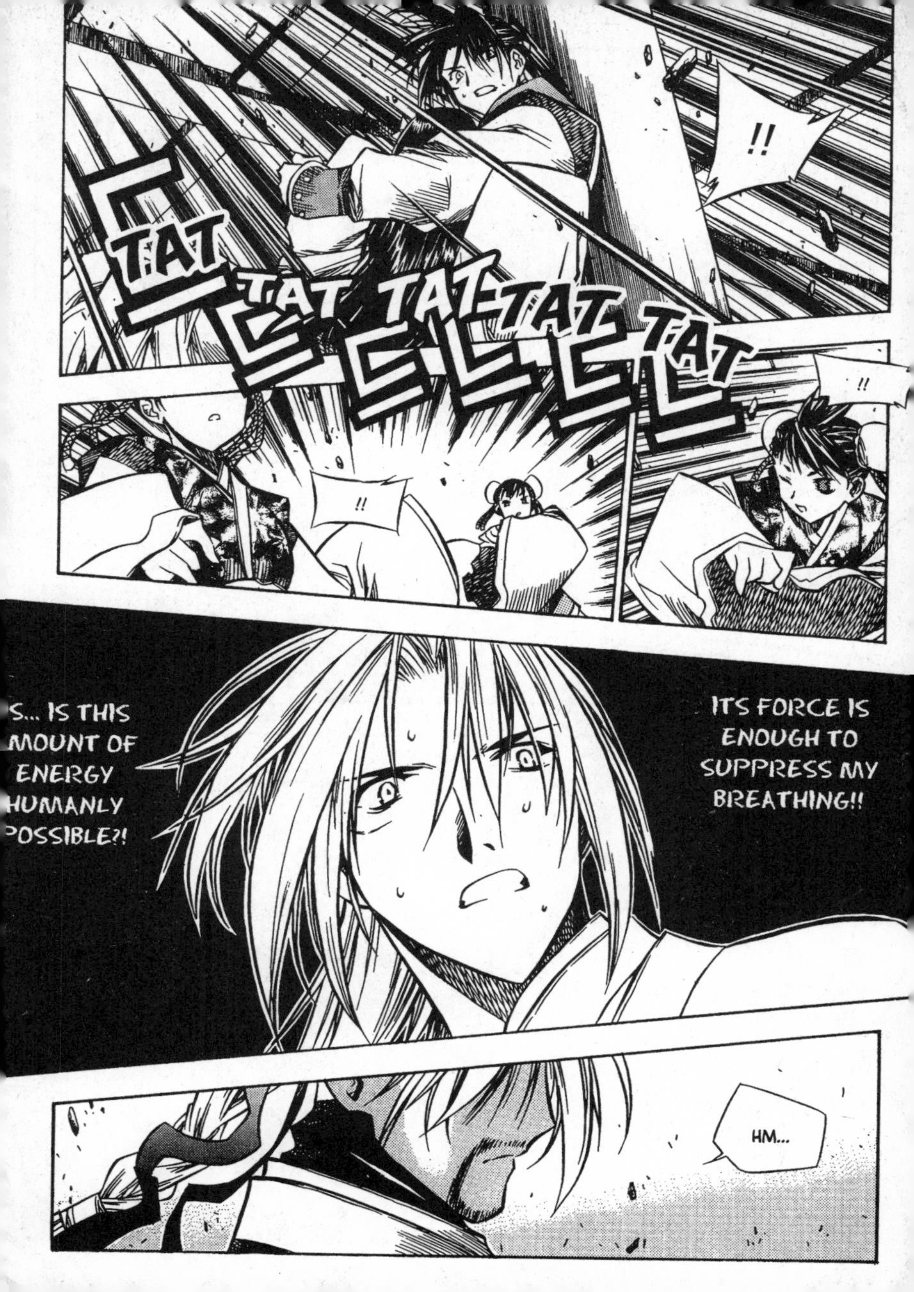
!!
TAT TAT TAT TAT TAT TAT
!!
!!
ITS FORCE IS ENOUGH TO SUPPRESS MY BREATHING!!
S... IS THIS MOUNT OF ENERGY HUMANLY OSSIBLE?!
HM...

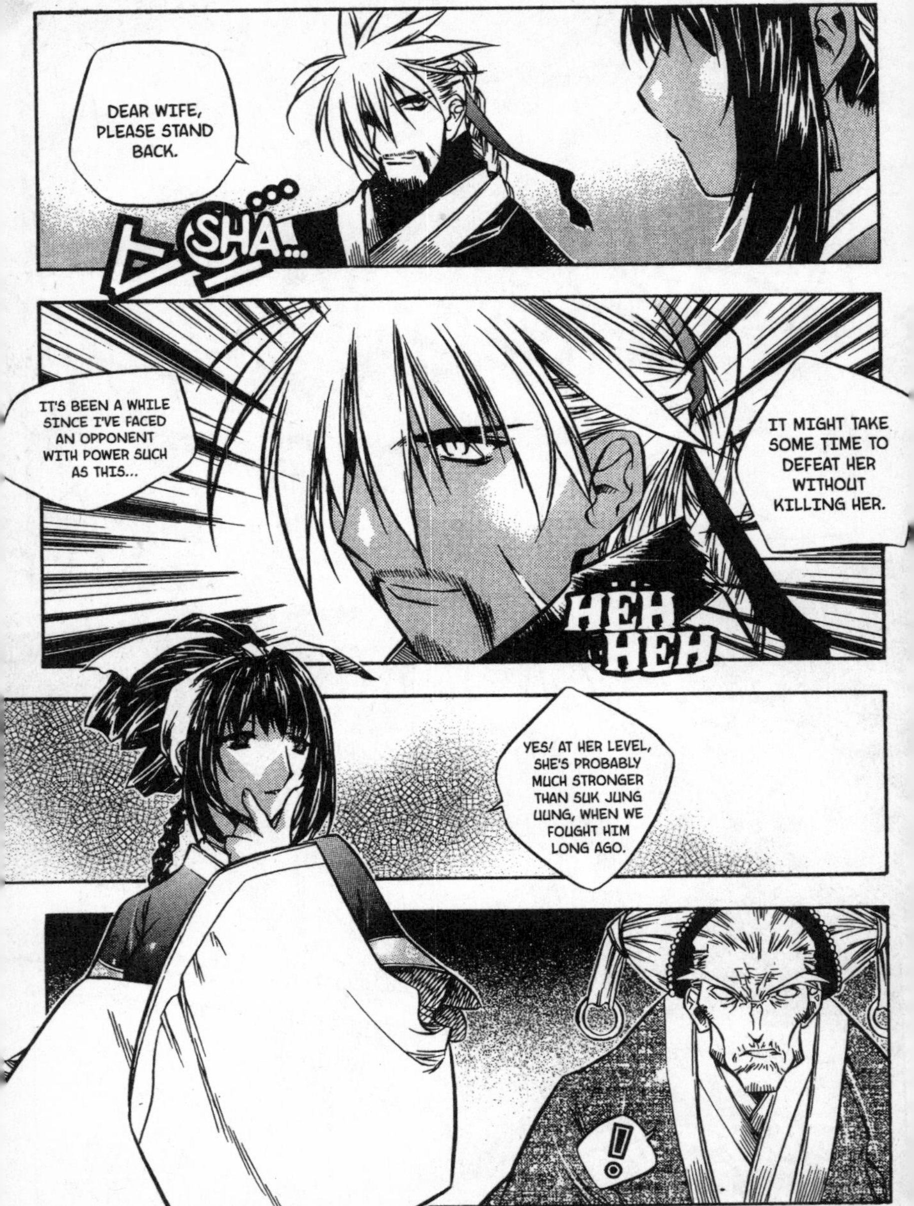

DEAR WIFE, PLEASE STAND BACK.
SHA...
IT MIGHT TAKE SOME TIME TO DEFEAT HER WITHOUT KILLING HER.
IT'S BEEN A WHILE SINCE I'VE FACED AN OPPONENT WITH POWER SUCH AS THIS...
HEH HEH
YES! AT HER LEVEL, SHE'S PROBABLY MUCH STRONGER THAN SUK JUNG UUNG, WHEN WE FOUGHT HIM LONG AGO.
!

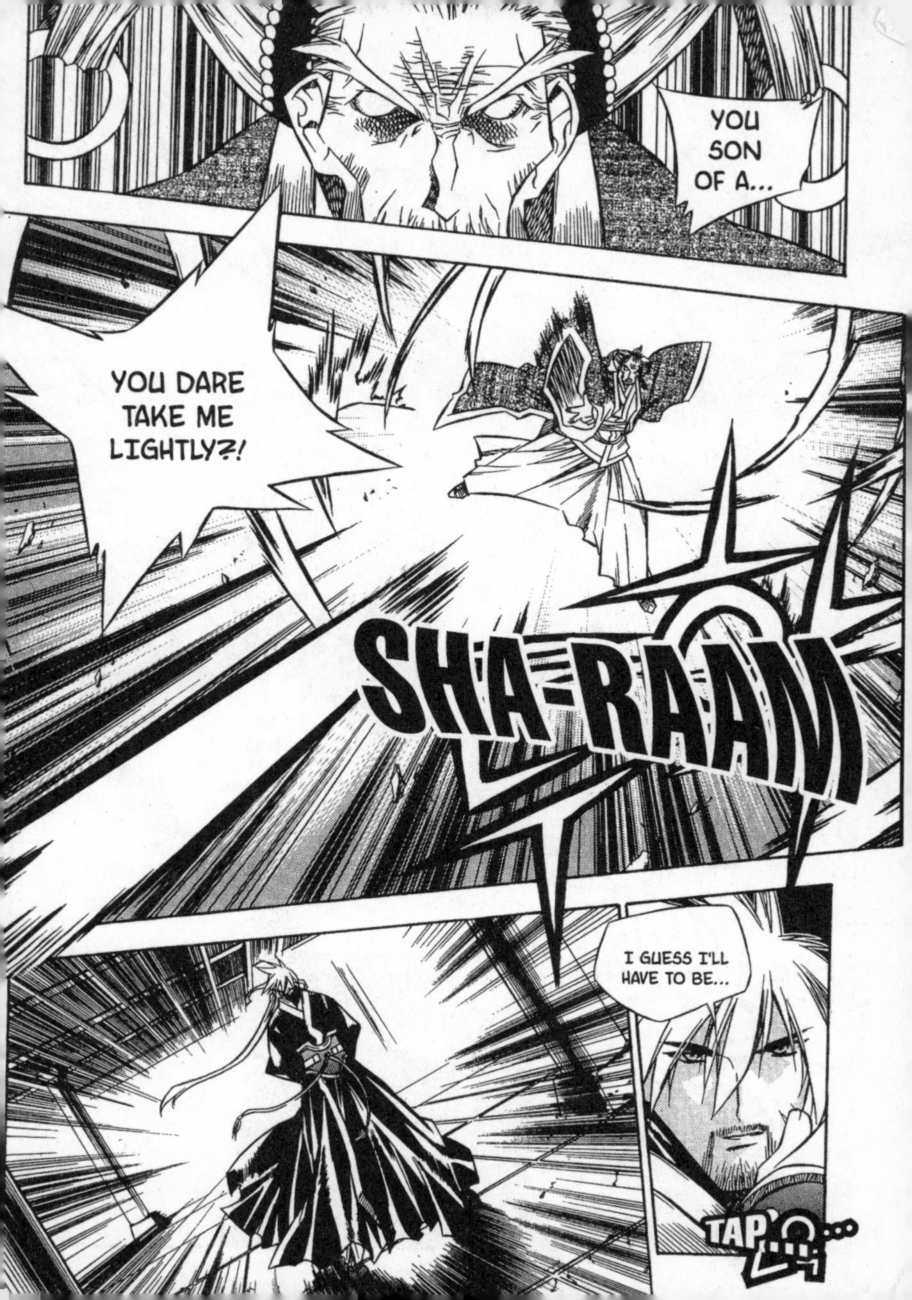
YOU SON OF A...
YOU DARE TAKE ME LIGHTLY?!
SHA-RAAM
I GUESS I'LL HAVE TO BE...
TAP

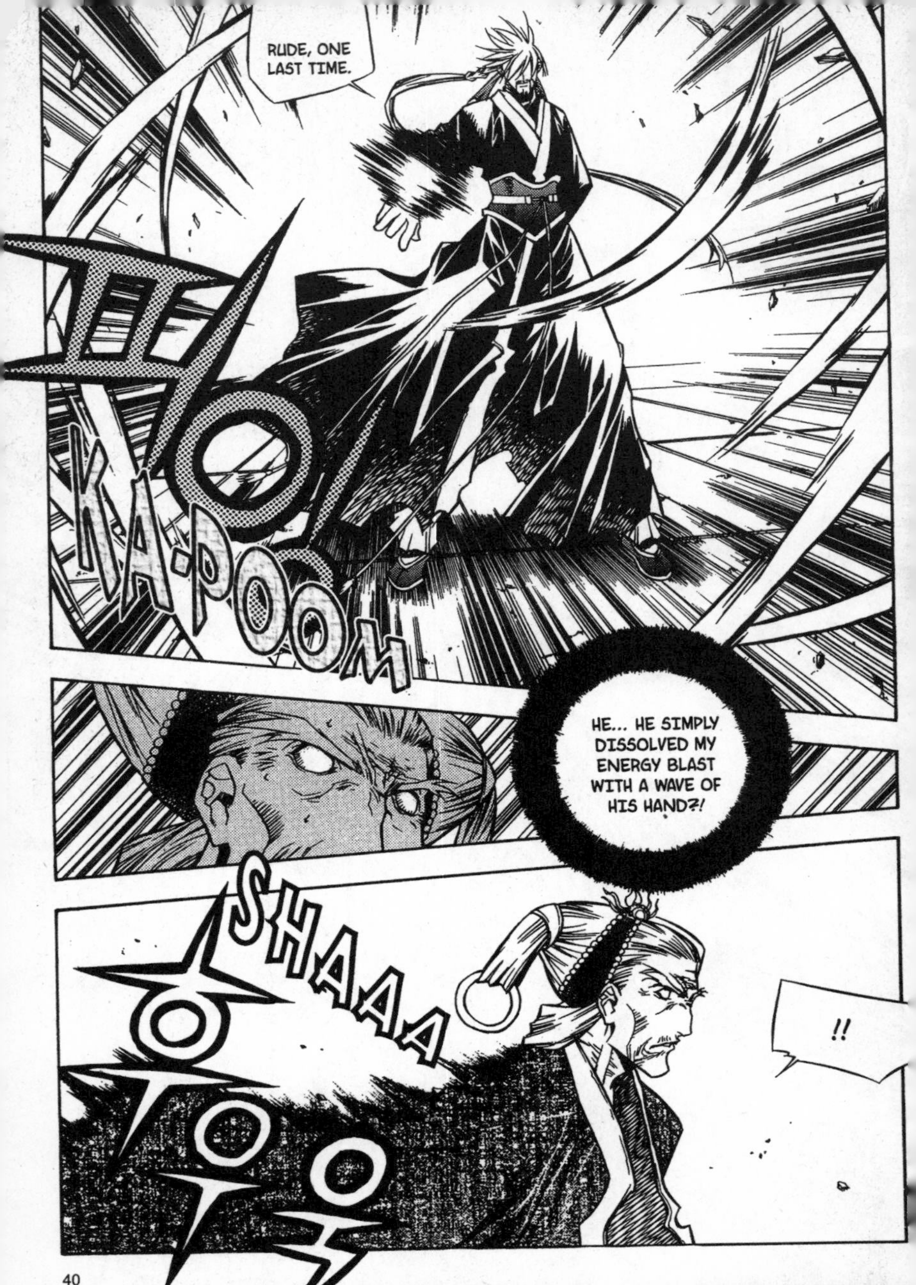
RUDE, ONE LAST TIME.
KA-POOOM
HE... HE SIMPLY DISSOLVED MY ENERGY BLAST WITH A WAVE OF HIS HAND?!
SHAAA
!!

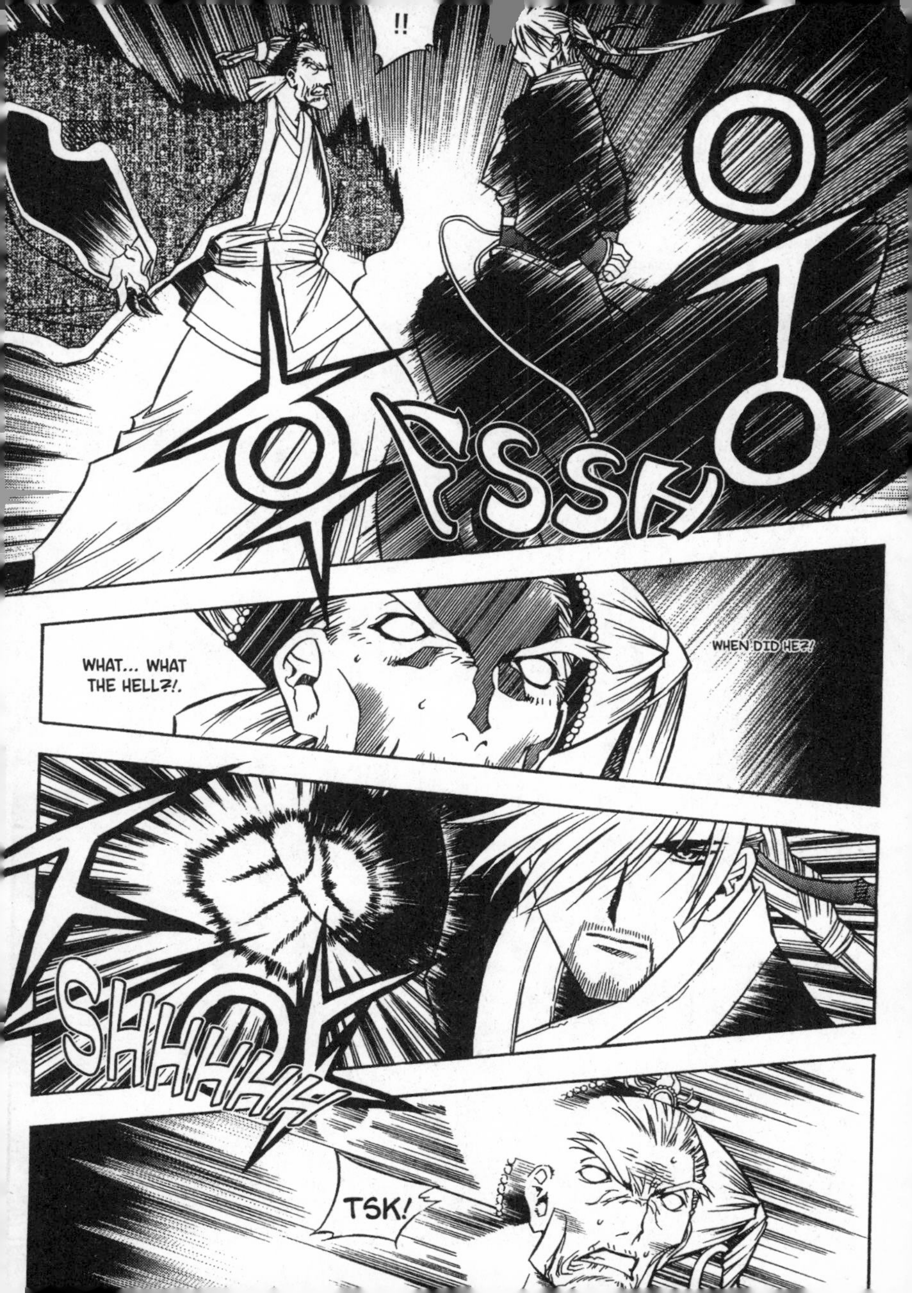
!!
FSSH
WHAT... WHAT THE HELL?!.
WHEN DID HE?!
SHHHHH
TSK!

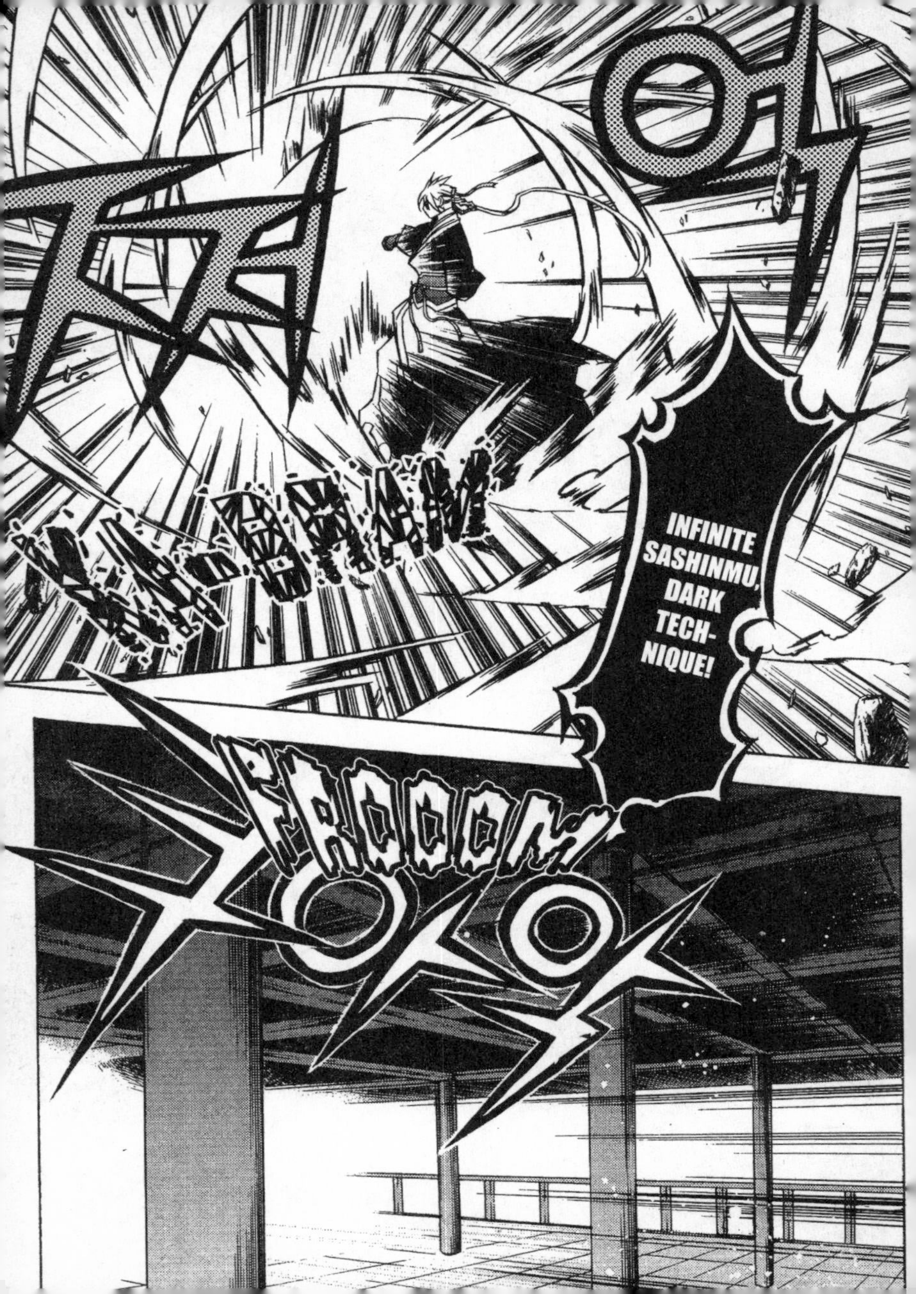
INFINITE SASHINMU, DARK TECHNIQUE!
FOOOOM

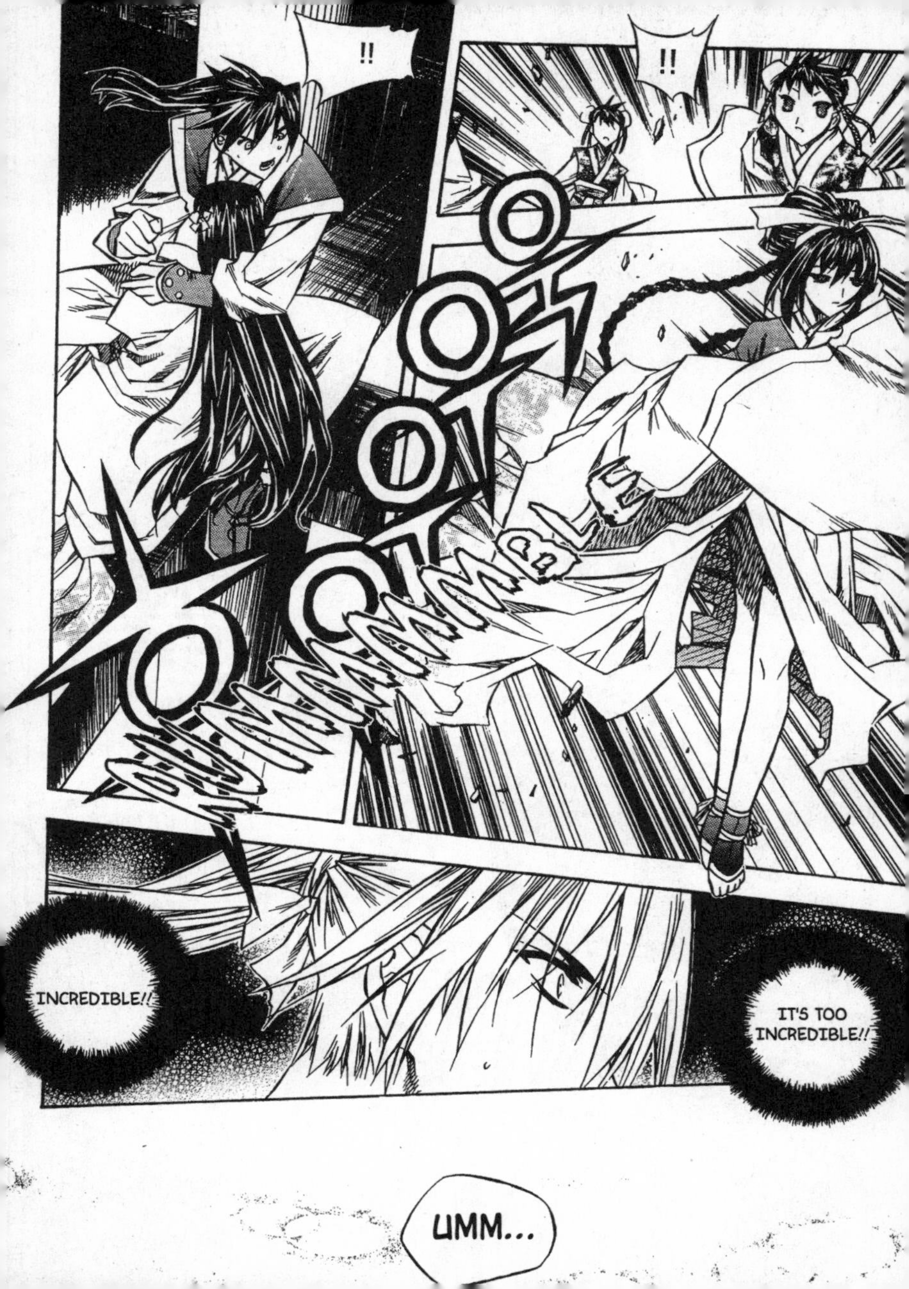
!!
!!
IT'S TOO INCREDIBLE!!
INCREDIBLE!!
UMM...

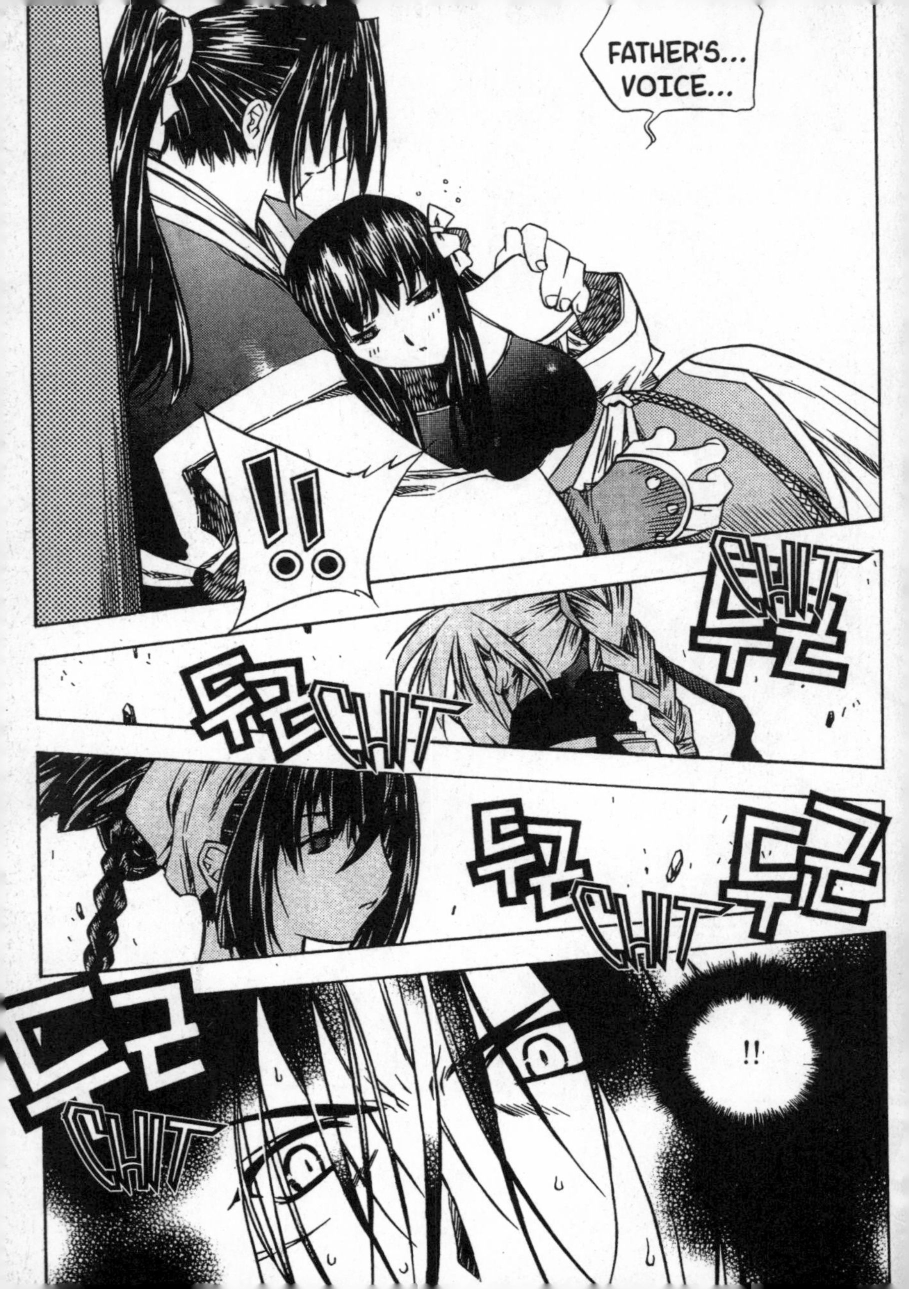
FATHER'S... VOICE...
!!
CHIT
CHIT
CHIT
CHIT
!!

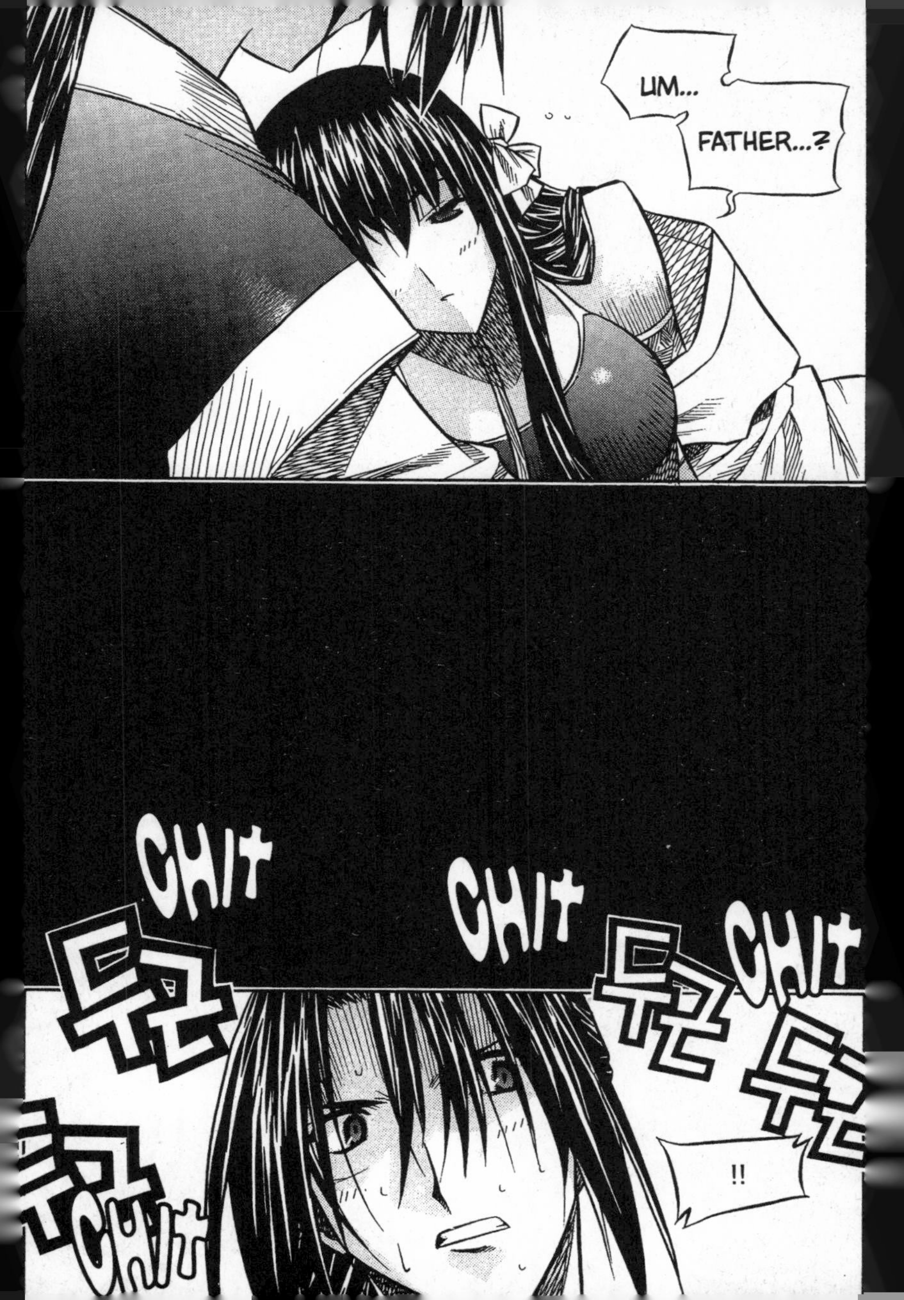

UM...
FATHER...?
CHIT
CHIT
CHIT
CHIT
!!

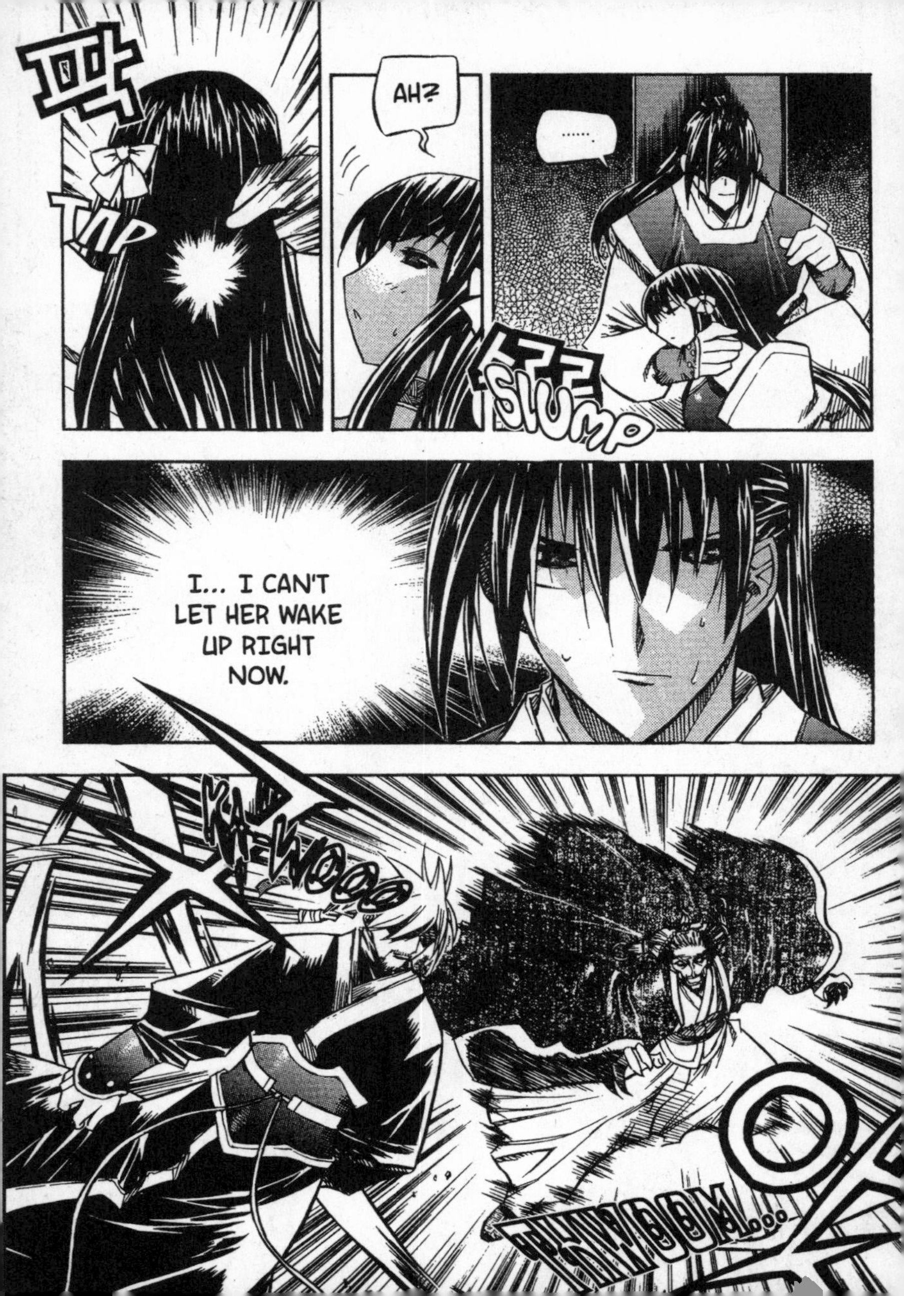
퍽
TAP
AH?
......
SLUMP
I... I CAN'T LET HER WAKE UP RIGHT NOW.

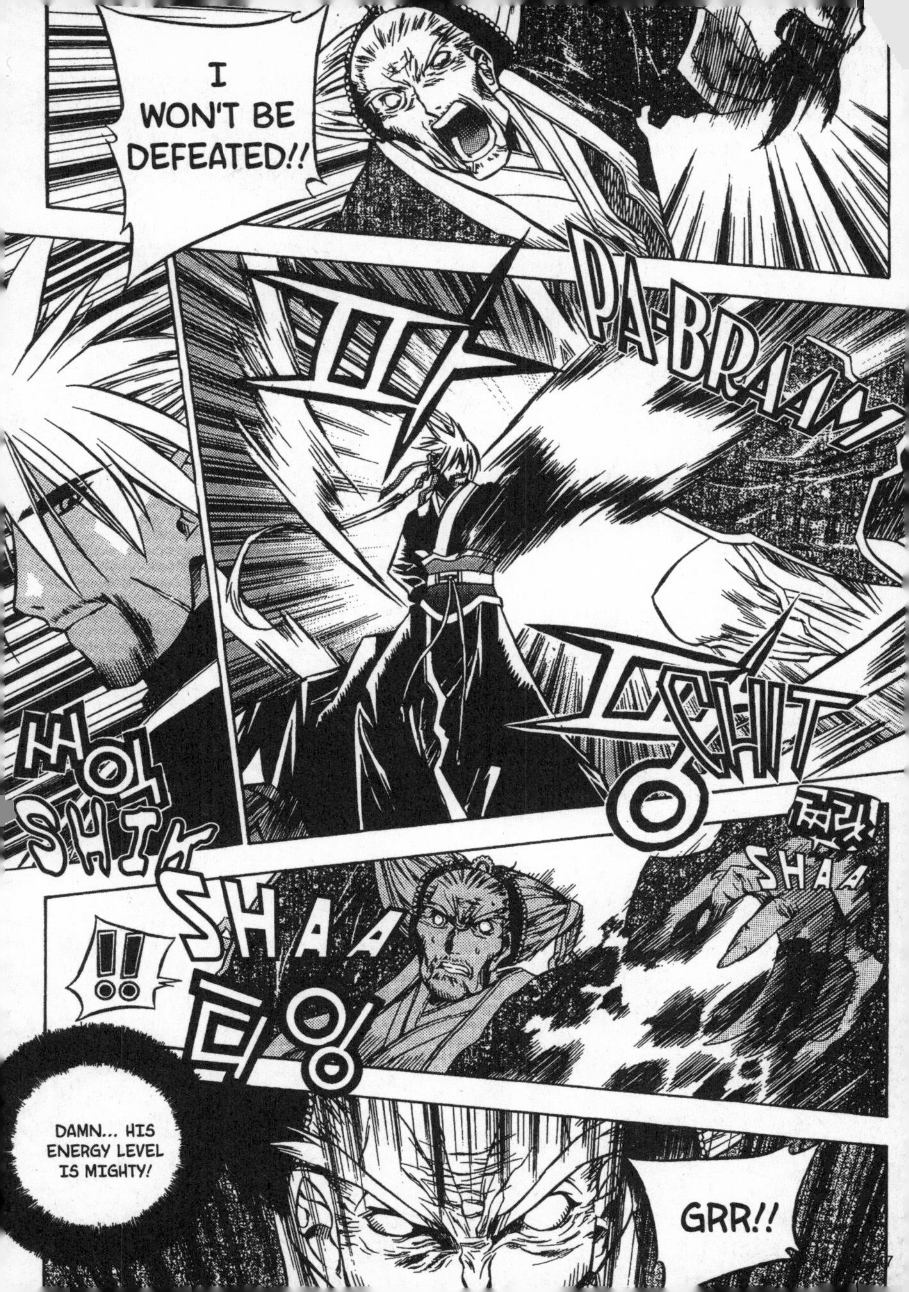
I WON'T BE DEFEATED!!
PA-BRAAM
ICHIT
SHIK
SHAA
!!
SHAA
DAMN... HIS ENERGY LEVEL IS MIGHTY!
GRR!!

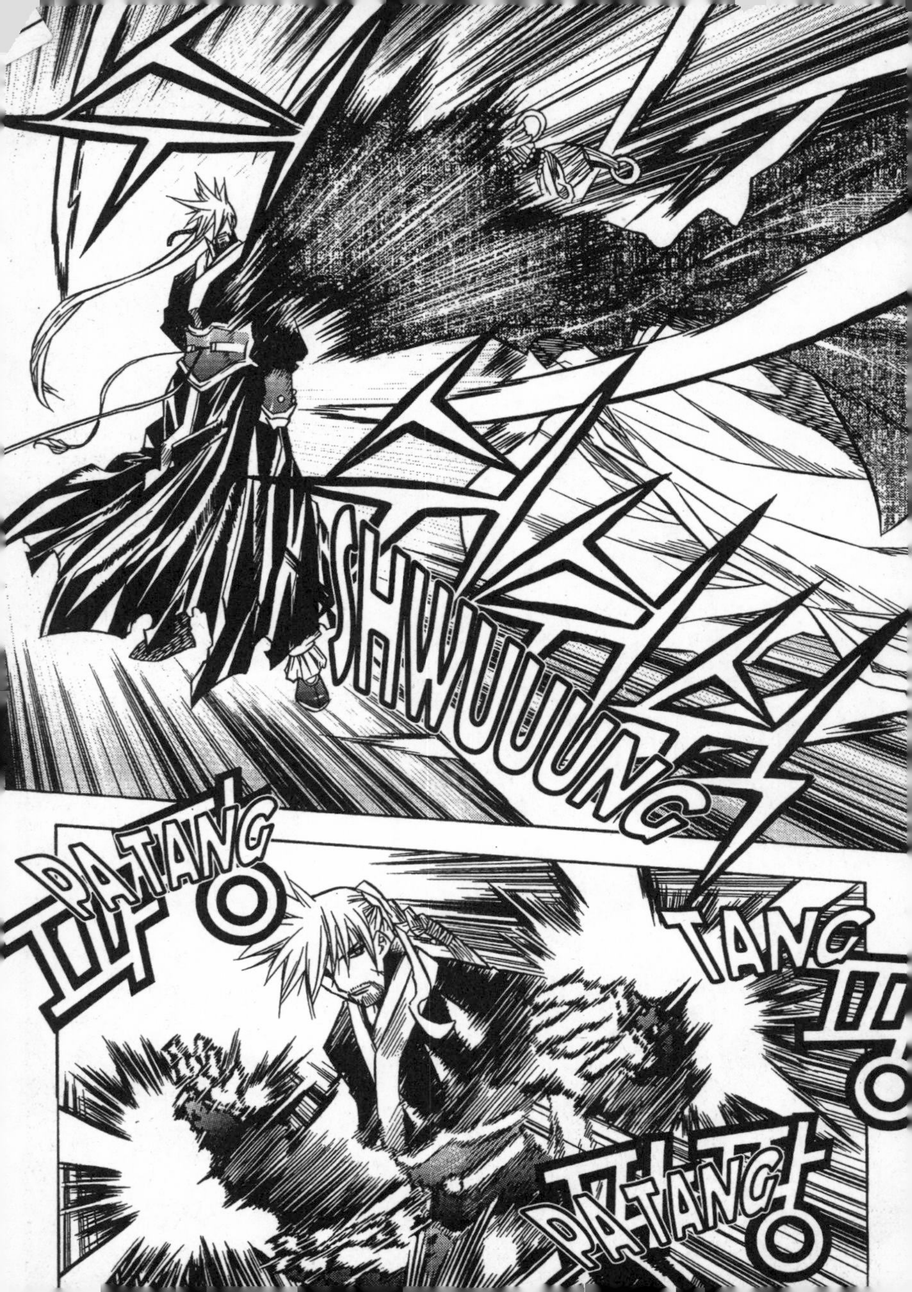
SHWUUUNG
PATANG
TANG
PATANG

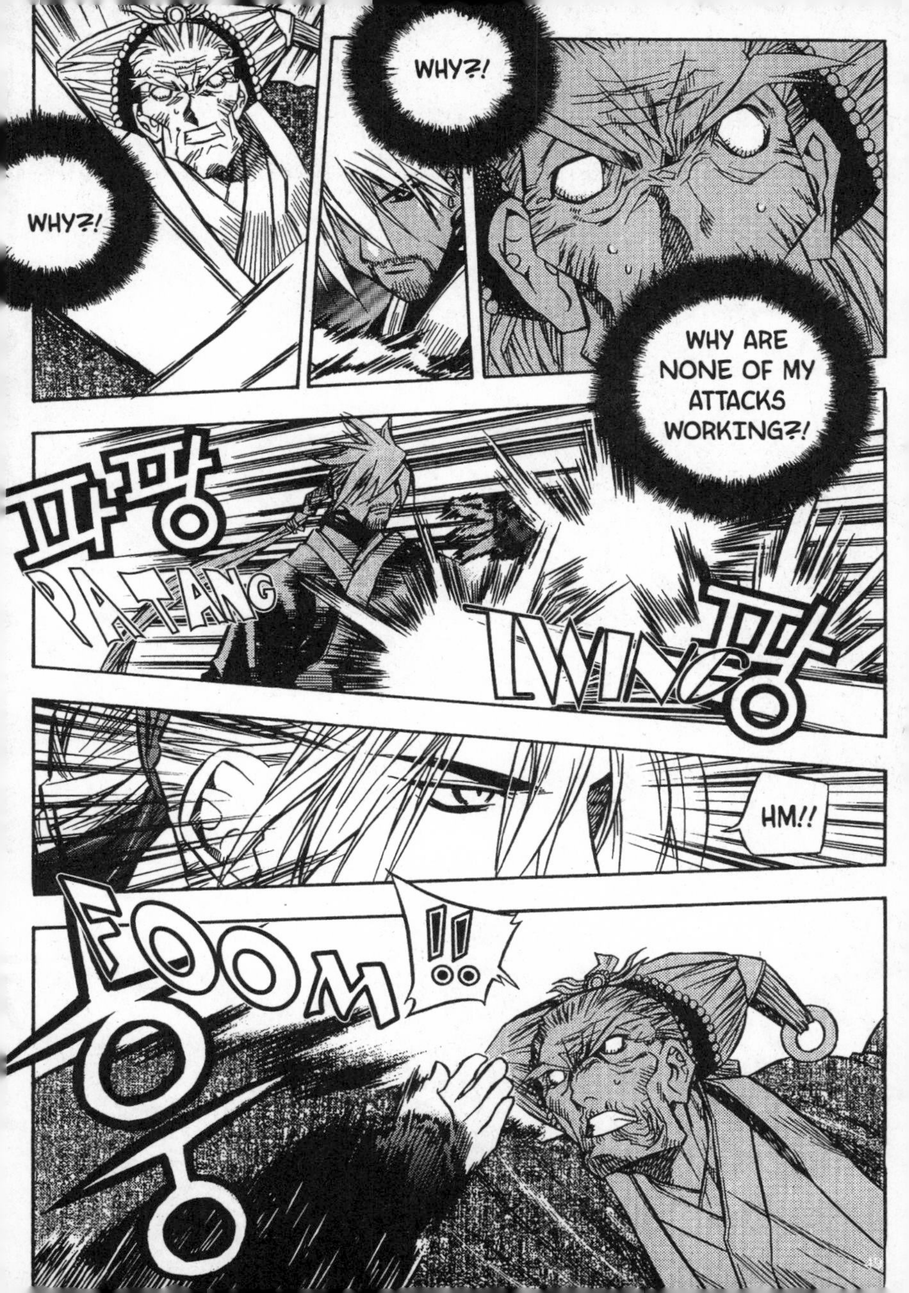
WHY?!
WHY?!
WHY ARE NONE OF MY ATTACKS WORKING?!
파팡
PA-TANG
TWING
HM!!
FOOM!!

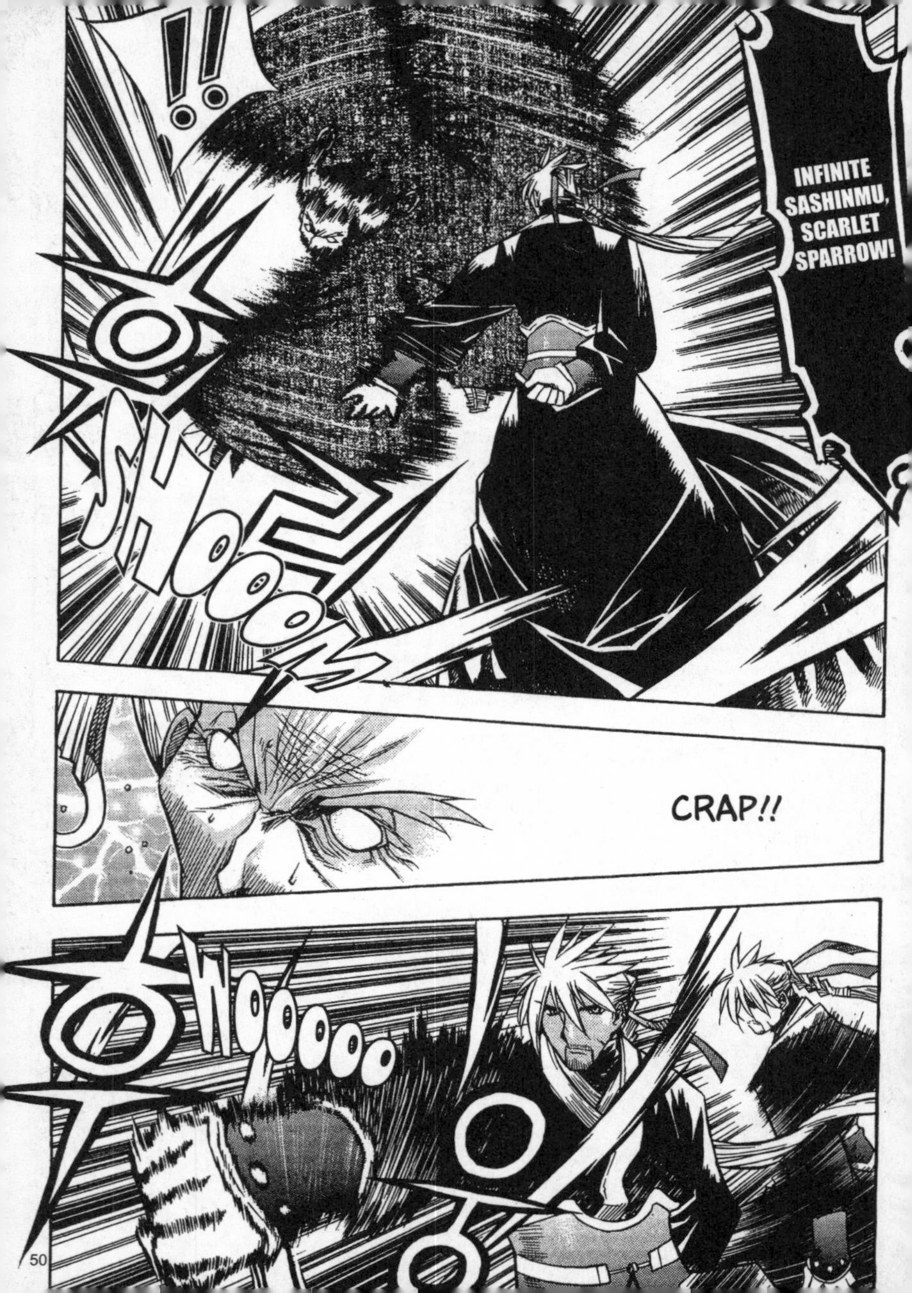
!!
INFINITE SASHINMU, SCARLET SPARROW!
SHOOOOM
CRAP!!
WOOOOOO

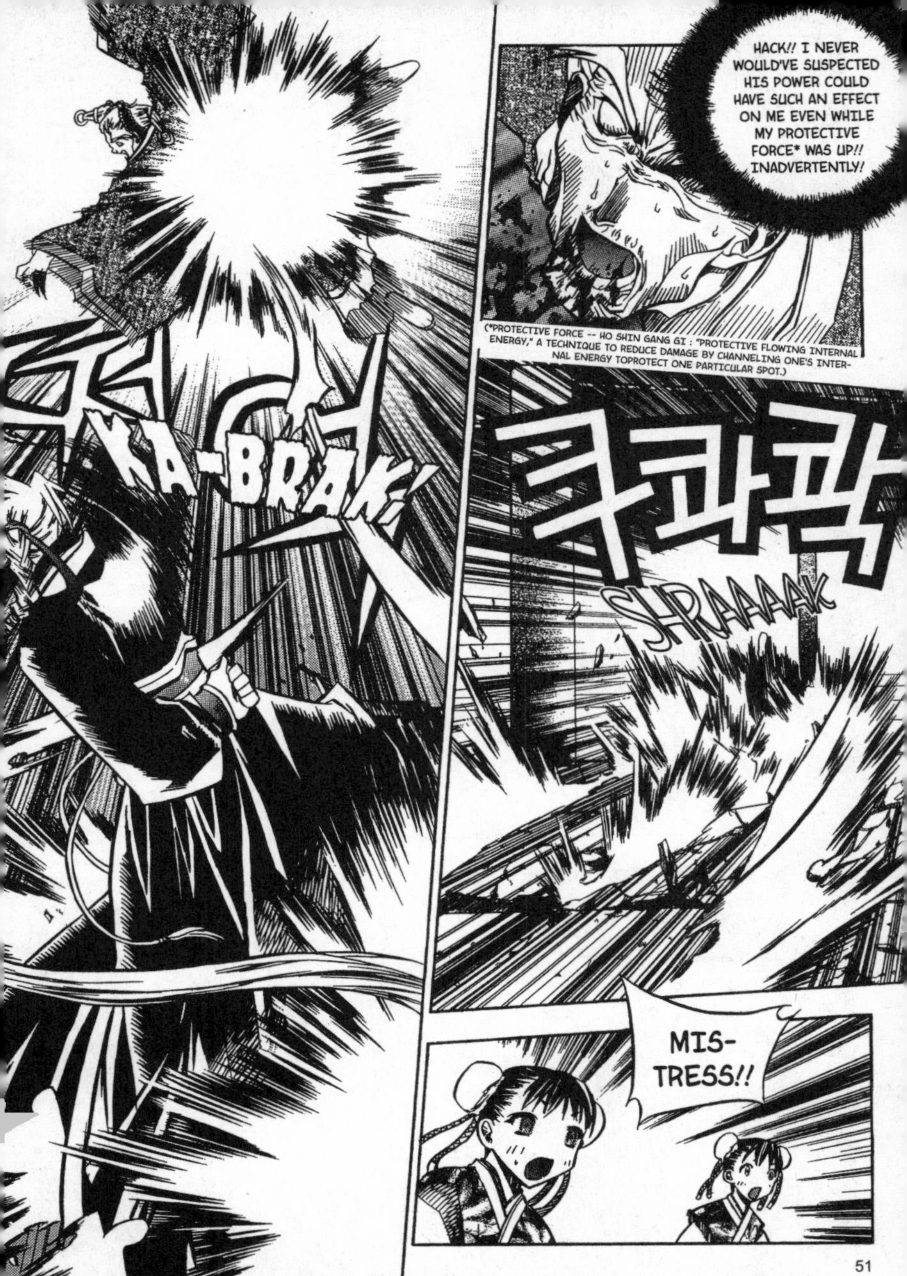
KA-BRAK!
HACK!! I NEVER WOULD'VE SUSPECTED HIS POWER COULD HAVE SUCH AN EFFECT ON ME EVEN WHILE MY PROTECTIVE FORCE* WAS UP!! INADVERTENTLY!
(*PROTECTIVE FORCE -- HO SHIN GANG GI : "PROTECTIVE FLOWING INTERNAL ENERGY," A TECHNIQUE TO REDUCE DAMAGE BY CHANNELING ONE'S INTERNAL ENERGY TOPROTECT ONE PARTICULAR SPOT.)
콰파팍
SHRAAAAK
MIS-TRESS!!

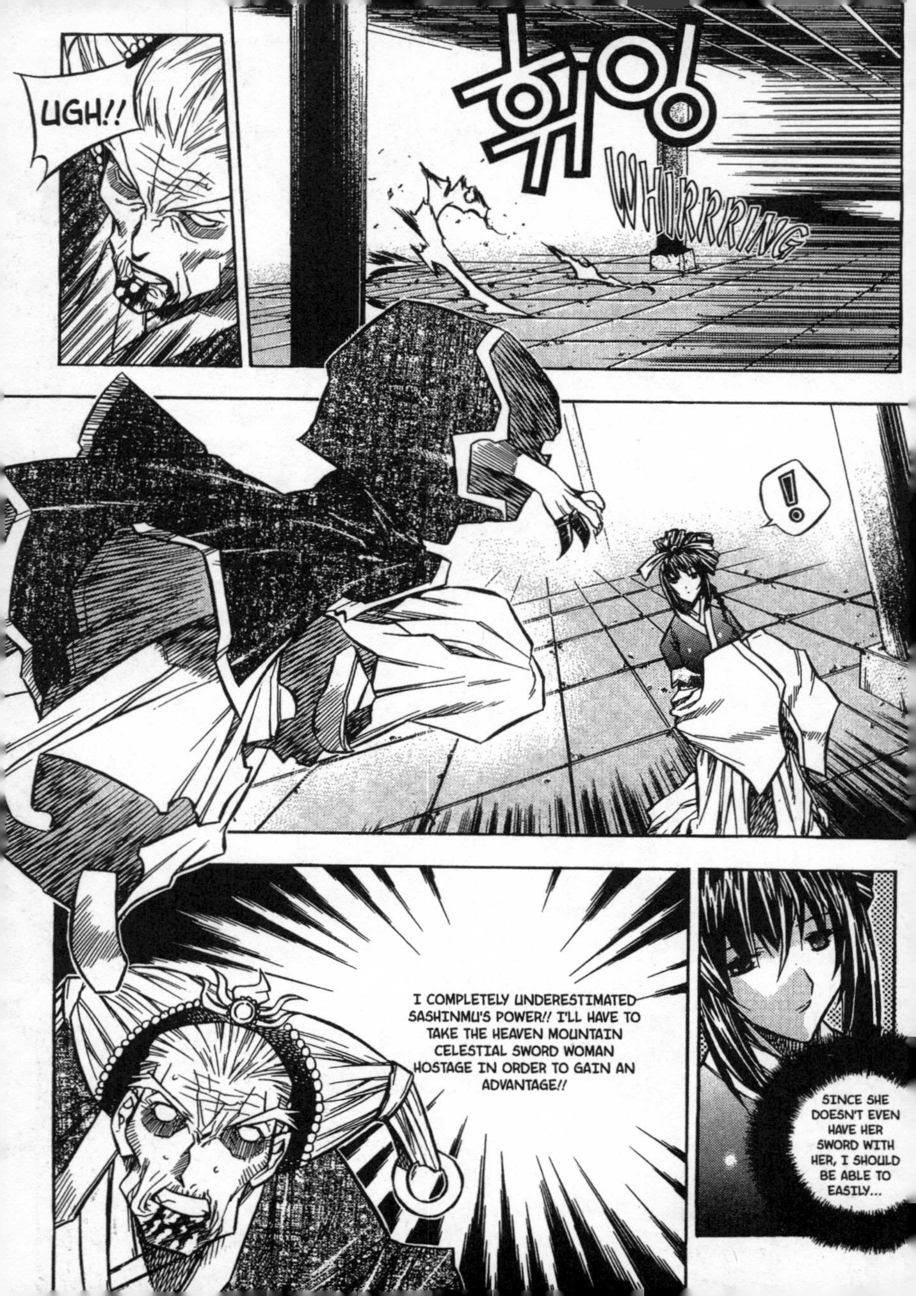
UGH!!
휘이잉
WHIRRRING
!
I COMPLETELY UNDERESTIMATED SASHINMU'S POWER!! I'LL HAVE TO TAKE THE HEAVEN MOUNTAIN CELESTIAL SWORD WOMAN HOSTAGE IN ORDER TO GAIN AN ADVANTAGE!!
SINCE SHE DOESN'T EVEN HAVE HER SWORD WITH HER, I SHOULD BE ABLE TO EASILY...

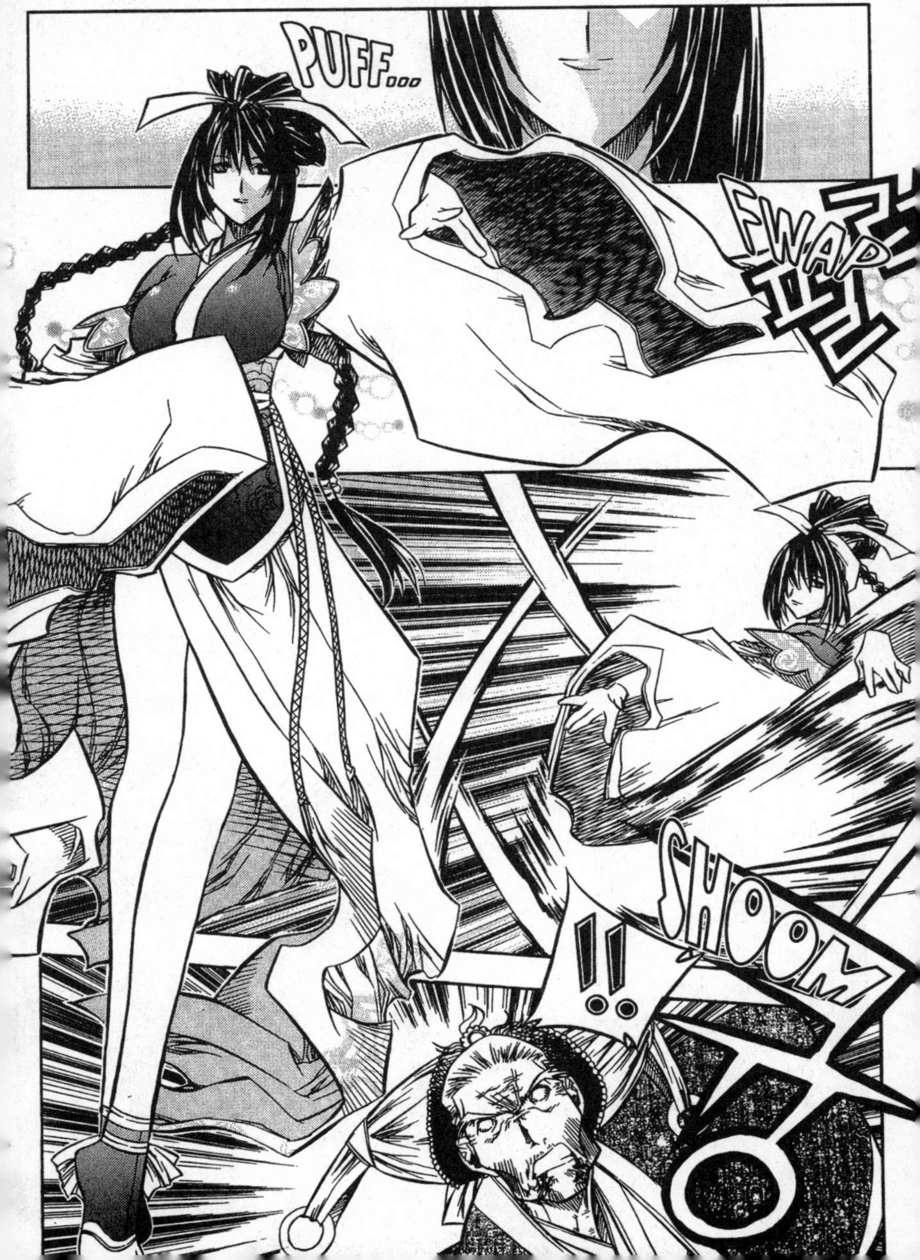
PUFF...
FWAP
SHOOM
!!

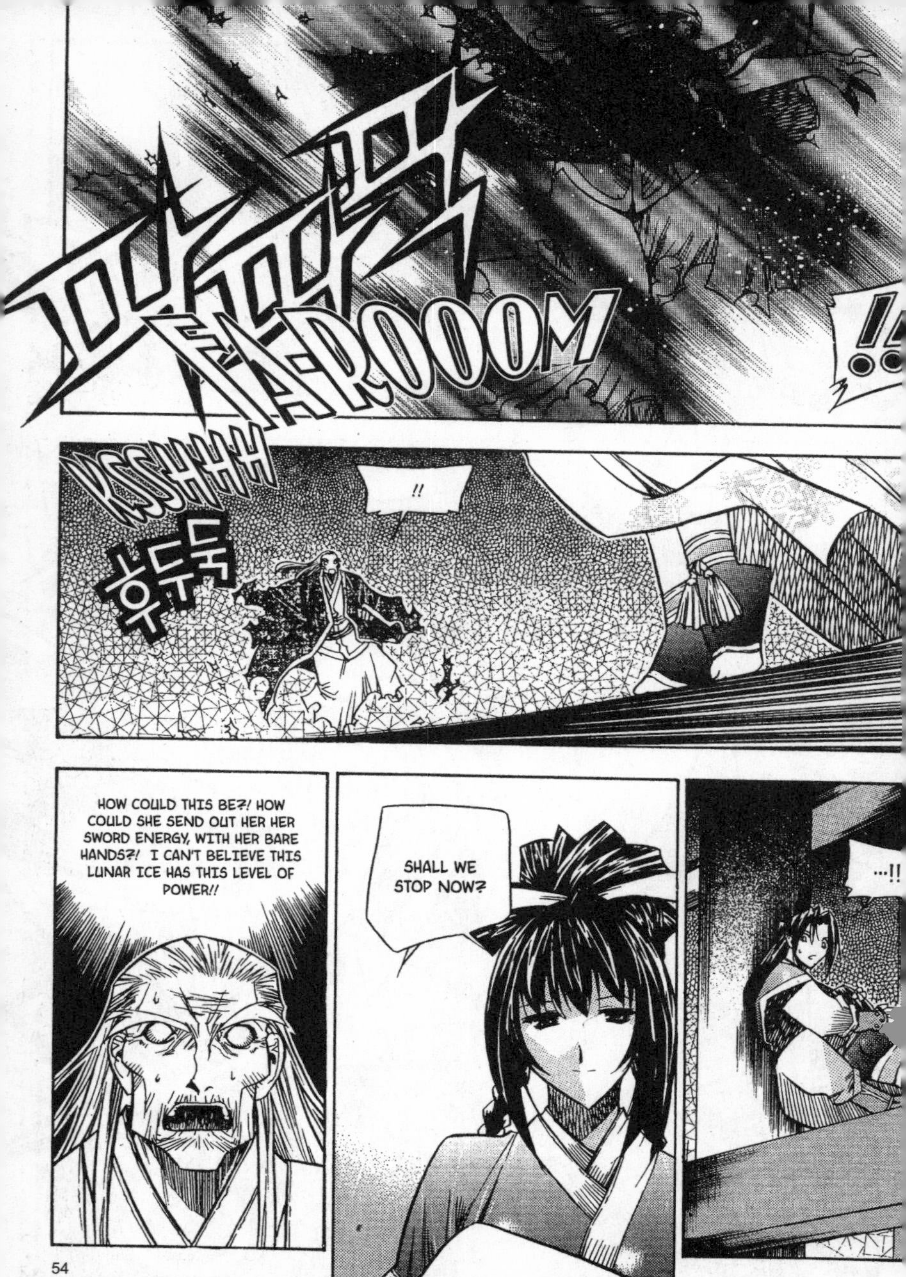

KA-ROOOM
!!
KSSHHH
!!
HOW COULD THIS BE?! HOW COULD SHE SEND OUT HER HER SWORD ENERGY, WITH HER BARE HANDS?! I CAN'T BELIEVE THIS LUNAR ICE HAS THIS LEVEL OF POWER!!
SHALL WE STOP NOW?
...!!

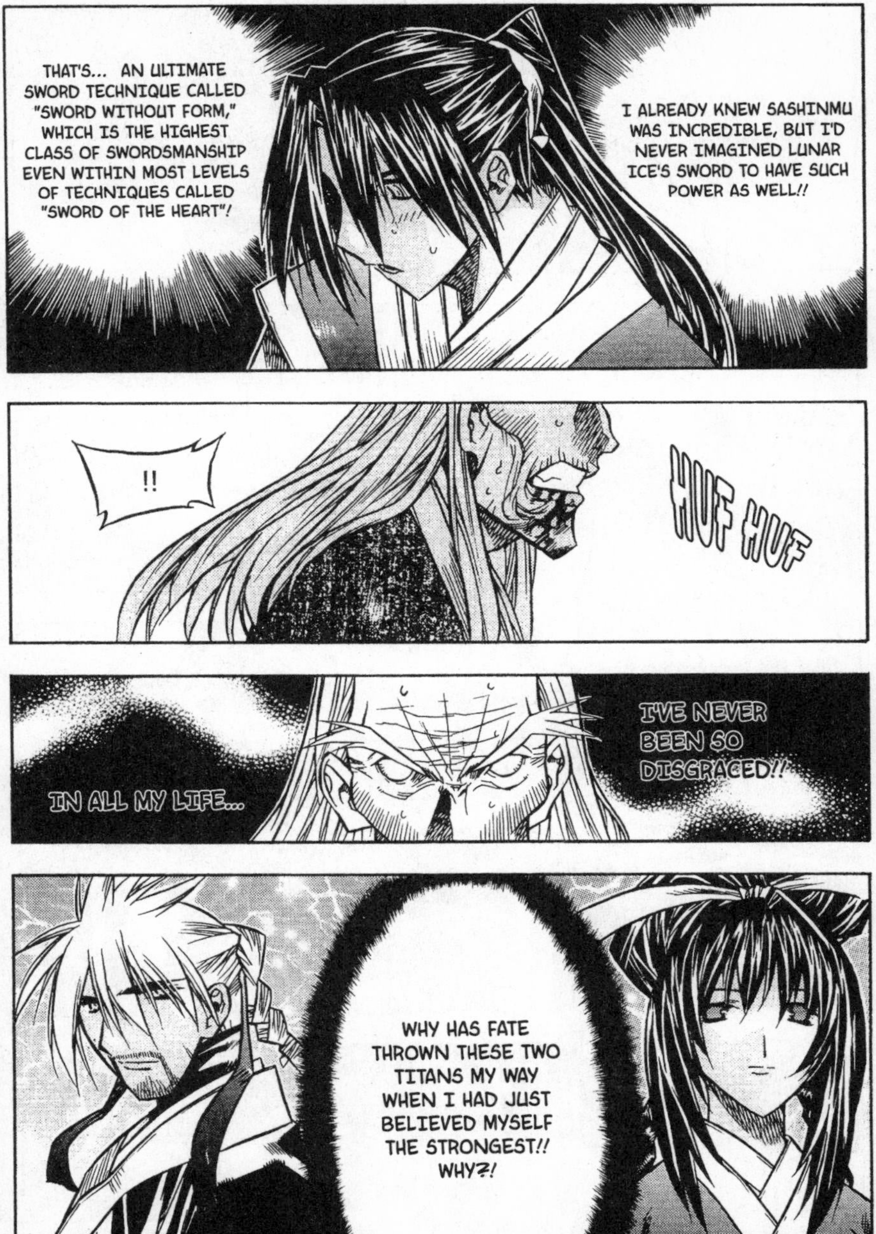
I ALREADY KNEW SASHINMU WAS INCREDIBLE, BUT I'D NEVER IMAGINED LUNAR ICE'S SWORD TO HAVE SUCH POWER AS WELL!!
THAT'S... AN ULTIMATE SWORD TECHNIQUE CALLED "SWORD WITHOUT FORM," WHICH IS THE HIGHEST CLASS OF SWORDSMANSHIP EVEN WITHIN MOST LEVELS OF TECHNIQUES CALLED "SWORD OF THE HEART"!
HUF HUF
!!
I'VE NEVER BEEN SO DISGRACED!!
IN ALL MY LIFE...
WHY HAS FATE THROWN THESE TWO TITANS MY WAY WHEN I HAD JUST BELIEVED MYSELF THE STRONGEST!! WHY?!

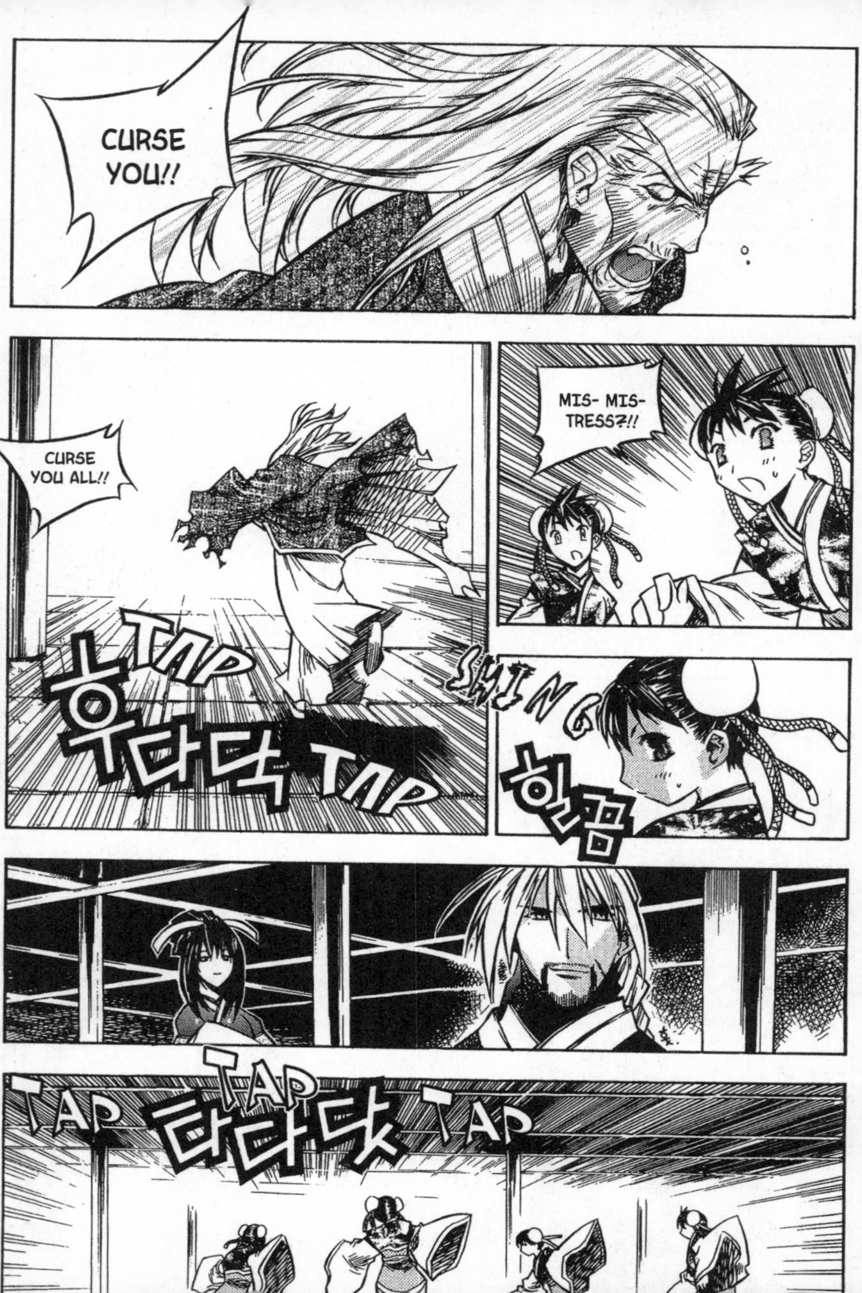
CURSE YOU!!
CURSE YOU ALL!!
MIS- MIS-TRESS?!!
TAP
후다닥
TAP
SWING
TAP
TAP
다다닥
TAP

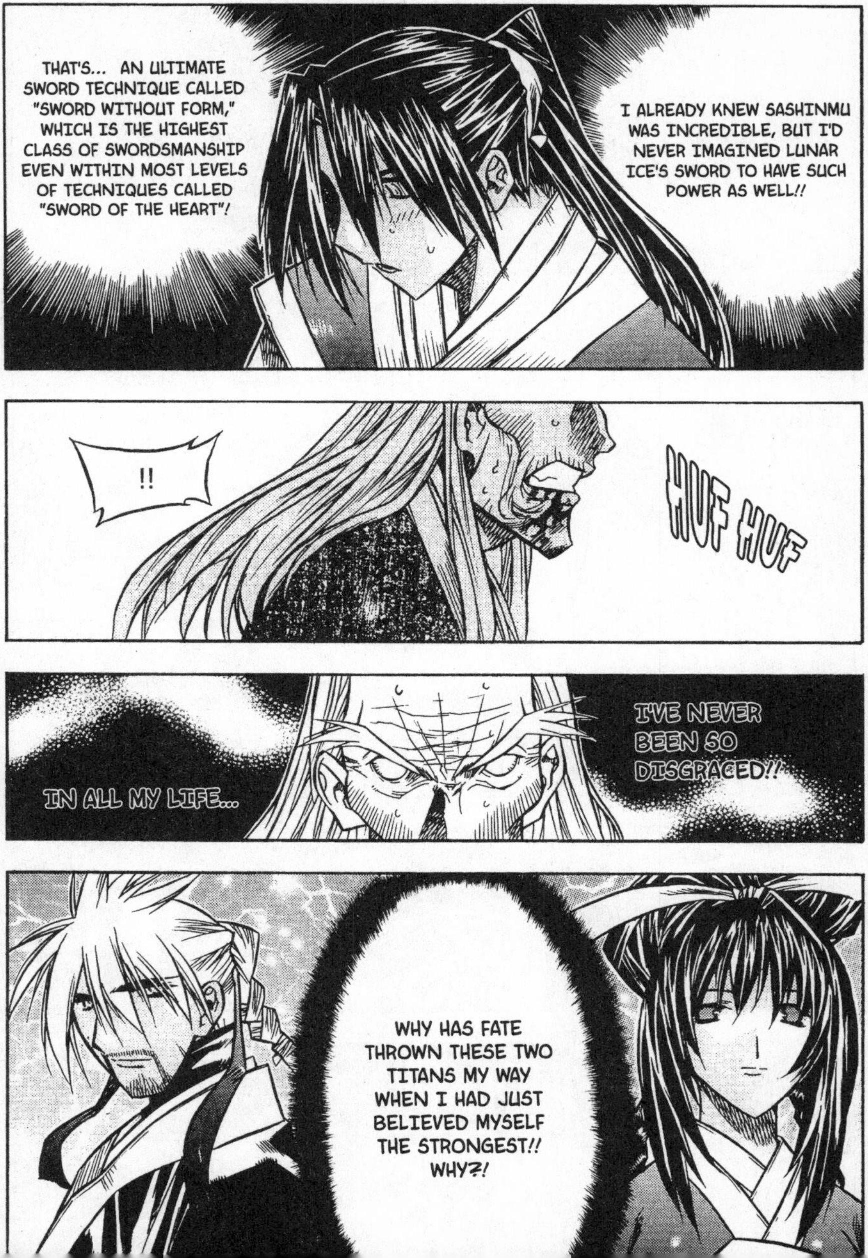
I ALREADY KNEW SASHINMU WAS INCREDIBLE, BUT I'D NEVER IMAGINED LUNAR ICE'S SWORD TO HAVE SUCH POWER AS WELL!!
THAT'S... AN ULTIMATE SWORD TECHNIQUE CALLED "SWORD WITHOUT FORM," WHICH IS THE HIGHEST CLASS OF SWORDSMANSHIP EVEN WITHIN MOST LEVELS OF TECHNIQUES CALLED "SWORD OF THE HEART"!
HUF HUF
!!
I'VE NEVER BEEN SO DISGRACED!!
IN ALL MY LIFE...
WHY HAS FATE THROWN THESE TWO TITANS MY WAY WHEN I HAD JUST BELIEVED MYSELF THE STRONGEST!! WHY?!

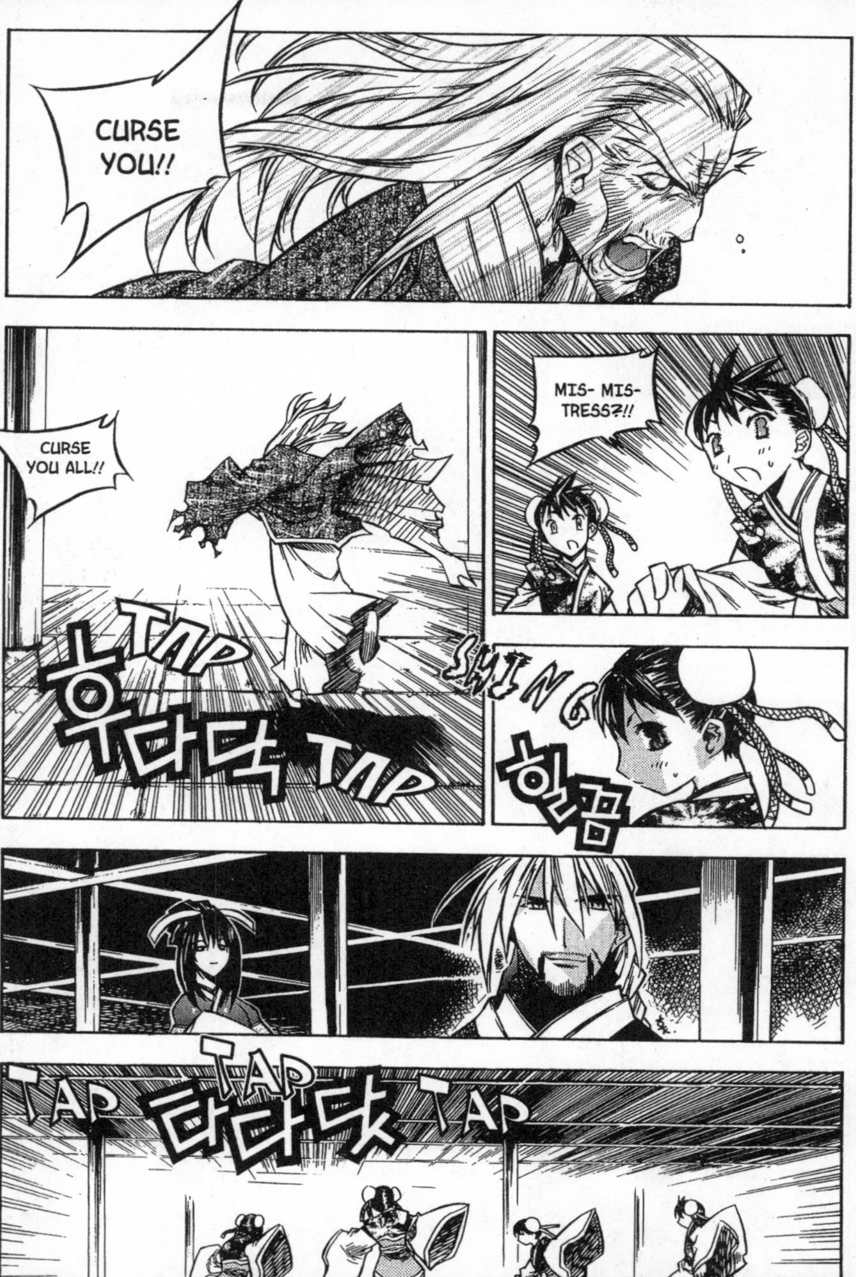
CURSE YOU!!
CURSE YOU ALL!!
TAP
후다닥
TAP
MIS- MIS- TRESS?!!
SWING
힐끔
TAP
TAP
다다닥
TAP

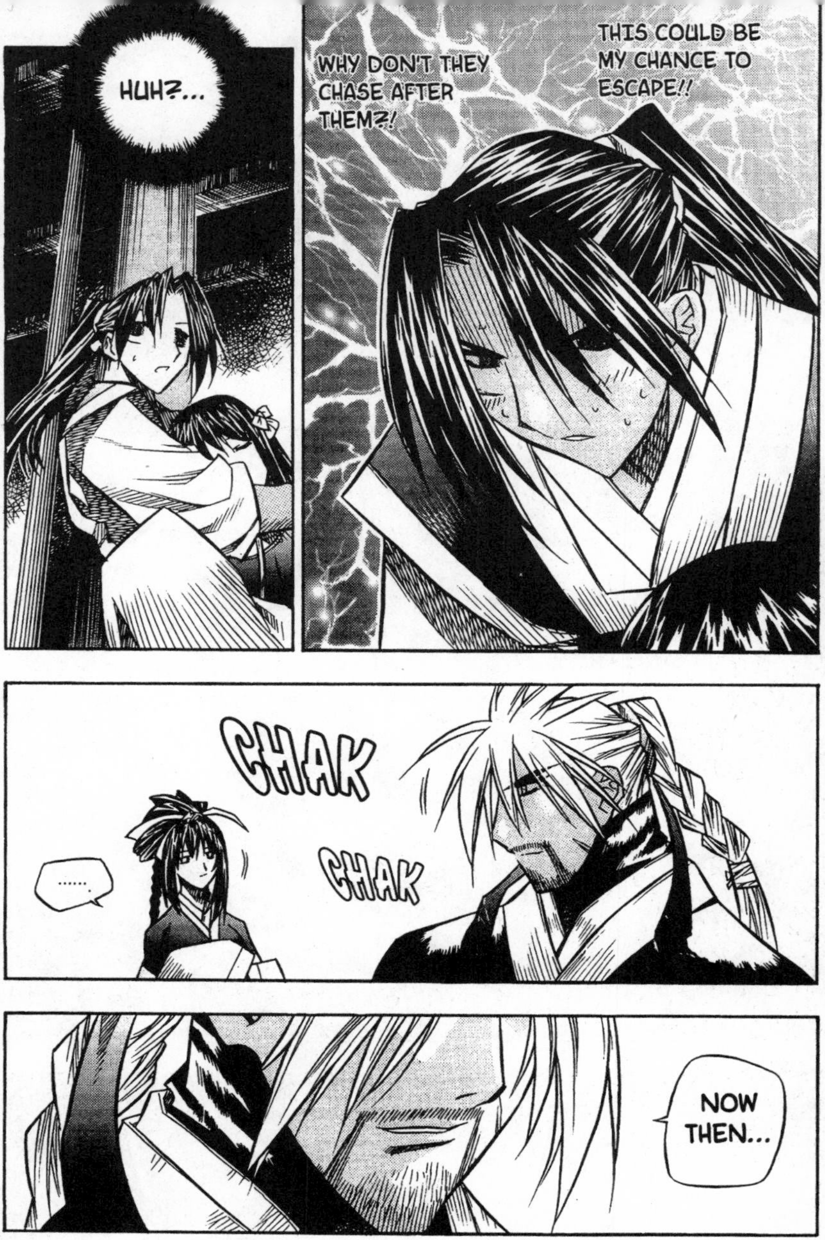
THIS COULD BE MY CHANCE TO ESCAPE!!
WHY DON'T THEY CHASE AFTER THEM?!
HUH?...
CHAK
CHAK
......
NOW THEN...

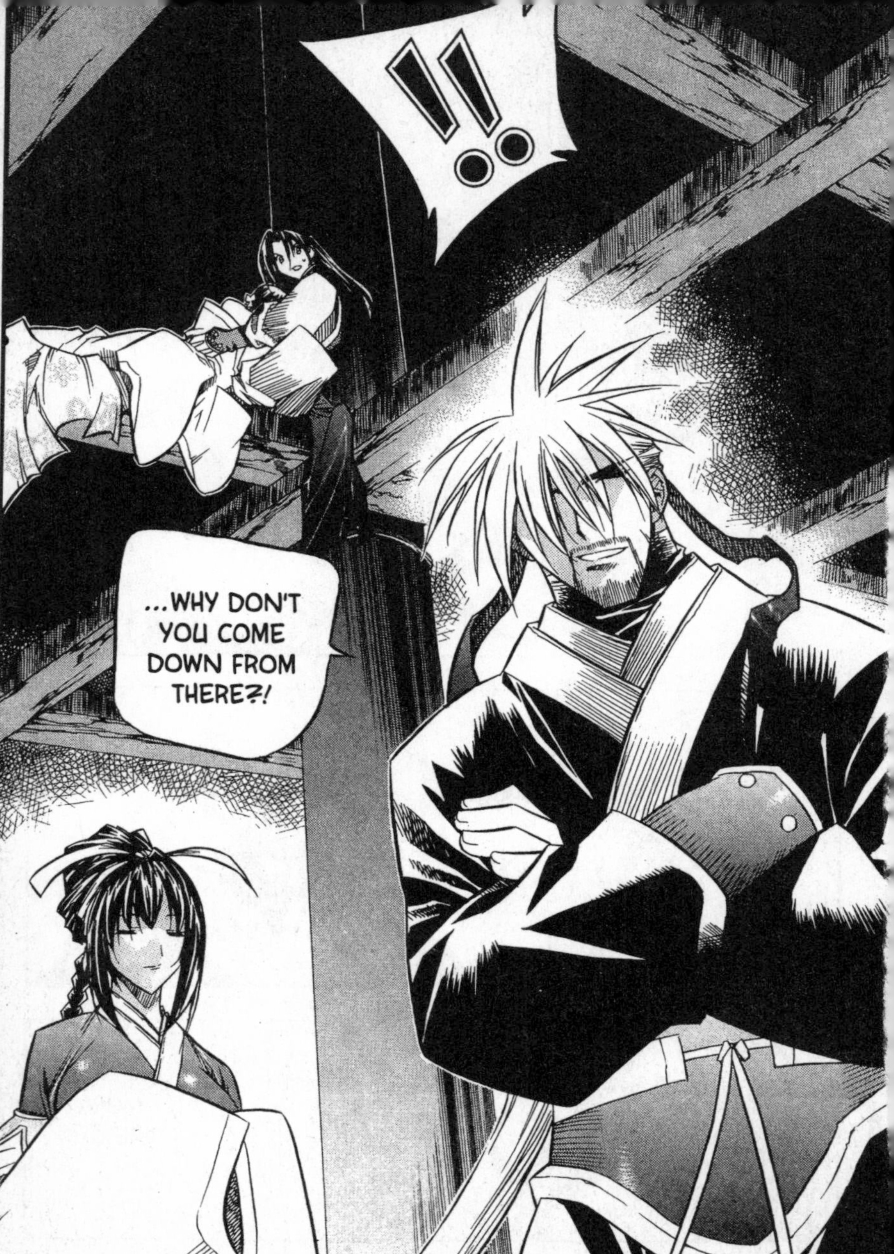
!!
...WHY DON'T YOU COME DOWN FROM THERE?!

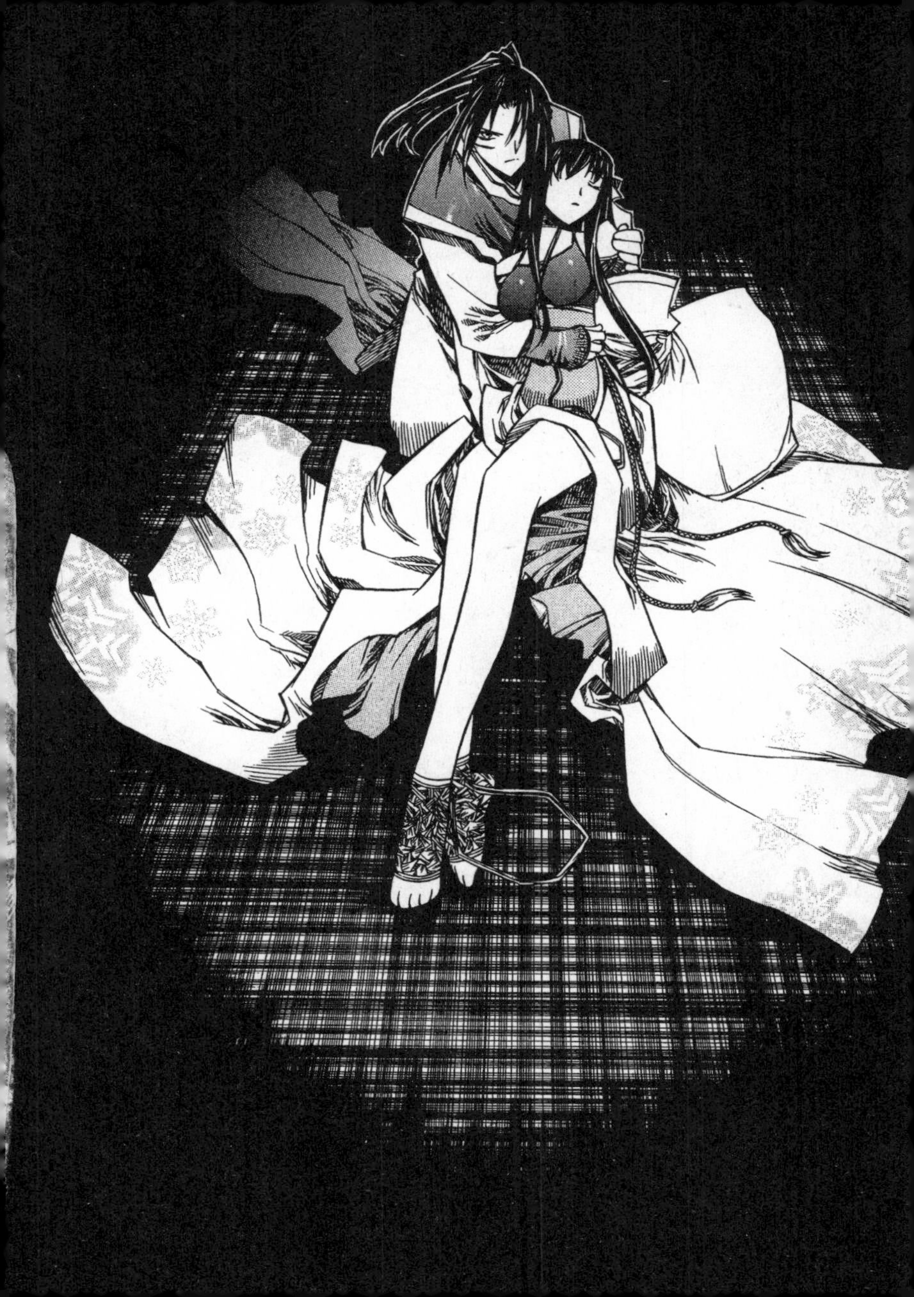

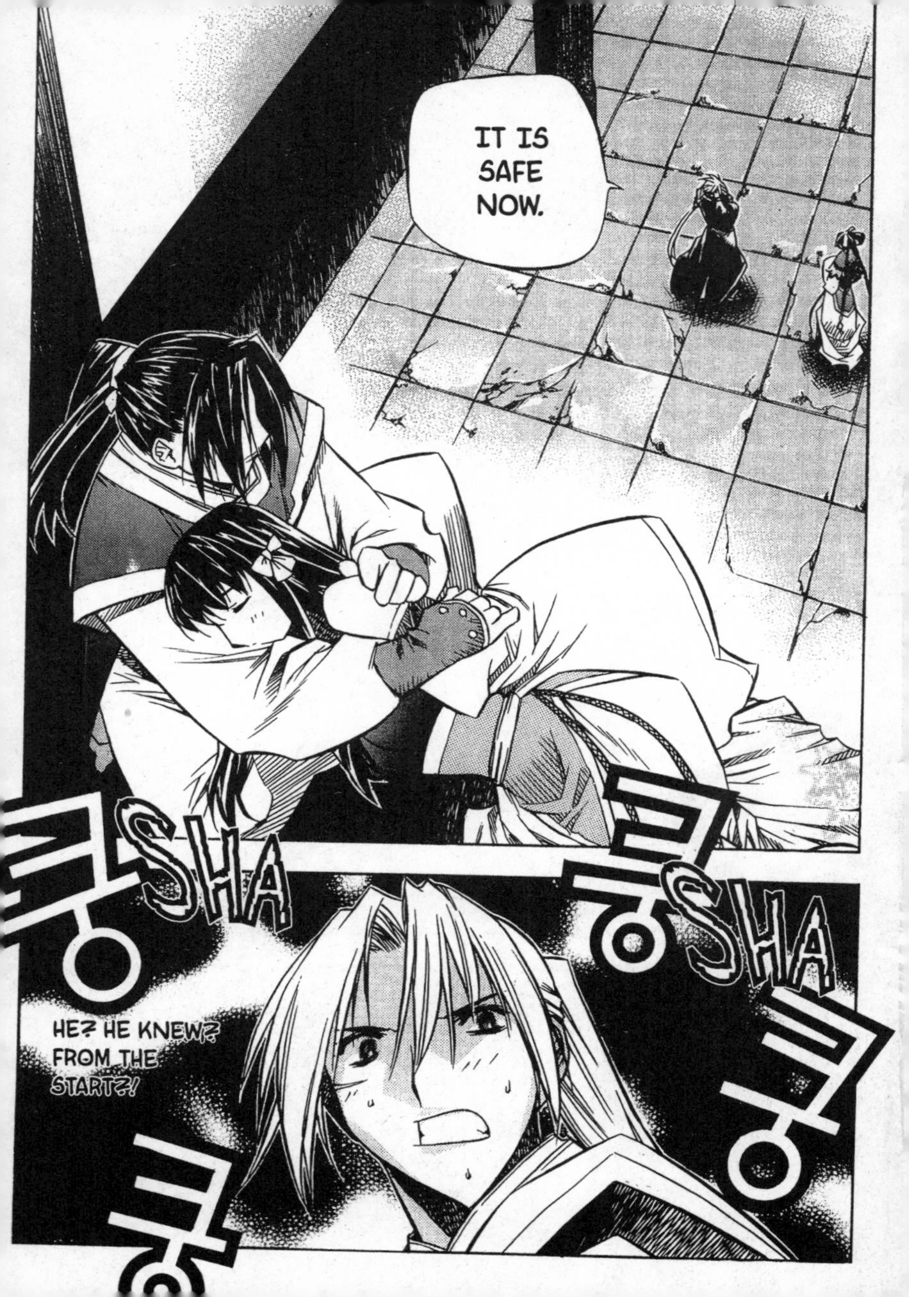
IT IS SAFE NOW.
SHA
SHA
HE? HE KNEW? FROM THE START?!

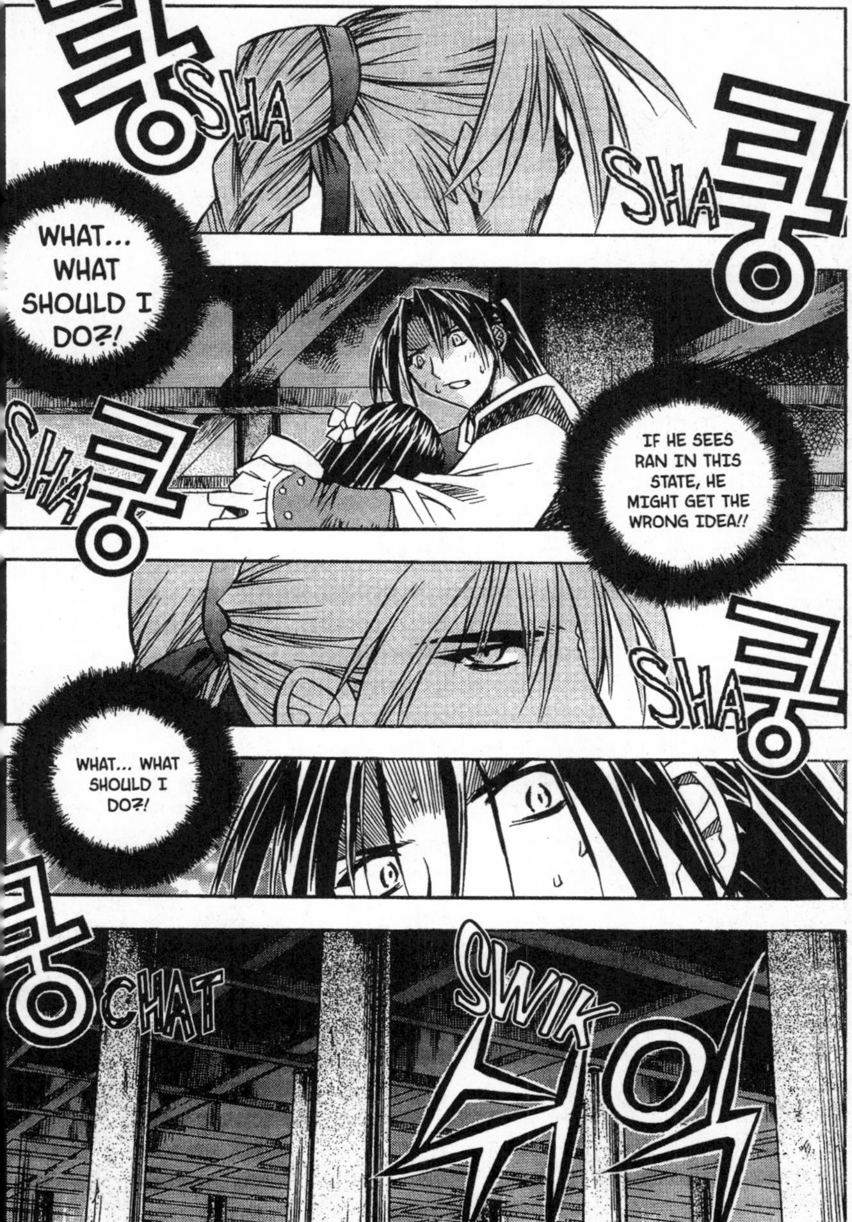
SHA
SHA
WHAT... WHAT SHOULD I DO?!
SHA
IF HE SEES RAN IN THIS STATE, HE MIGHT GET THE WRONG IDEA!!
SHA
WHAT... WHAT SHOULD I DO?!
CHAT
SWIK

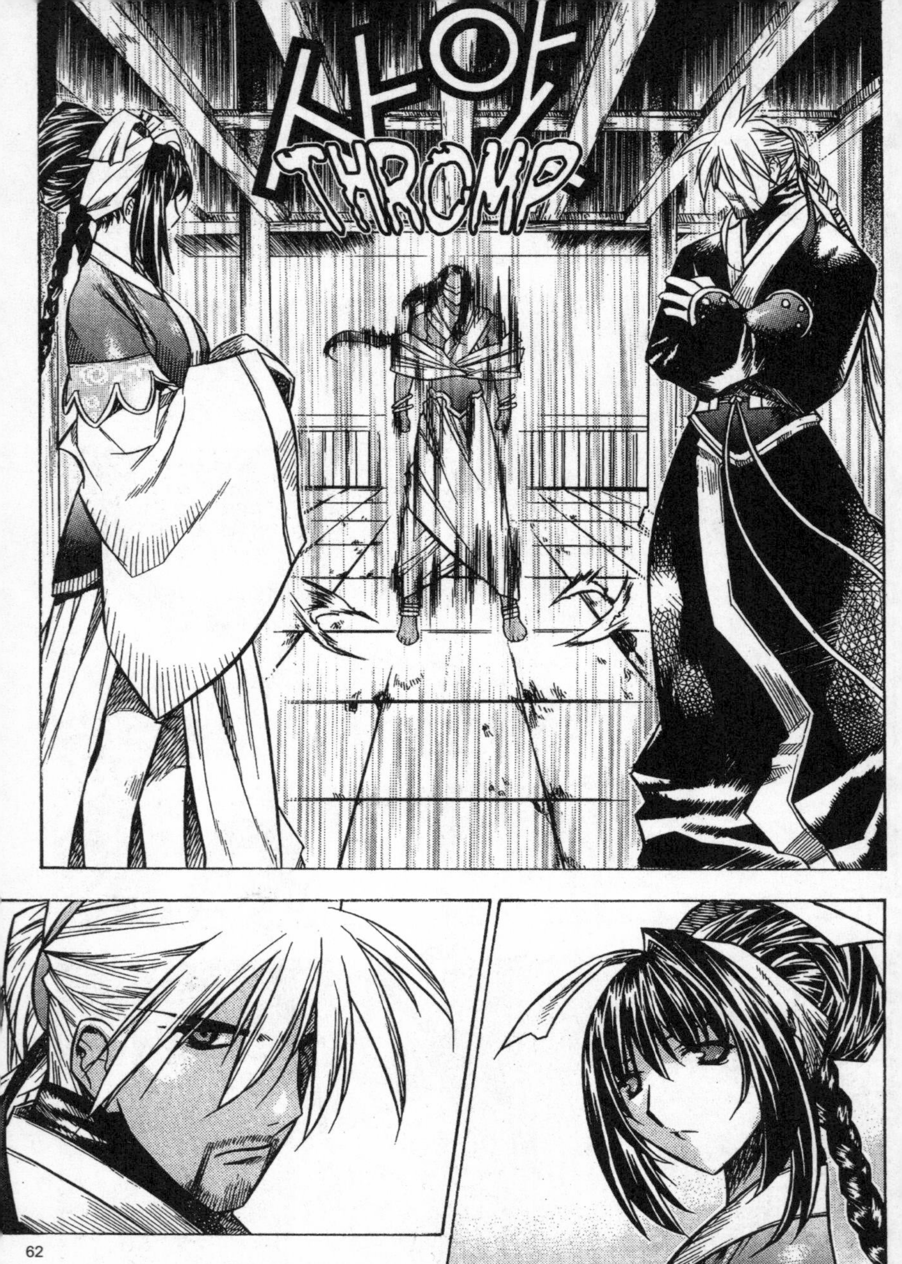
THROMP

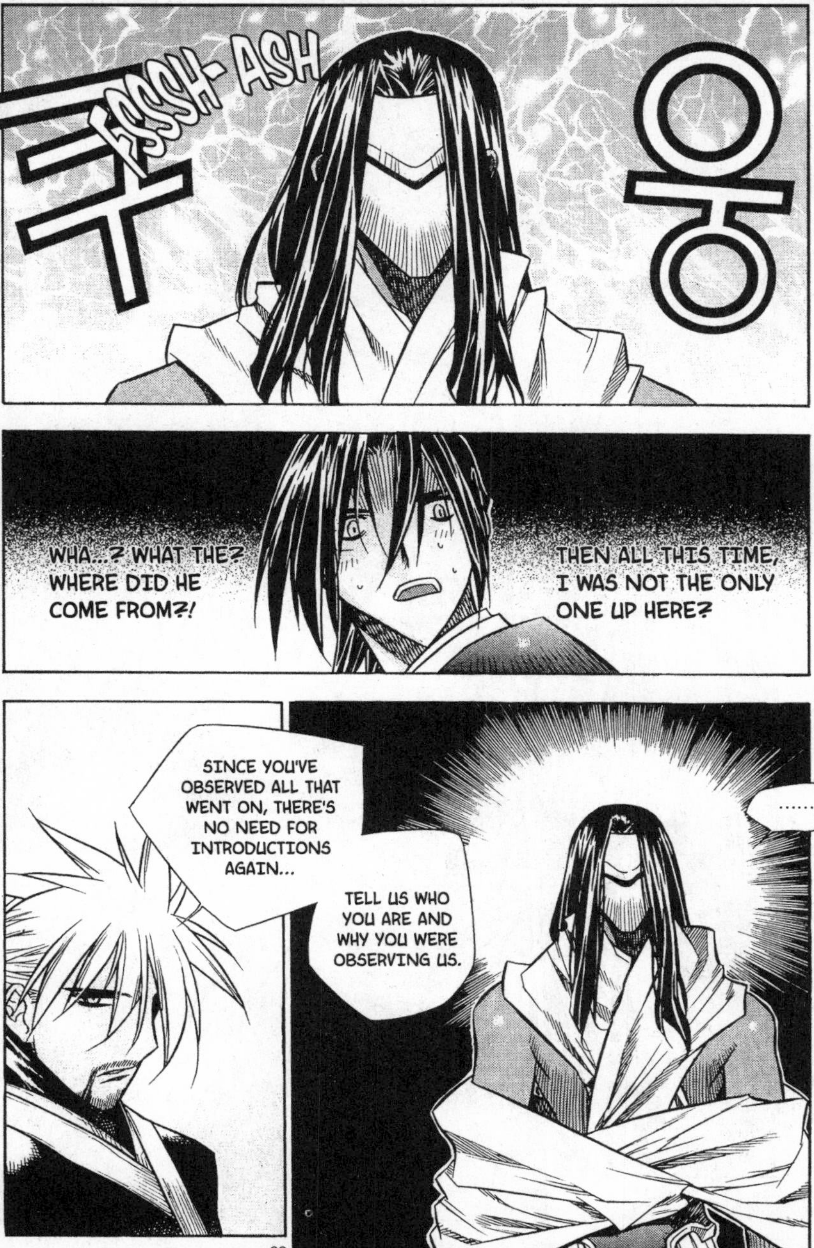
FSSSH-ASH
쿠웅
WHA...? WHAT THE? WHERE DID HE COME FROM?!
THEN ALL THIS TIME, I WAS NOT THE ONLY ONE UP HERE?
SINCE YOU'VE OBSERVED ALL THAT WENT ON, THERE'S NO NEED FOR INTRODUCTIONS AGAIN...
TELL US WHO YOU ARE AND WHY YOU WERE OBSERVING US.
.......

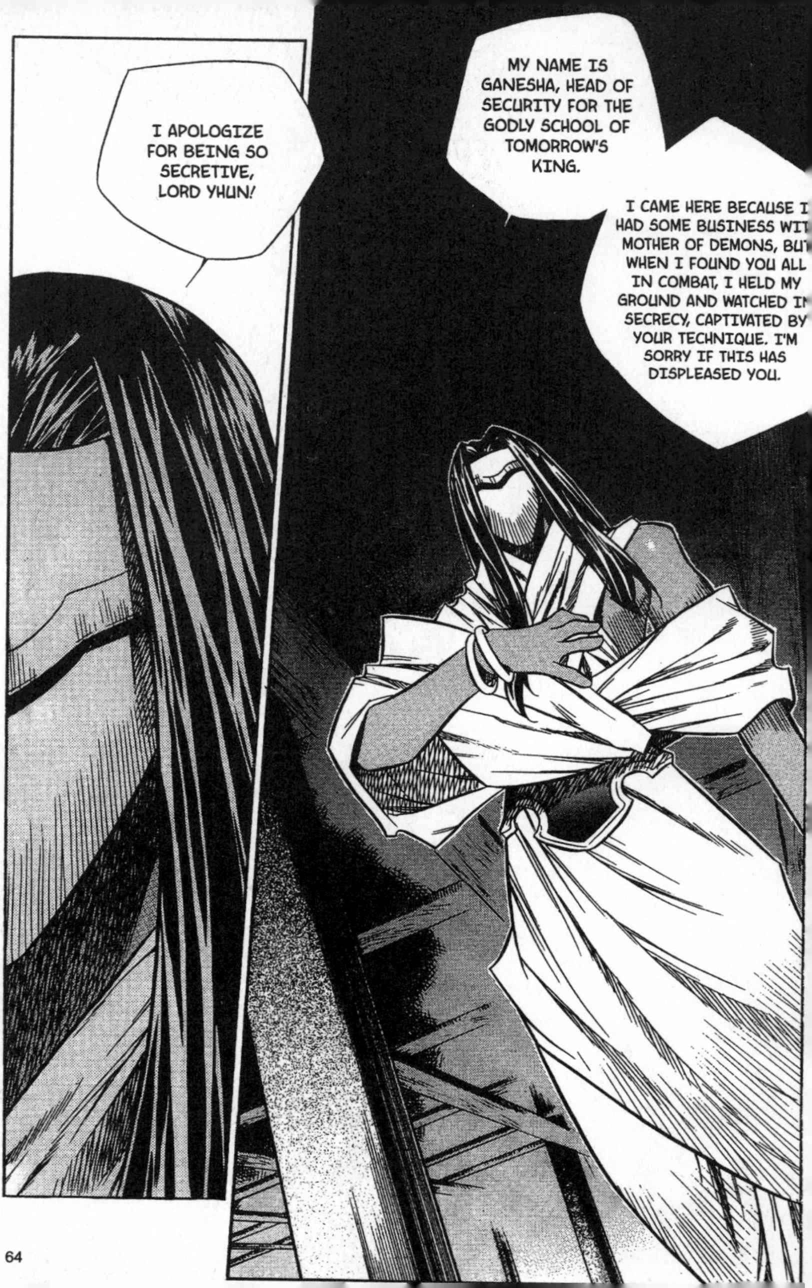
I APOLOGIZE FOR BEING SO SECRETIVE, LORD YHUN!
MY NAME IS GANESHA, HEAD OF SECURITY FOR THE GODLY SCHOOL OF TOMORROW'S KING.
I CAME HERE BECAUSE I HAD SOME BUSINESS WIT MOTHER OF DEMONS, BUT WHEN I FOUND YOU ALL IN COMBAT, I HELD MY GROUND AND WATCHED IN SECRECY, CAPTIVATED BY YOUR TECHNIQUE. I'M SORRY IF THIS HAS DISPLEASED YOU.

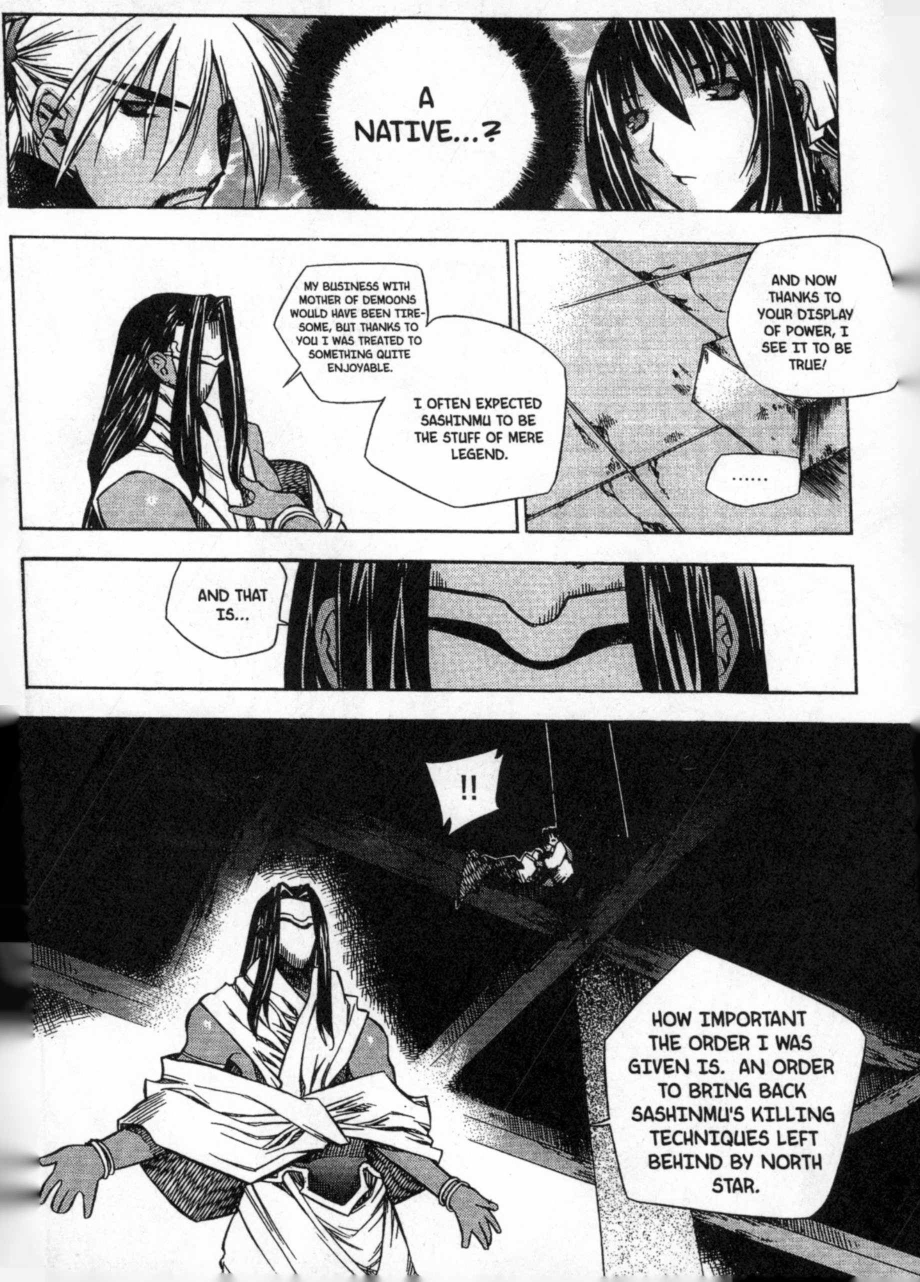
A NATIVE...?
AND NOW THANKS TO YOUR DISPLAY OF POWER, I SEE IT TO BE TRUE!
......
MY BUSINESS WITH MOTHER OF DEMOONS WOULD HAVE BEEN TIRE-SOME, BUT THANKS TO YOU I WAS TREATED TO SOMETHING QUITE ENJOYABLE.
I OFTEN EXPECTED SASHINMU TO BE THE STUFF OF MERE LEGEND.
AND THAT IS...
!!
HOW IMPORTANT THE ORDER I WAS GIVEN IS. AN ORDER TO BRING BACK SASHINMU'S KILLING TECHNIQUES LEFT BEHIND BY NORTH STAR.

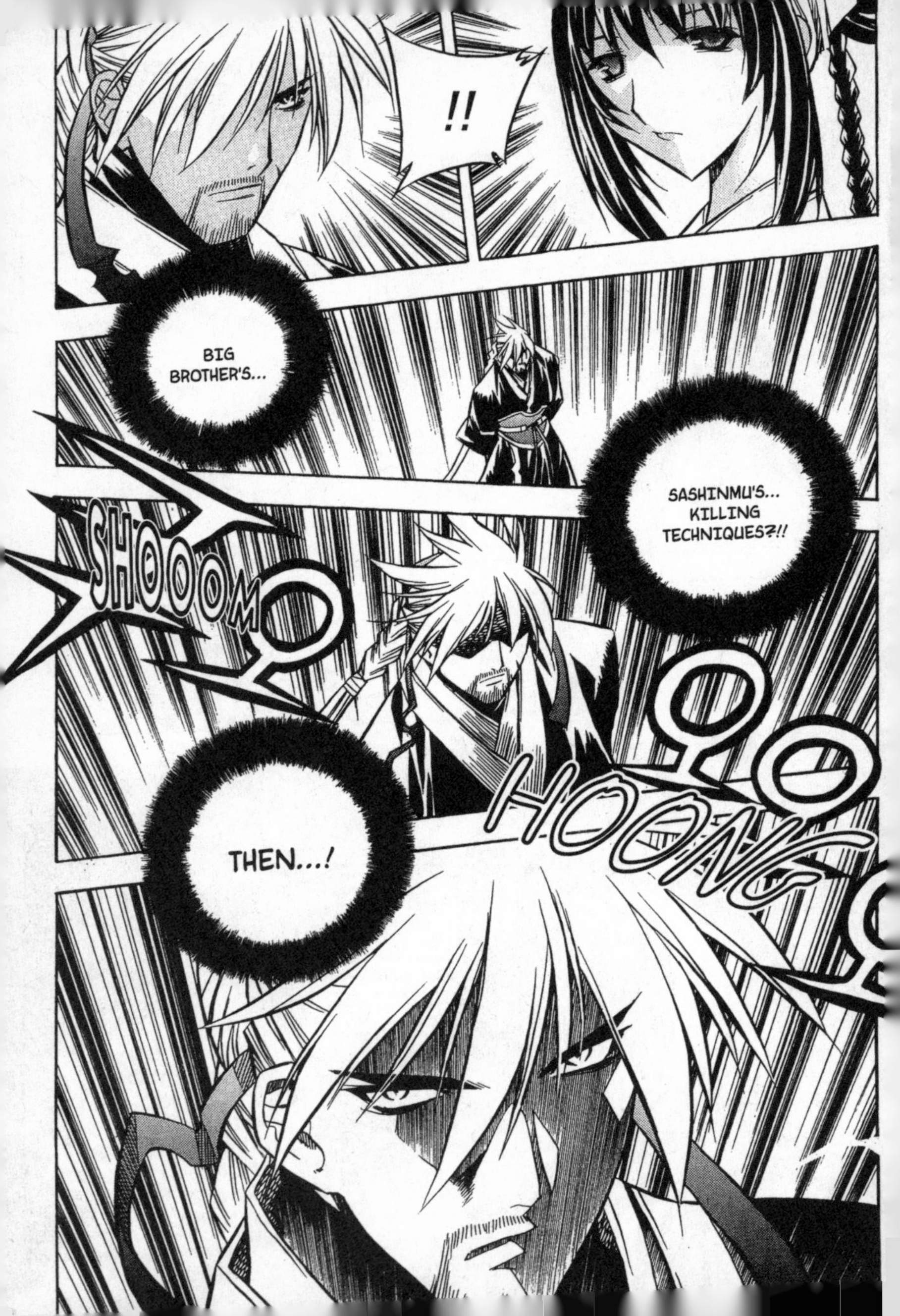

!!
BIG BROTHER'S...
SASHINMU'S... KILLING TECHNIQUES?!!
SHOOOM
THEN...!
HOONG

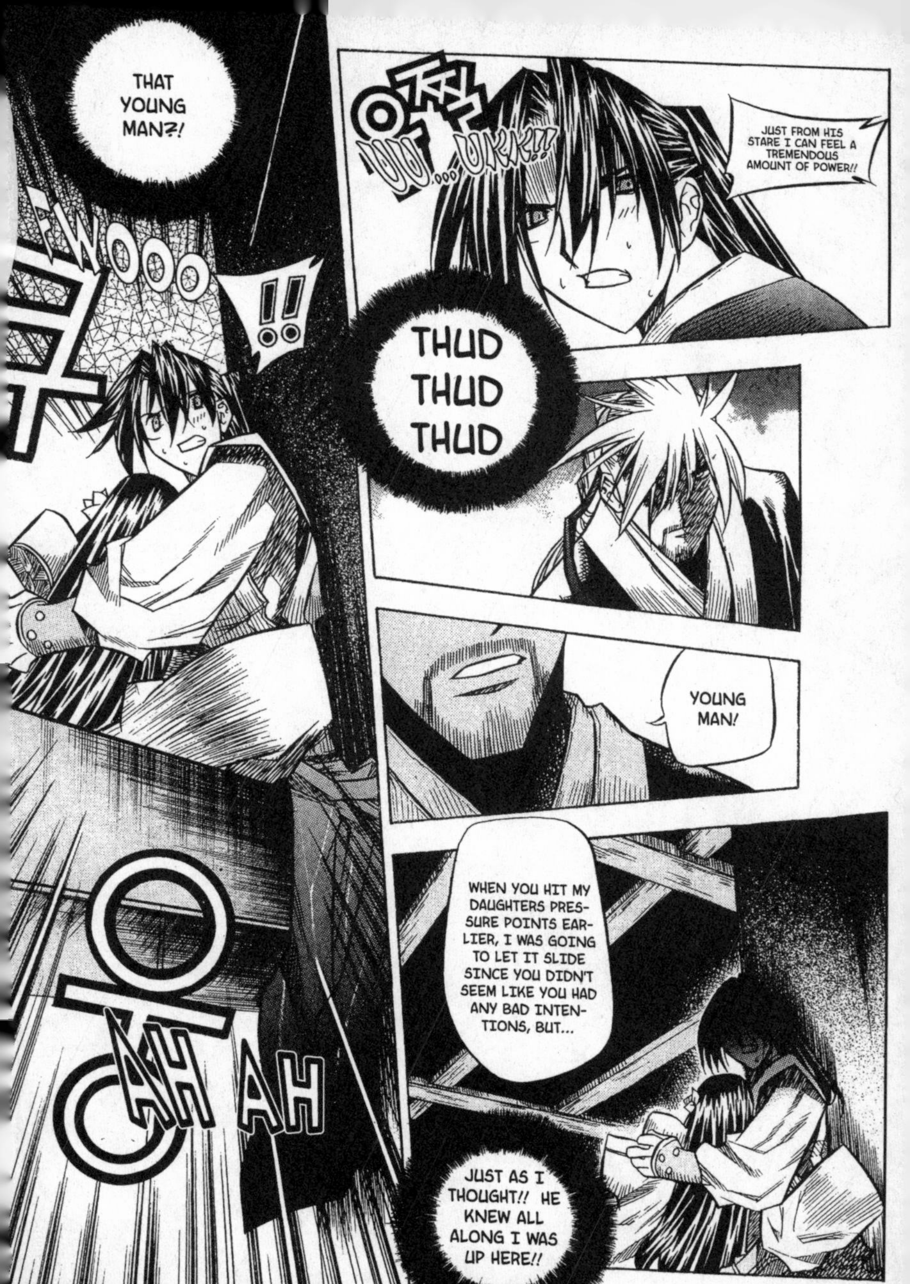
THAT YOUNG MAN?!
FWOOO
!!
AH AH
UU... UKK!!
JUST FROM HIS STARE I CAN FEEL A TREMENDOUS AMOUNT OF POWER!!
THUD THUD THUD
YOUNG MAN!
WHEN YOU HIT MY DAUGHTERS PRESSURE POINTS EARLIER, I WAS GOING TO LET IT SLIDE SINCE YOU DIDN'T SEEM LIKE YOU HAD ANY BAD INTENTIONS, BUT...
JUST AS I THOUGHT!! HE KNEW ALL ALONG I WAS UP HERE!!

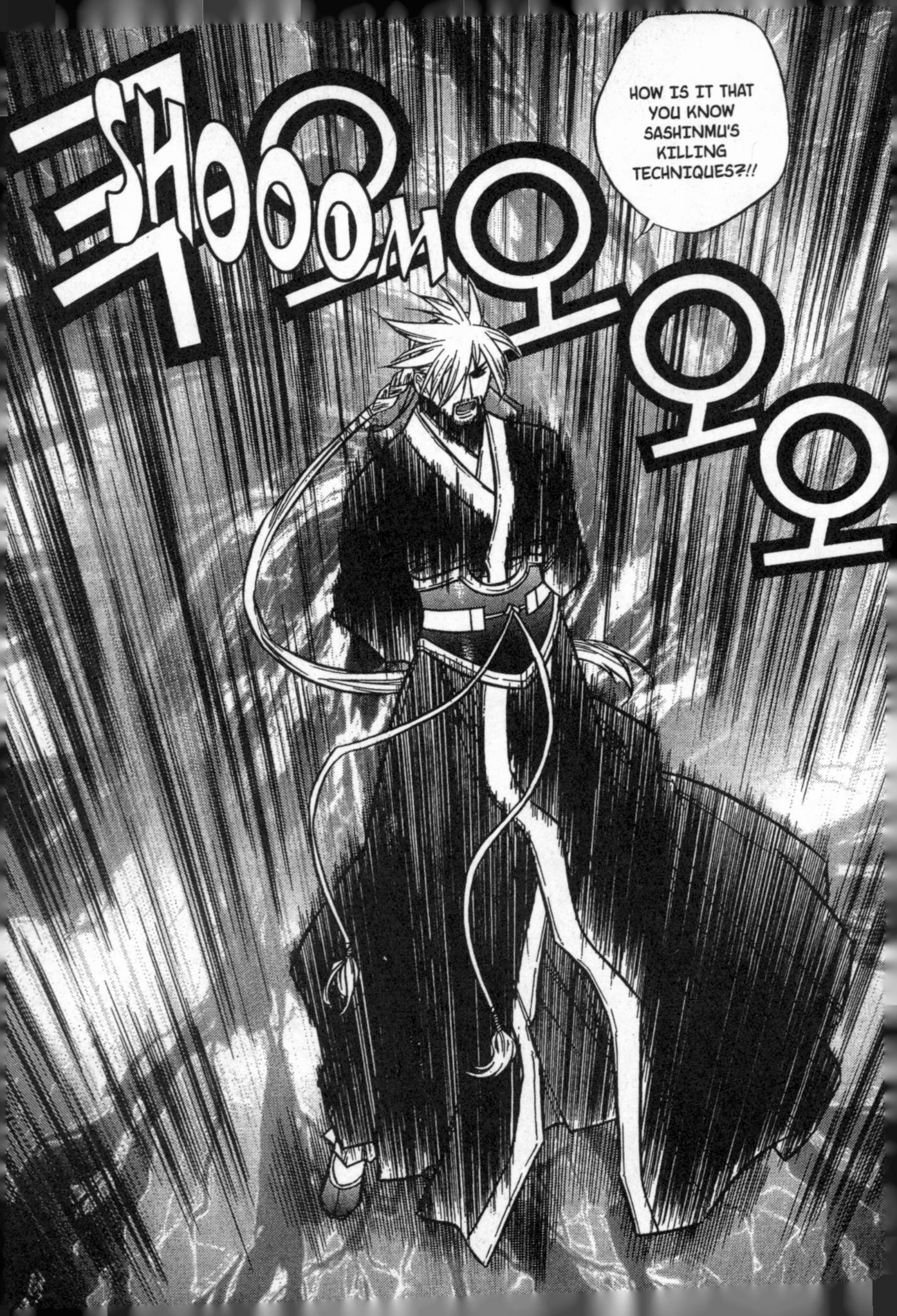
SHOOOMOOOO
HOW IS IT THAT YOU KNOW SASHINMU'S KILLING TECHNIQUES?!!

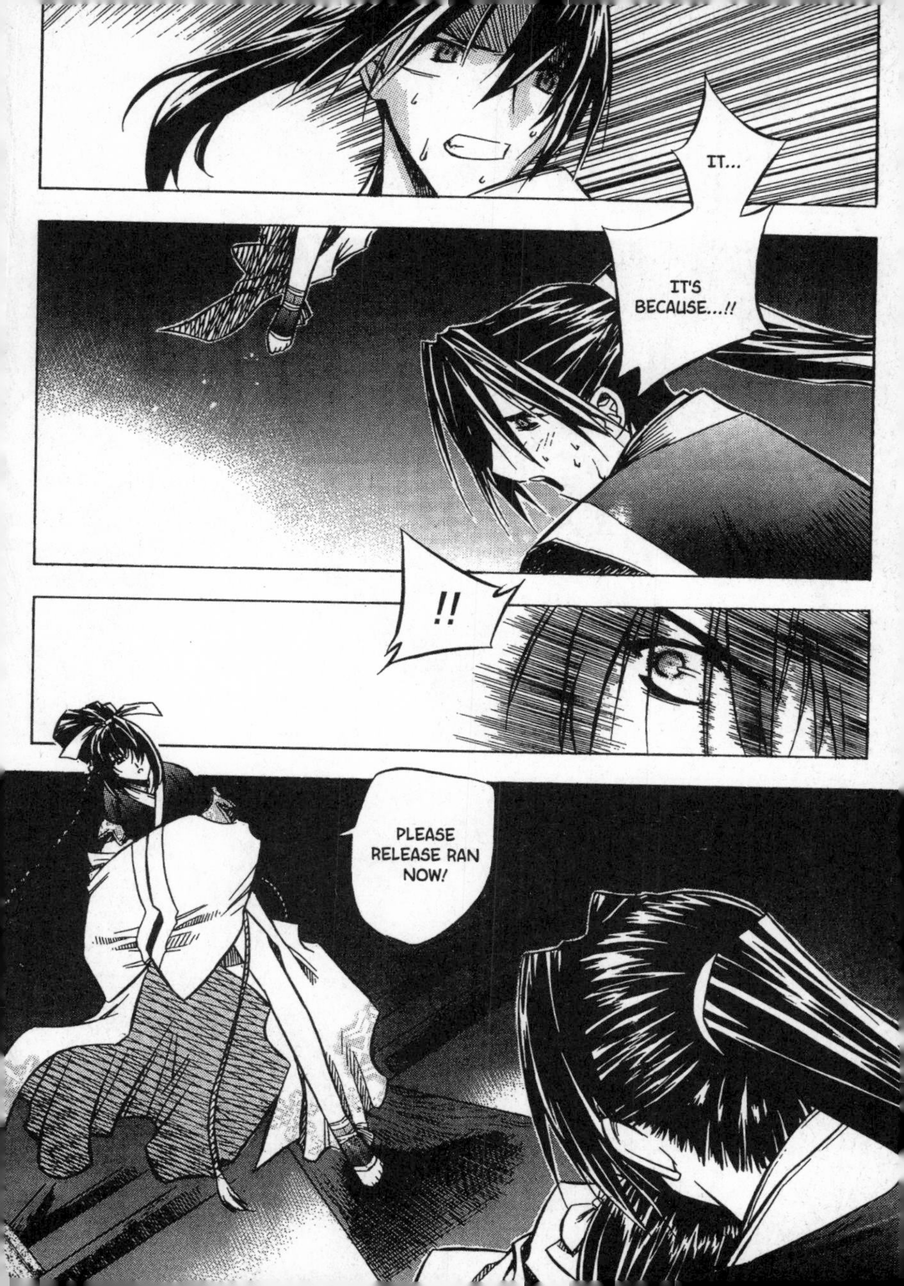
IT...
IT'S BECAUSE...!!
!!
PLEASE RELEASE RAN NOW!

I... I...

EH?

SWSSSSH OK

THAT MIGHT BE DIFFICULT, LADY YHUN!

JUST AS I SAID A MOMENT AGO...

I'M REQUIRED TO BRING BACK THE KILLING TECHNIQUES OF SASHINMU!

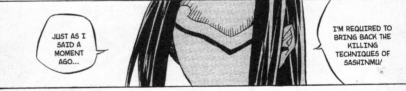

ALTHOUGH I DIDN'T ORIGINALLY PLAN ON TAKING MISS YHUN, THIS YOUNG MAN SEEMS TO HAVE FORMED A UNIQUE RELATIONSHIP WITH HER DURING HIS SASHINMU TRAINING. THEREFORE, I MUST BE RUDE AND TAKE HER ALONG AS WELL!

!!

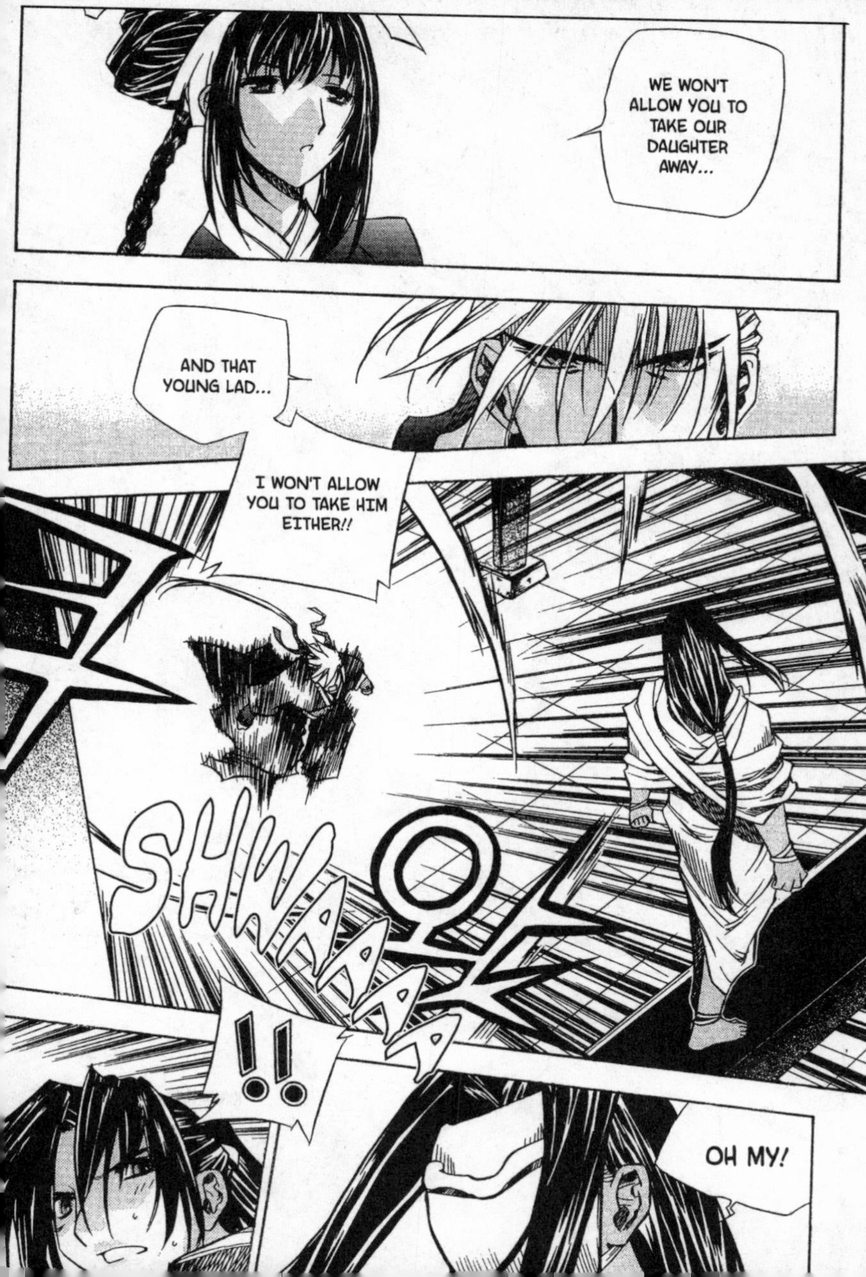
WE WON'T ALLOW YOU TO TAKE OUR DAUGHTER AWAY...
AND THAT YOUNG LAD...
I WON'T ALLOW YOU TO TAKE HIM EITHER!!
SHWAAAAAA
!!
OH MY!

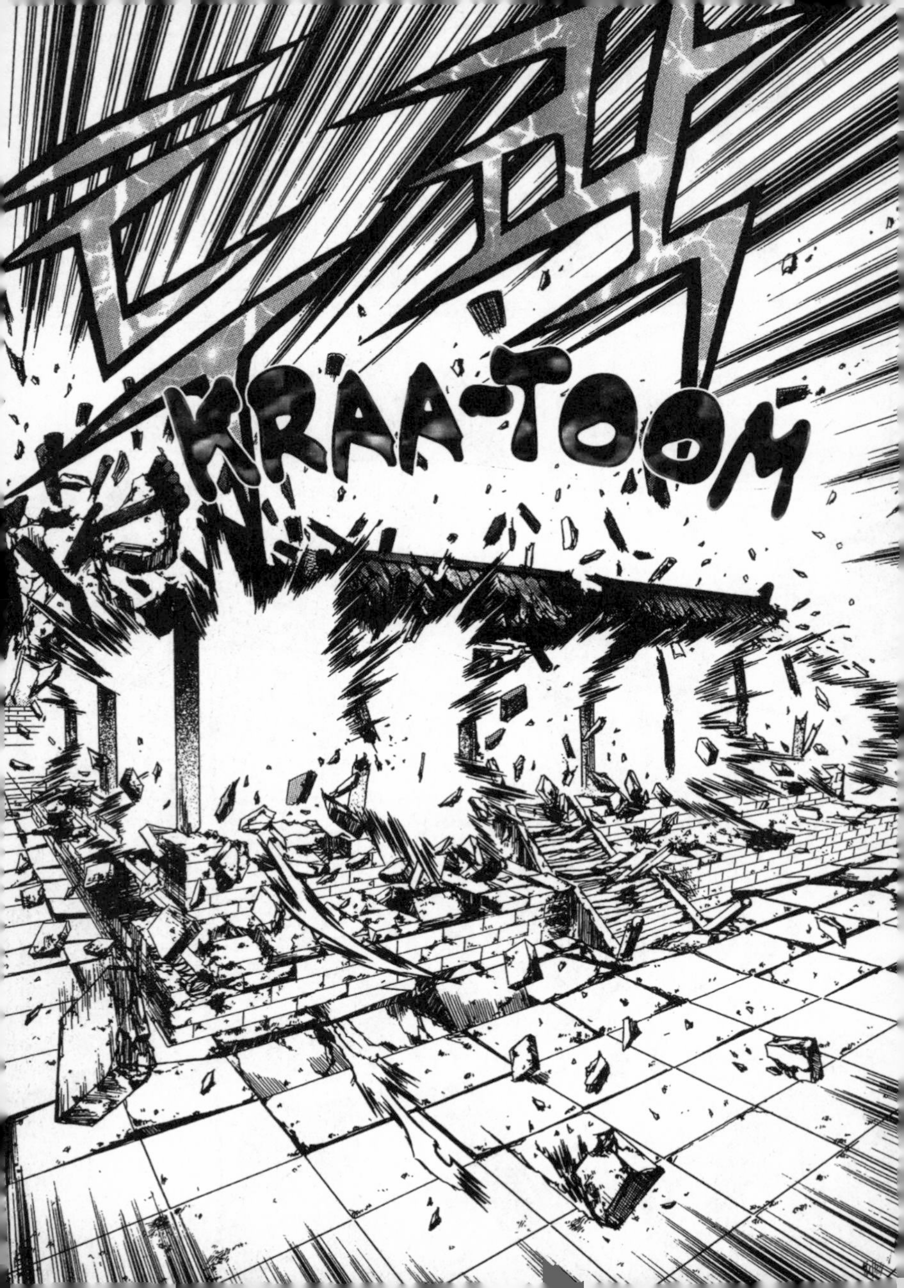
KRAA-TOOM

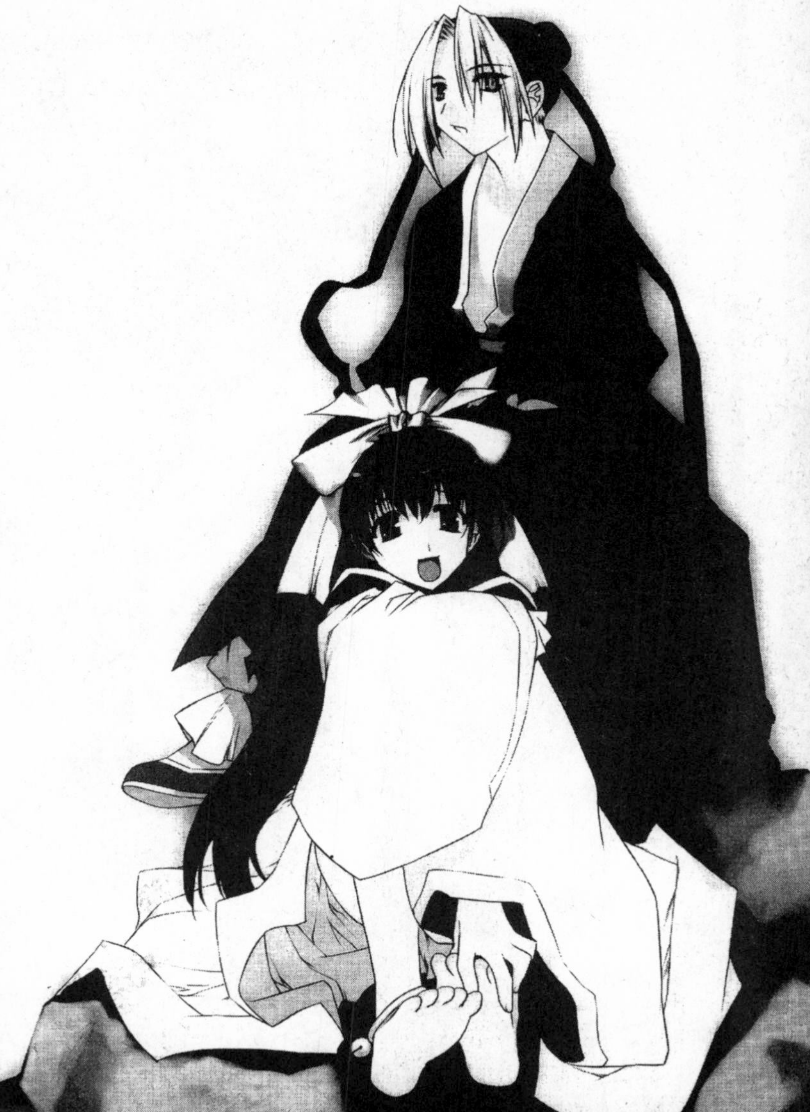

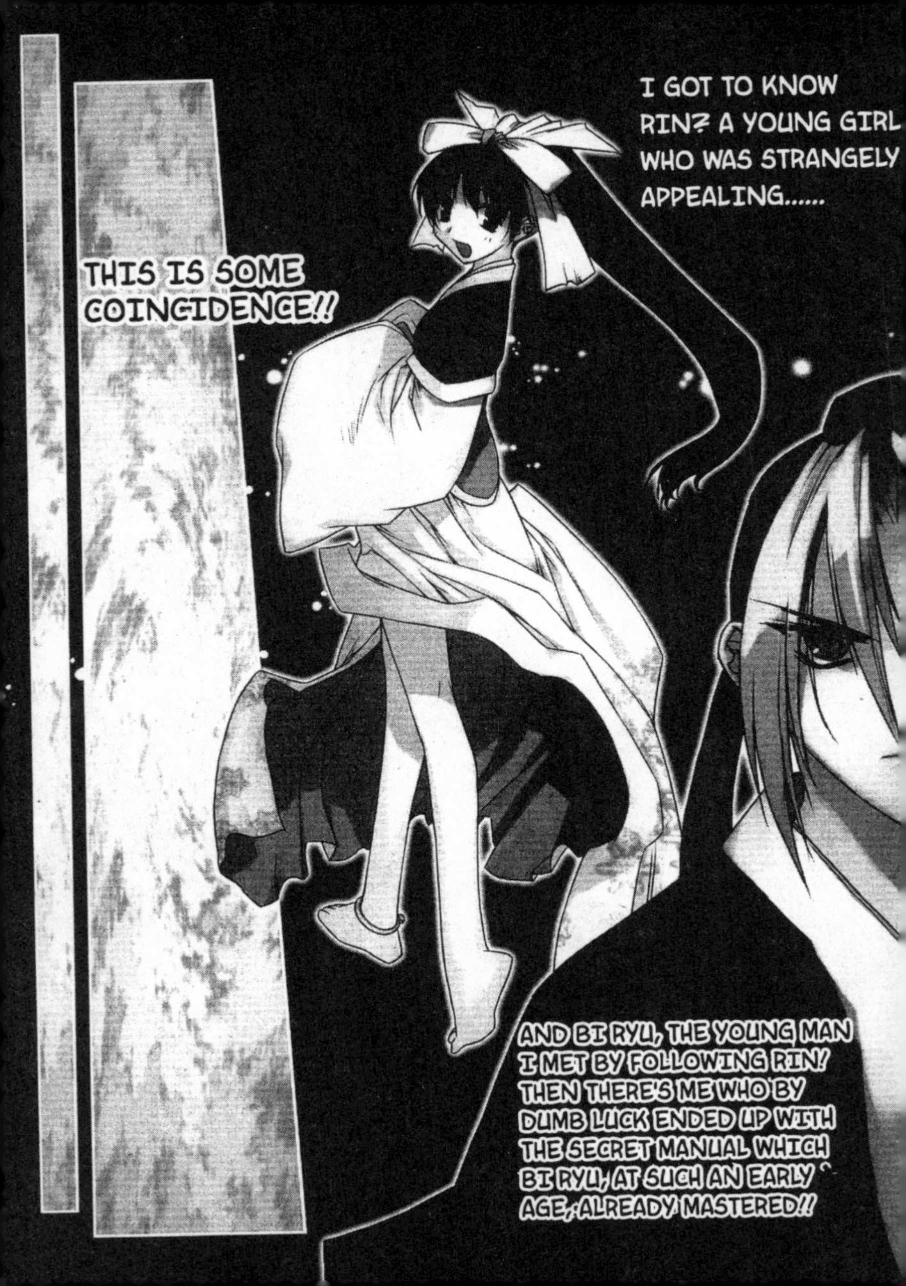
I GOT TO KNOW RIN? A YOUNG GIRL WHO WAS STRANGELY APPEALING......
THIS IS SOME COINCIDENCE!!
AND BI RYU, THE YOUNG MAN I MET BY FOLLOWING RIN! THEN THERE'S ME WHO BY DUMB LUCK ENDED UP WITH THE SECRET MANUAL WHICH BI RYU, AT SUCH AN EARLY AGE, ALREADY MASTERED!!

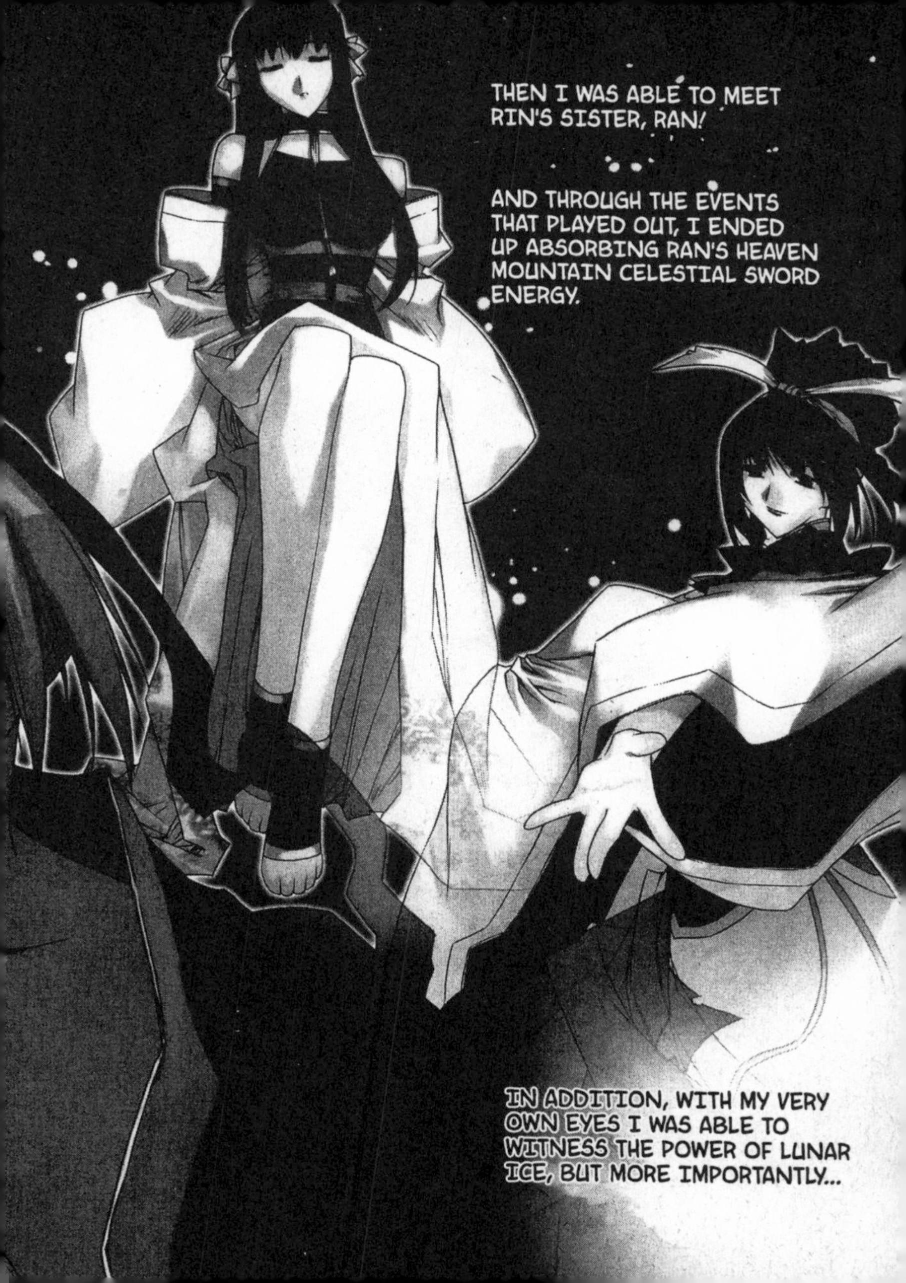
THEN I WAS ABLE TO MEET RIN'S SISTER, RAN!
AND THROUGH THE EVENTS THAT PLAYED OUT, I ENDED UP ABSORBING RAN'S HEAVEN MOUNTAIN CELESTIAL SWORD ENERGY.
IN ADDITION, WITH MY VERY OWN EYES I WAS ABLE TO WITNESS THE POWER OF LUNAR ICE, BUT MORE IMPORTANTLY...

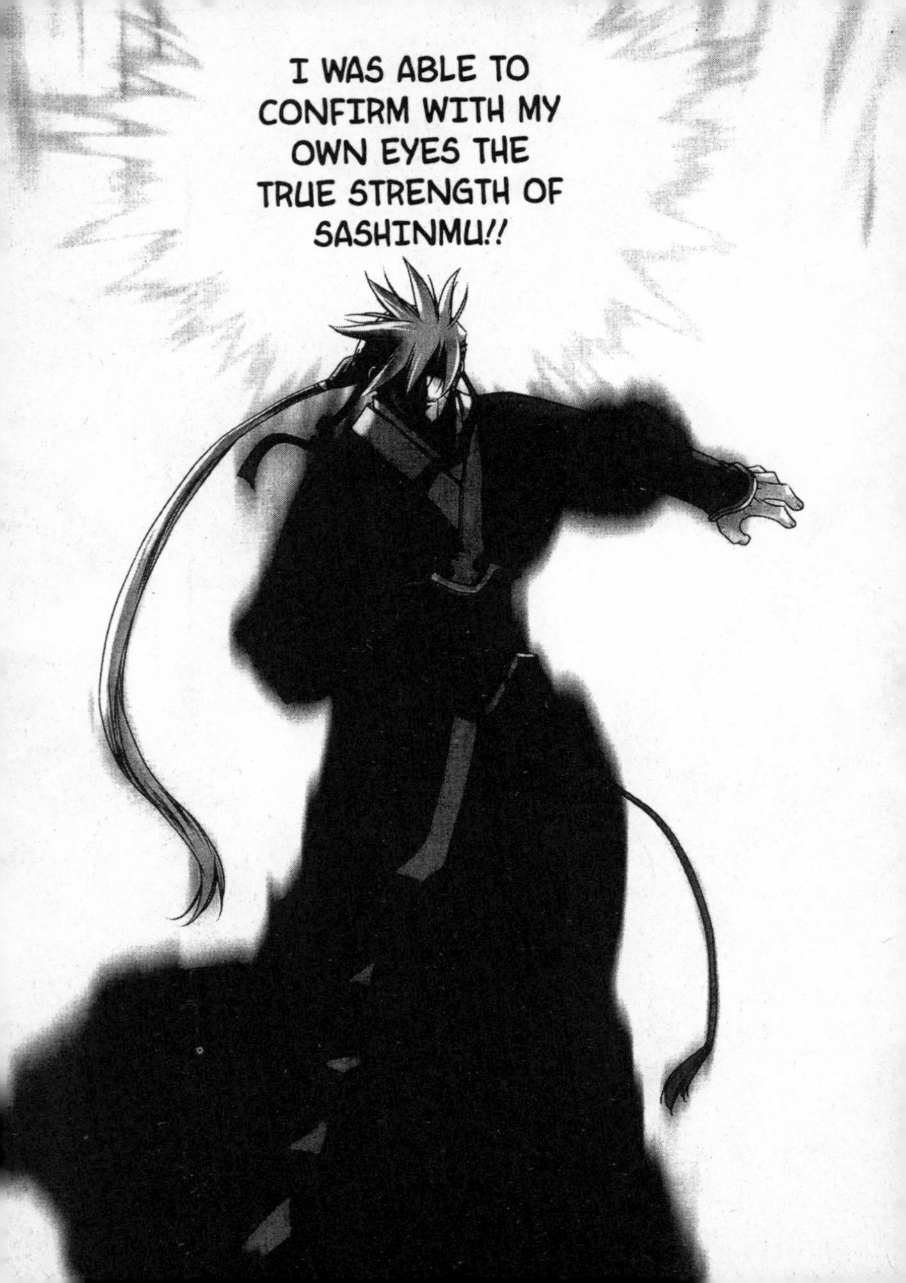
I WAS ABLE TO CONFIRM WITH MY OWN EYES THE TRUE STRENGTH OF SASHINMU!!

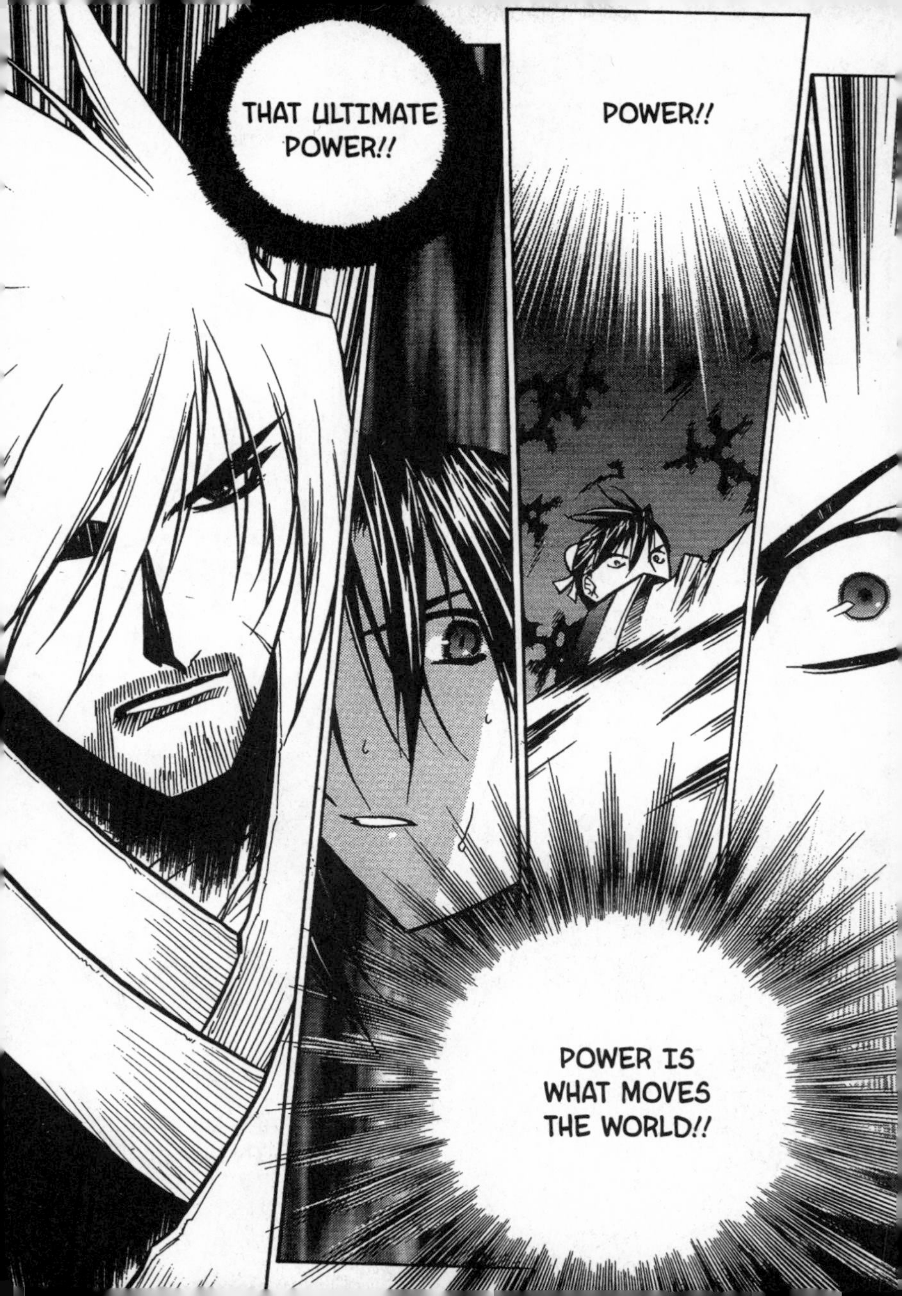
POWER!!
THAT ULTIMATE POWER!!
POWER IS WHAT MOVES THE WORLD!!

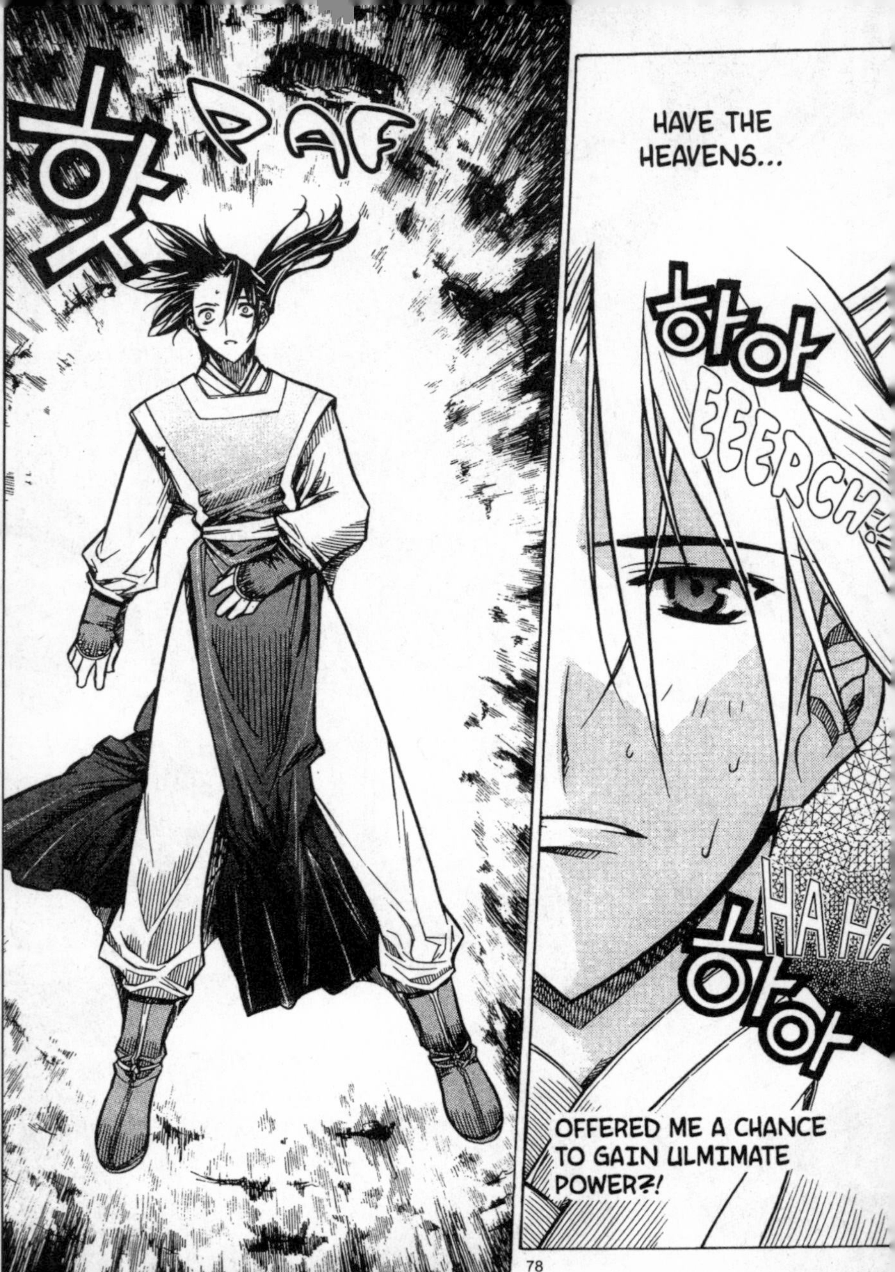
PAF
HAVE THE HEAVENS...
하아
EEERCH!
HAHA
하아
OFFERED ME A CHANCE TO GAIN ULMIMATE POWER?!

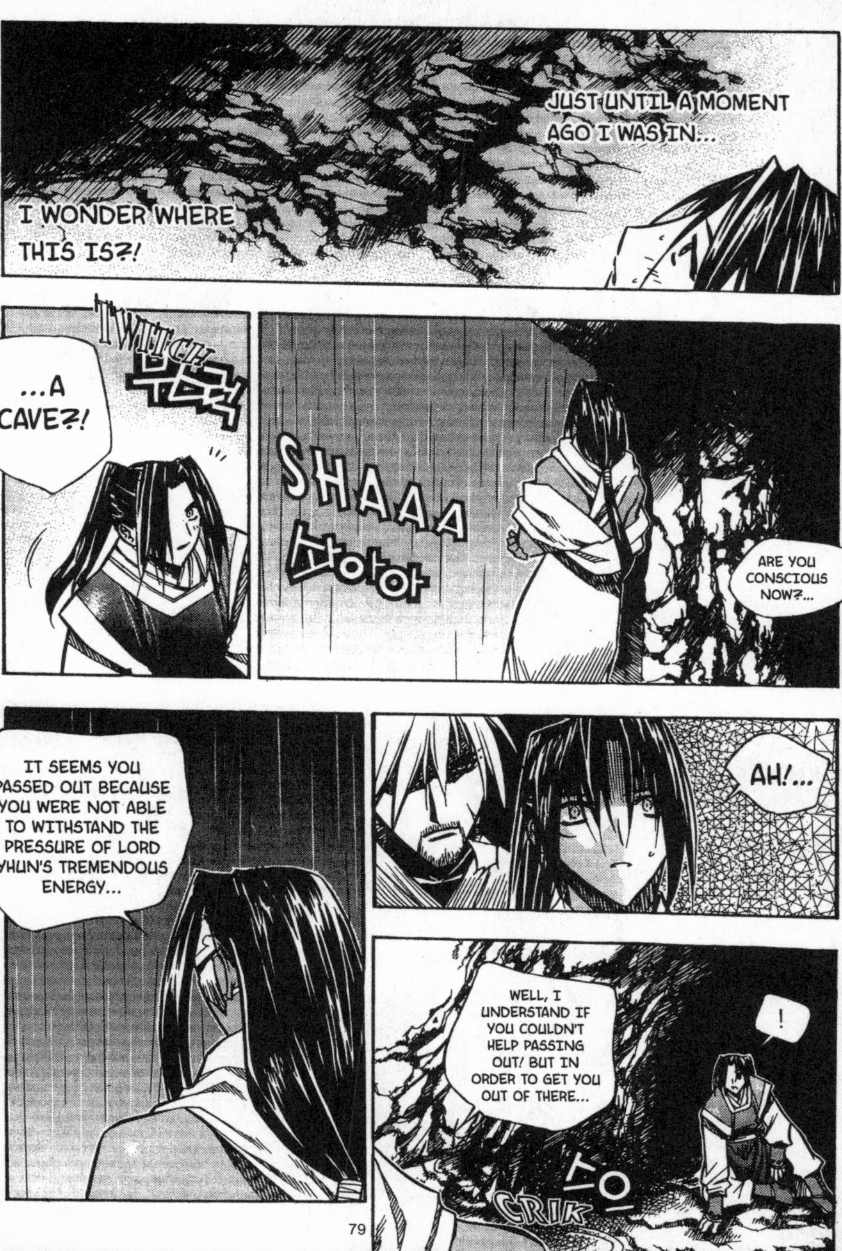
JUST UNTIL A MOMENT AGO I WAS IN...
I WONDER WHERE THIS IS?!
TWITCH
...A CAVE?!
SHAAAA
ARE YOU CONSCIOUS NOW?...
IT SEEMS YOU PASSED OUT BECAUSE YOU WERE NOT ABLE TO WITHSTAND THE PRESSURE OF LORD YHUN'S TREMENDOUS ENERGY...
AH!...
WELL, I UNDERSTAND IF YOU COULDN'T HELP PASSING OUT! BUT IN ORDER TO GET YOU OUT OF THERE...
!
CRIK

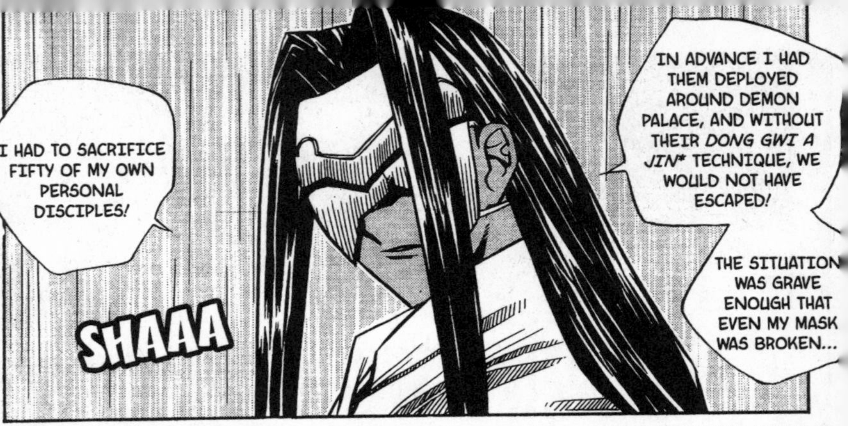

I HAD TO SACRIFICE FIFTY OF MY OWN PERSONAL DISCIPLES!
IN ADVANCE I HAD THEM DEPLOYED AROUND DEMON PALACE, AND WITHOUT THEIR *DONG GWI A JIN** TECHNIQUE, WE WOULD NOT HAVE ESCAPED!
SHAAA
THE SITUATION WAS GRAVE ENOUGH THAT EVEN MY MASK WAS BROKEN...


**DONG GWI A JIN: A SUICIDE ATTACK IN WHICH AN OPPONENT KILLS HIS TARGET AND HIMSELF.*

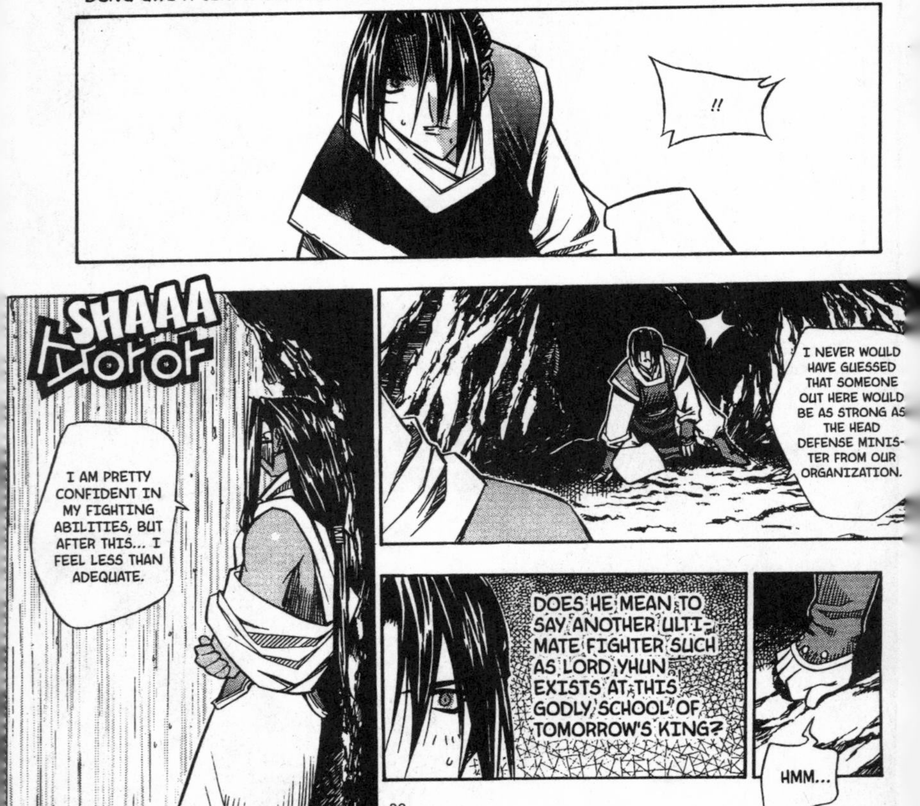

!!
SHAAA
I AM PRETTY CONFIDENT IN MY FIGHTING ABILITIES, BUT AFTER THIS... I FEEL LESS THAN ADEQUATE.
I NEVER WOULD HAVE GUESSED THAT SOMEONE OUT HERE WOULD BE AS STRONG AS THE HEAD DEFENSE MINISTER FROM OUR ORGANIZATION.
DOES HE MEAN TO SAY ANOTHER ULTIMATE FIGHTER SUCH AS LORD YHUN EXISTS AT THIS GODLY SCHOOL OF TOMORROW'S KING?
HMM...

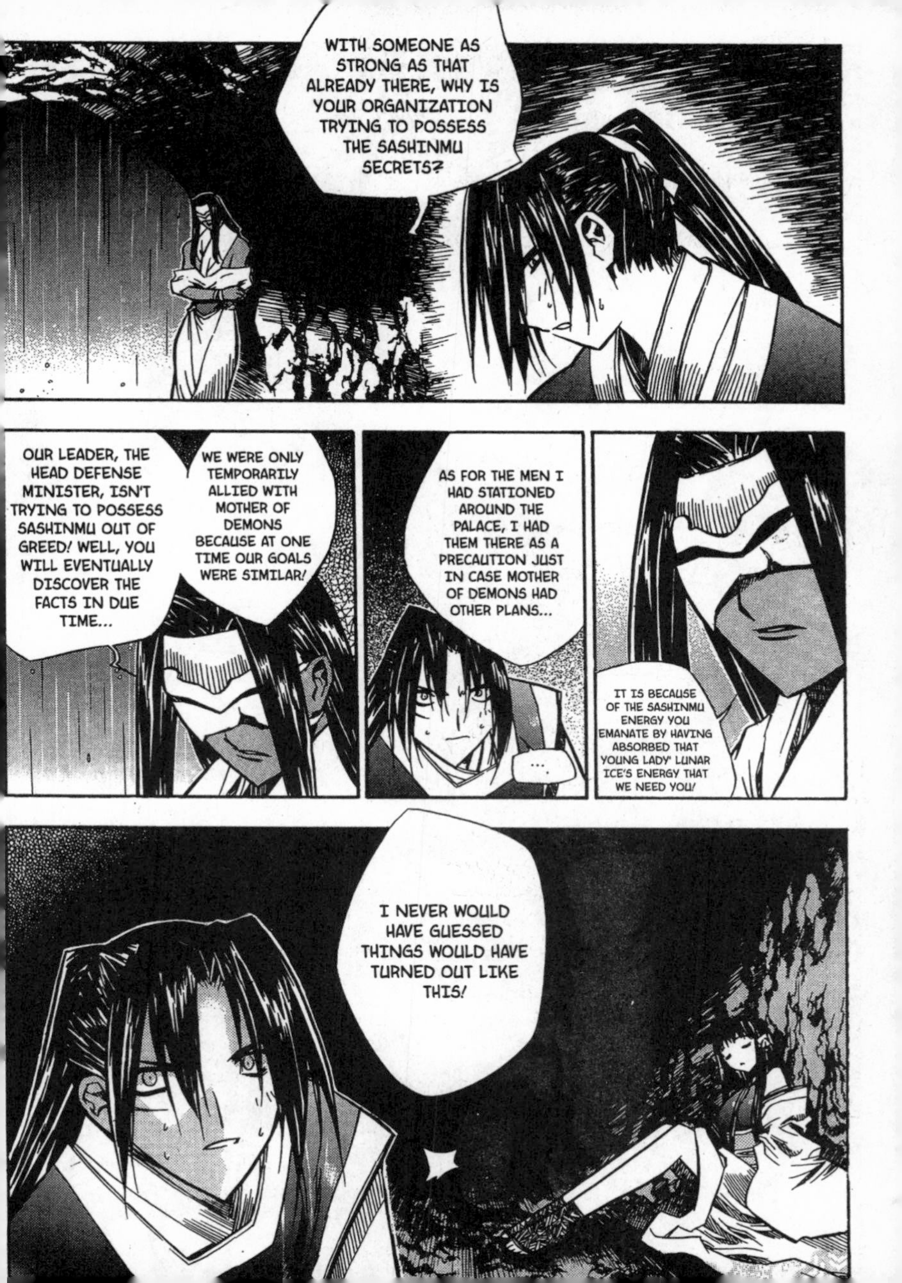

WITH SOMEONE AS STRONG AS THAT ALREADY THERE, WHY IS YOUR ORGANIZATION TRYING TO POSSESS THE SASHINMU SECRETS?
OUR LEADER, THE HEAD DEFENSE MINISTER, ISN'T TRYING TO POSSESS SASHINMU OUT OF GREED! WELL, YOU WILL EVENTUALLY DISCOVER THE FACTS IN DUE TIME...
WE WERE ONLY TEMPORARILY ALLIED WITH MOTHER OF DEMONS BECAUSE AT ONE TIME OUR GOALS WERE SIMILAR!
AS FOR THE MEN I HAD STATIONED AROUND THE PALACE, I HAD THEM THERE AS A PRECAUTION JUST IN CASE MOTHER OF DEMONS HAD OTHER PLANS...
...
IT IS BECAUSE OF THE SASHINMU ENERGY YOU EMANATE BY HAVING ABSORBED THAT YOUNG LADY' LUNAR ICE'S ENERGY THAT WE NEED YOU!
I NEVER WOULD HAVE GUESSED THINGS WOULD HAVE TURNED OUT LIKE THIS!

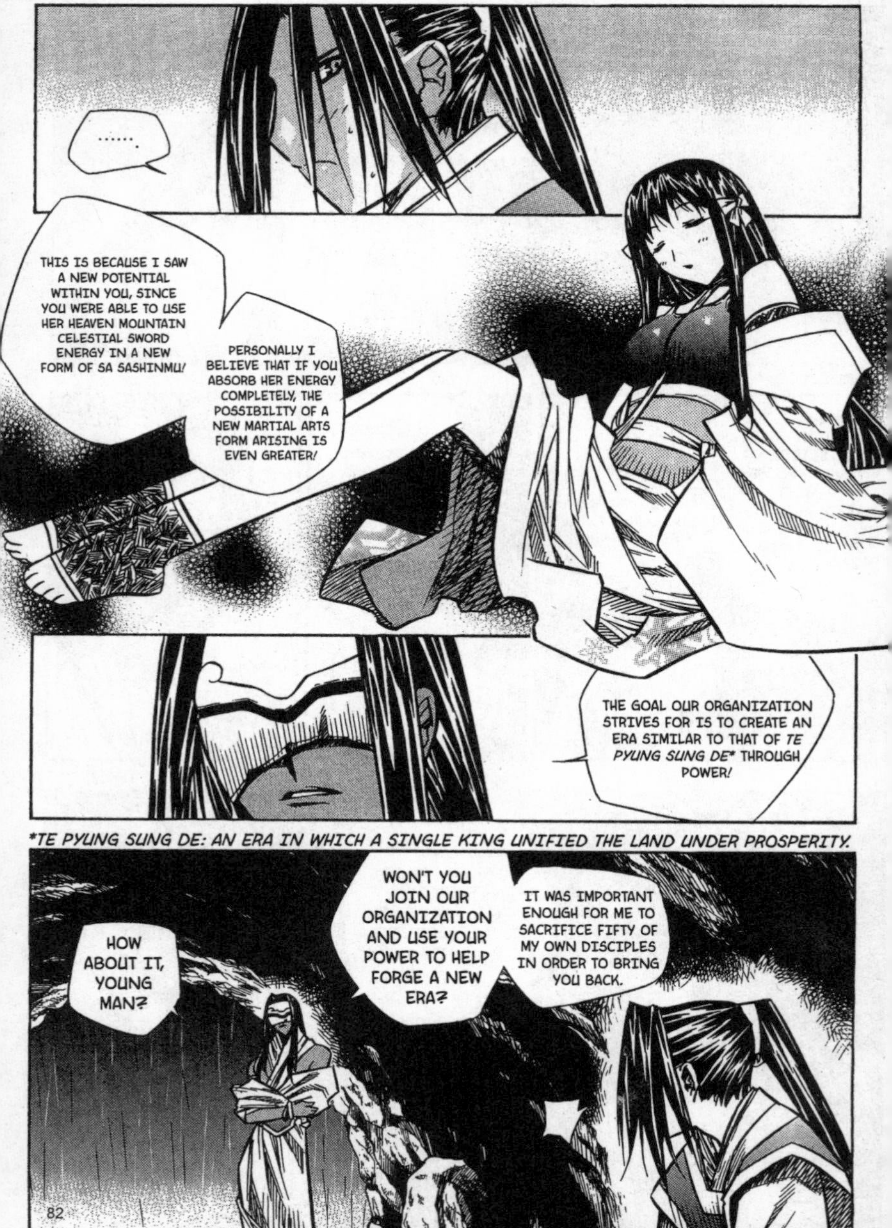
......
THIS IS BECAUSE I SAW A NEW POTENTIAL WITHIN YOU, SINCE YOU WERE ABLE TO USE HER HEAVEN MOUNTAIN CELESTIAL SWORD ENERGY IN A NEW FORM OF SA SASHINMU!
PERSONALLY I BELIEVE THAT IF YOU ABSORB HER ENERGY COMPLETELY, THE POSSIBILITY OF A NEW MARTIAL ARTS FORM ARISING IS EVEN GREATER!
THE GOAL OUR ORGANIZATION STRIVES FOR IS TO CREATE AN ERA SIMILAR TO THAT OF *TE PYUNG SUNG DE** THROUGH POWER!
*TE PYUNG SUNG DE: AN ERA IN WHICH A SINGLE KING UNIFIED THE LAND UNDER PROSPERITY.
IT WAS IMPORTANT ENOUGH FOR ME TO SACRIFICE FIFTY OF MY OWN DISCIPLES IN ORDER TO BRING YOU BACK.
WON'T YOU JOIN OUR ORGANIZATION AND USE YOUR POWER TO HELP FORGE A NEW ERA?
HOW ABOUT IT, YOUNG MAN?

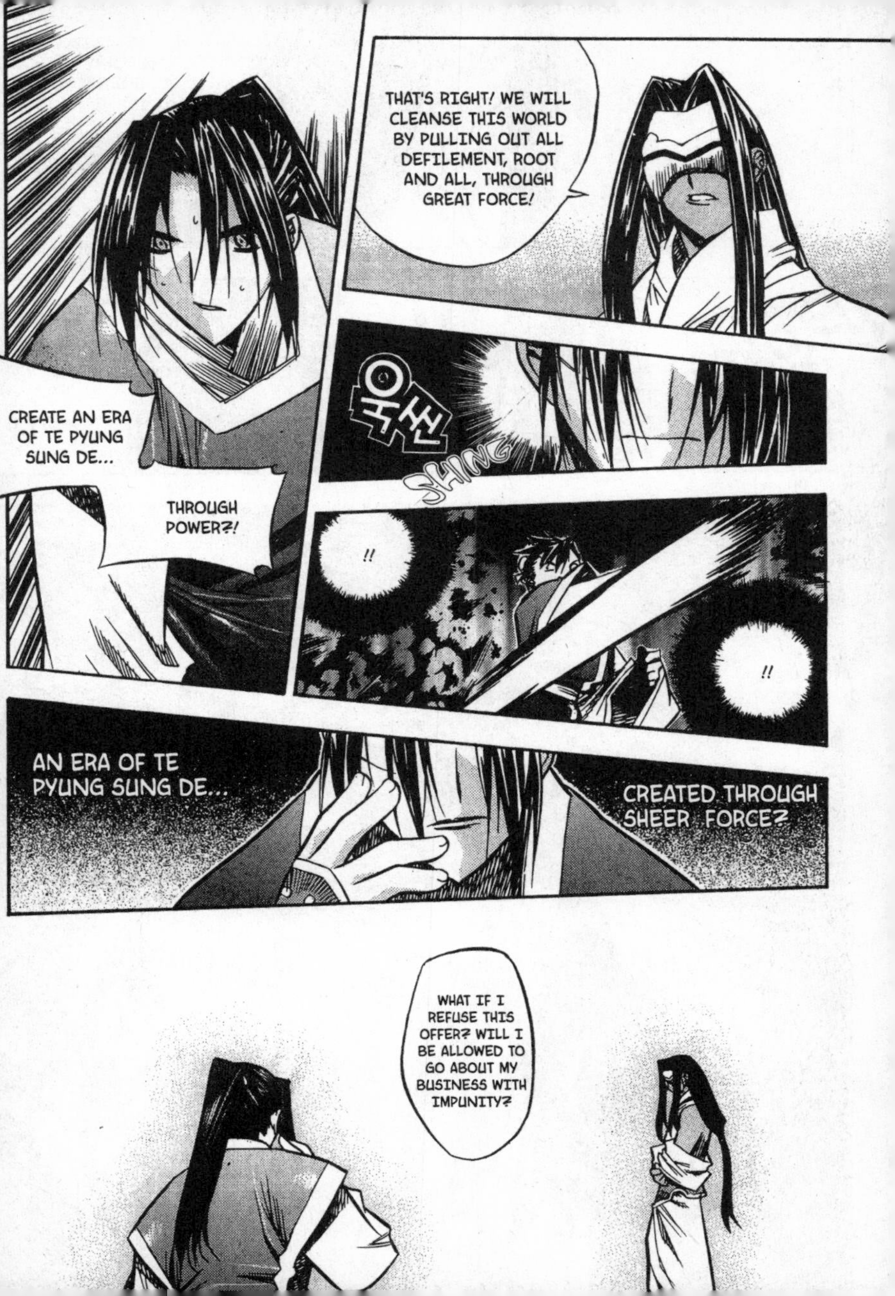
CREATE AN ERA OF TE PYUNG SUNG DE...
THROUGH POWER?!
THAT'S RIGHT! WE WILL CLEANSE THIS WORLD BY PULLING OUT ALL DEFILEMENT, ROOT AND ALL, THROUGH GREAT FORCE!
SHING
!!
!!
AN ERA OF TE PYUNG SUNG DE...
CREATED THROUGH SHEER FORCE?
WHAT IF I REFUSE THIS OFFER? WILL I BE ALLOWED TO GO ABOUT MY BUSINESS WITH IMPUNITY?

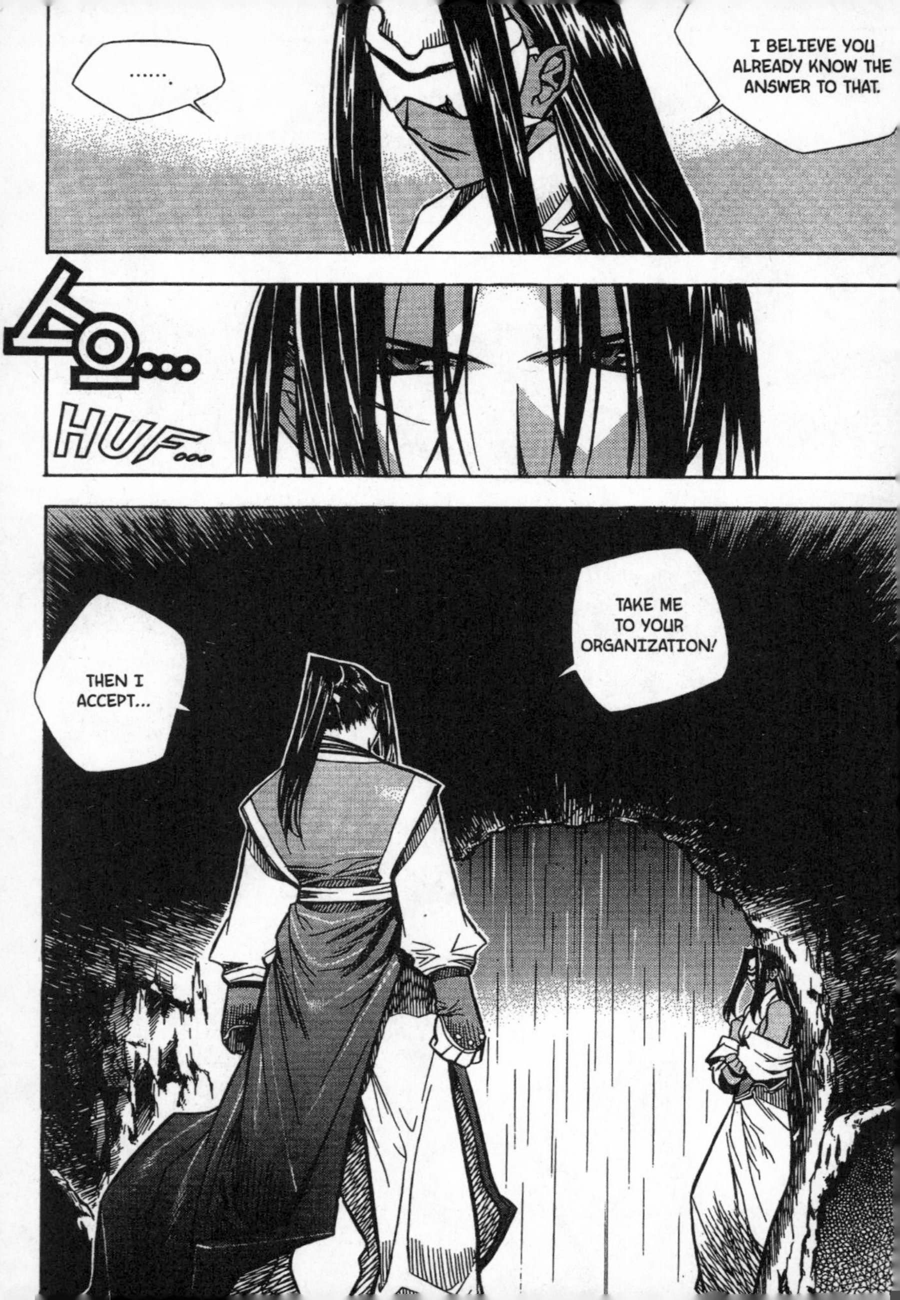
I BELIEVE YOU ALREADY KNOW THE ANSWER TO THAT.
.......
HUF...
TAKE ME TO YOUR ORGANIZATION!
THEN I ACCEPT...

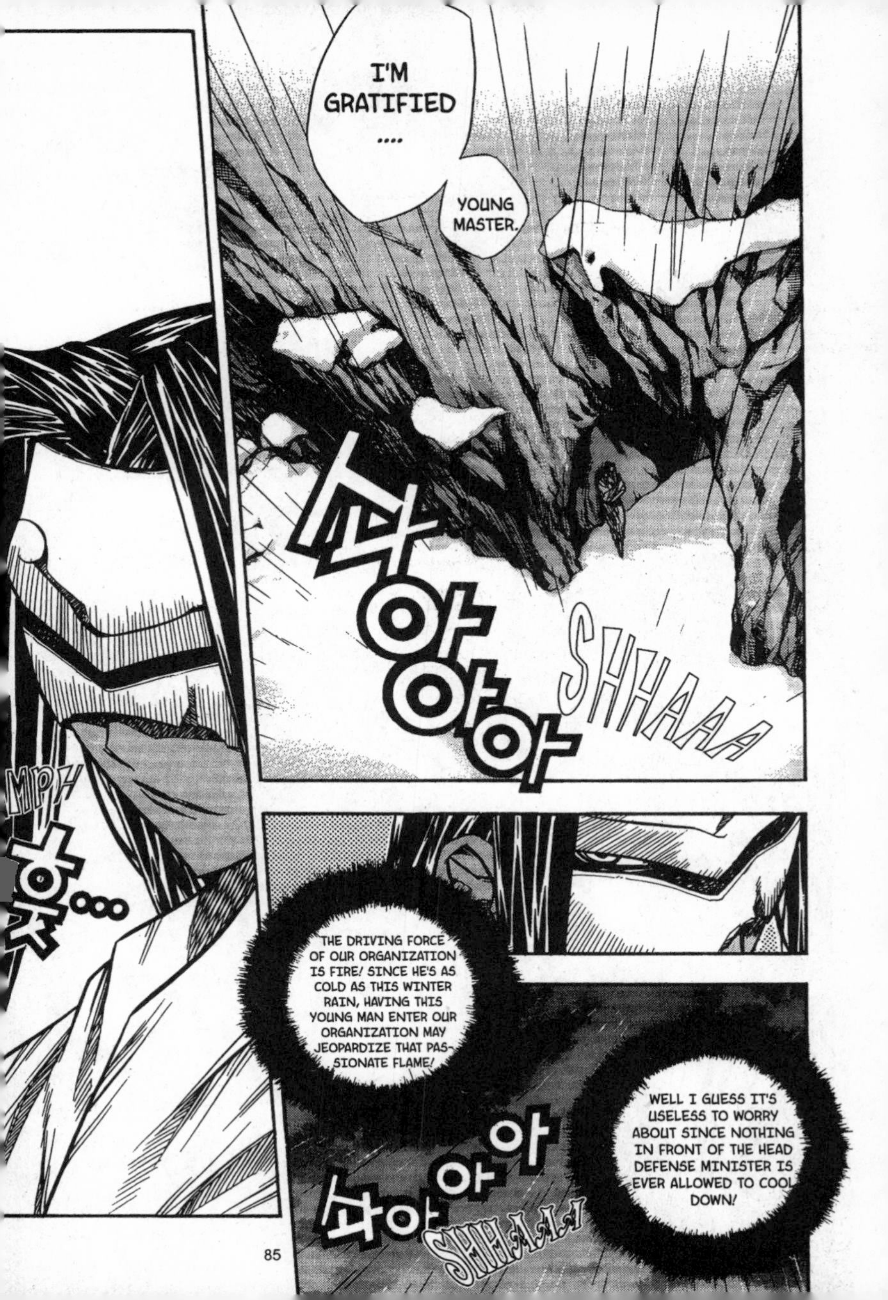
I'M GRATIFIED ....
YOUNG MASTER.
SHHAAA
MPH
THE DRIVING FORCE OF OUR ORGANIZATION IS FIRE! SINCE HE'S AS COLD AS THIS WINTER RAIN, HAVING THIS YOUNG MAN ENTER OUR ORGANIZATION MAY JEOPARDIZE THAT PAS-SIONATE FLAME!
WELL I GUESS IT'S USELESS TO WORRY ABOUT SINCE NOTHING IN FRONT OF THE HEAD DEFENSE MINISTER IS EVER ALLOWED TO COOL DOWN!
SHHAAA

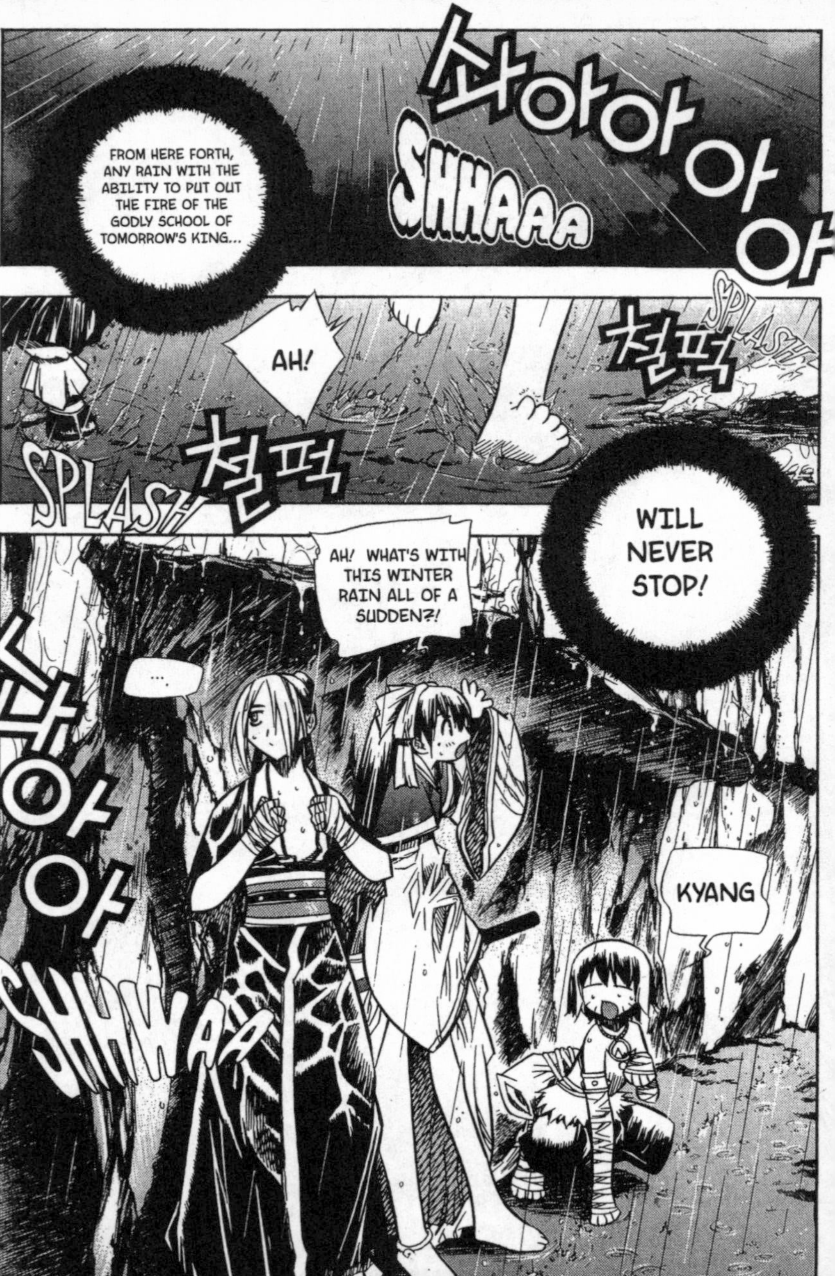

FROM HERE FORTH, ANY RAIN WITH THE ABILITY TO PUT OUT THE FIRE OF THE GODLY SCHOOL OF TOMORROW'S KING...
쏴아아아아
SHHAAA
AH!
철퍽
SPLASH
철퍽
SPLASH
WILL NEVER STOP!
AH! WHAT'S WITH THIS WINTER RAIN ALL OF A SUDDEN?!
...
쏴아아
SHHWAA
KYANG

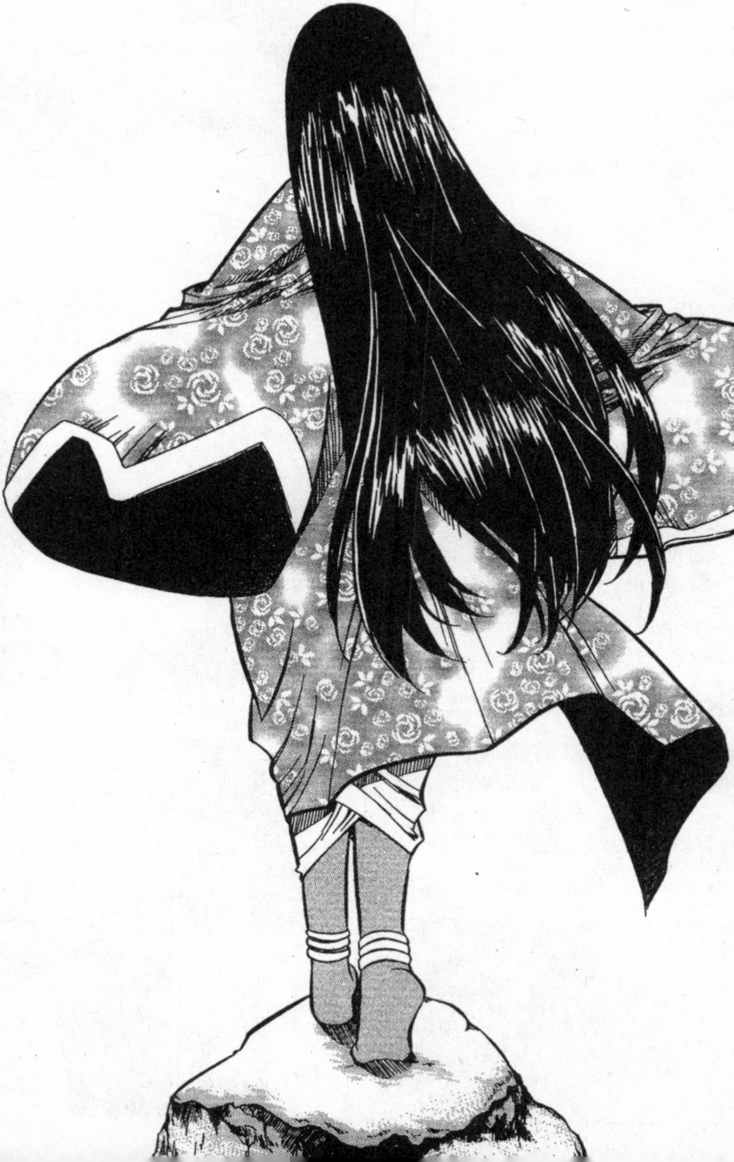

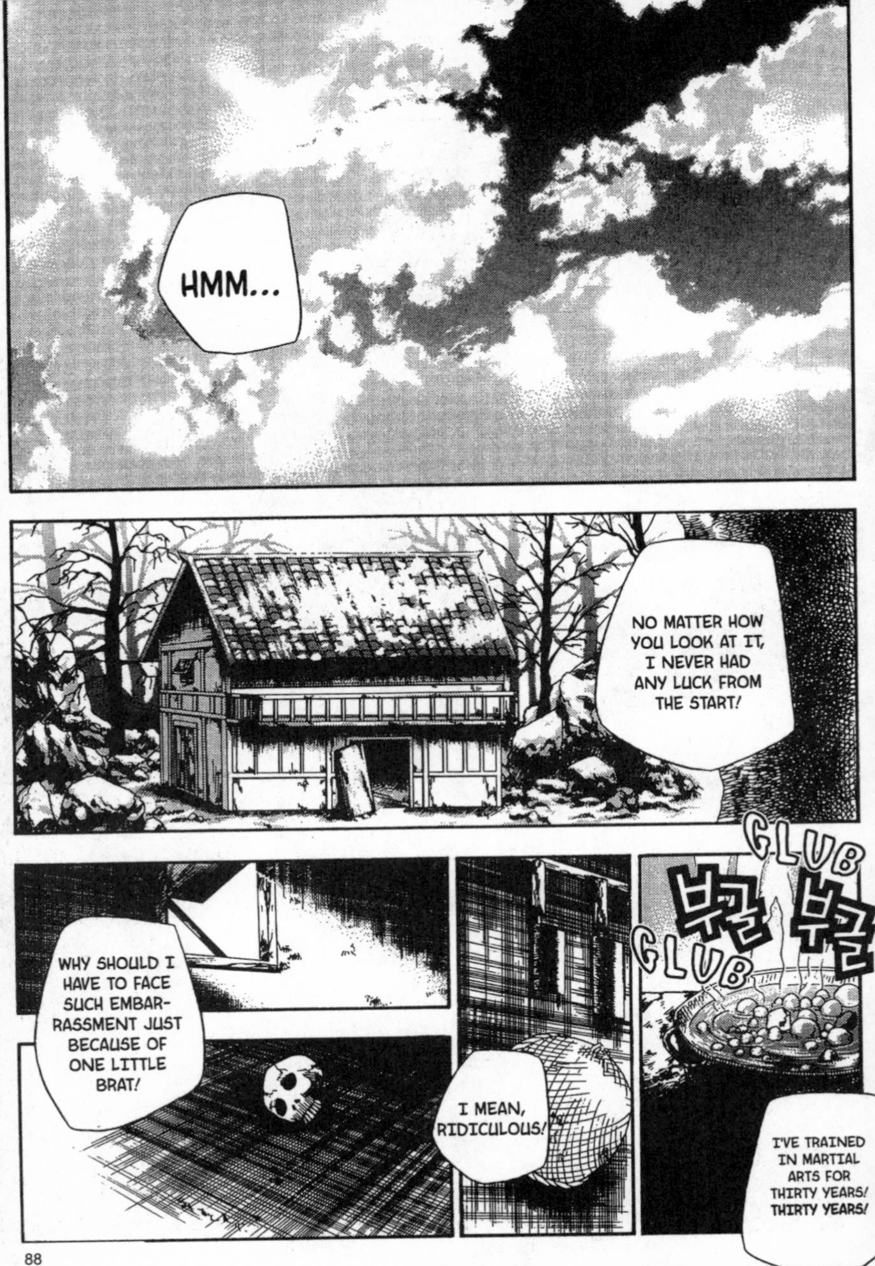
HMM...
NO MATTER HOW YOU LOOK AT IT, I NEVER HAD ANY LUCK FROM THE START!
WHY SHOULD I HAVE TO FACE SUCH EMBAR-RASSMENT JUST BECAUSE OF ONE LITTLE BRAT!
I MEAN, RIDICULOUS!
GLUB
부글 부글
GLUB
I'VE TRAINED IN MARTIAL ARTS FOR THIRTY YEARS! THIRTY YEARS!

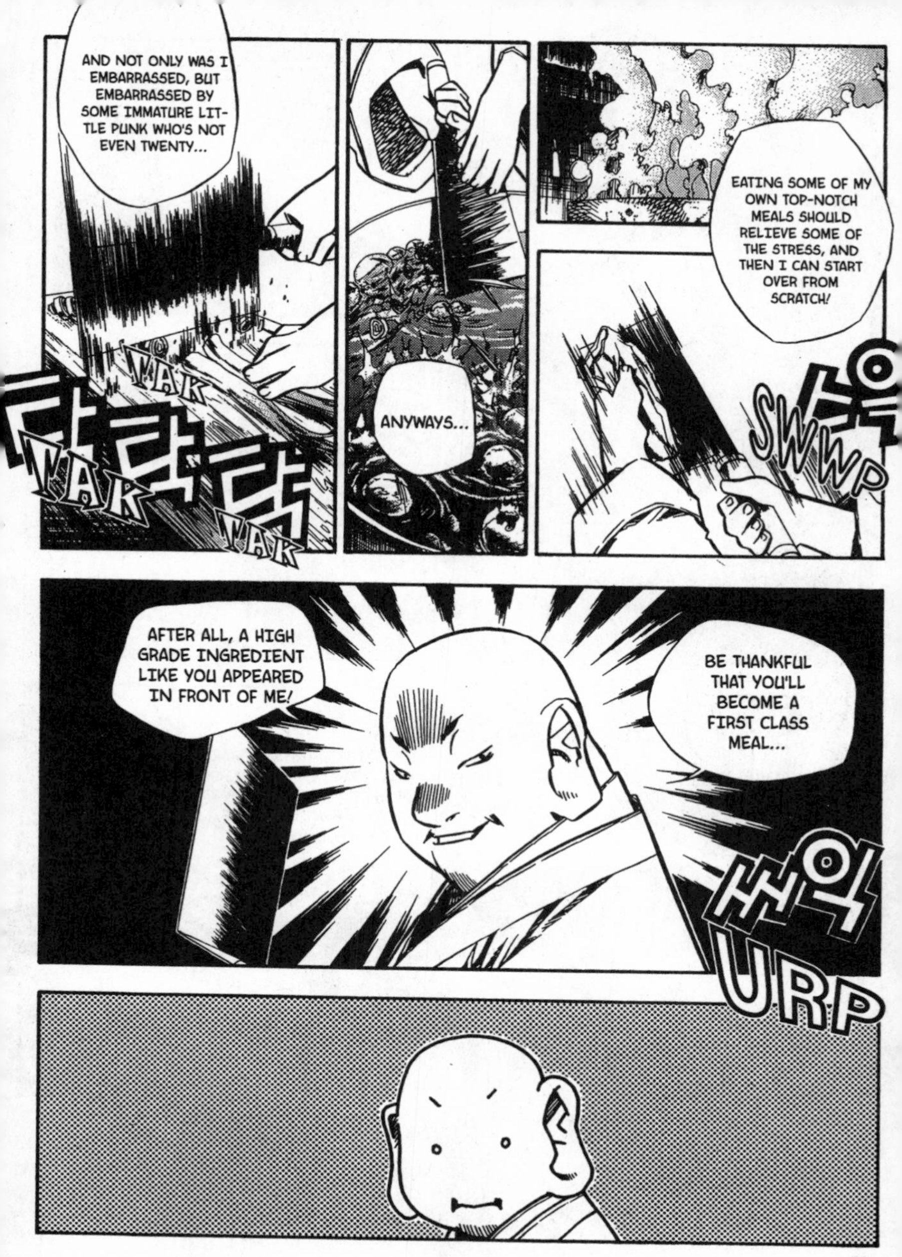
AND NOT ONLY WAS I EMBARRASSED, BUT EMBARRASSED BY SOME IMMATURE LITTLE PUNK WHO'S NOT EVEN TWENTY...
TAK
TAK
TAK
ANYWAYS...
EATING SOME OF MY OWN TOP-NOTCH MEALS SHOULD RELIEVE SOME OF THE STRESS, AND THEN I CAN START OVER FROM SCRATCH!
SWWP
AFTER ALL, A HIGH GRADE INGREDIENT LIKE YOU APPEARED IN FRONT OF ME!
BE THANKFUL THAT YOU'LL BECOME A FIRST CLASS MEAL...
URP

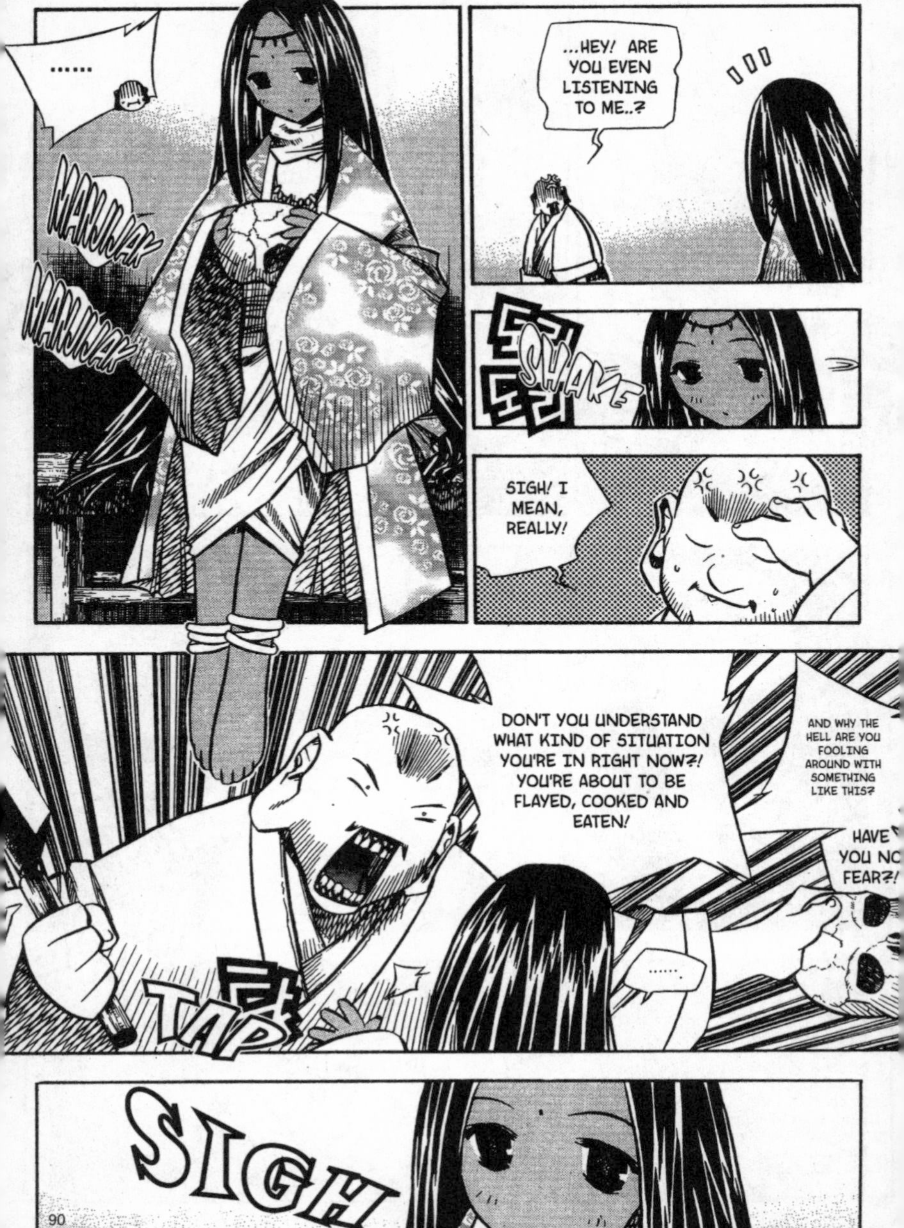
......
MAKUWAK
MAKUWAK
...HEY! ARE YOU EVEN LISTENING TO ME..?!
SHAKE
SIGH! I MEAN, REALLY!
AND WHY THE HELL ARE YOU FOOLING AROUND WITH SOMETHING LIKE THIS?!
HAVE YOU NO FEAR?!
DON'T YOU UNDERSTAND WHAT KIND OF SITUATION YOU'RE IN RIGHT NOW?! YOU'RE ABOUT TO BE FLAYED, COOKED AND EATEN!
......
TAP
SIGH

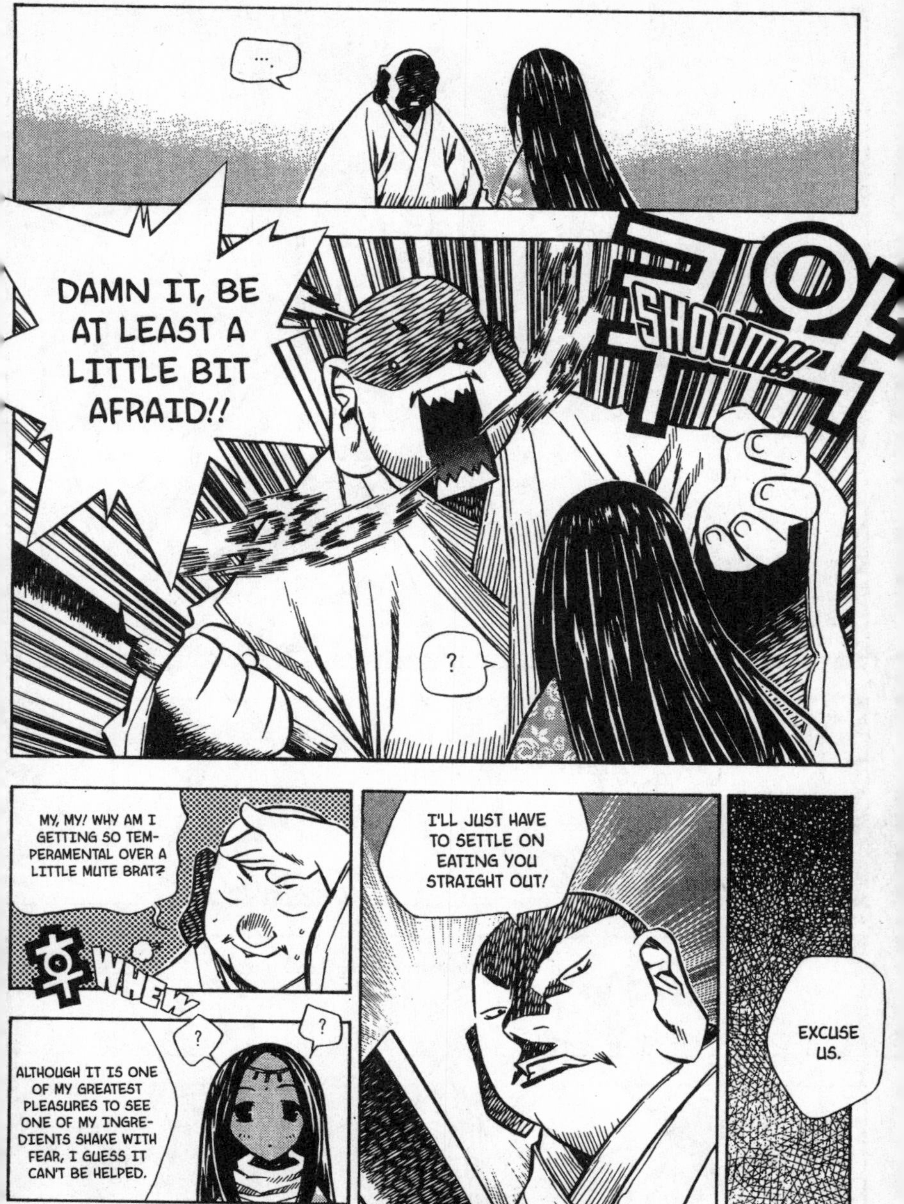
....
DAMN IT, BE AT LEAST A LITTLE BIT AFRAID!!
SHOOM!!
?
MY, MY! WHY AM I GETTING SO TEMPERAMENTAL OVER A LITTLE MUTE BRAT?
WHEW
?
?
ALTHOUGH IT IS ONE OF MY GREATEST PLEASURES TO SEE ONE OF MY INGREDIENTS SHAKE WITH FEAR, I GUESS IT CAN'T BE HELPED.
I'LL JUST HAVE TO SETTLE ON EATING YOU STRAIGHT OUT!
EXCUSE US.

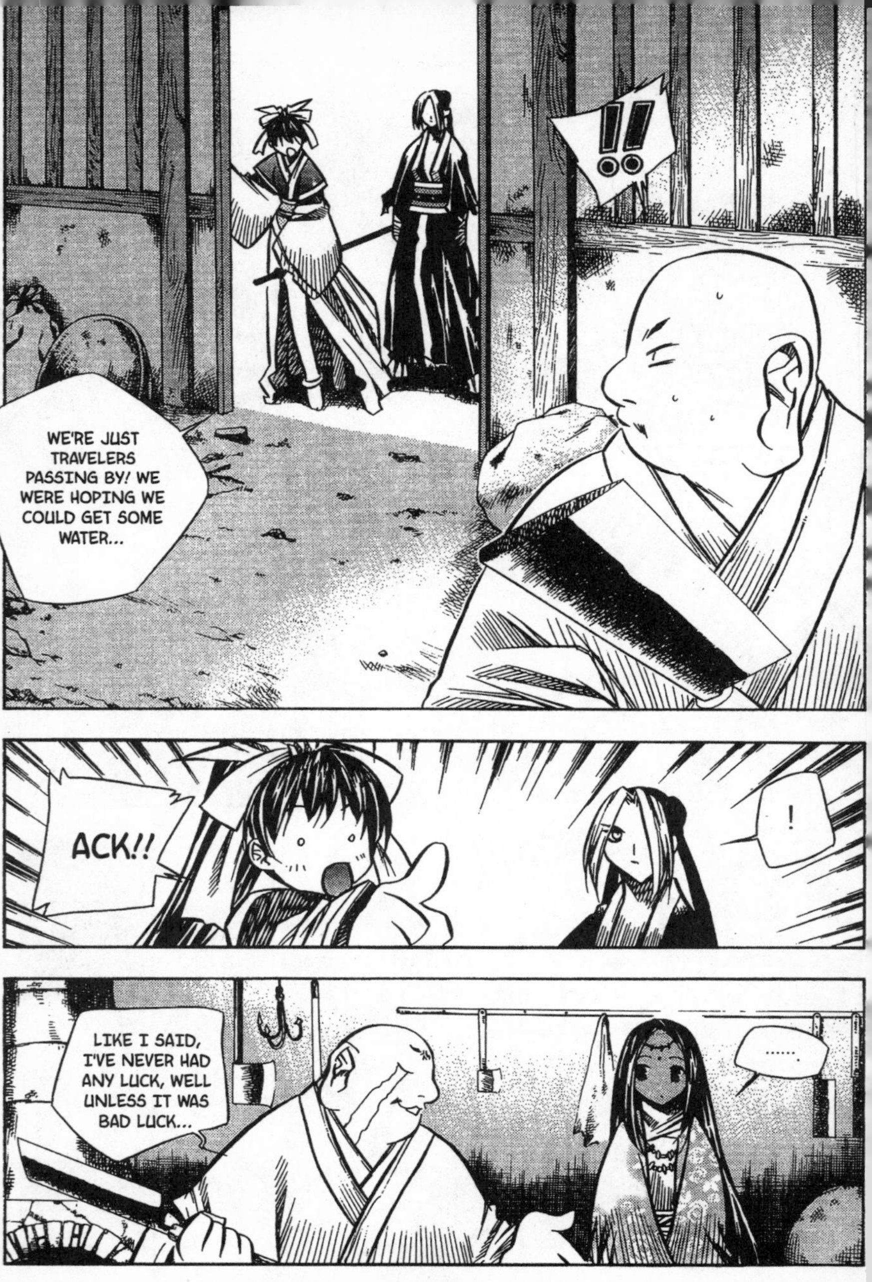
!!
WE'RE JUST TRAVELERS PASSING BY! WE WERE HOPING WE COULD GET SOME WATER...
!
ACK!!
......
LIKE I SAID, I'VE NEVER HAD ANY LUCK, WELL UNLESS IT WAS BAD LUCK...

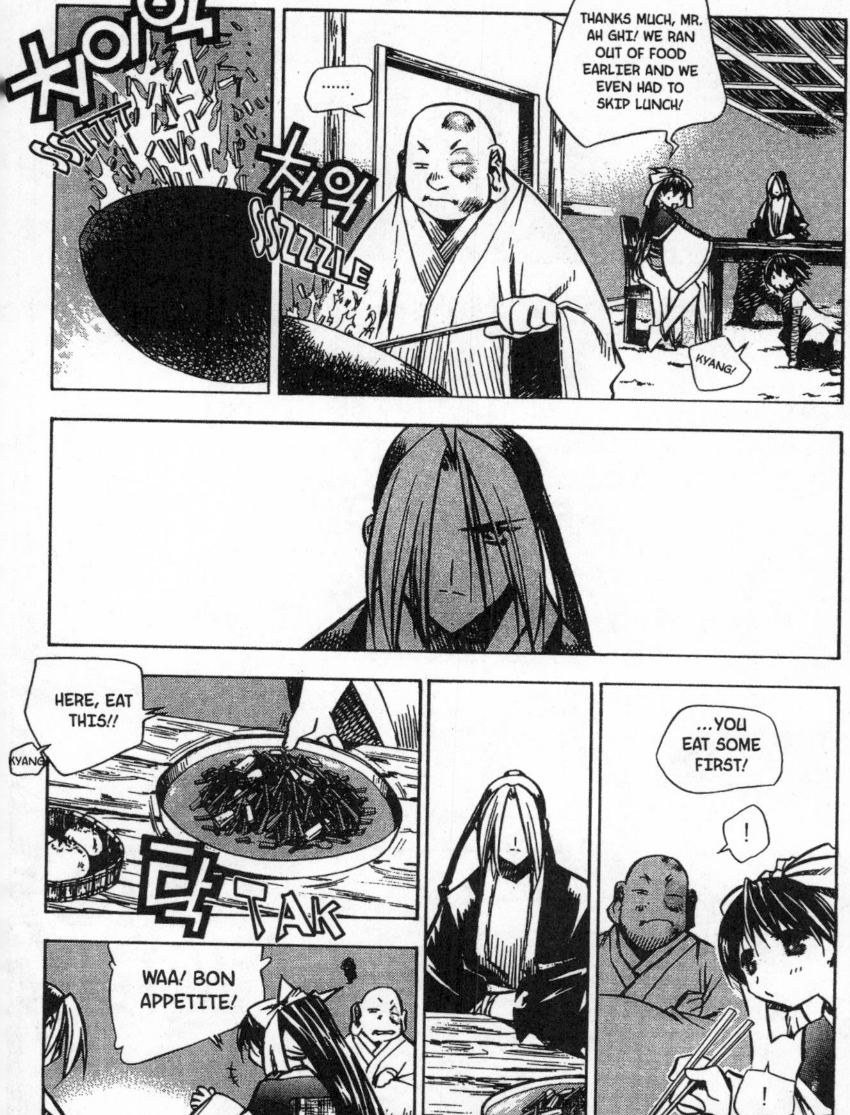

치이익
SSSTTTTT
치익
SSSZZZZLE
......
THANKS MUCH, MR. AH GHI! WE RAN OUT OF FOOD EARLIER AND WE EVEN HAD TO SKIP LUNCH!
KYANG!
HERE, EAT THIS!!
KYANG
탁
TAK
WAA! BON APPETITE!
...YOU EAT SOME FIRST!
!
!

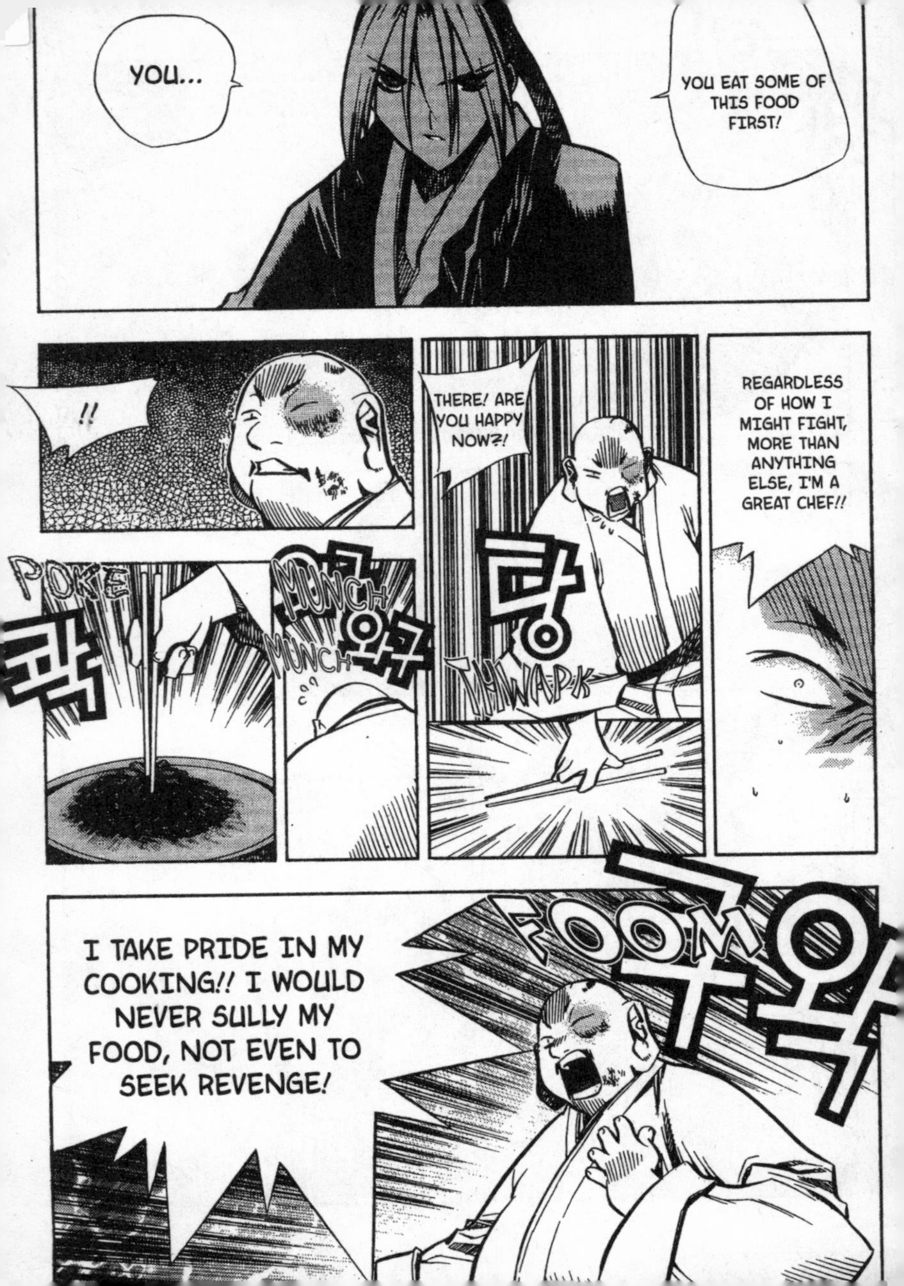
YOU...
YOU EAT SOME OF THIS FOOD FIRST!
!!
POKE
MUNCH
MUNCH
THERE! ARE YOU HAPPY NOW?!
THWAPK
REGARDLESS OF HOW I MIGHT FIGHT, MORE THAN ANYTHING ELSE, I'M A GREAT CHEF!!
FOOM
I TAKE PRIDE IN MY COOKING!! I WOULD NEVER SULLY MY FOOD, NOT EVEN TO SEEK REVENGE!

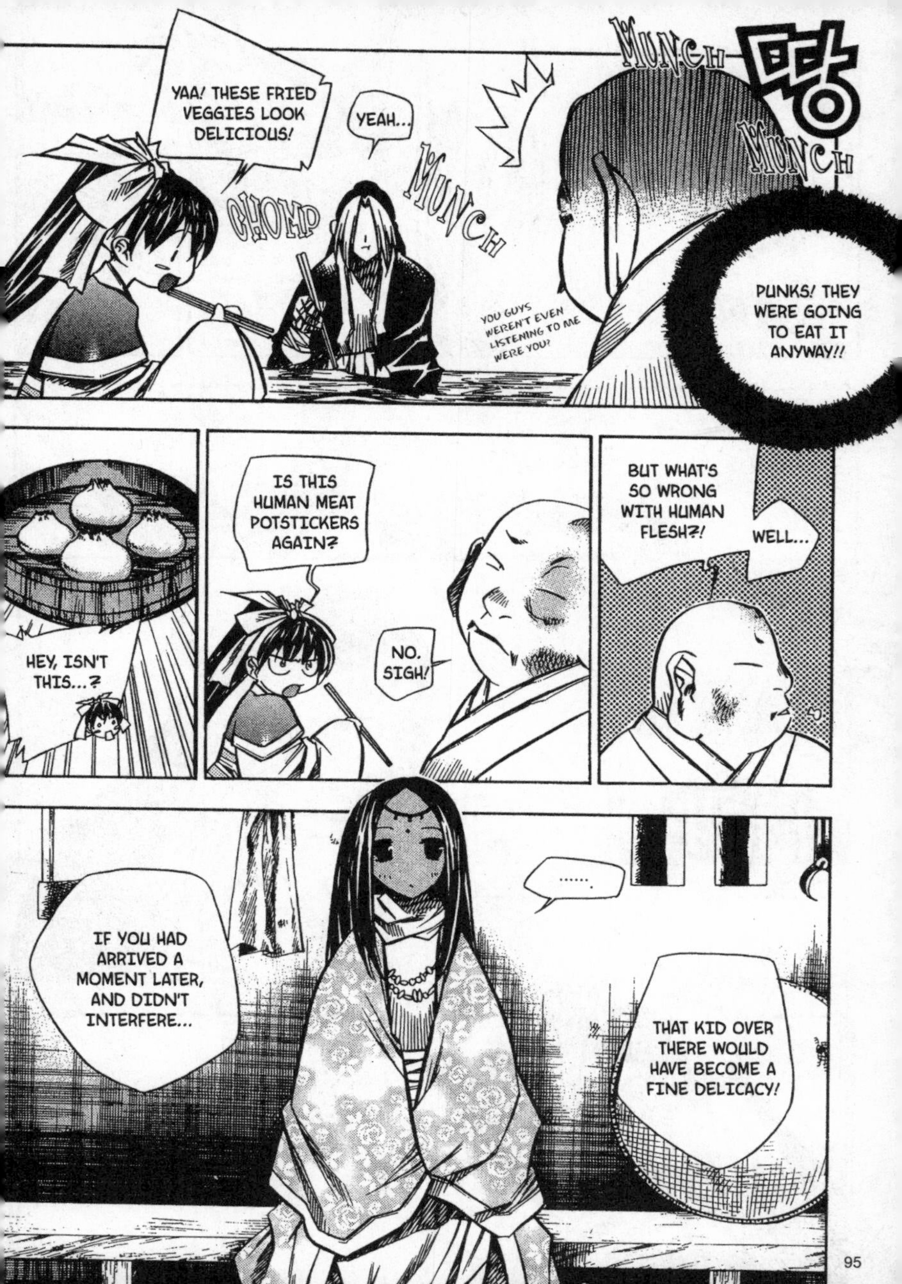

YAA! THESE FRIED VEGGIES LOOK DELICIOUS!
YEAH...
CHOMP
MUNCH
MUNCH
MUNCH
YOU GUYS WEREN'T EVEN LISTENING TO ME WERE YOU?
PUNKS! THEY WERE GOING TO EAT IT ANYWAY!!
HEY, ISN'T THIS...?
IS THIS HUMAN MEAT POTSTICKERS AGAIN?
NO. SIGH!
BUT WHAT'S SO WRONG WITH HUMAN FLESH?!
WELL...
......
IF YOU HAD ARRIVED A MOMENT LATER, AND DIDN'T INTERFERE...
THAT KID OVER THERE WOULD HAVE BECOME A FINE DELICACY!

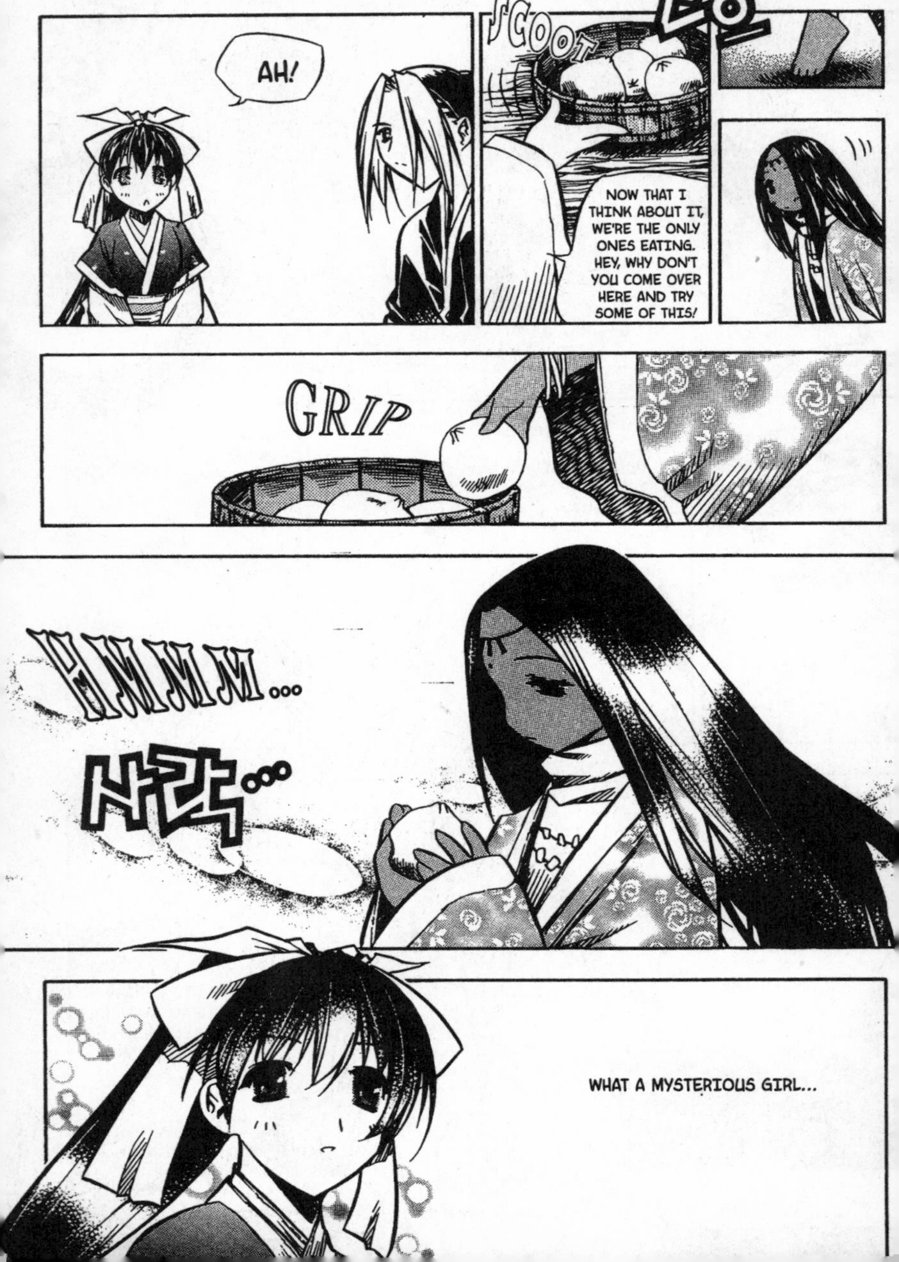
SCOOT
NOW THAT I THINK ABOUT IT, WE'RE THE ONLY ONES EATING. HEY, WHY DON'T YOU COME OVER HERE AND TRY SOME OF THIS!
AH!
GRIP
HMMM...
WHAT A MYSTERIOUS GIRL...

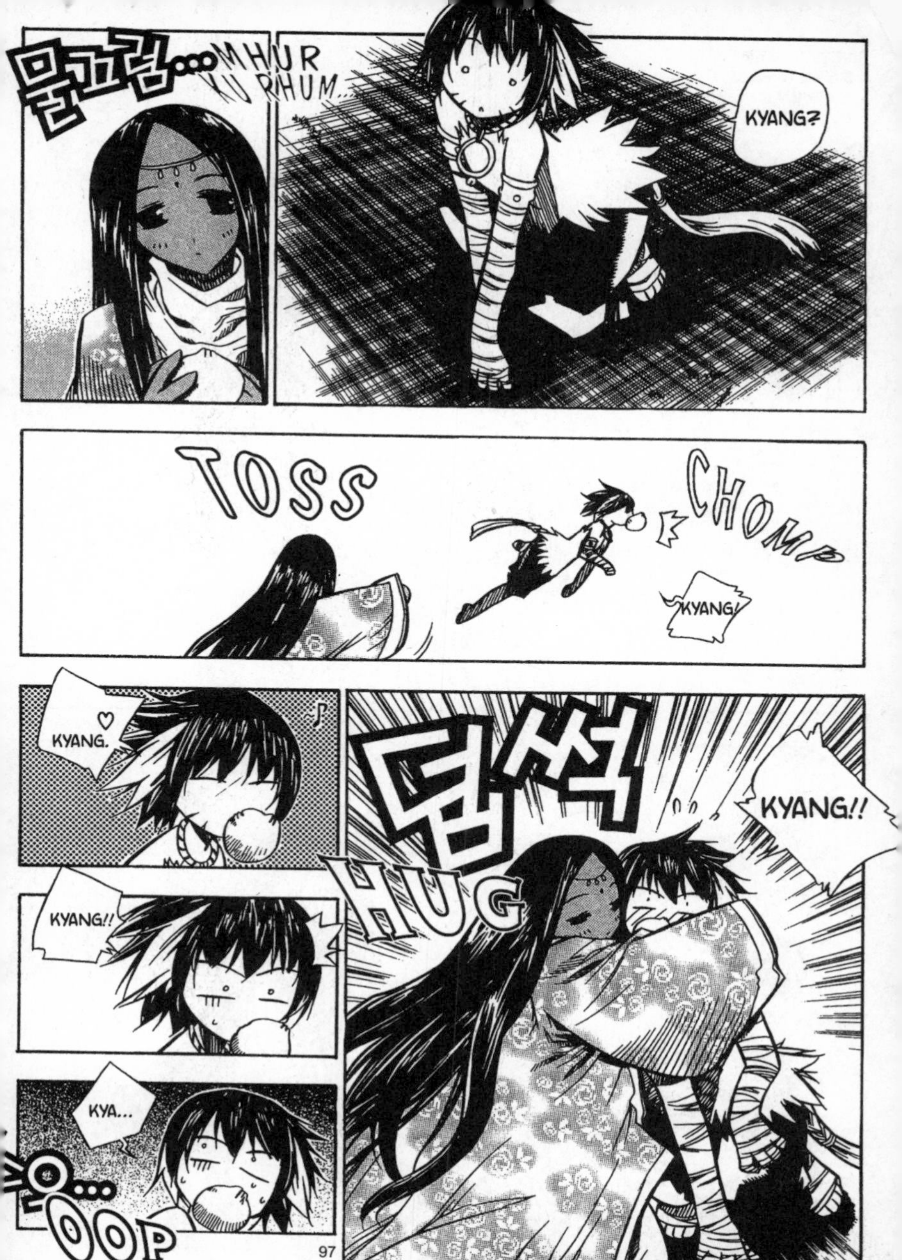
물끄럼... MHUR KU RHUM...
KYANG?
TOSS
CHOMP
KYANG!
KYANG.
KYANG!!
KYA...
읍... OOP
덥석 HUG
KYANG!!

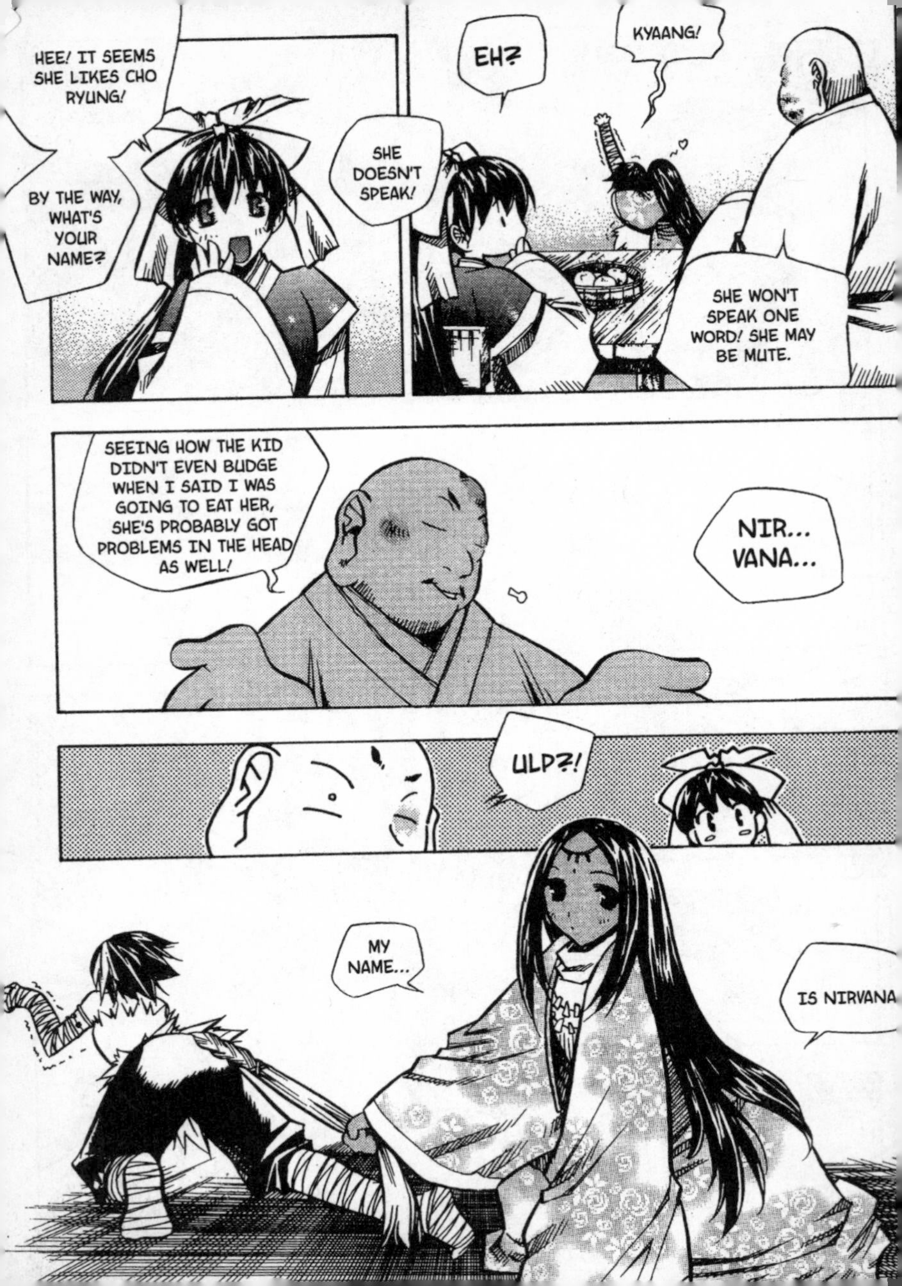
HEE! IT SEEMS SHE LIKES CHO RYUNG!
BY THE WAY, WHAT'S YOUR NAME?
SHE DOESN'T SPEAK!
EH?
KYAANG!
SHE WON'T SPEAK ONE WORD! SHE MAY BE MUTE.
SEEING HOW THE KID DIDN'T EVEN BUDGE WHEN I SAID I WAS GOING TO EAT HER, SHE'S PROBABLY GOT PROBLEMS IN THE HEAD AS WELL!
NIR... VANA...
ULP?!
MY NAME...
IS NIRVANA

YOU CAN SPEAK?!

...

HEY, THAT'S A UNIQUE NAME! JUST AS I THOUGHT, YOU'RE NOT FROM AROUND HERE ARE YOU?!

OOP?!

NOW THAT I THINK ABOUT IT, I SHOULDN'T BLOW ANYMORE TIME WITH THESE KIDS!

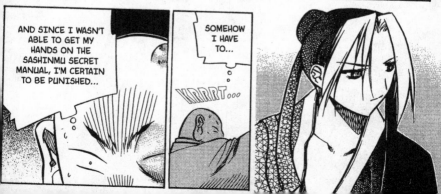

AND SINCE I WASN'T ABLE TO GET MY HANDS ON THE SASHINMU SECRET MANUAL, I'M CERTAIN TO BE PUNISHED...

SOMEHOW I HAVE TO...

KRRRT...

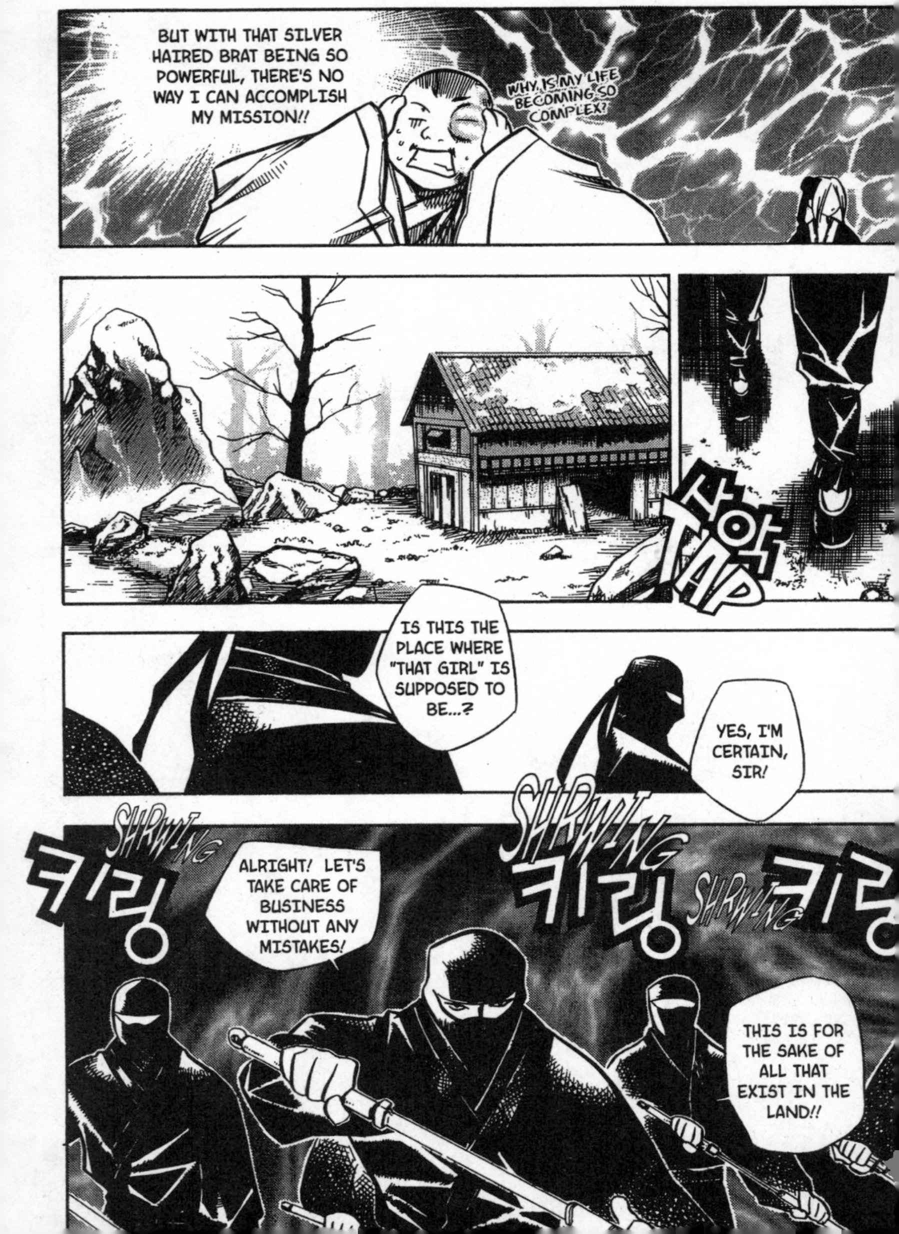

BUT WITH THAT SILVER HAIRED BRAT BEING SO POWERFUL, THERE'S NO WAY I CAN ACCOMPLISH MY MISSION!!
WHY IS MY LIFE BECOMING SO COMPLEX?
사악
TAP
IS THIS THE PLACE WHERE "THAT GIRL" IS SUPPOSED TO BE...?
YES, I'M CERTAIN, SIR!
SHRWING
키링
ALRIGHT! LET'S TAKE CARE OF BUSINESS WITHOUT ANY MISTAKES!
SHRWING
키링
SHRWING
키링
THIS IS FOR THE SAKE OF ALL THAT EXIST IN THE LAND!!

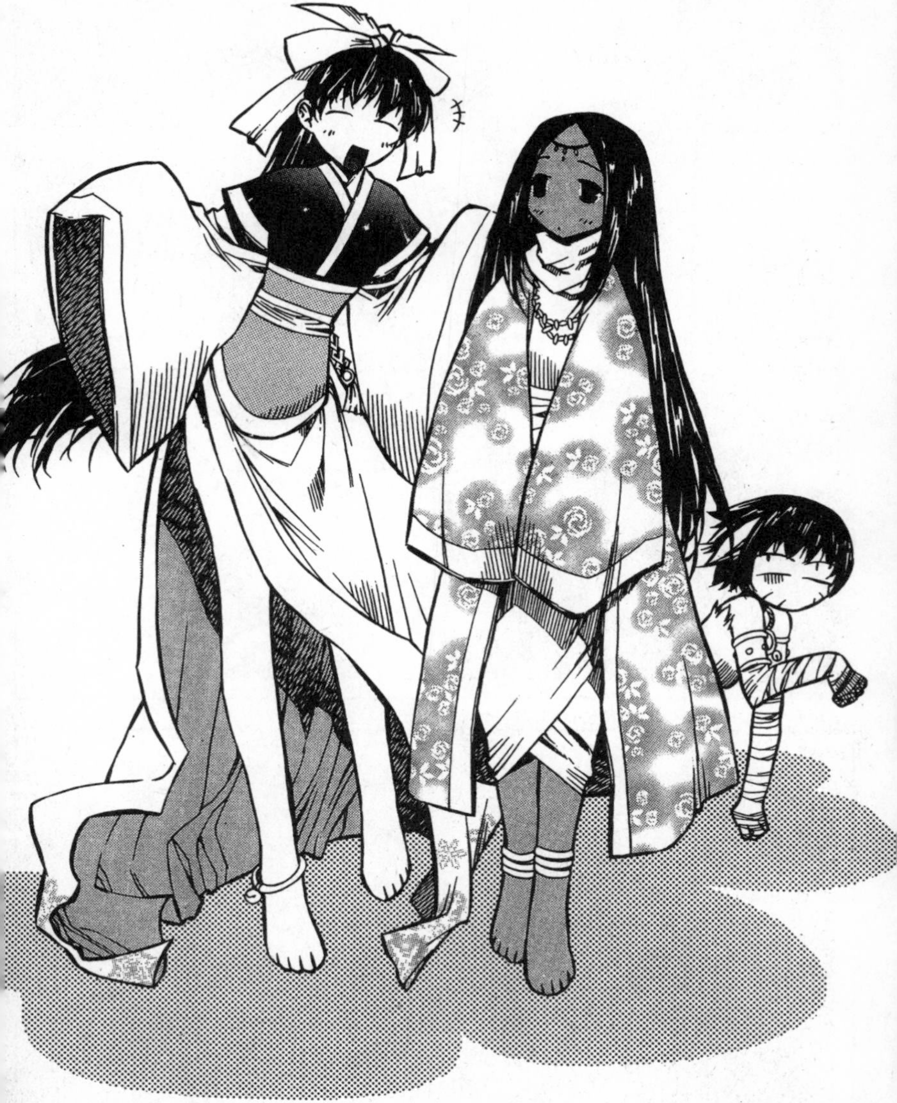

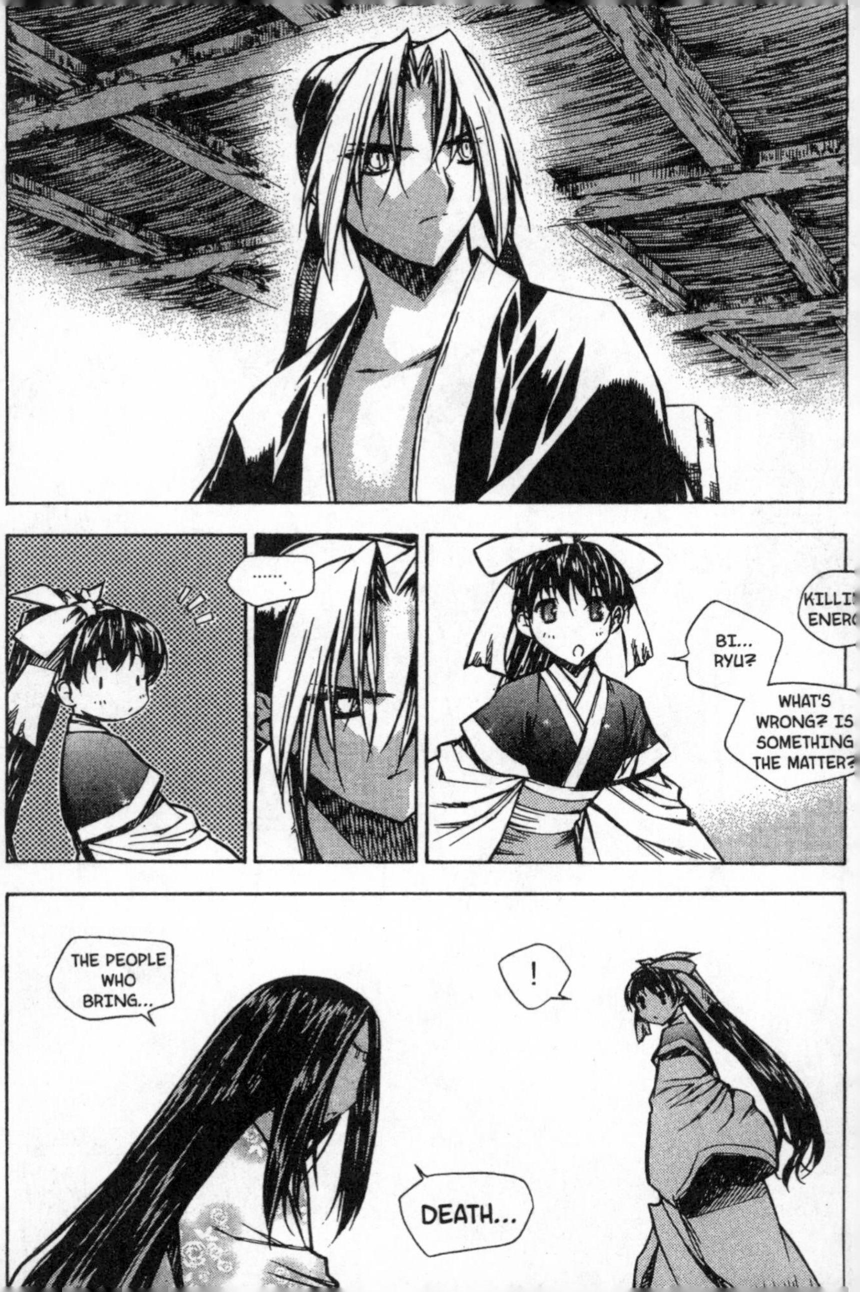
BI... RYU?
WHAT'S WRONG? IS SOMETHING THE MATTER?
......
!
THE PEOPLE WHO BRING...
DEATH...

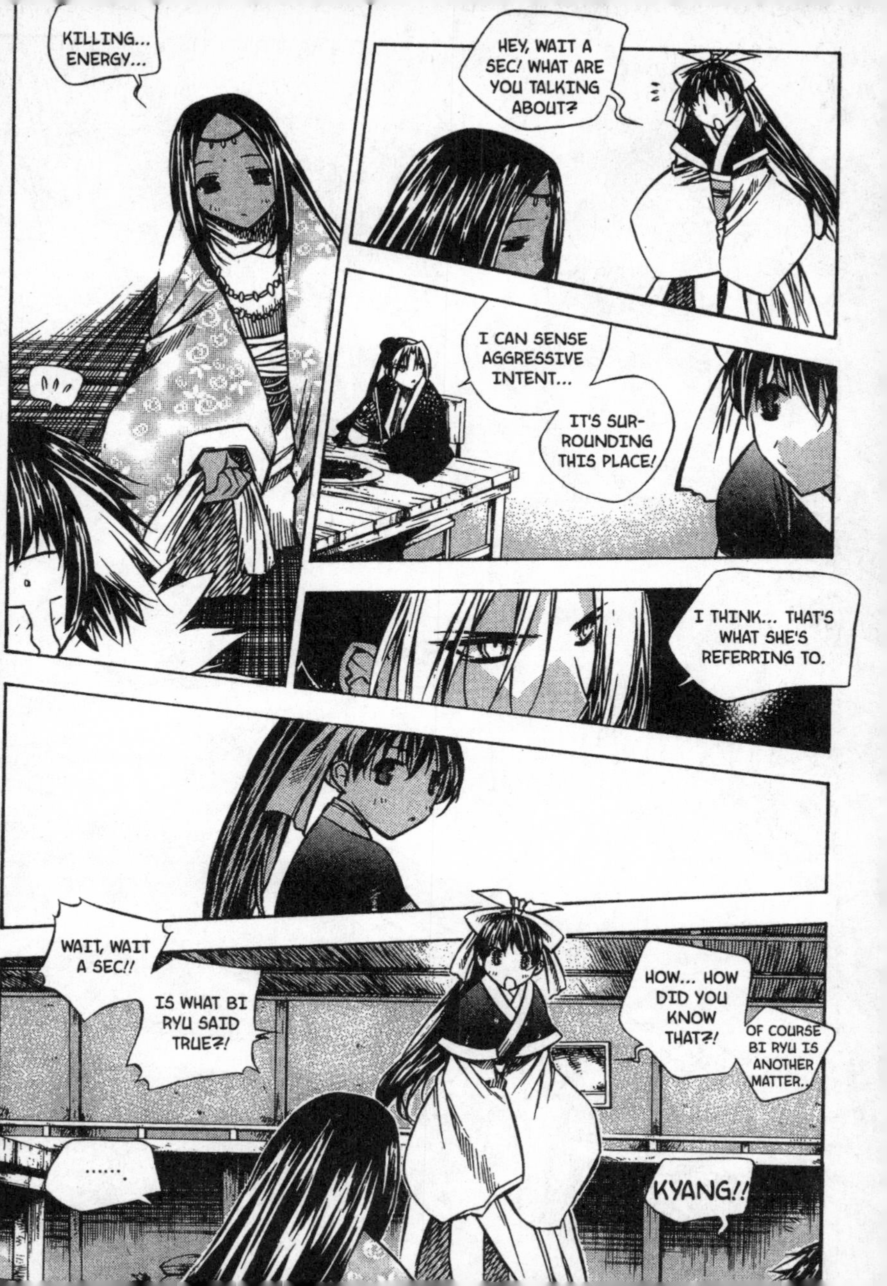
HEY, WAIT A SEC! WHAT ARE YOU TALKING ABOUT?
KILLING... ENERGY...
I CAN SENSE AGGRESSIVE INTENT...
IT'S SUR-ROUNDING THIS PLACE!
I THINK... THAT'S WHAT SHE'S REFERRING TO.
OF COURSE BI RYU IS ANOTHER MATTER...
HOW... HOW DID YOU KNOW THAT?!
WAIT, WAIT A SEC!!
IS WHAT BI RYU SAID TRUE?!
KYANG!!
......

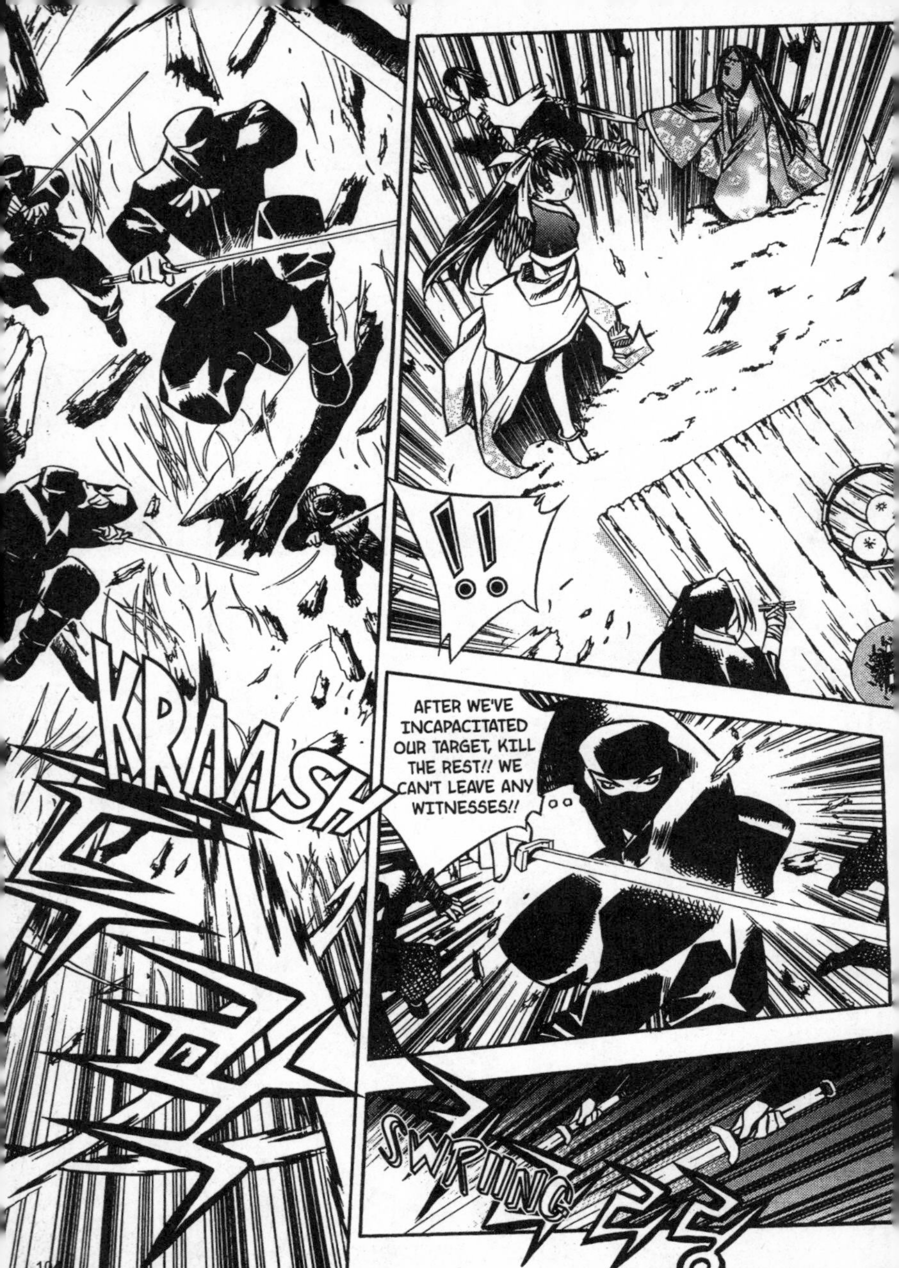
!!
AFTER WE'VE INCAPACITATED OUR TARGET, KILL THE REST!! WE CAN'T LEAVE ANY WITNESSES!!
KRAASH

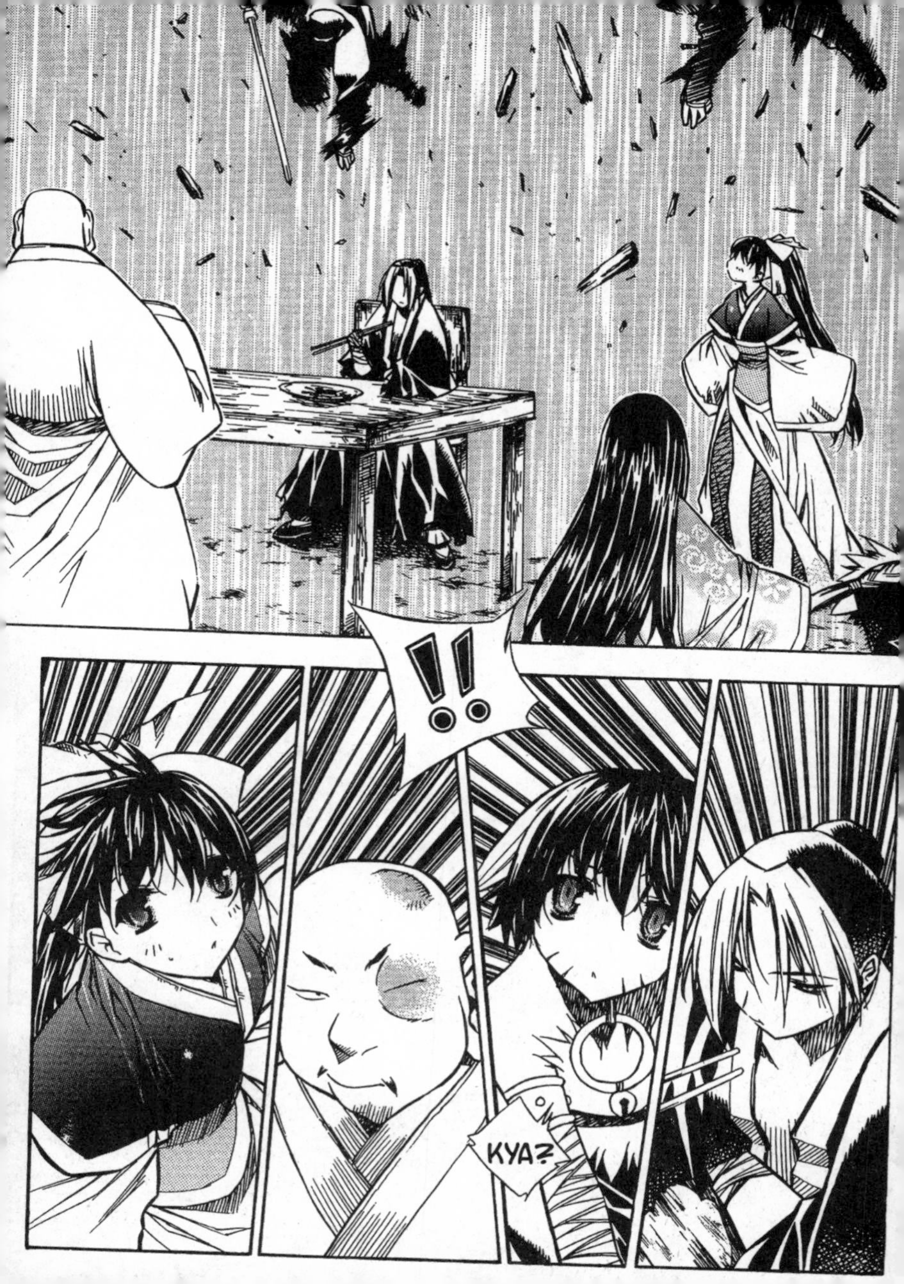
!!
KYA?

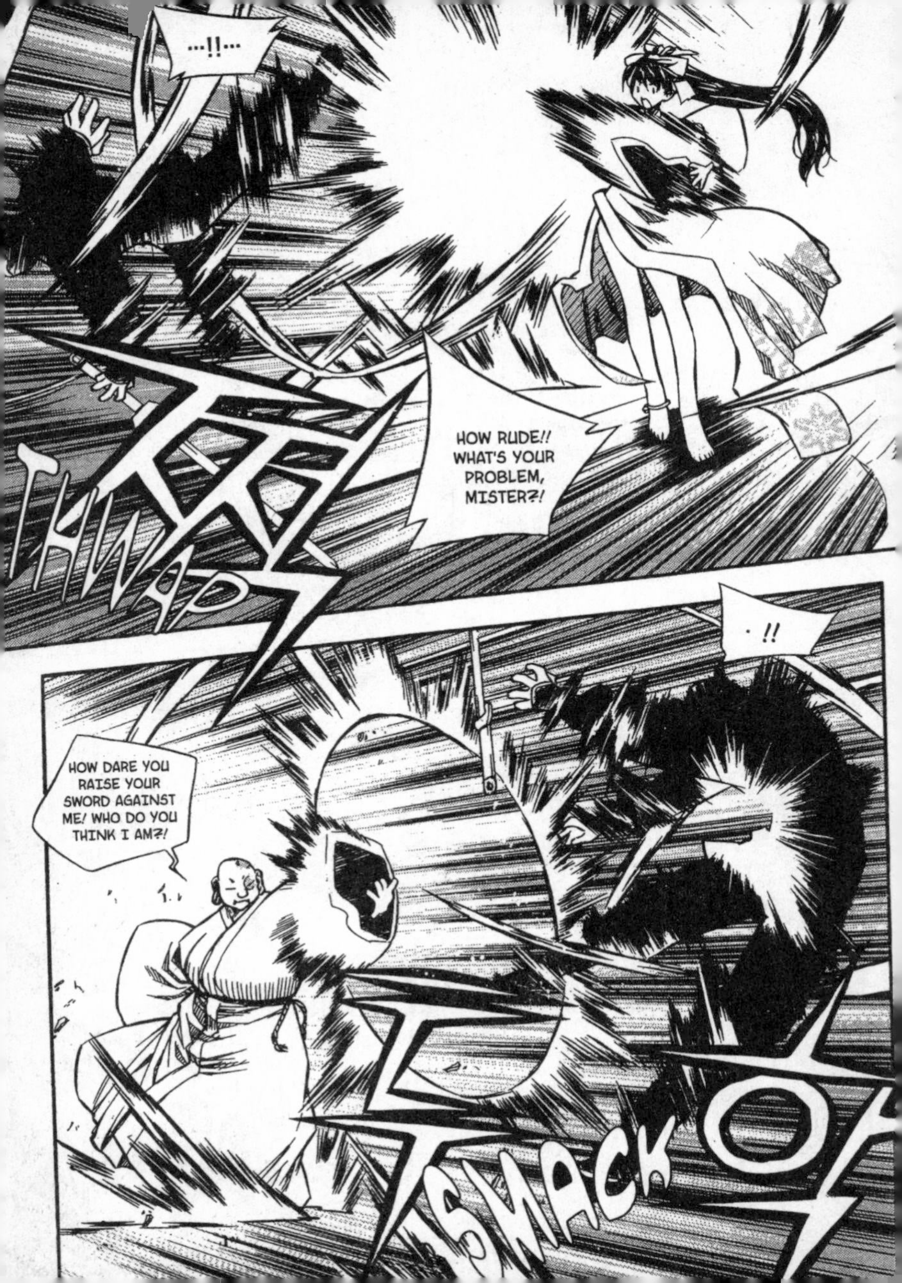

...!!...
HOW RUDE!! WHAT'S YOUR PROBLEM, MISTER?!
THWAP
·!!
HOW DARE YOU RAISE YOUR SWORD AGAINST ME! WHO DO YOU THINK I AM?!
SMACK

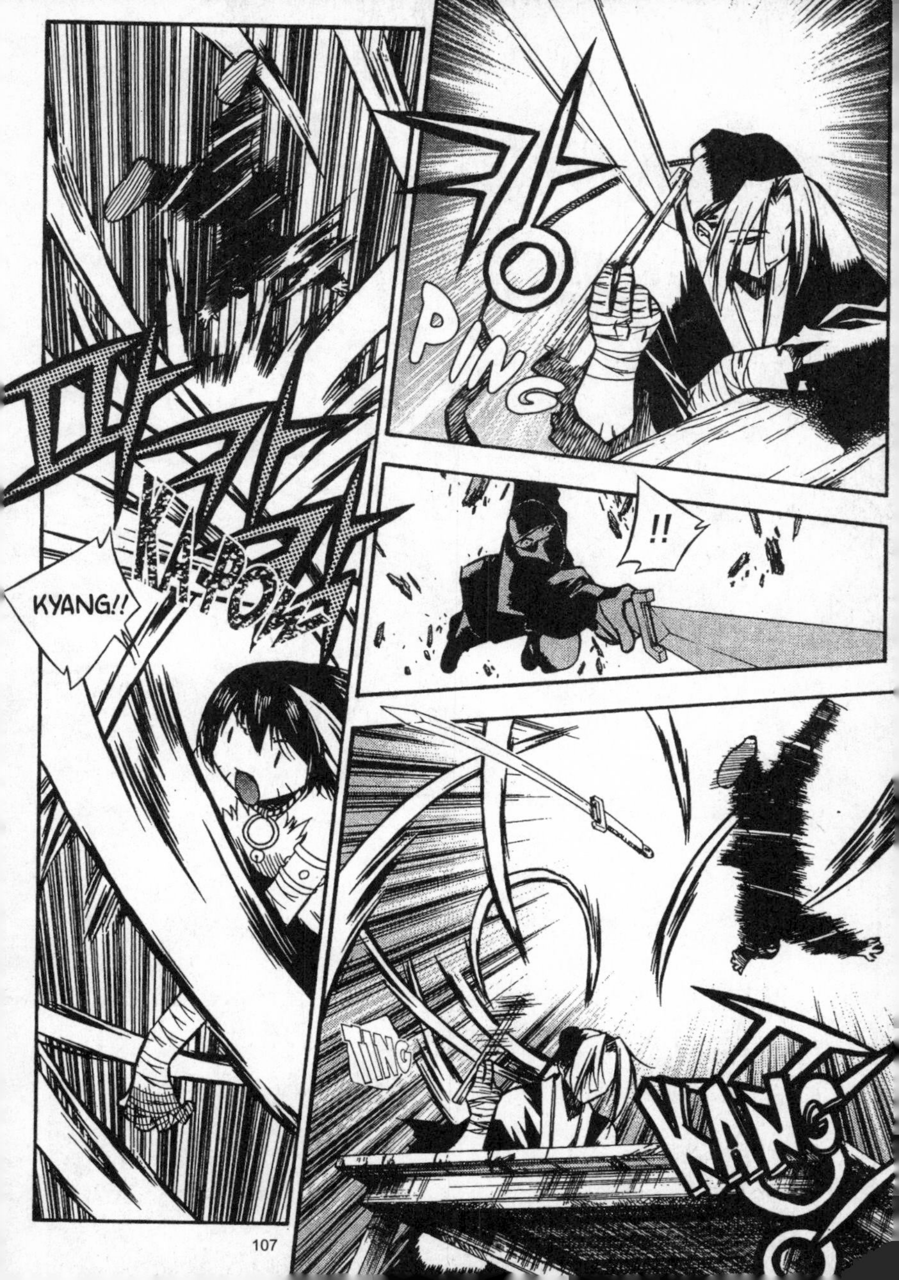
PING
!!
KYANG!!
TING

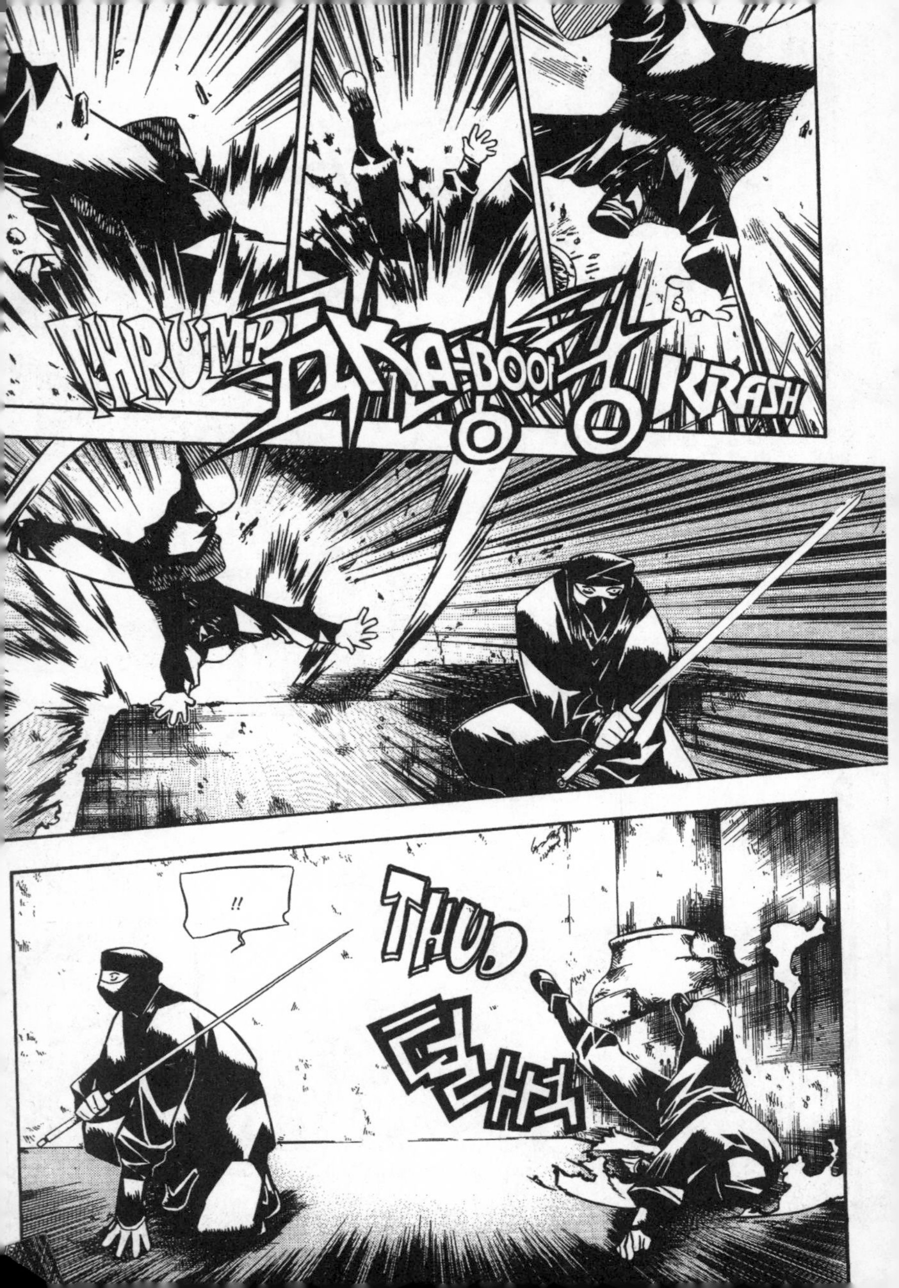
THRUMP
KA-BOOOOM
KRASH
!!
THUD

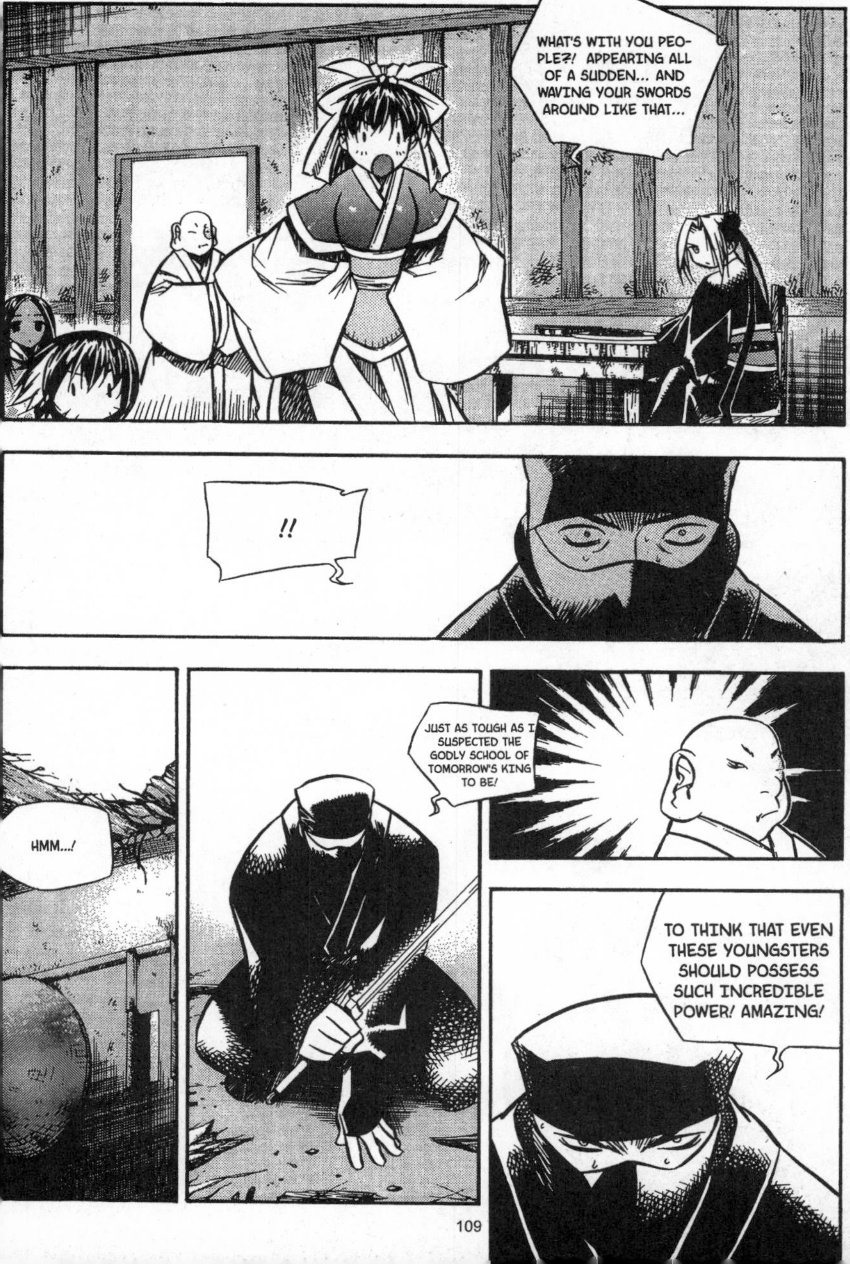
WHAT'S WITH YOU PEOPLE?! APPEARING ALL OF A SUDDEN... AND WAVING YOUR SWORDS AROUND LIKE THAT...
!!
HMM...!
JUST AS TOUGH AS I SUSPECTED THE GODLY SCHOOL OF TOMORROW'S KING TO BE!
TO THINK THAT EVEN THESE YOUNGSTERS SHOULD POSSESS SUCH INCREDIBLE POWER! AMAZING!

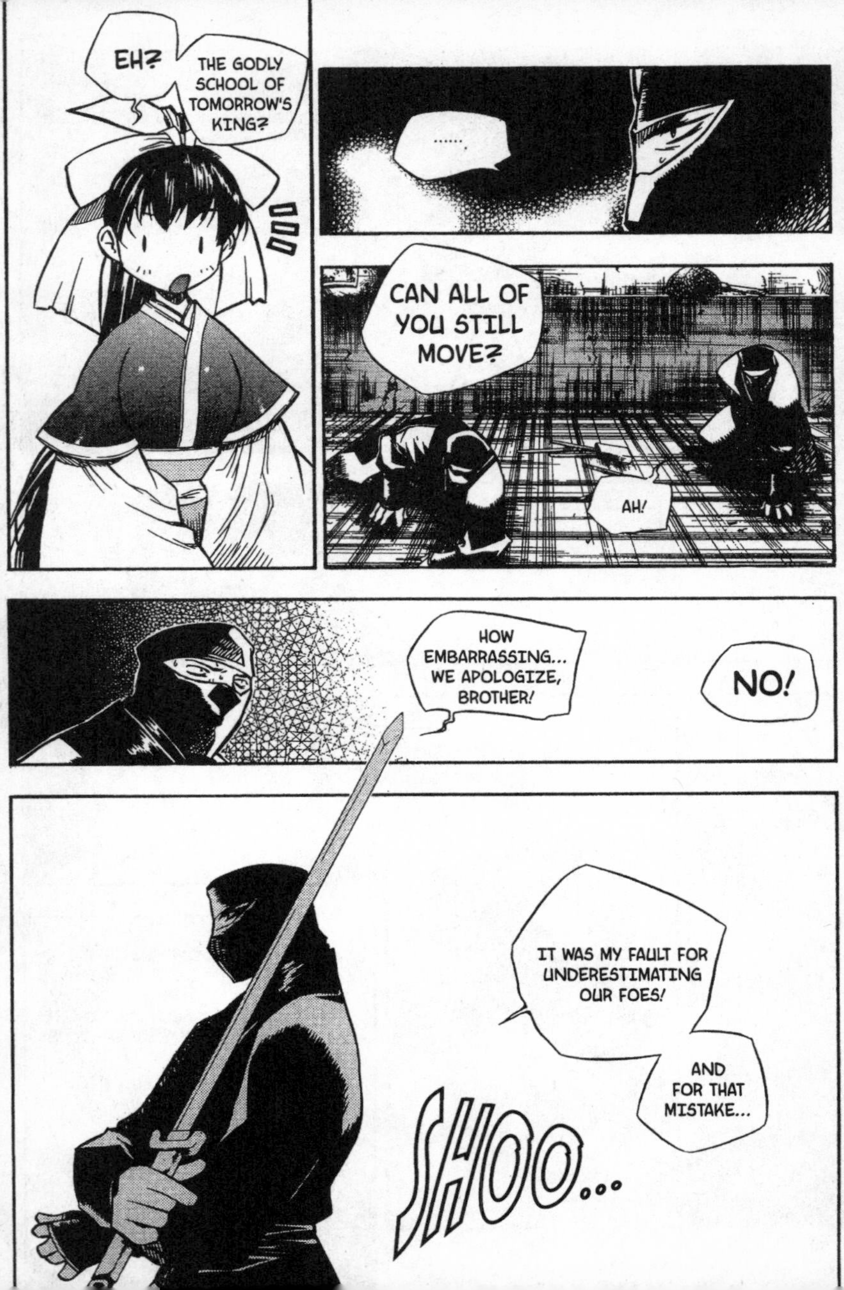
EH?
THE GODLY SCHOOL OF TOMORROW'S KING?
......
CAN ALL OF YOU STILL MOVE?
AH!
HOW EMBARRASSING... WE APOLOGIZE, BROTHER!
NO!
IT WAS MY FAULT FOR UNDERESTIMATING OUR FOES!
AND FOR THAT MISTAKE...
SHOO...

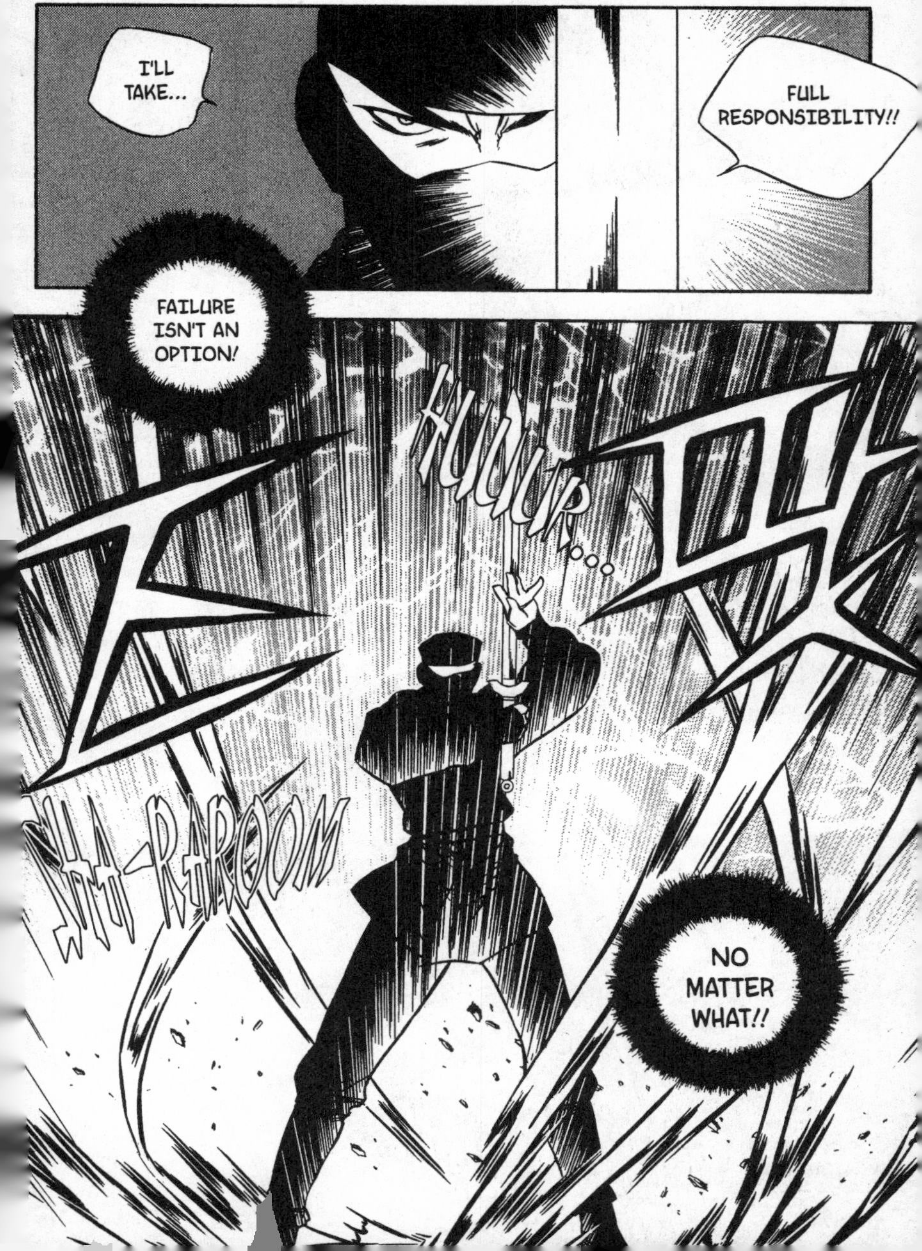
I'LL TAKE...
FULL RESPONSIBILITY!!
FAILURE ISN'T AN OPTION!
HUUUR...
SHA-RAROOM
NO MATTER WHAT!!

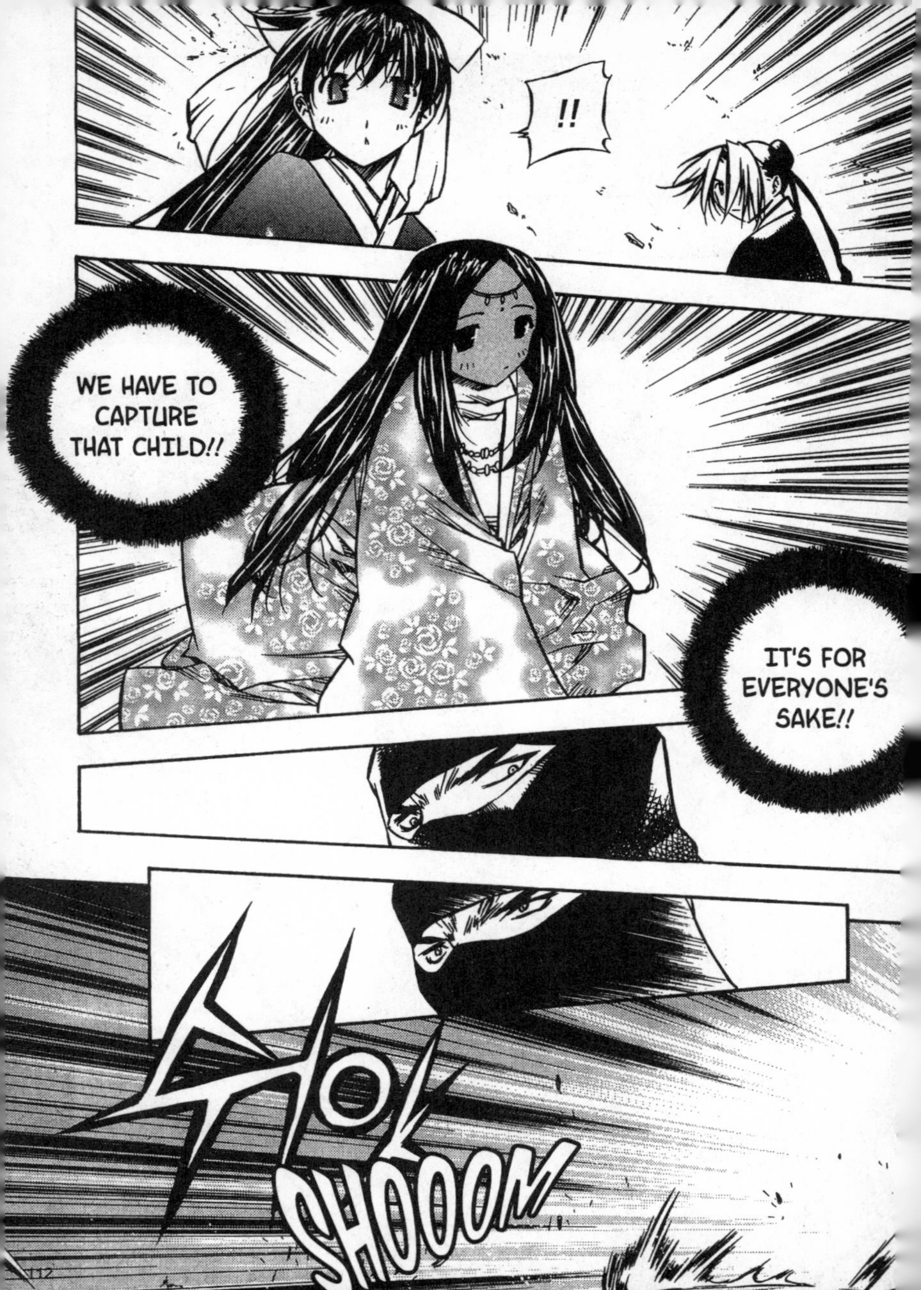
!!
WE HAVE TO CAPTURE THAT CHILD!!
IT'S FOR EVERYONE'S SAKE!!
SHOOOM

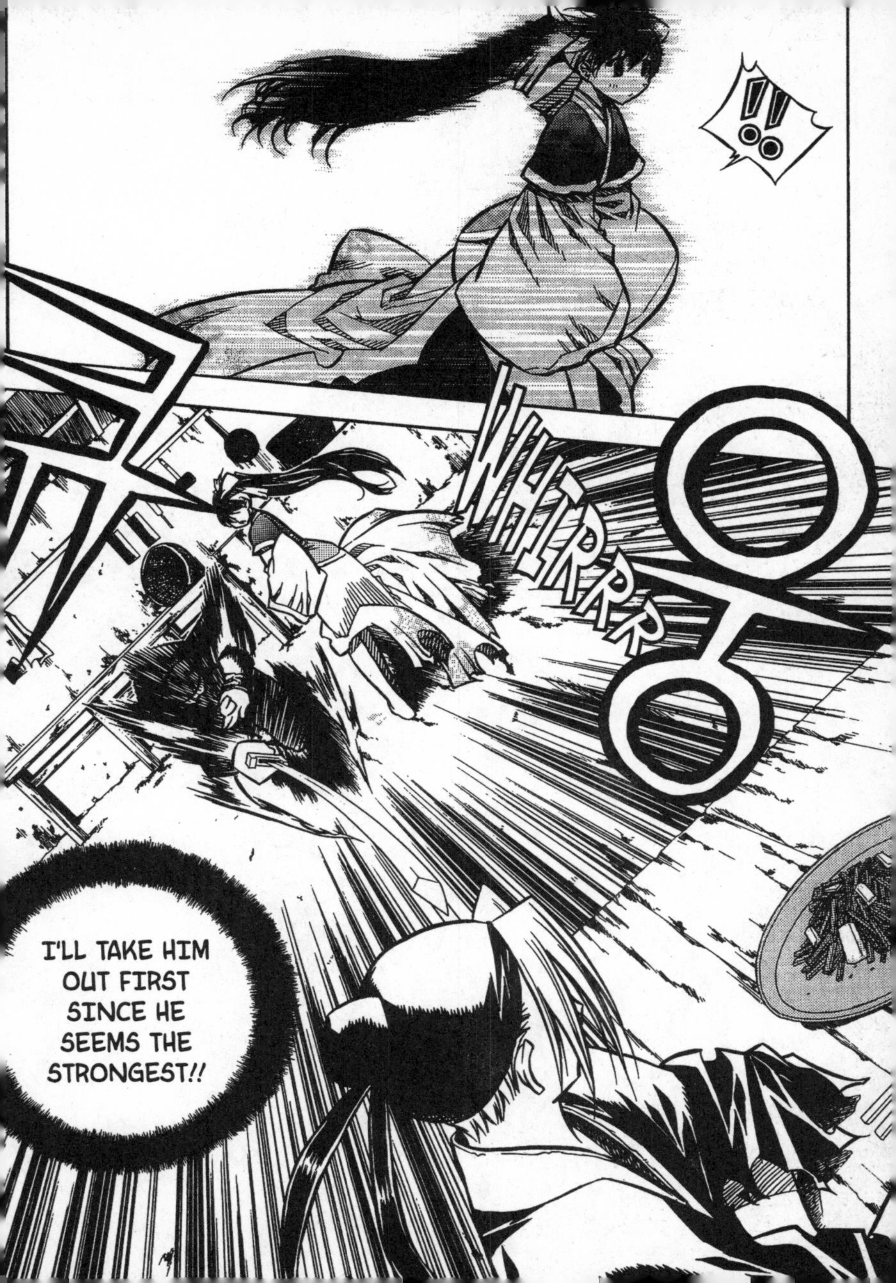
!!
WHIRRR
I'LL TAKE HIM OUT FIRST SINCE HE SEEMS THE STRONGEST!!

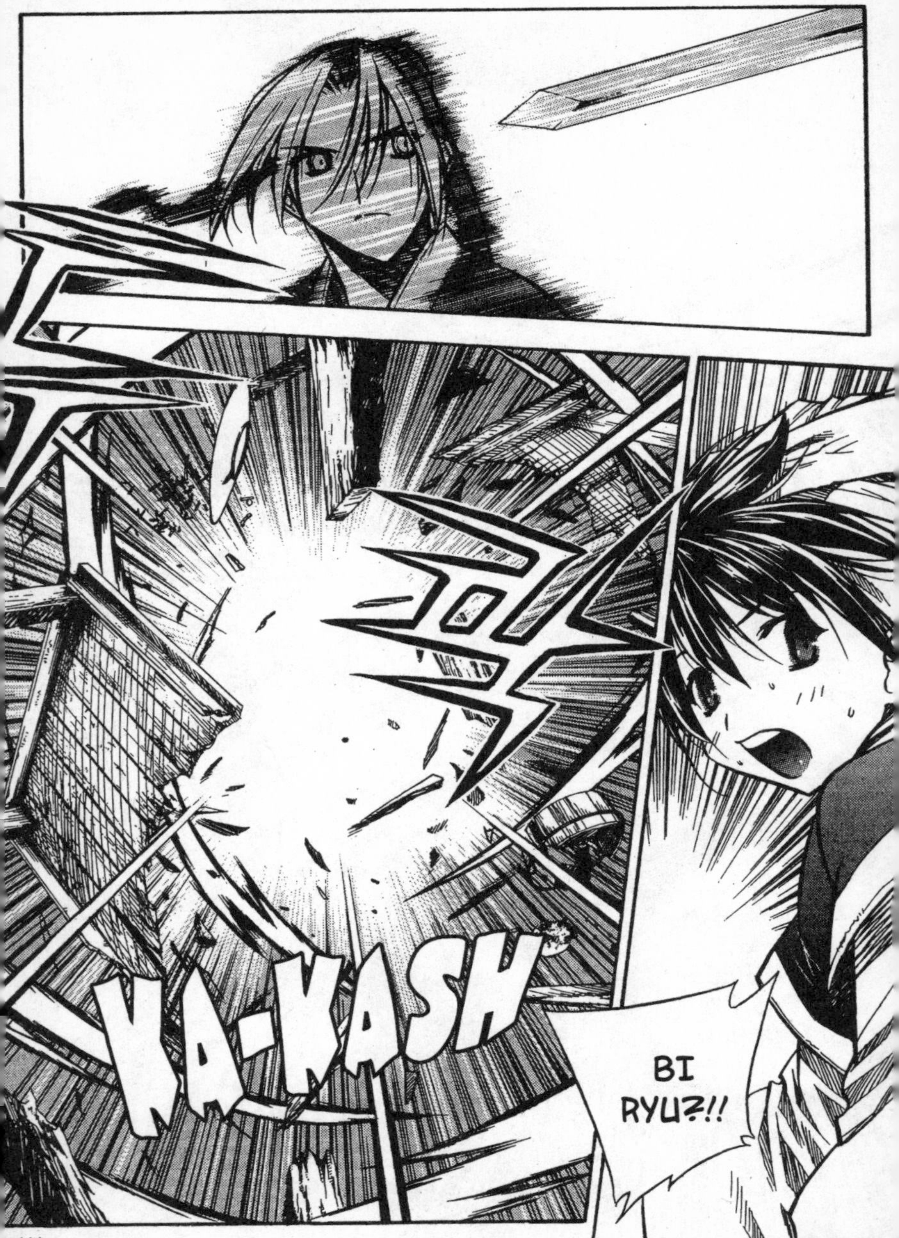
KA-KASH
BI
RYU?!!

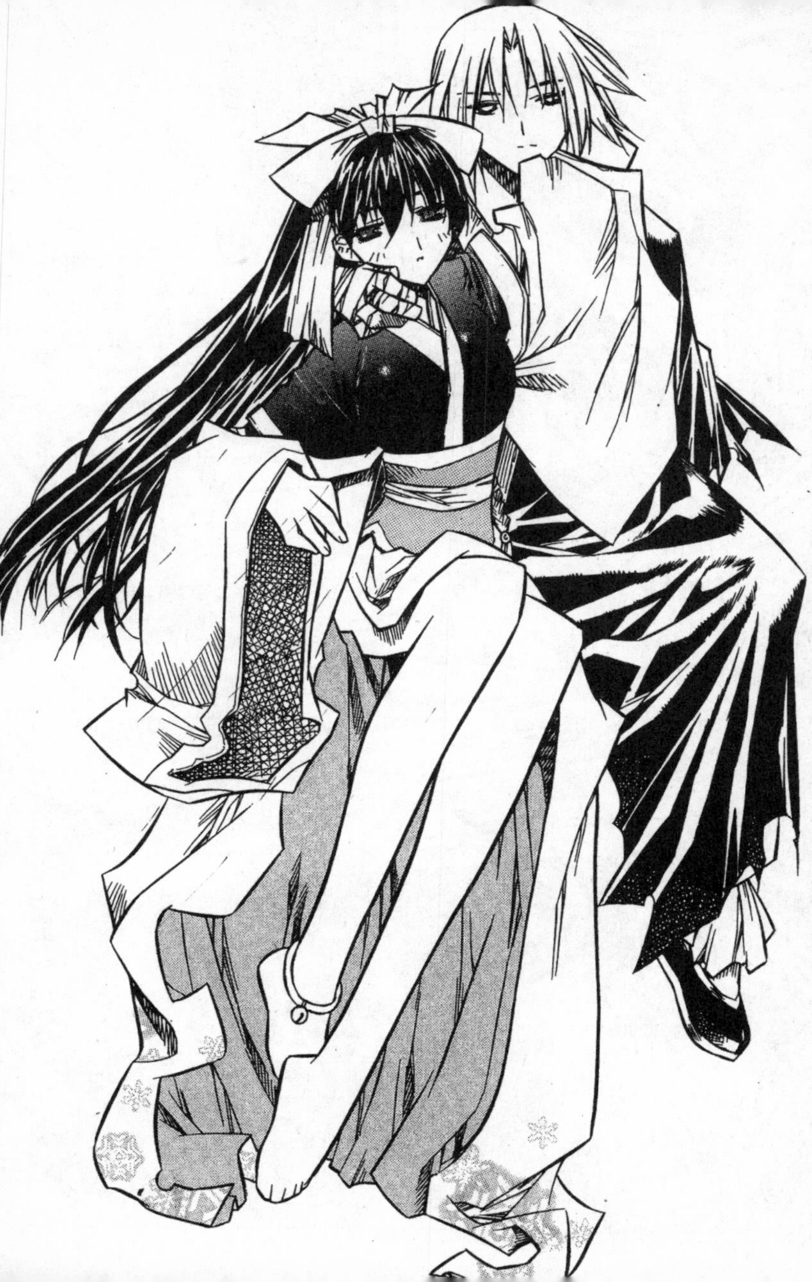

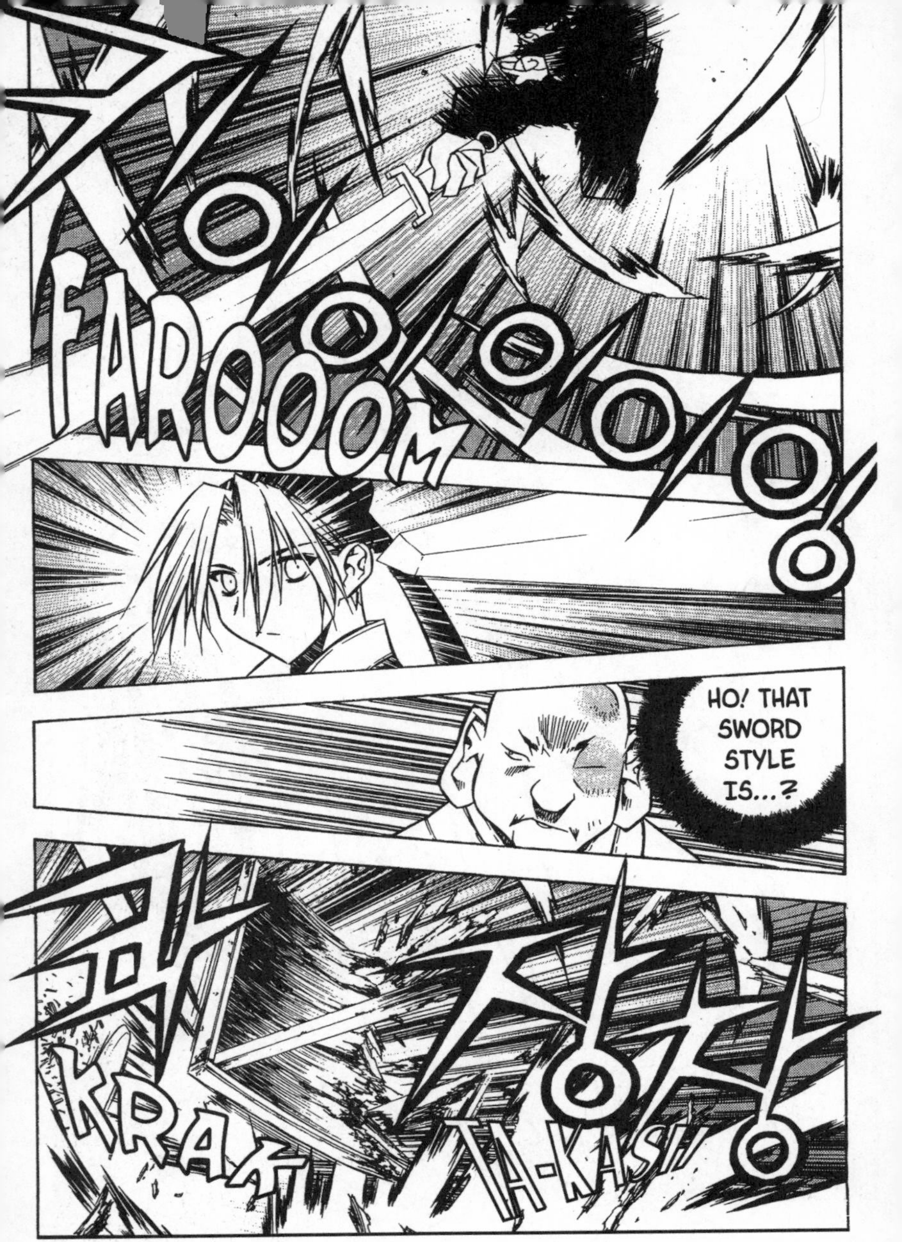
FAROOOOM
HO! THAT SWORD STYLE IS...?
KRAK
TA-KASH

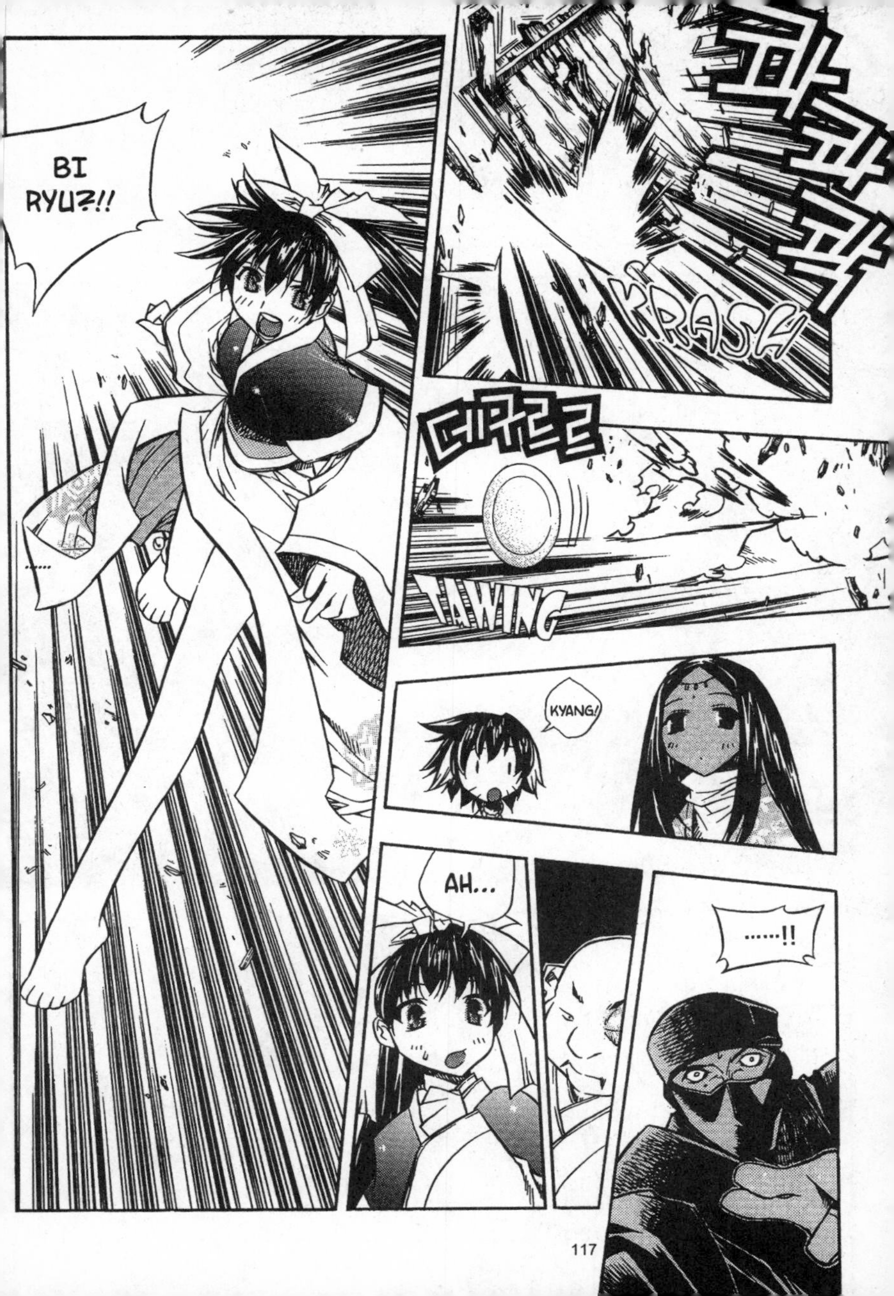
BI RYU?!!
......
KRASH
TAWING
KYANG!
AH...
......!!

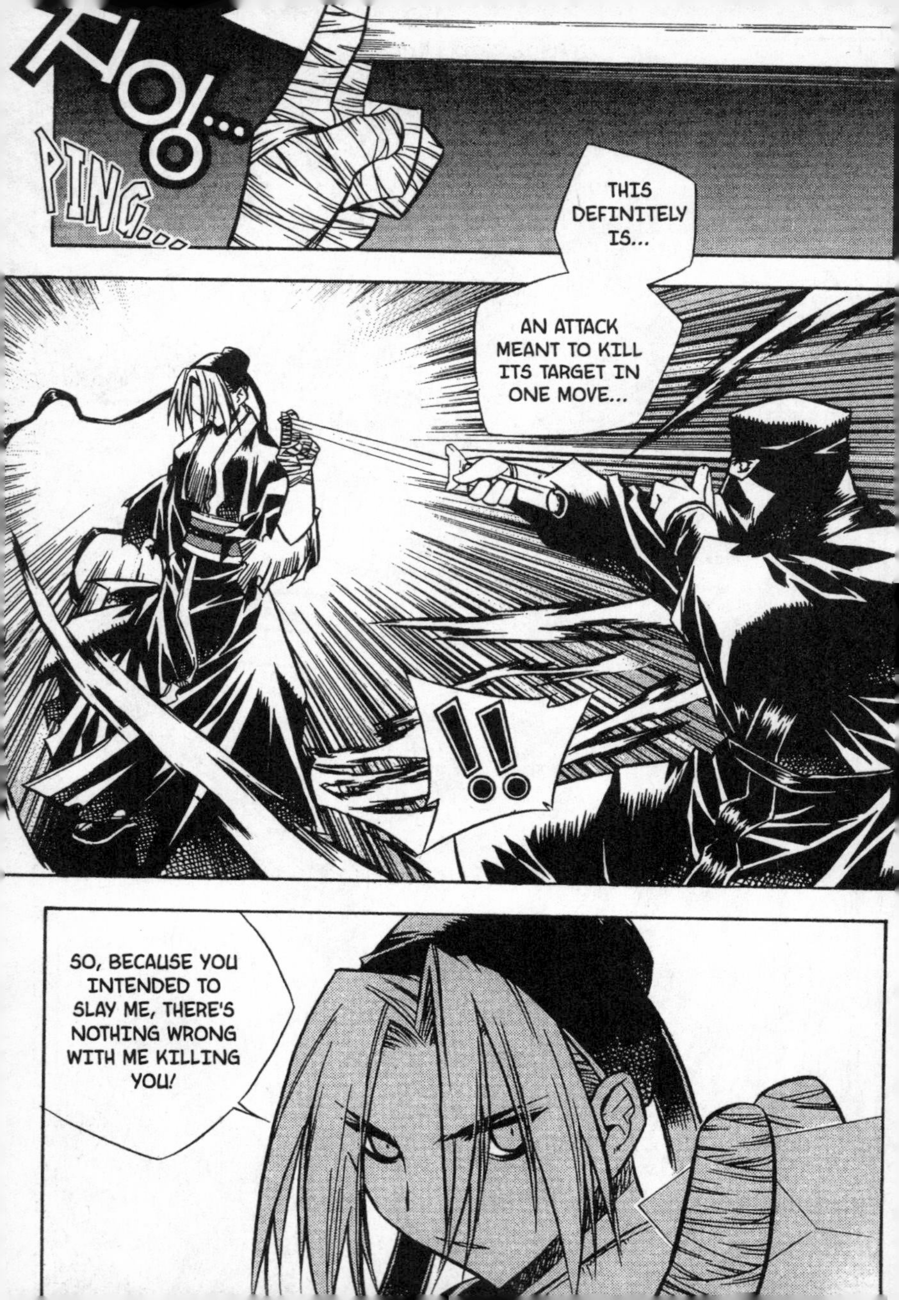
HOO...
PING...
THIS DEFINITELY IS...
AN ATTACK MEANT TO KILL ITS TARGET IN ONE MOVE...
!!
SO, BECAUSE YOU INTENDED TO SLAY ME, THERE'S NOTHING WRONG WITH ME KILLING YOU!

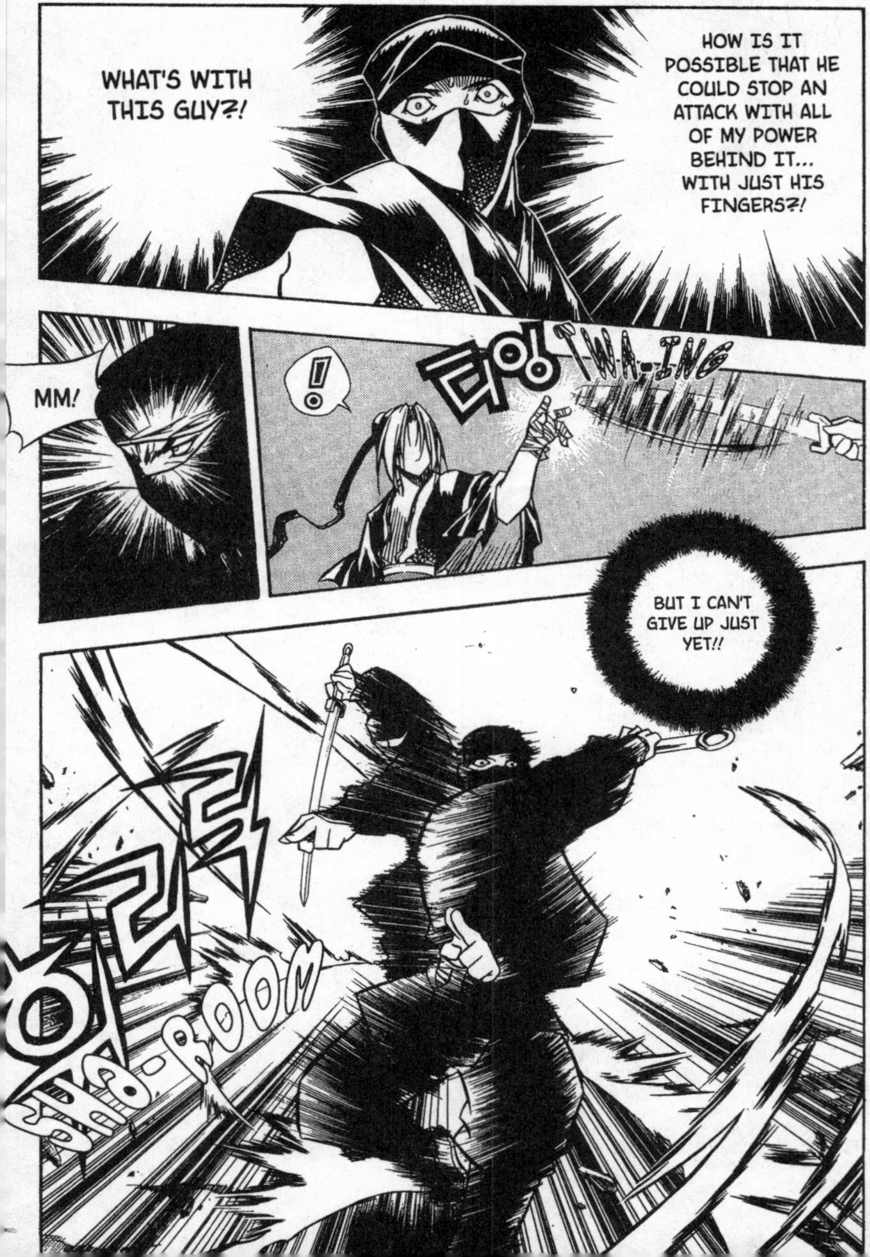
HOW IS IT POSSIBLE THAT HE COULD STOP AN ATTACK WITH ALL OF MY POWER BEHIND IT... WITH JUST HIS FINGERS?!
WHAT'S WITH THIS GUY?!
TWA-ING
!
MM!
BUT I CAN'T GIVE UP JUST YET!!
SHO-BOOM

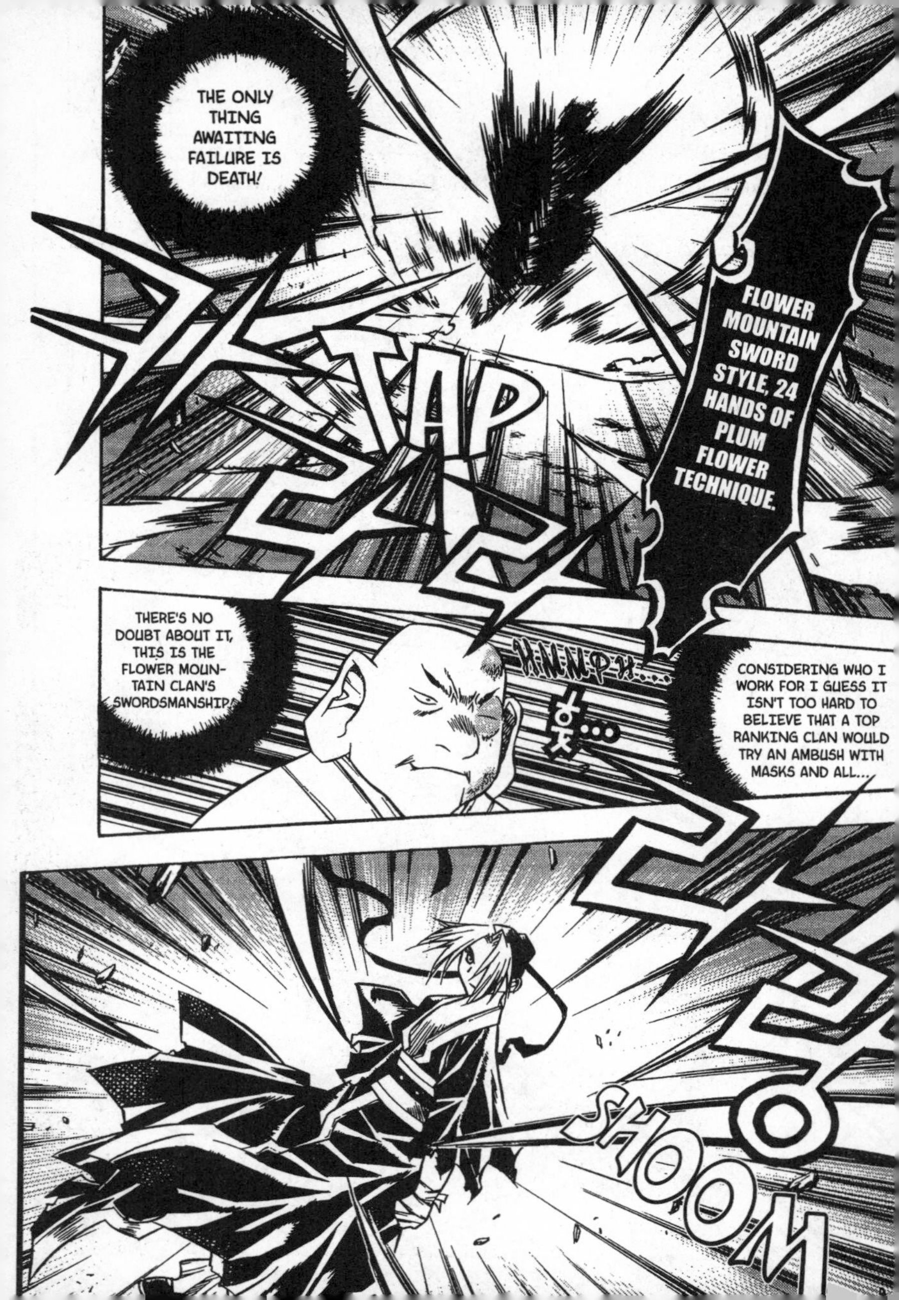
THE ONLY THING AWAITING FAILURE IS DEATH!
TAP
FLOWER MOUNTAIN SWORD STYLE, 24 HANDS OF PLUM FLOWER TECHNIQUE.
THERE'S NO DOUBT ABOUT IT, THIS IS THE FLOWER MOUN-TAIN CLAN'S SWORDSMANSHIP!
HMMPH...
CONSIDERING WHO I WORK FOR I GUESS IT ISN'T TOO HARD TO BELIEVE THAT A TOP RANKING CLAN WOULD TRY AN AMBUSH WITH MASKS AND ALL...
SHOOM

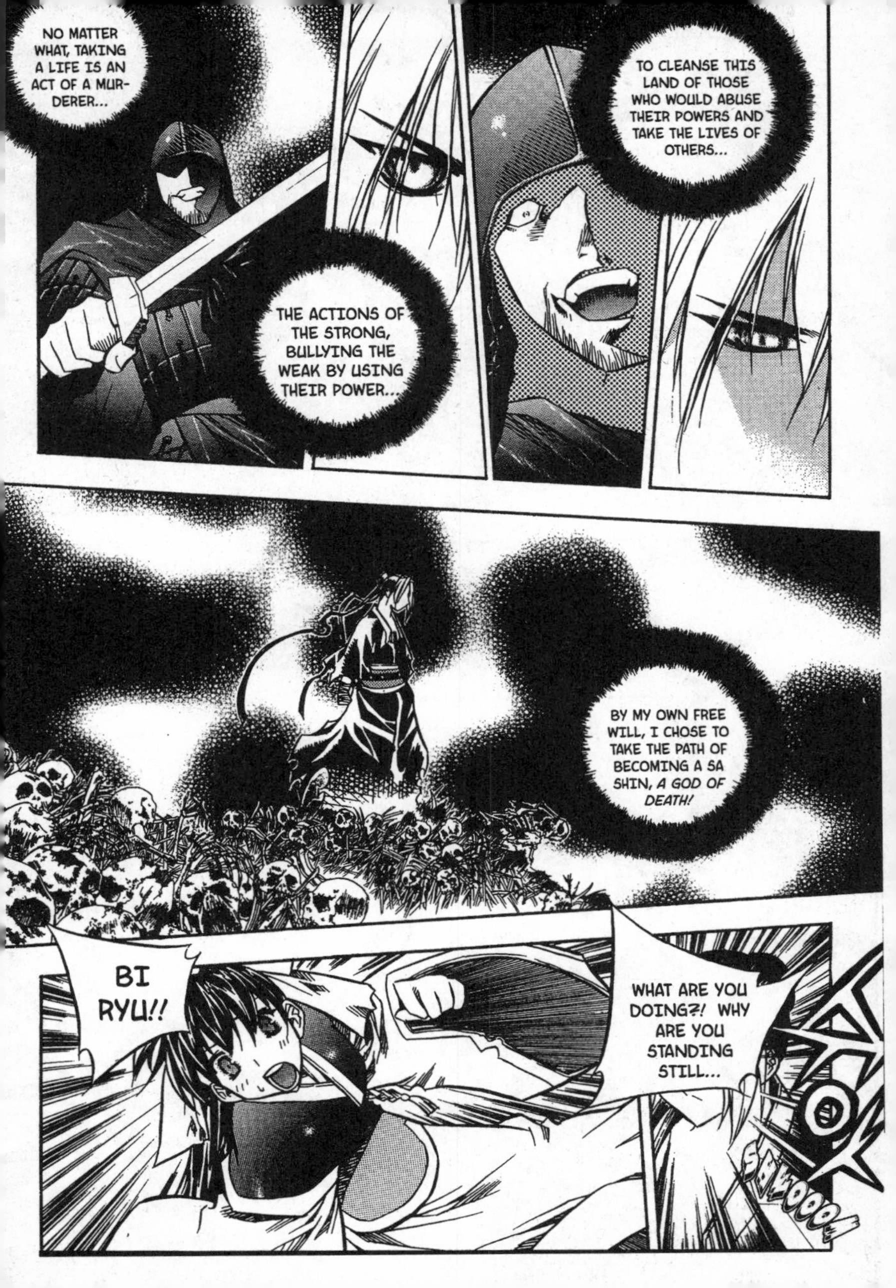
NO MATTER WHAT, TAKING A LIFE IS AN ACT OF A MURDERER...
TO CLEANSE THIS LAND OF THOSE WHO WOULD ABUSE THEIR POWERS AND TAKE THE LIVES OF OTHERS...
THE ACTIONS OF THE STRONG, BULLYING THE WEAK BY USING THEIR POWER...
BY MY OWN FREE WILL, I CHOSE TO TAKE THE PATH OF BECOMING A SA SHIN, *A GOD OF DEATH!*
BI RYU!!
WHAT ARE YOU DOING?! WHY ARE YOU STANDING STILL...

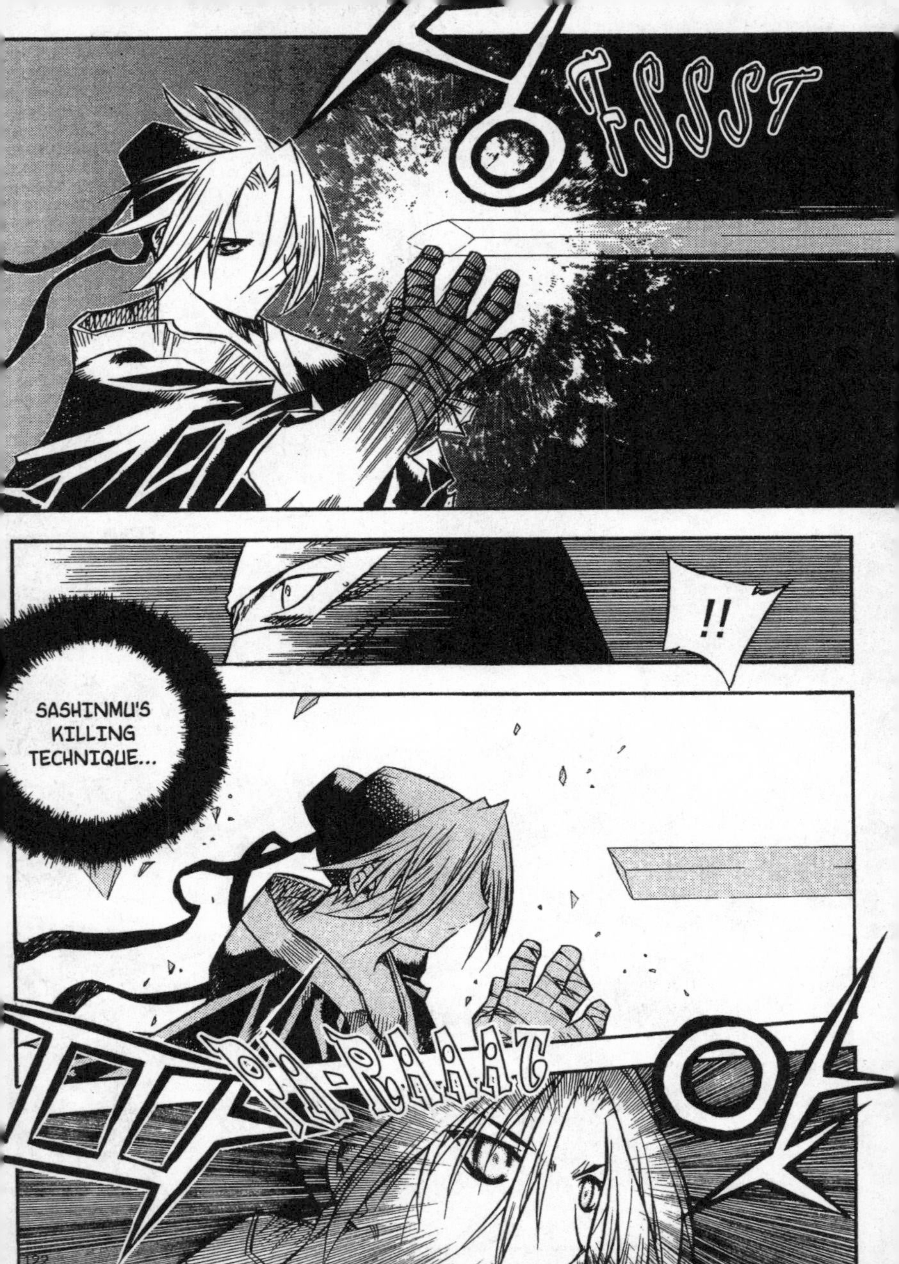
FSSST
!!
SASHINMU'S KILLING TECHNIQUE...
SH-RAAAT

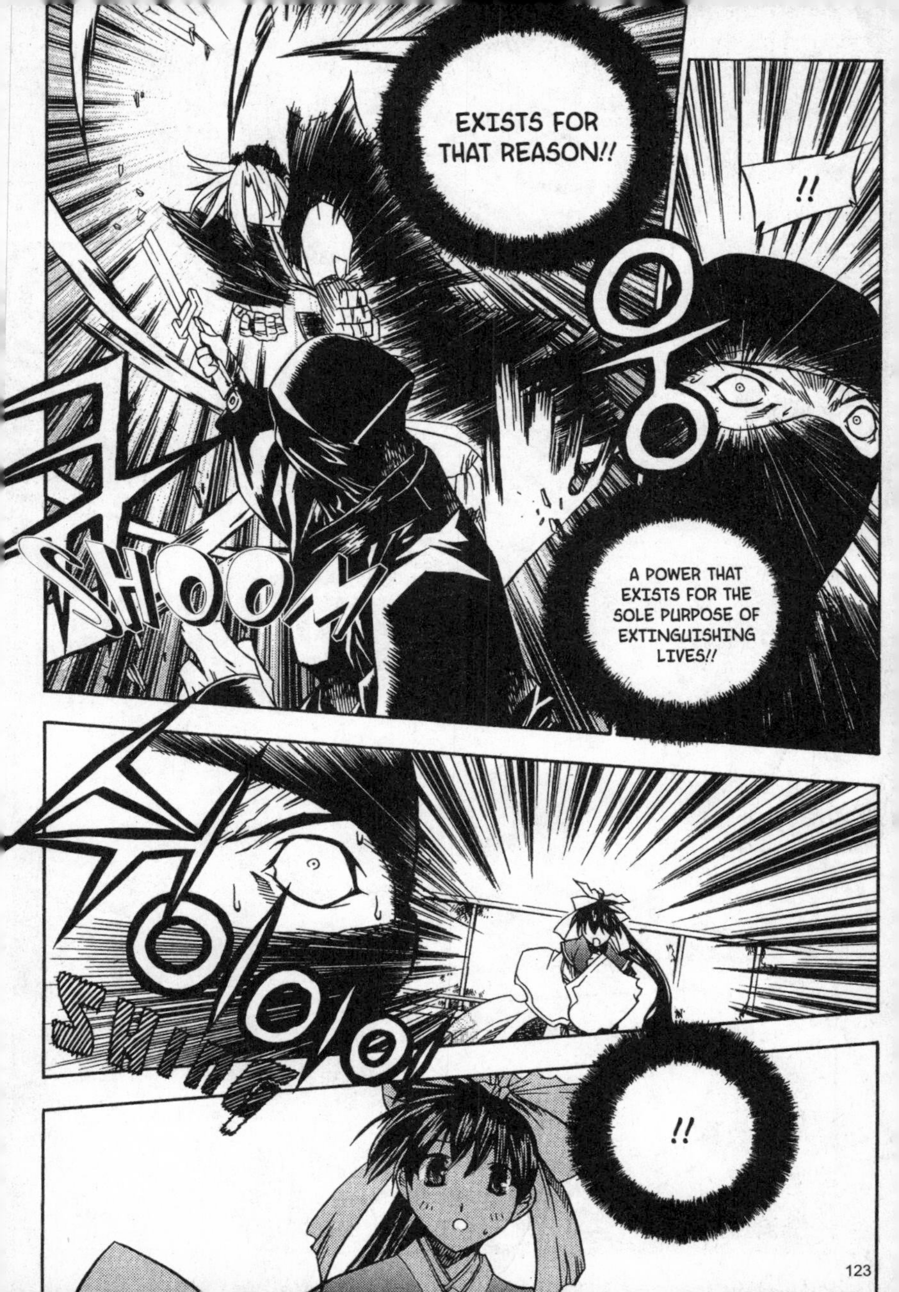
!!
EXISTS FOR THAT REASON!!
A POWER THAT EXISTS FOR THE SOLE PURPOSE OF EXTINGUISHING LIVES!!
SHOOM
SHING
!!

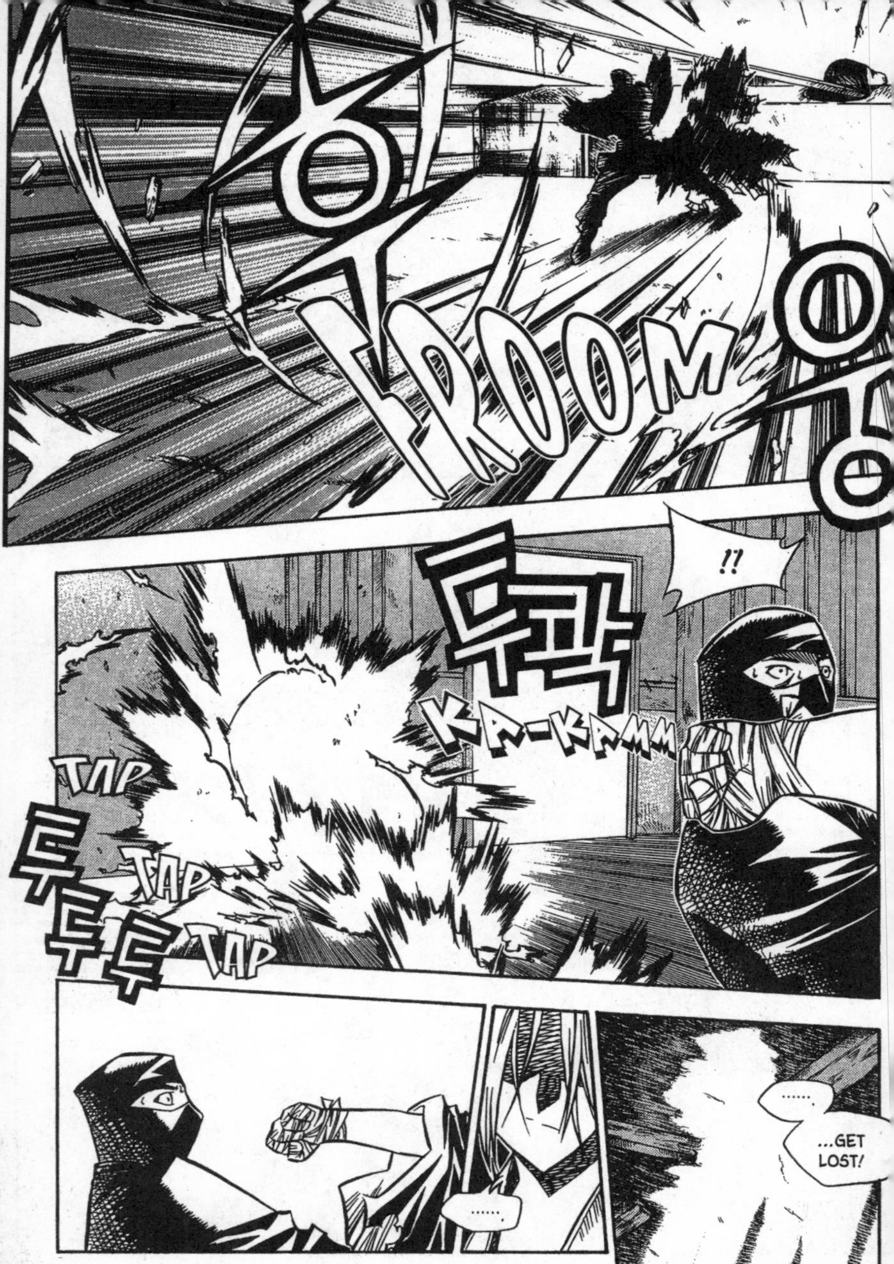

KROOM
!?
KA-KAMM
TAP
TAP
TAP
......
......
...GET LOST!

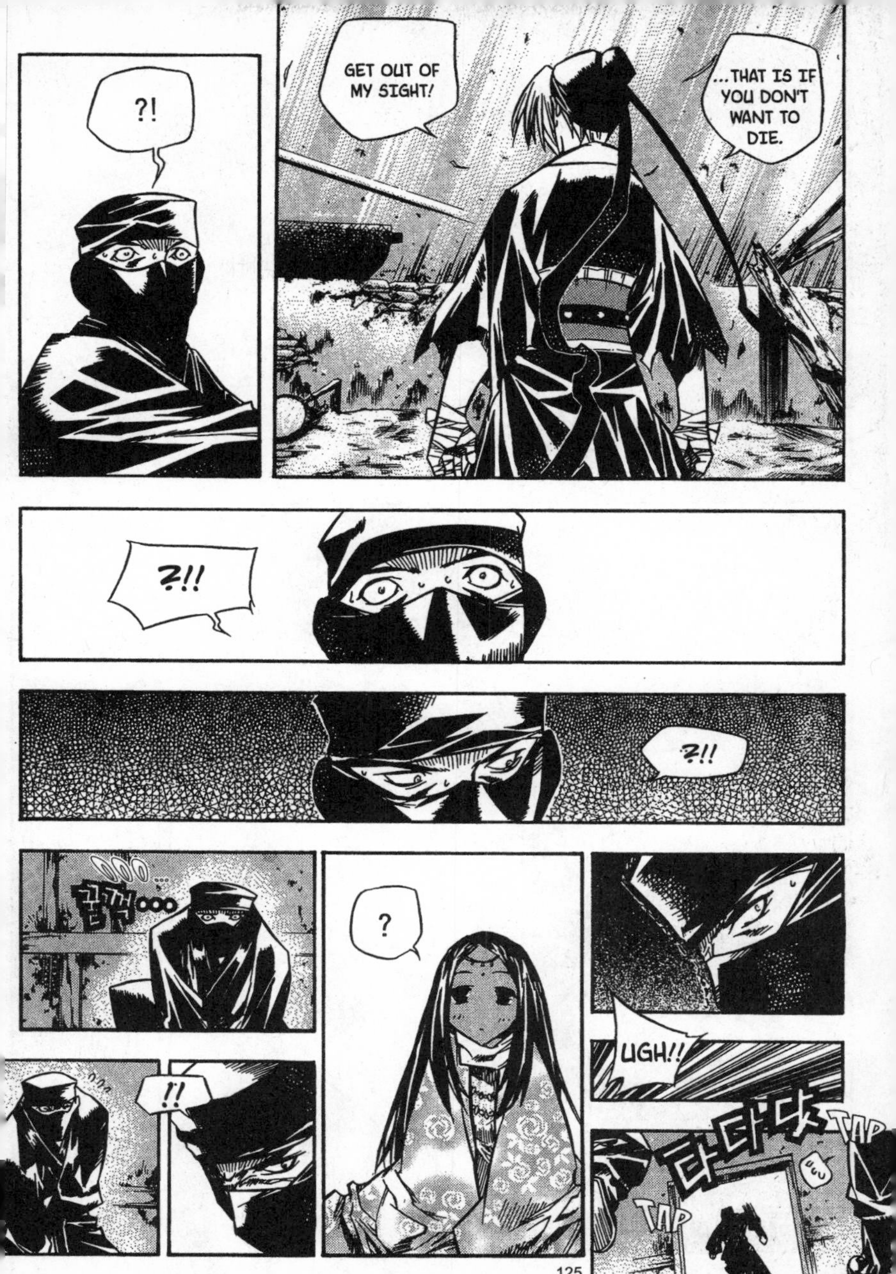

GET OUT OF MY SIGHT!
...THAT IS IF YOU DON'T WANT TO DIE.
?!
?!!
?!!
?
UGH!!
!!
TAP
TAP

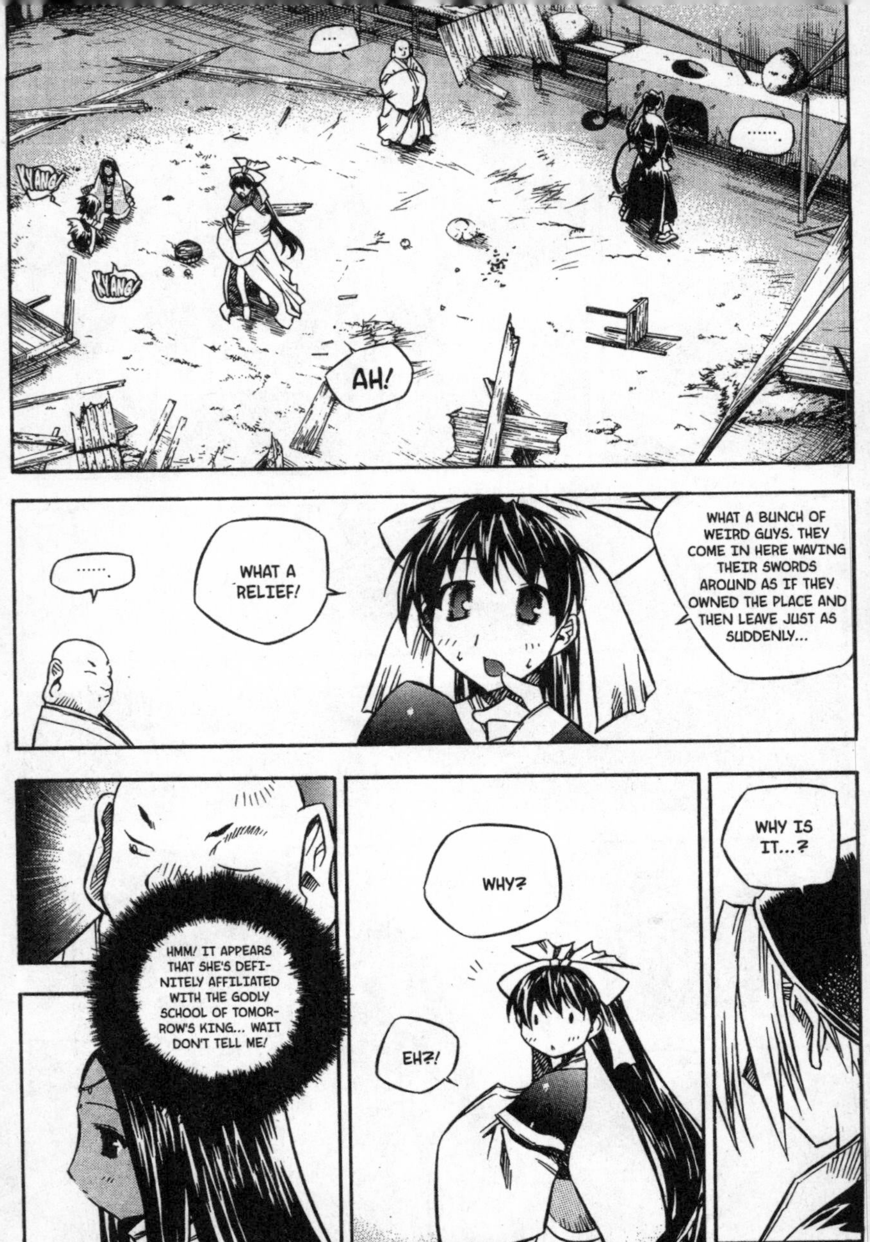
...
......
KYANG!
KYANG!
AH!
......
WHAT A RELIEF!
WHAT A BUNCH OF WEIRD GUYS. THEY COME IN HERE WAVING THEIR SWORDS AROUND AS IF THEY OWNED THE PLACE AND THEN LEAVE JUST AS SUDDENLY...
HMM! IT APPEARS THAT SHE'S DEFINITELY AFFILIATED WITH THE GODLY SCHOOL OF TOMORROW'S KING... WAIT DON'T TELL ME!
WHY?
EH?!
WHY IS IT...?

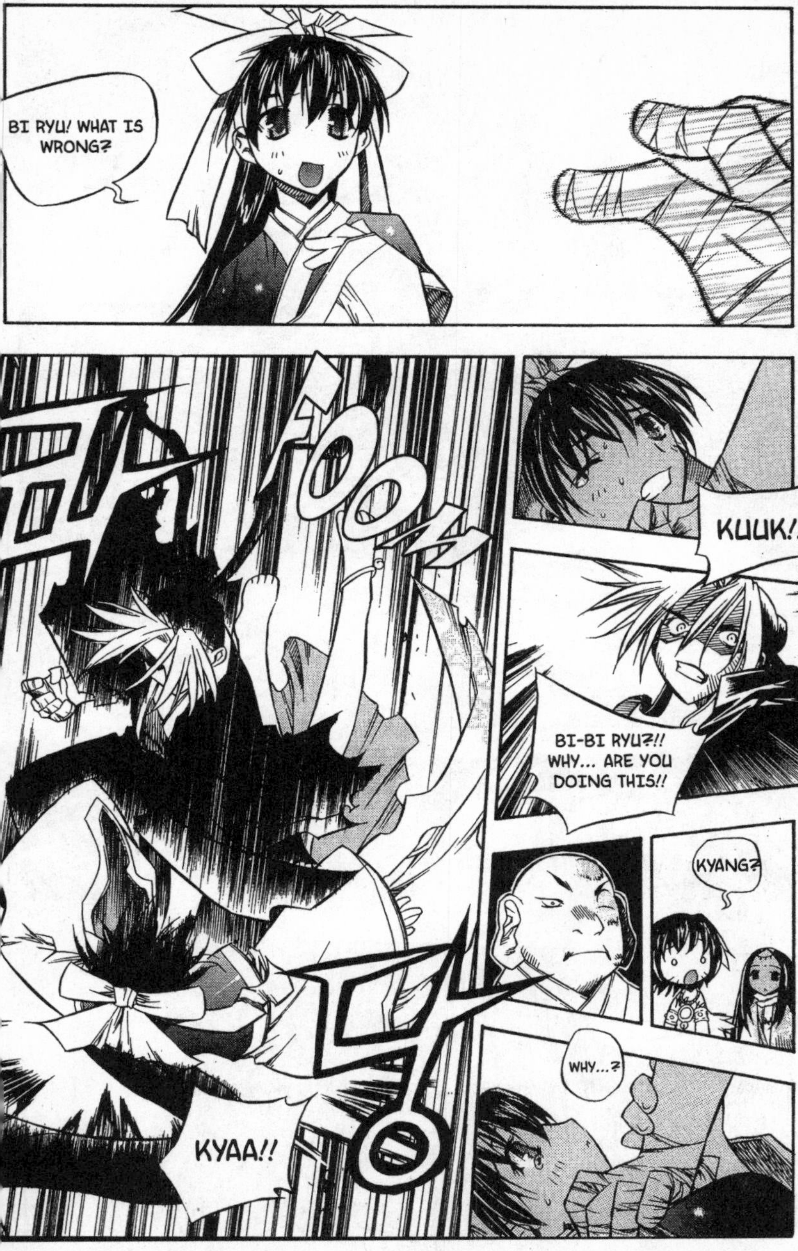
BI RYU! WHAT IS WRONG?
KYAA!!
KUUK!!
BI-BI RYU?!! WHY... ARE YOU DOING THIS!!
KYANG?
WHY...?

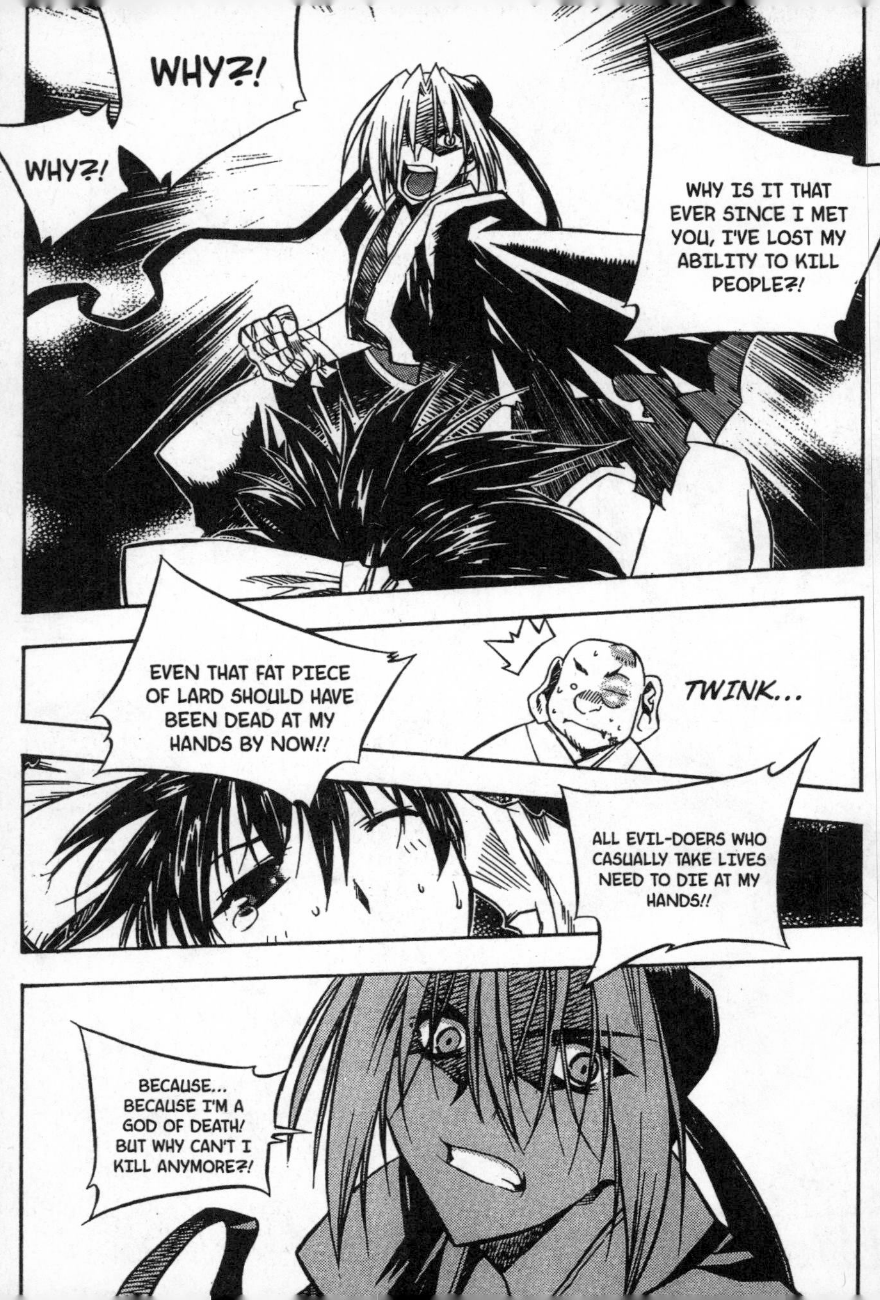

WHY?!
WHY?!
WHY IS IT THAT EVER SINCE I MET YOU, I'VE LOST MY ABILITY TO KILL PEOPLE?!
EVEN THAT FAT PIECE OF LARD SHOULD HAVE BEEN DEAD AT MY HANDS BY NOW!!
TWINK...
ALL EVIL-DOERS WHO CASUALLY TAKE LIVES NEED TO DIE AT MY HANDS!!
BECAUSE... BECAUSE I'M A GOD OF DEATH! BUT WHY CAN'T I KILL ANYMORE?!

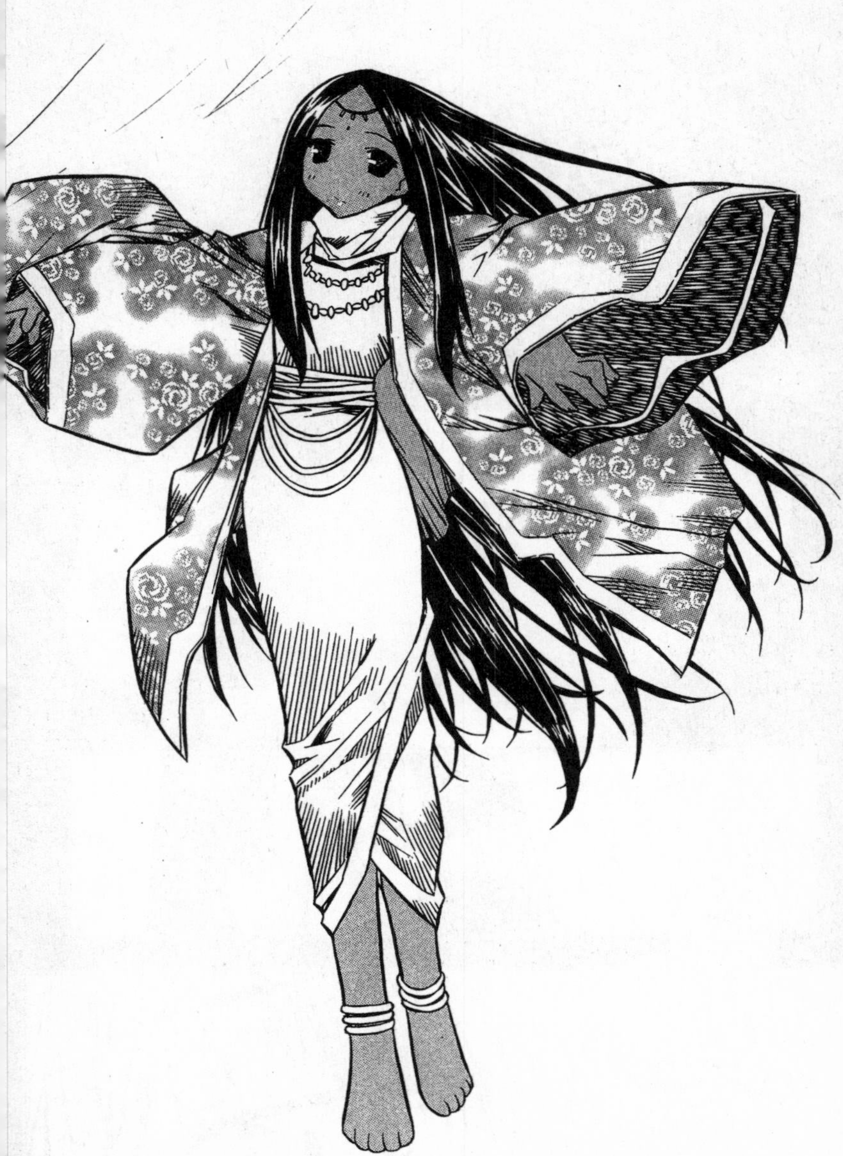

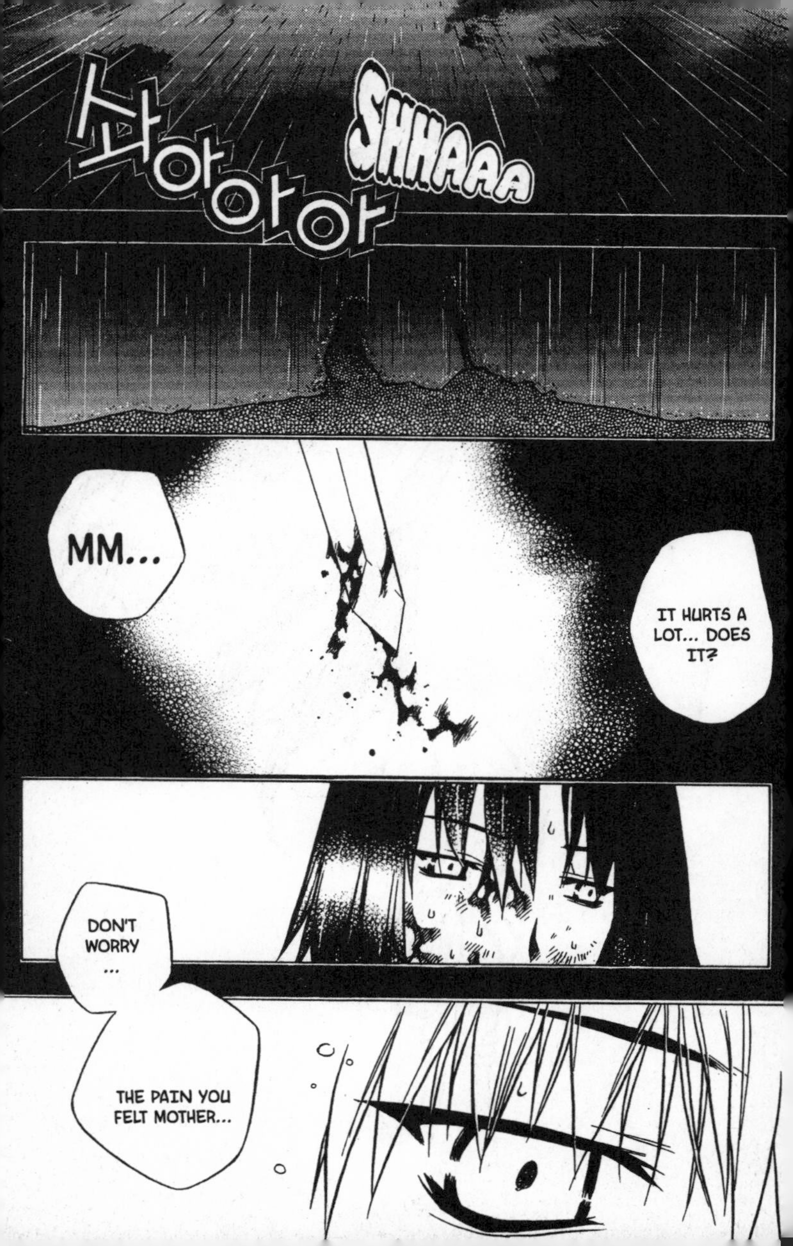

쏴아아아
SHHAAA
MM...
IT HURTS A LOT... DOES IT?
DON'T WORRY ...
THE PAIN YOU FELT MOTHER...

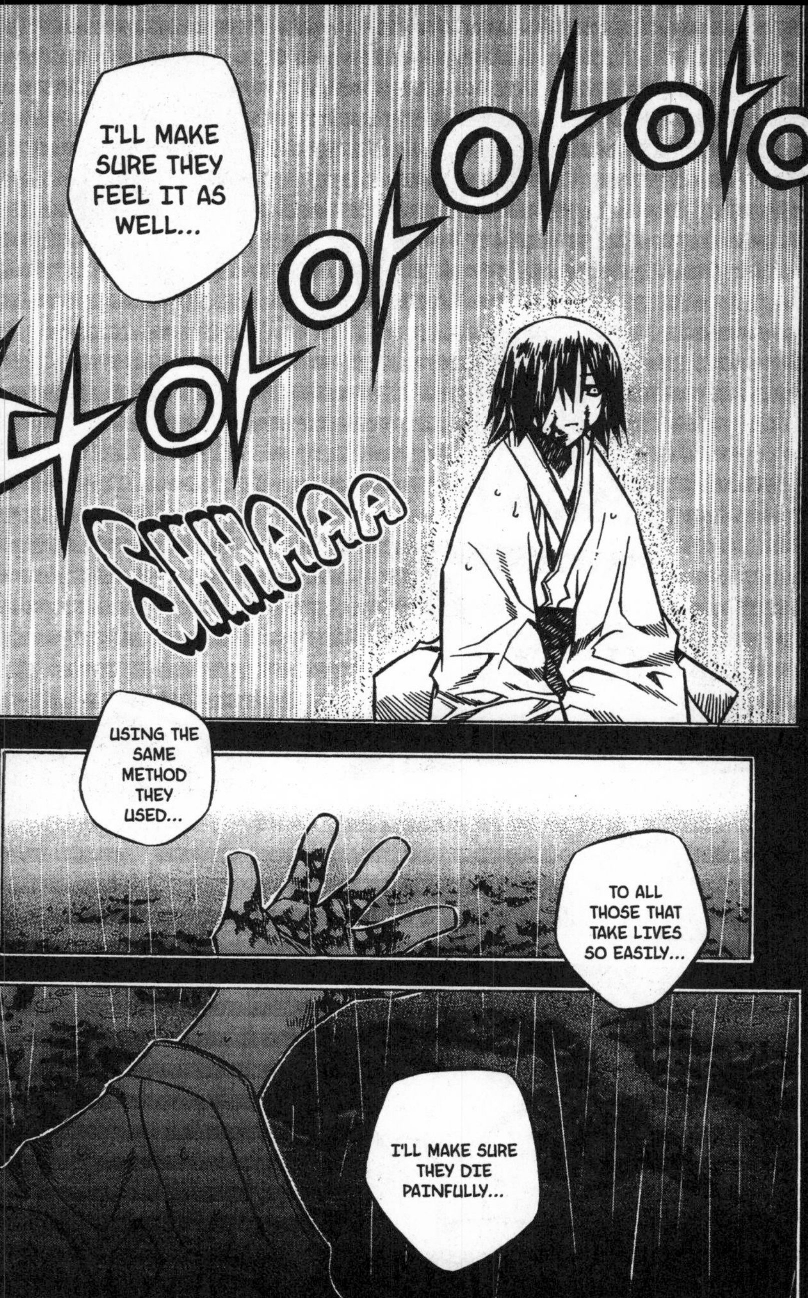
I'LL MAKE SURE THEY FEEL IT AS WELL...
SHHAAA
USING THE SAME METHOD THEY USED...
TO ALL THOSE THAT TAKE LIVES SO EASILY...
I'LL MAKE SURE THEY DIE PAINFULLY...

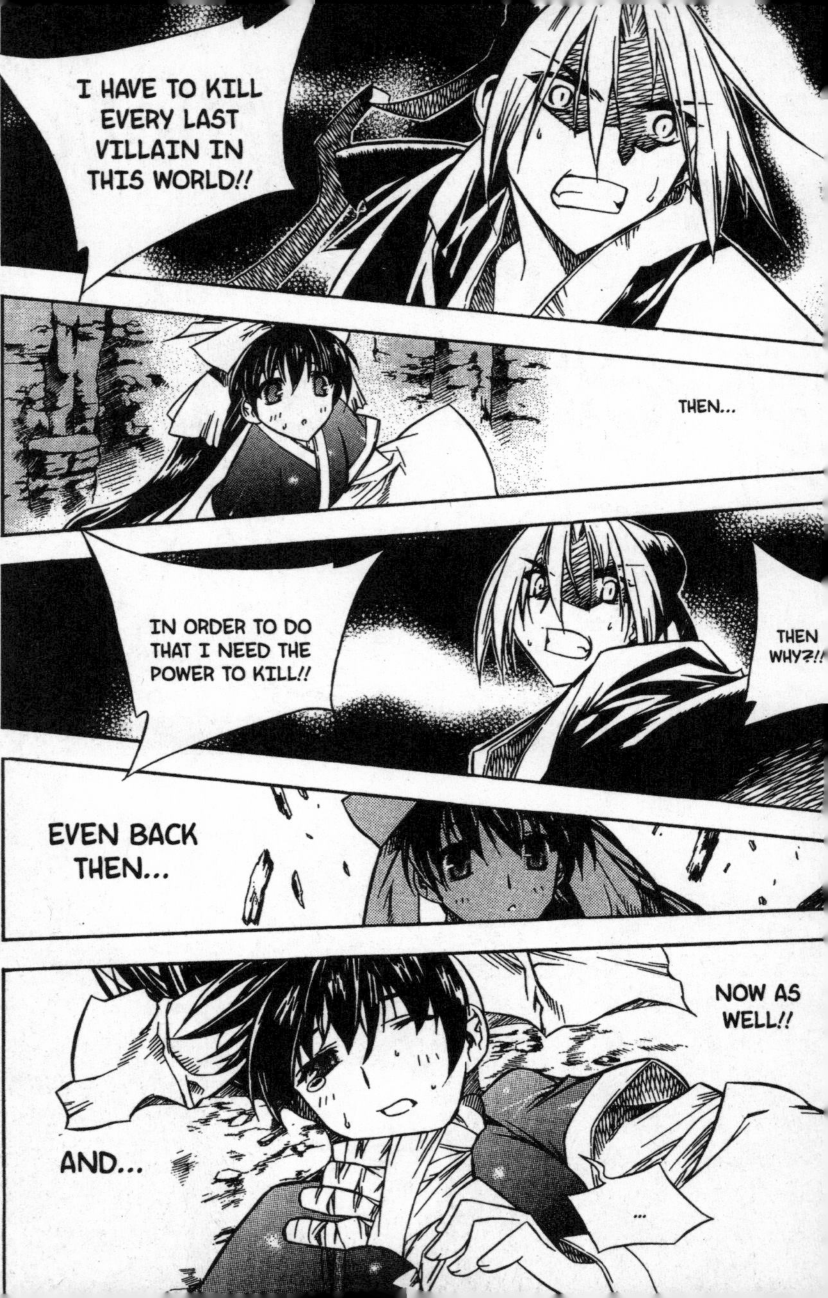
I HAVE TO KILL EVERY LAST VILLAIN IN THIS WORLD!!
THEN...
THEN WHY?!!
IN ORDER TO DO THAT I NEED THE POWER TO KILL!!
EVEN BACK THEN...
NOW AS WELL!!
...
AND...

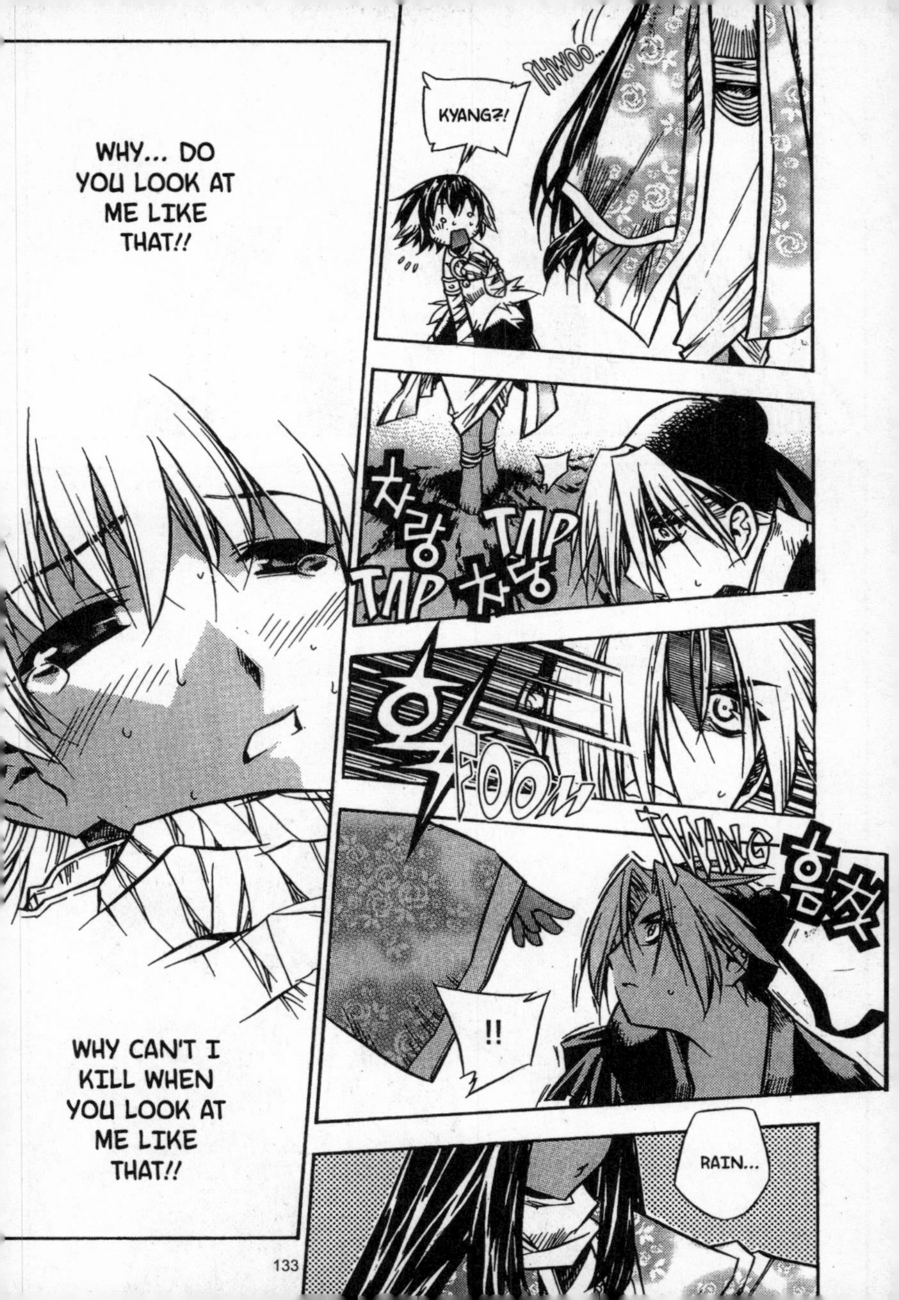

THWOO...
KYANG?!
차랑
TAP TAP
차당
후
FOOM
TWANG
흠칫
!!
RAIN...
WHY... DO YOU LOOK AT ME LIKE THAT!!
WHY CAN'T I KILL WHEN YOU LOOK AT ME LIKE THAT!!

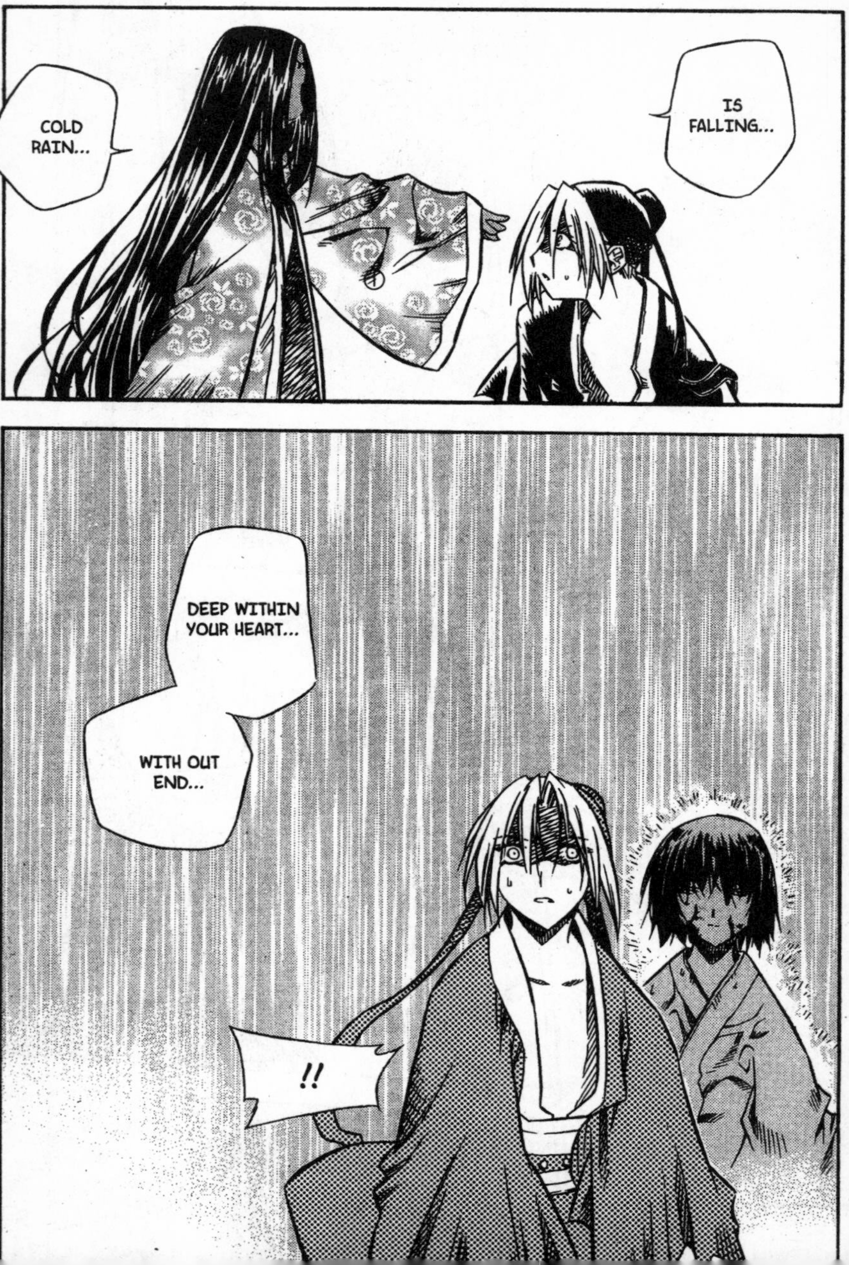
COLD RAIN...
IS FALLING...
DEEP WITHIN YOUR HEART...
WITH OUT END...
!!

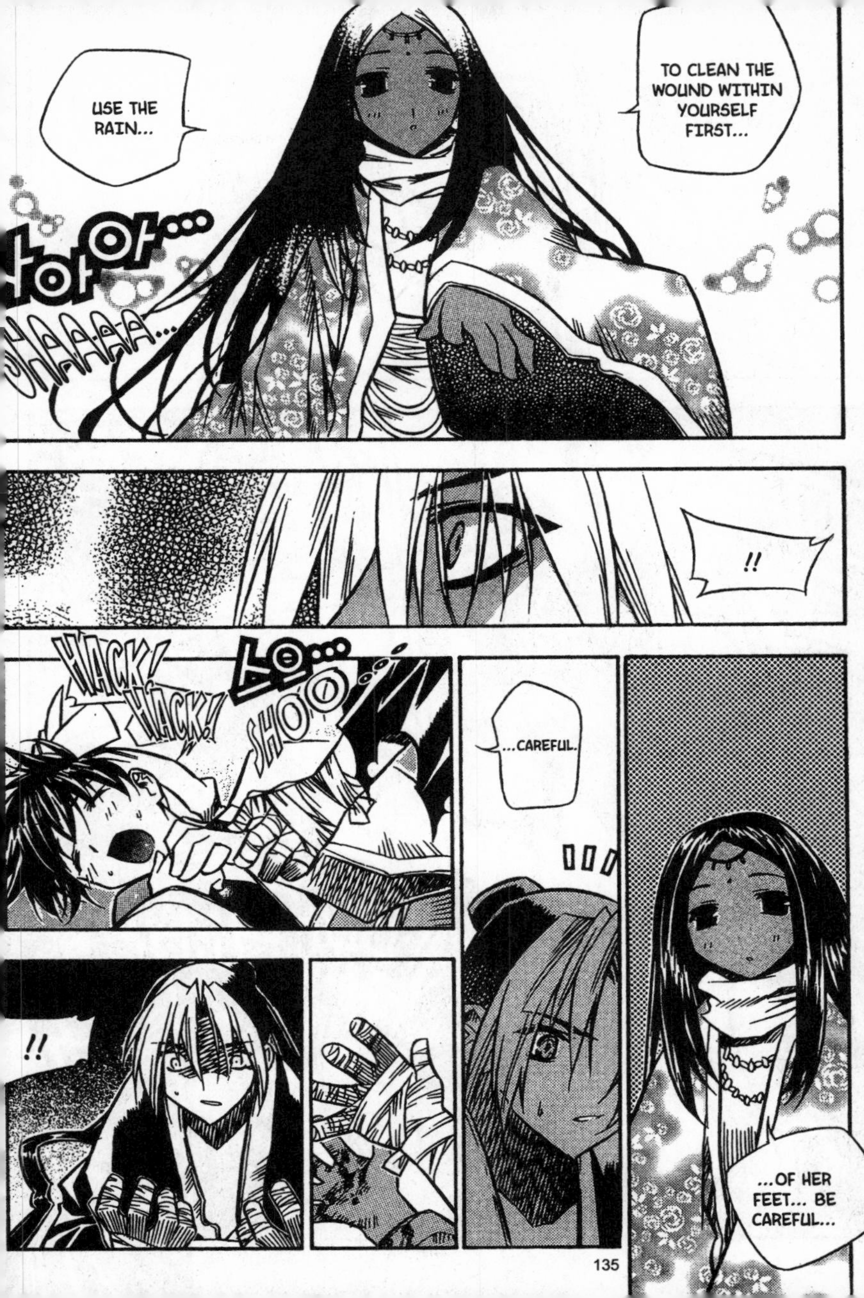
USE THE RAIN...
TO CLEAN THE WOUND WITHIN YOURSELF FIRST...
SHAAAAA...
!!
...CAREFUL.
HACK! HACK!
SHOO...
!!
...OF HER FEET... BE CAREFUL...

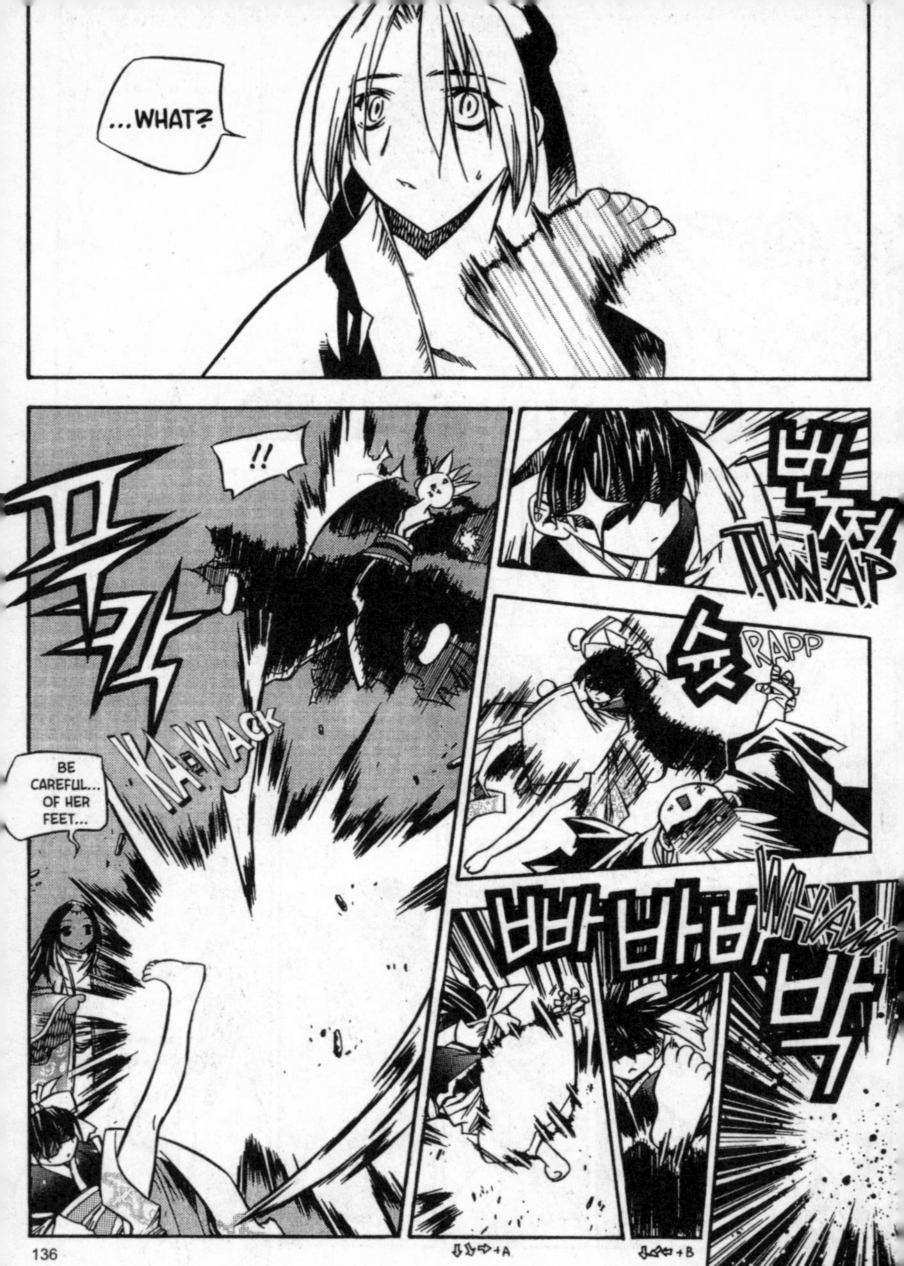
...WHAT?
THWAP
RAPP
WHAM
!!
KAWACK
BE CAREFUL... OF HER FEET...

⇩↘⇨+A ⇩↙⇦+B

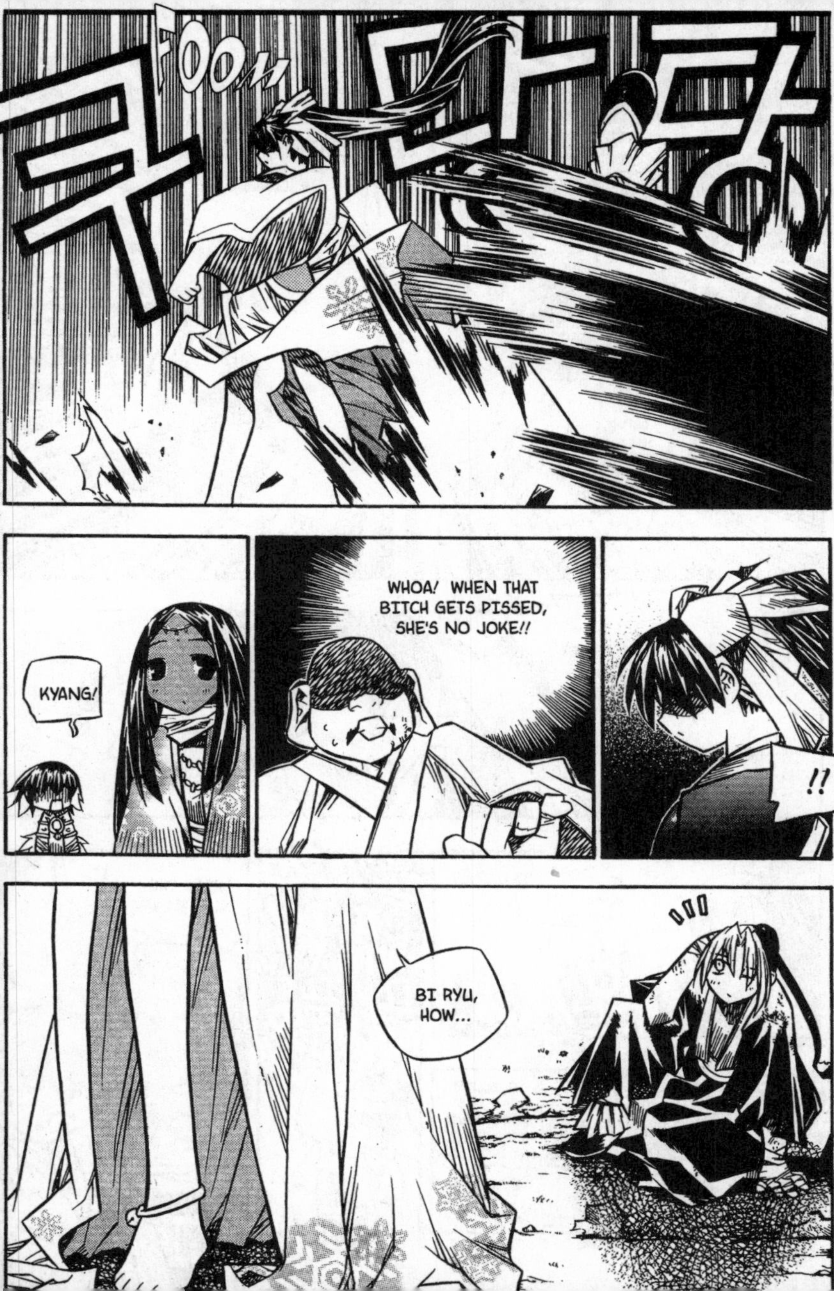
FOOM
KYANG!
WHOA! WHEN THAT BITCH GETS PISSED, SHE'S NO JOKE!!
!!
BI RYU, HOW...

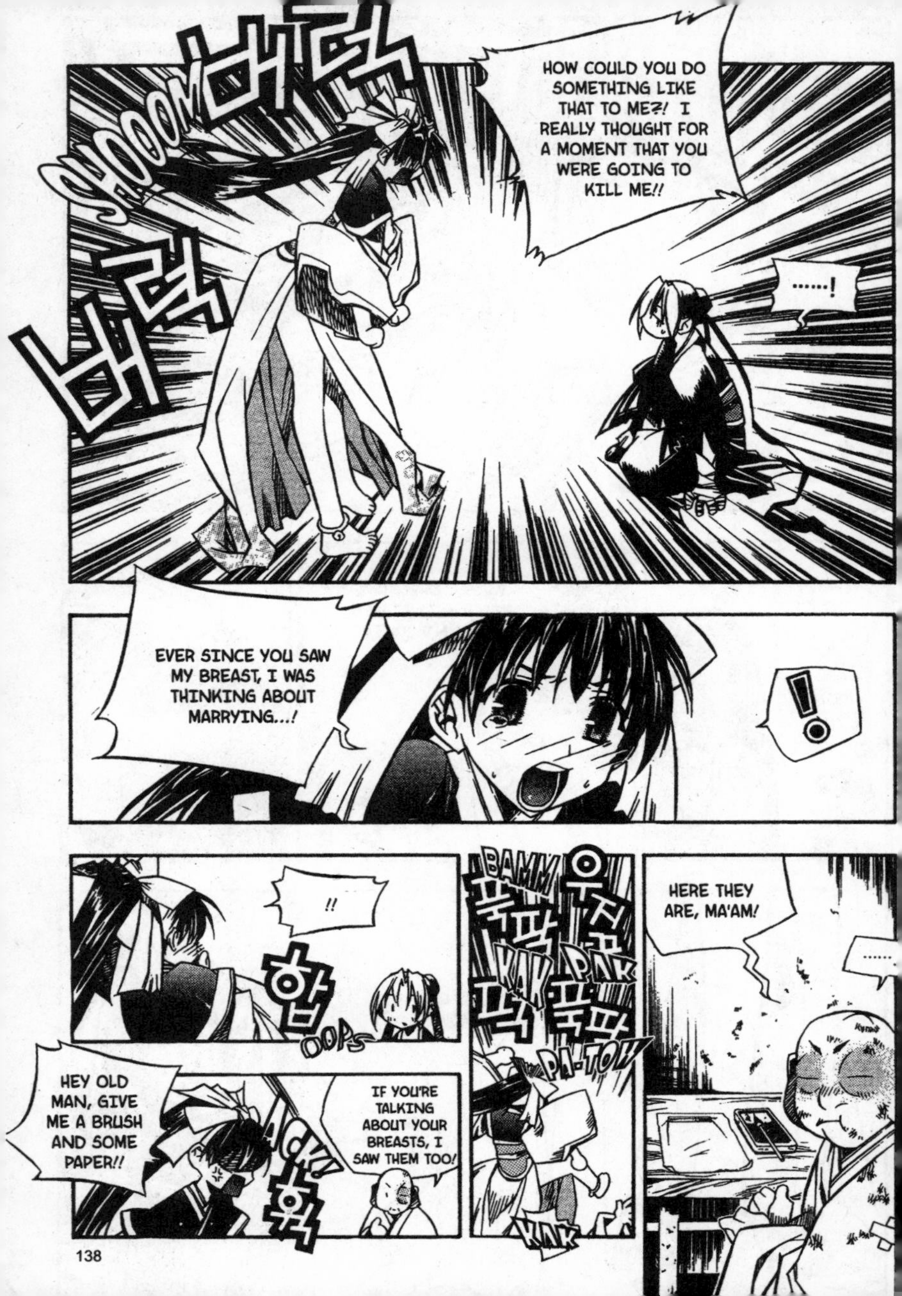
SHOOOM
HOW COULD YOU DO SOMETHING LIKE THAT TO ME?! I REALLY THOUGHT FOR A MOMENT THAT YOU WERE GOING TO KILL ME!!
......!
EVER SINCE YOU SAW MY BREAST, I WAS THINKING ABOUT MARRYING...!
!
!!
합
OOPS
HEY OLD MAN, GIVE ME A BRUSH AND SOME PAPER!!
ACK!
IF YOU'RE TALKING ABOUT YOUR BREASTS, I SAW THEM TOO!
BAMM
PAK
KAK
PI-TOW
KAK
HERE THEY ARE, MA'AM!
......

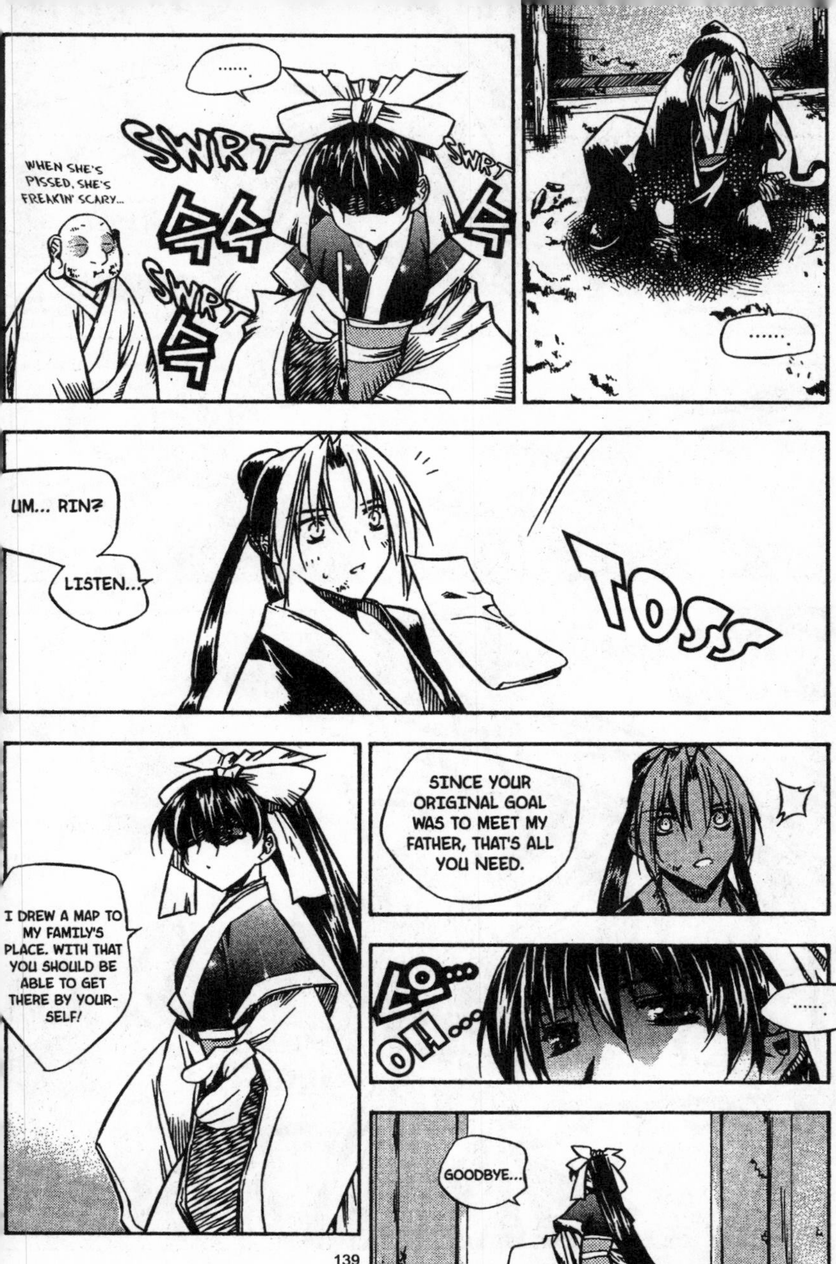
......
SWRT
SWRT
SWRT
WHEN SHE'S PISSED, SHE'S FREAKIN' SCARY...
......
UM... RIN?
LISTEN...
TOSS
I DREW A MAP TO MY FAMILY'S PLACE. WITH THAT YOU SHOULD BE ABLE TO GET THERE BY YOUR-SELF!
SINCE YOUR ORIGINAL GOAL WAS TO MEET MY FATHER, THAT'S ALL YOU NEED.
......
GOODBYE...

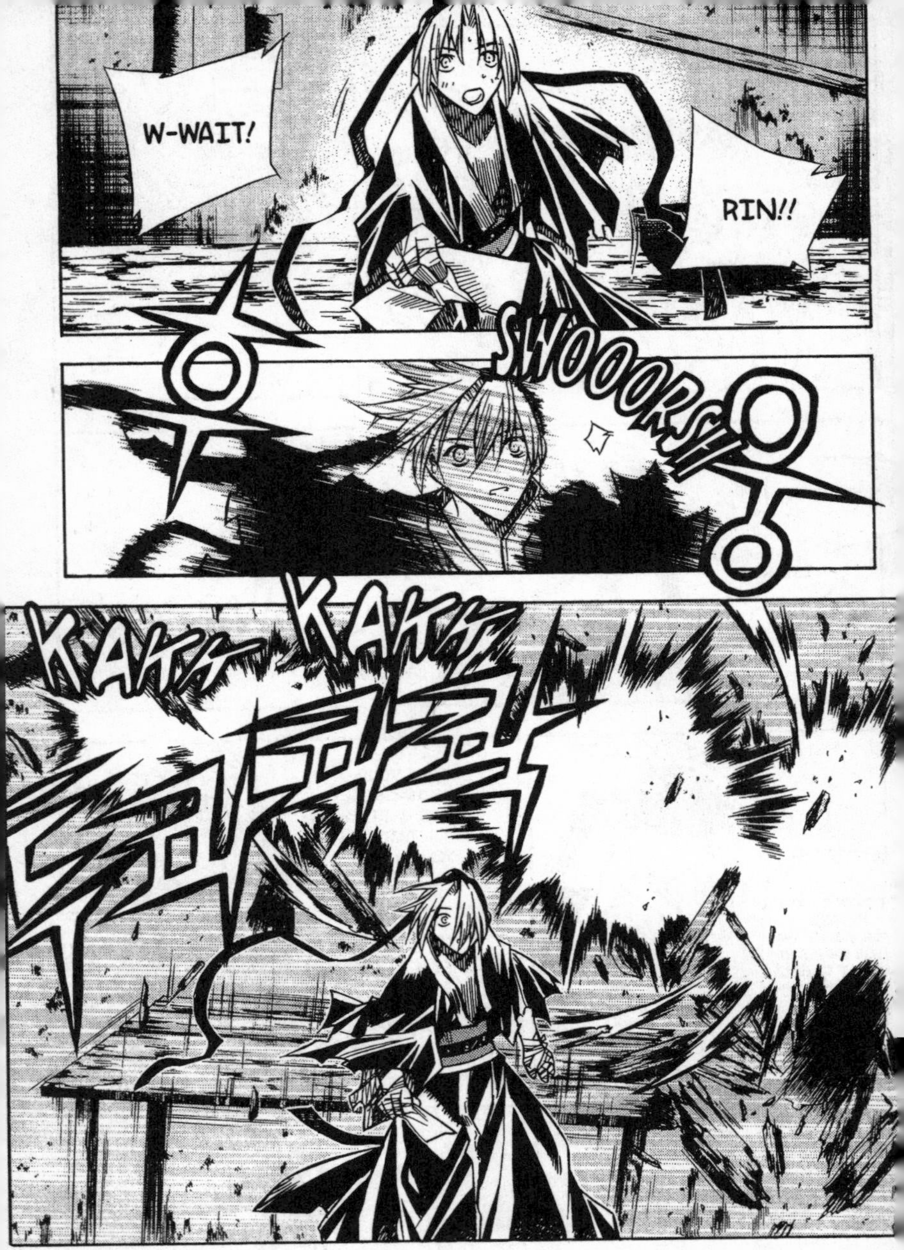
RIN!!
W-WAIT!
SWOOORSH!!

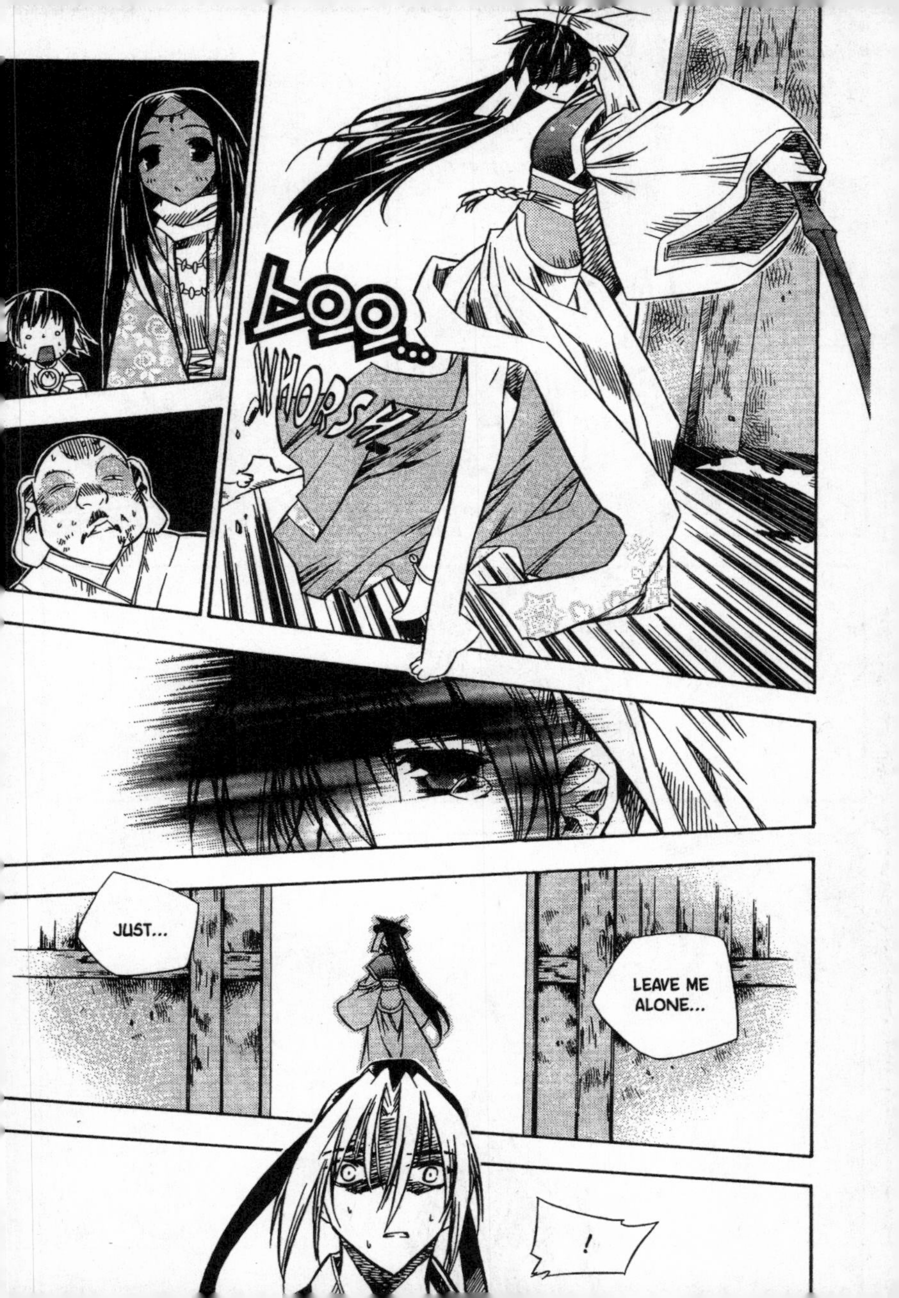
FOO...
WHORSH
JUST...
LEAVE ME ALONE...
!

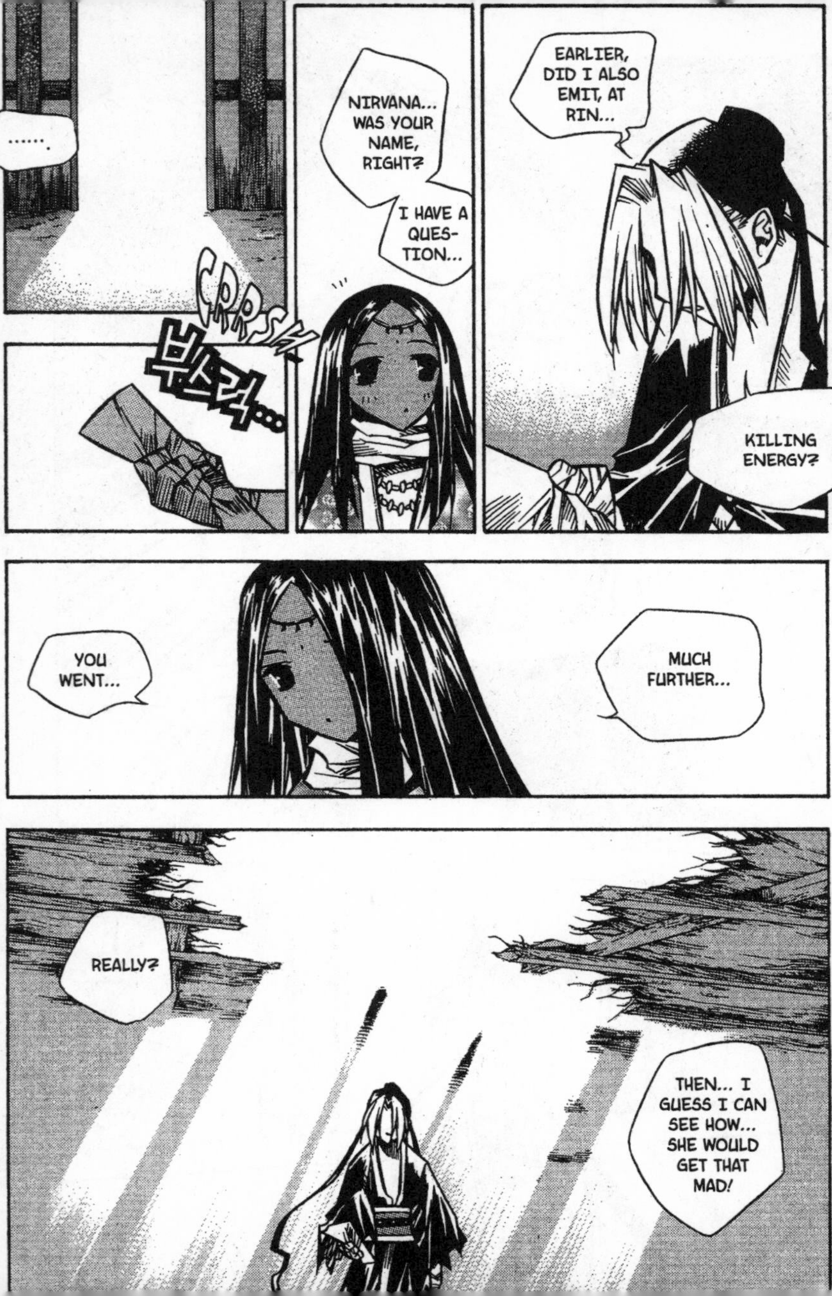

.......
CRRSH
NIRVANA... WAS YOUR NAME, RIGHT?
I HAVE A QUES-TION...
EARLIER, DID I ALSO EMIT, AT RIN...
KILLING ENERGY?
YOU WENT...
MUCH FURTHER...
REALLY?
THEN... I GUESS I CAN SEE HOW... SHE WOULD GET THAT MAD!

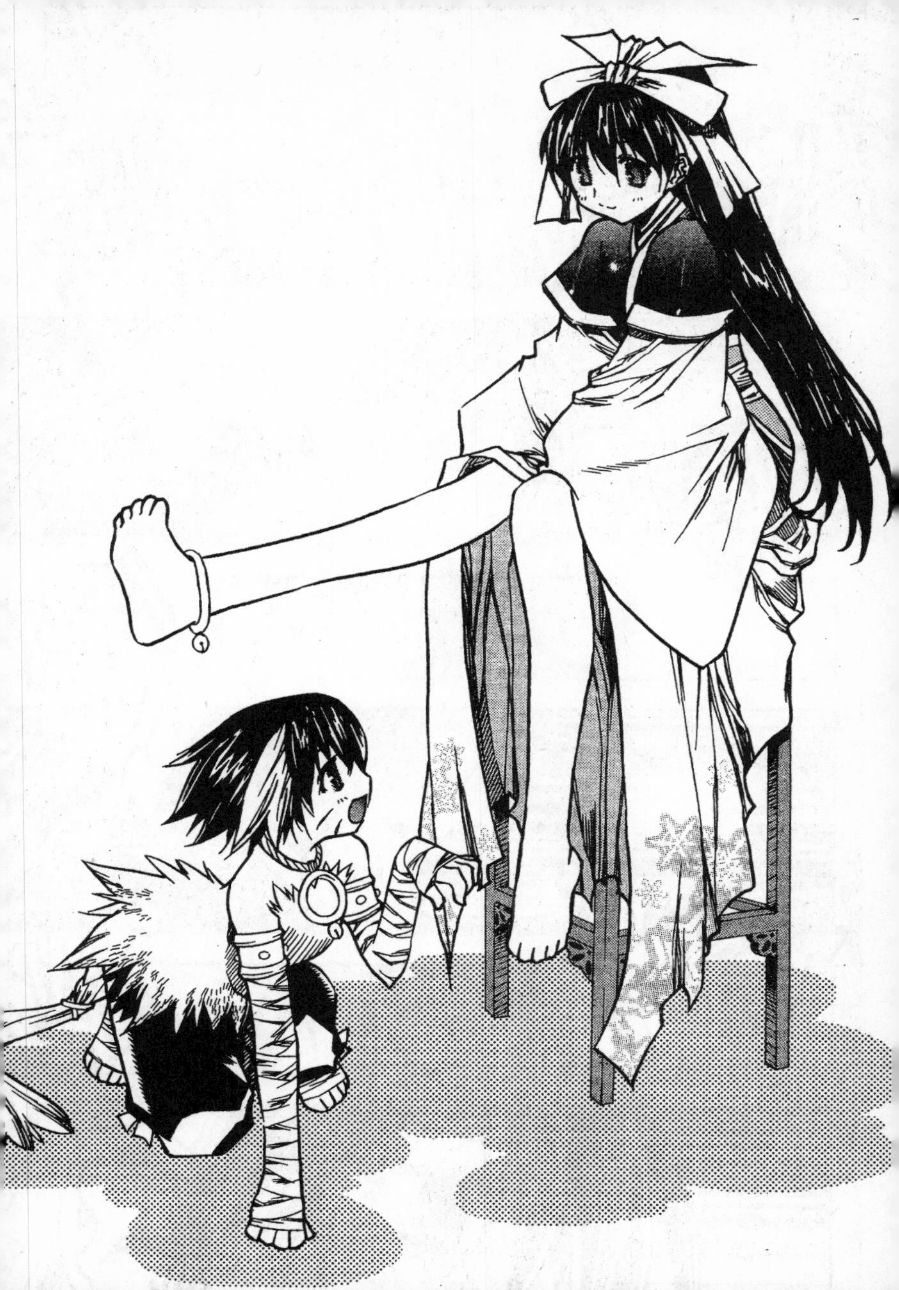

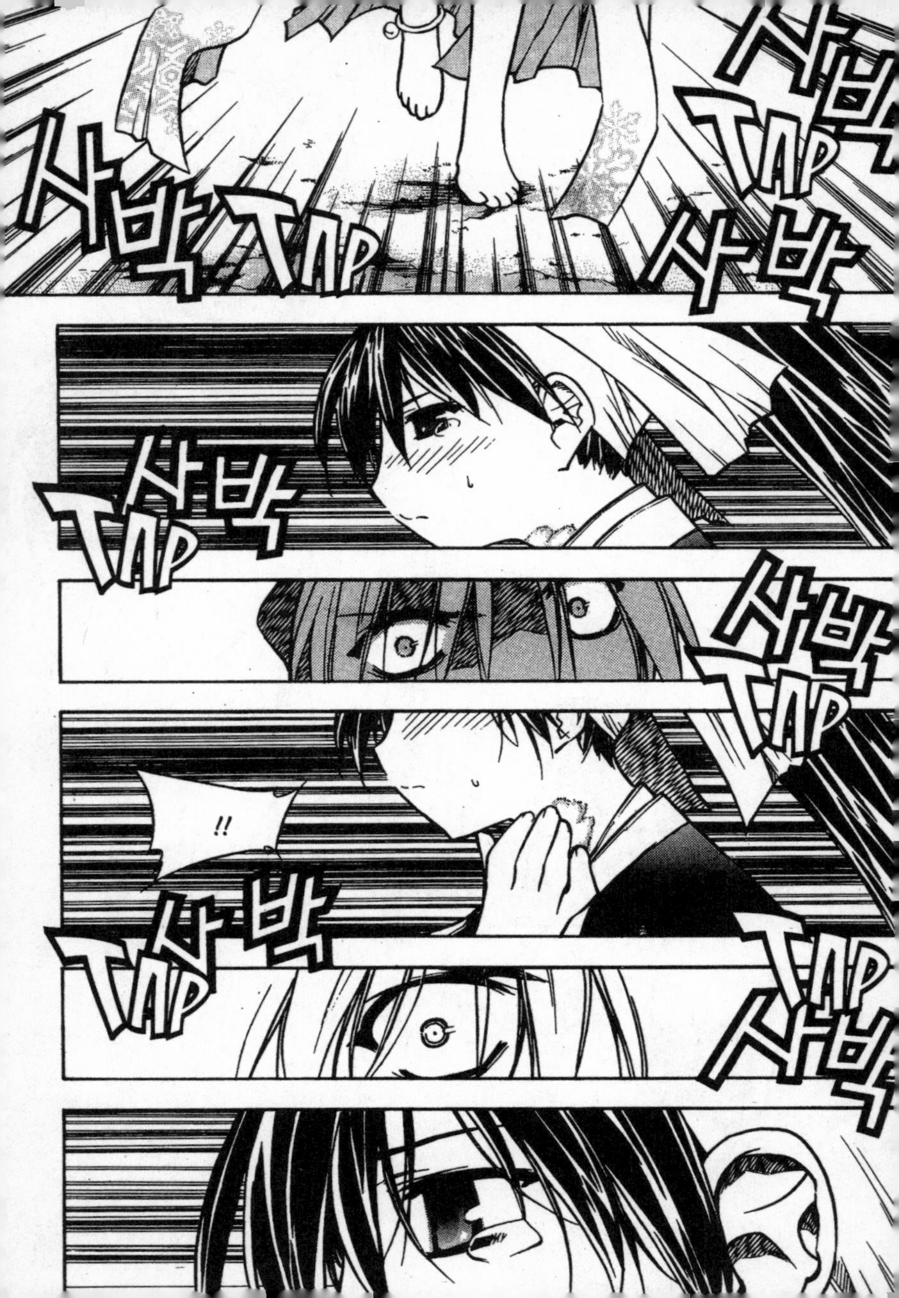
사박
TAP
사박
사박
TAP
사박
TAP
사박
TAP
!!
TAP
사박
사박
TAP

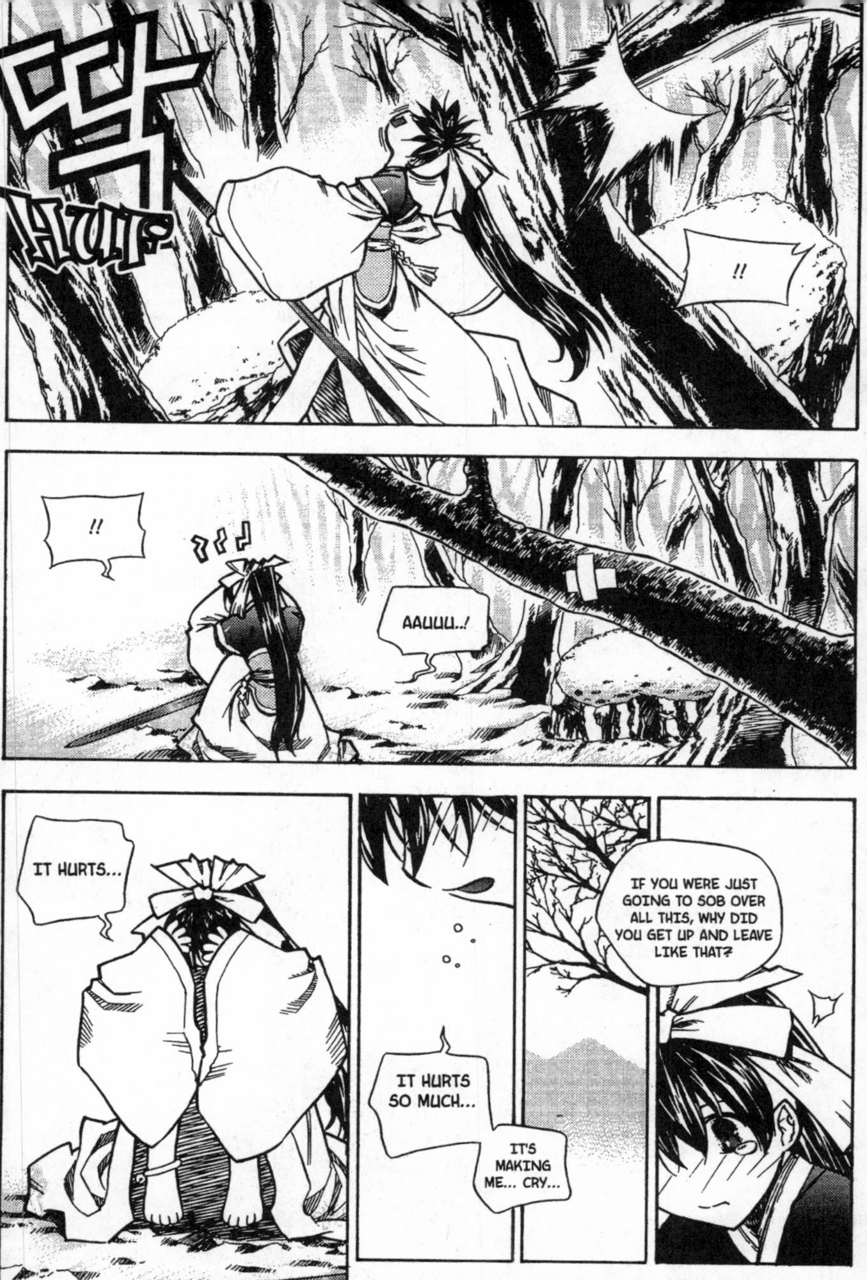
!!
AAUUU..!
!!
IF YOU WERE JUST GOING TO SOB OVER ALL THIS, WHY DID YOU GET UP AND LEAVE LIKE THAT?
IT HURTS SO MUCH...
IT'S MAKING ME... CRY...
IT HURTS...

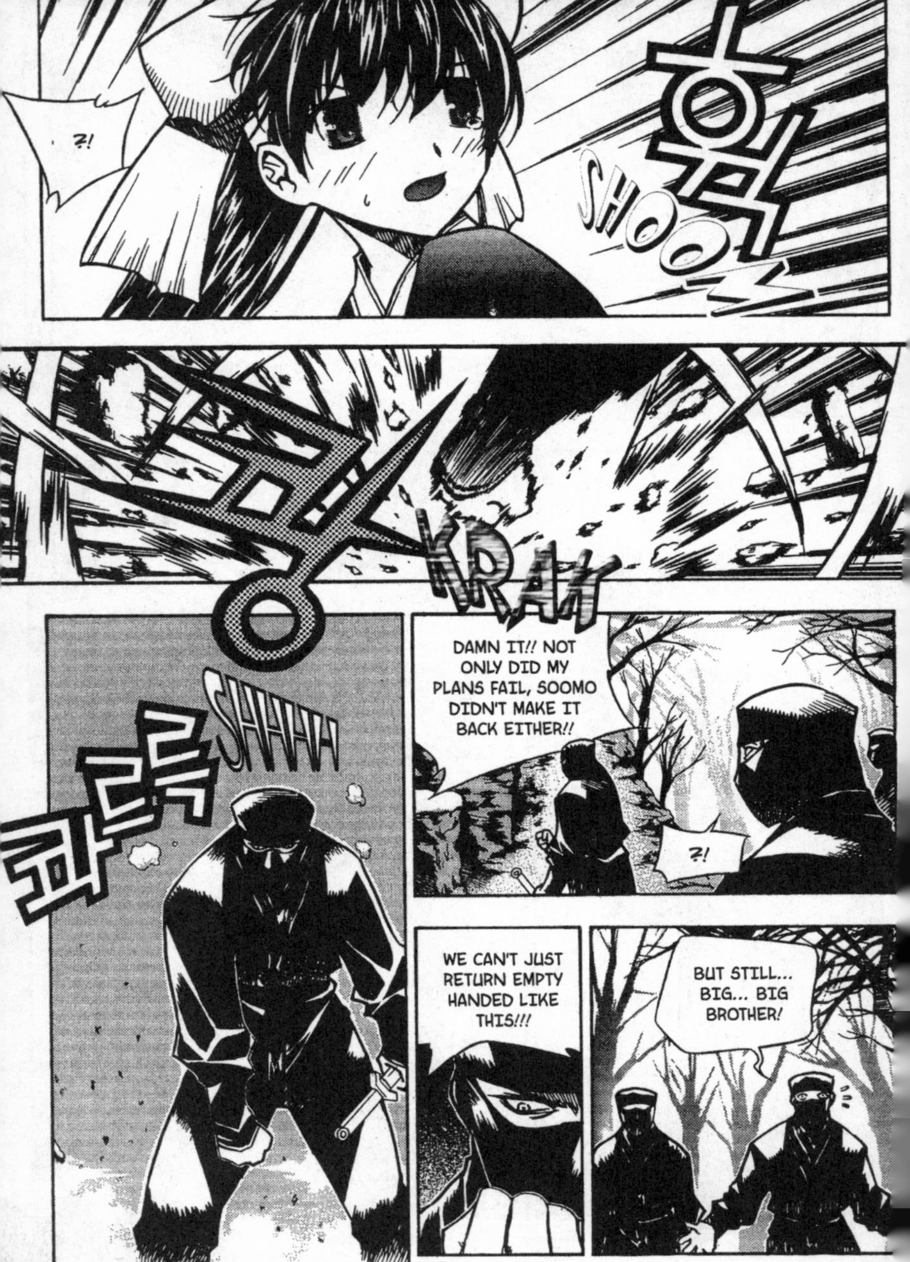
?!
SHOOM
DAMN IT!! NOT ONLY DID MY PLANS FAIL, SOOMO DIDN'T MAKE IT BACK EITHER!!
?!
WE CAN'T JUST RETURN EMPTY HANDED LIKE THIS!!!
BUT STILL... BIG... BIG BROTHER!

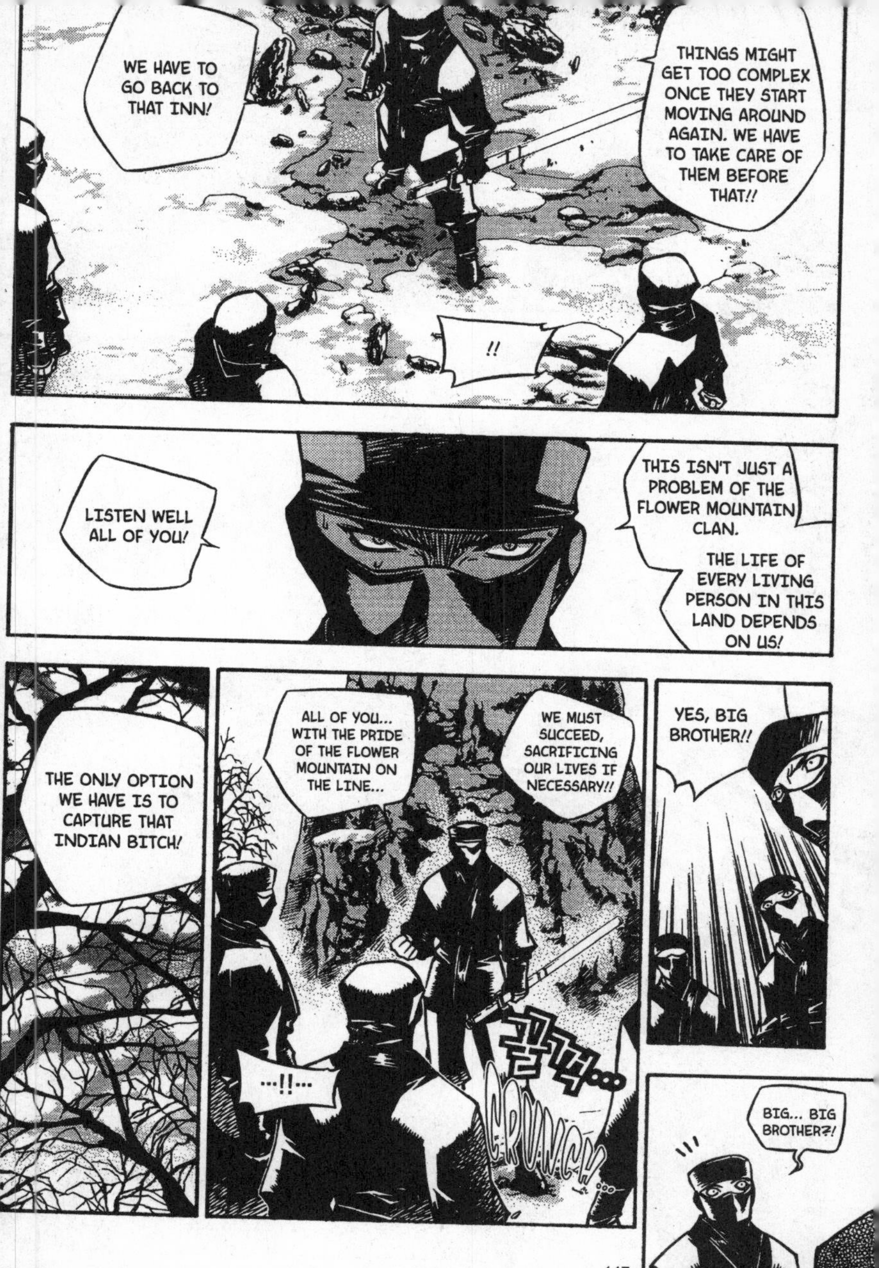
WE HAVE TO GO BACK TO THAT INN!
THINGS MIGHT GET TOO COMPLEX ONCE THEY START MOVING AROUND AGAIN. WE HAVE TO TAKE CARE OF THEM BEFORE THAT!!
!!
LISTEN WELL ALL OF YOU!
THIS ISN'T JUST A PROBLEM OF THE FLOWER MOUNTAIN CLAN.
THE LIFE OF EVERY LIVING PERSON IN THIS LAND DEPENDS ON US!
THE ONLY OPTION WE HAVE IS TO CAPTURE THAT INDIAN BITCH!
ALL OF YOU... WITH THE PRIDE OF THE FLOWER MOUNTAIN ON THE LINE...
WE MUST SUCCEED, SACRIFICING OUR LIVES IF NECESSARY!!
YES, BIG BROTHER!!
...!!...
CRUNCH
BIG... BIG BROTHER?!

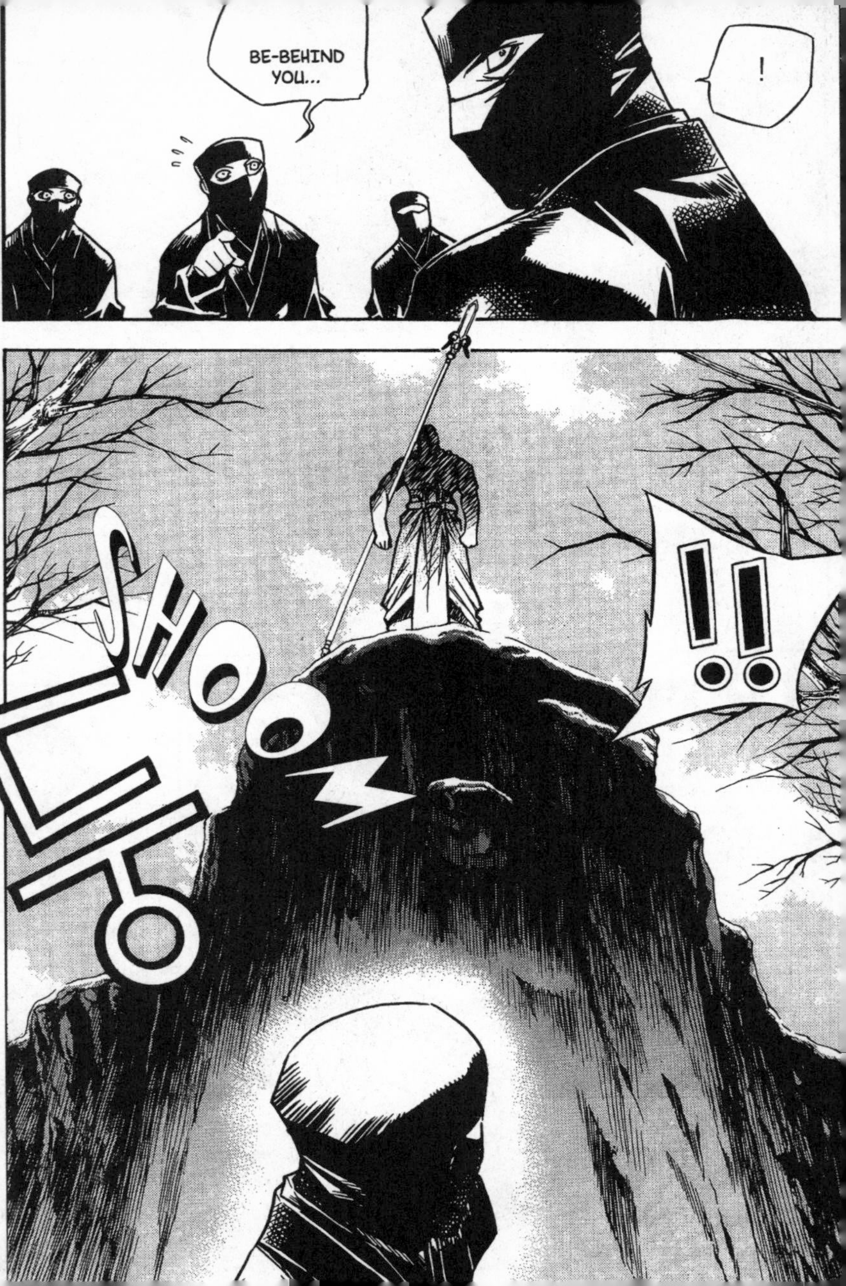
BE-BEHIND YOU...
!
SHOO
!!

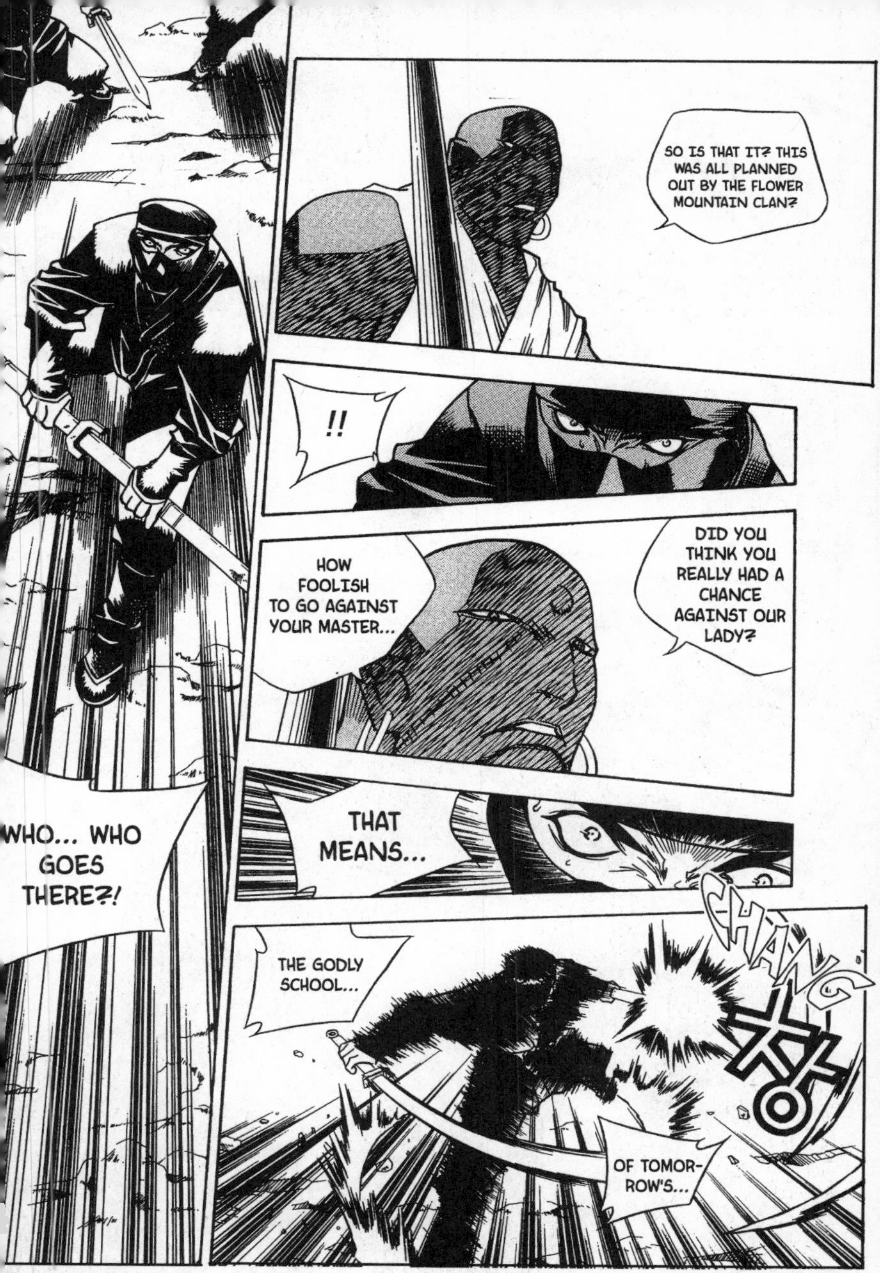

WHO... WHO GOES THERE?!
SO IS THAT IT? THIS WAS ALL PLANNED OUT BY THE FLOWER MOUNTAIN CLAN?
!!
HOW FOOLISH TO GO AGAINST YOUR MASTER...
DID YOU THINK YOU REALLY HAD A CHANCE AGAINST OUR LADY?
THAT MEANS...
THE GODLY SCHOOL...
CHANG
OF TOMOR-ROW'S...

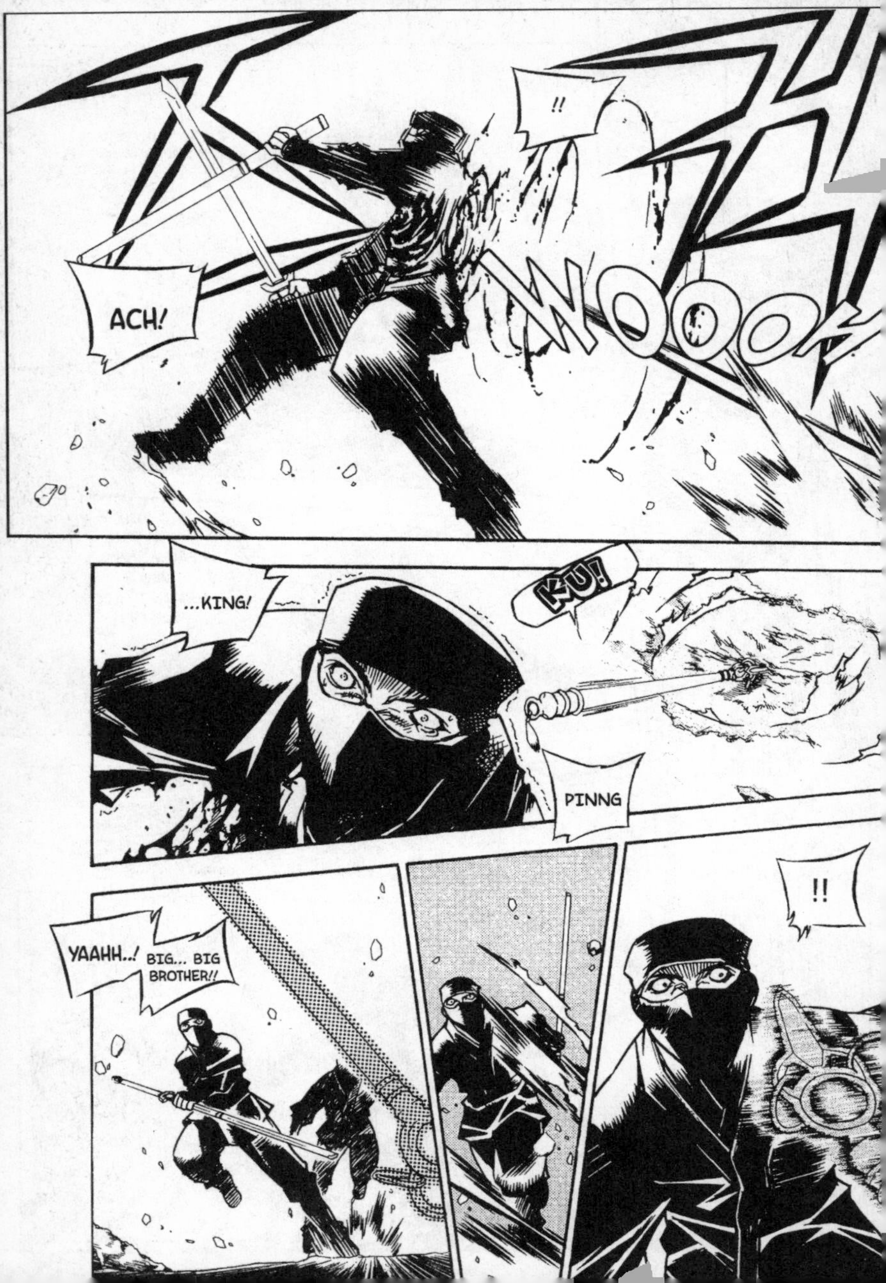
!!
ACH!
WOOOK
...KING!
KU!
PINNG
!!
BIG... BIG BROTHER!!
YAAHH...!

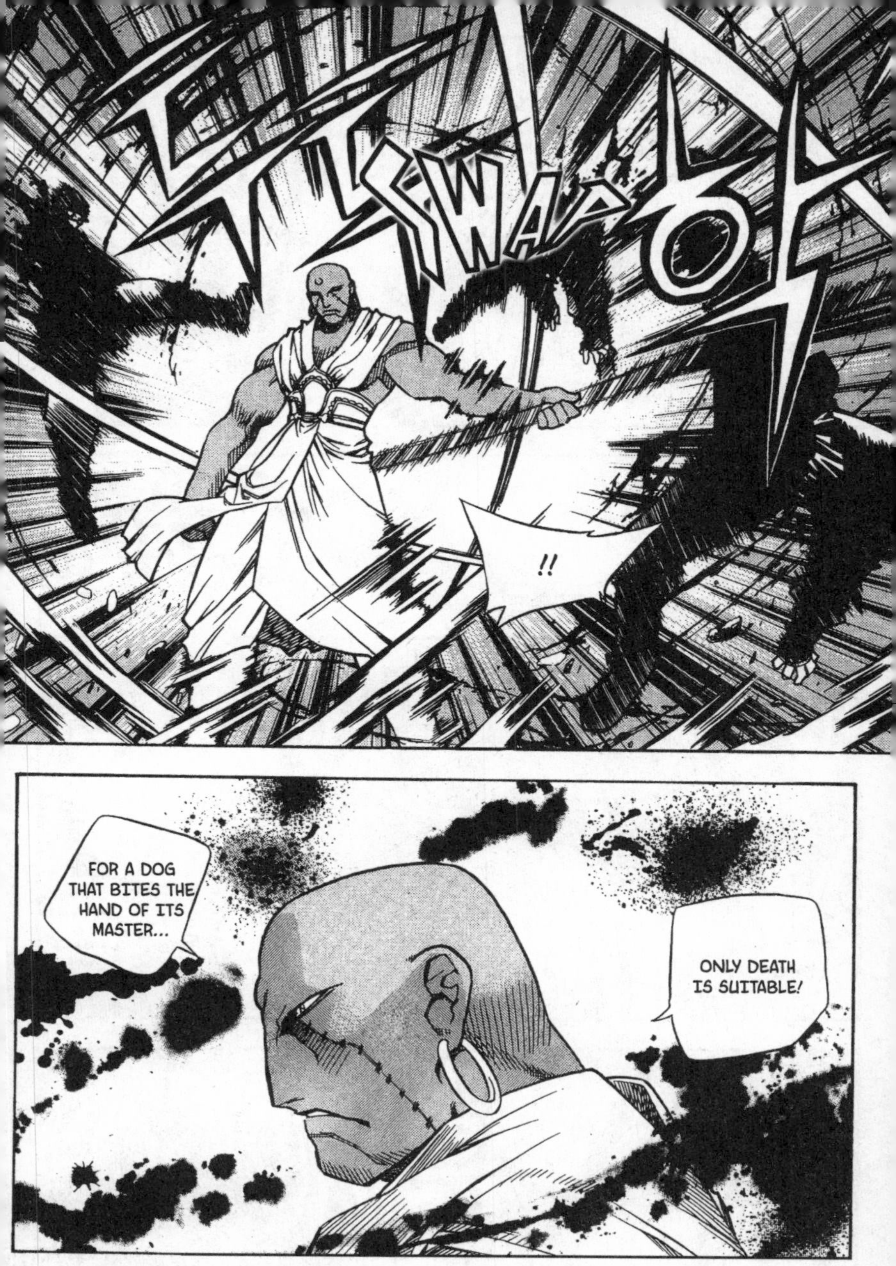
!!
FOR A DOG THAT BITES THE HAND OF ITS MASTER...
ONLY DEATH IS SUITABLE!

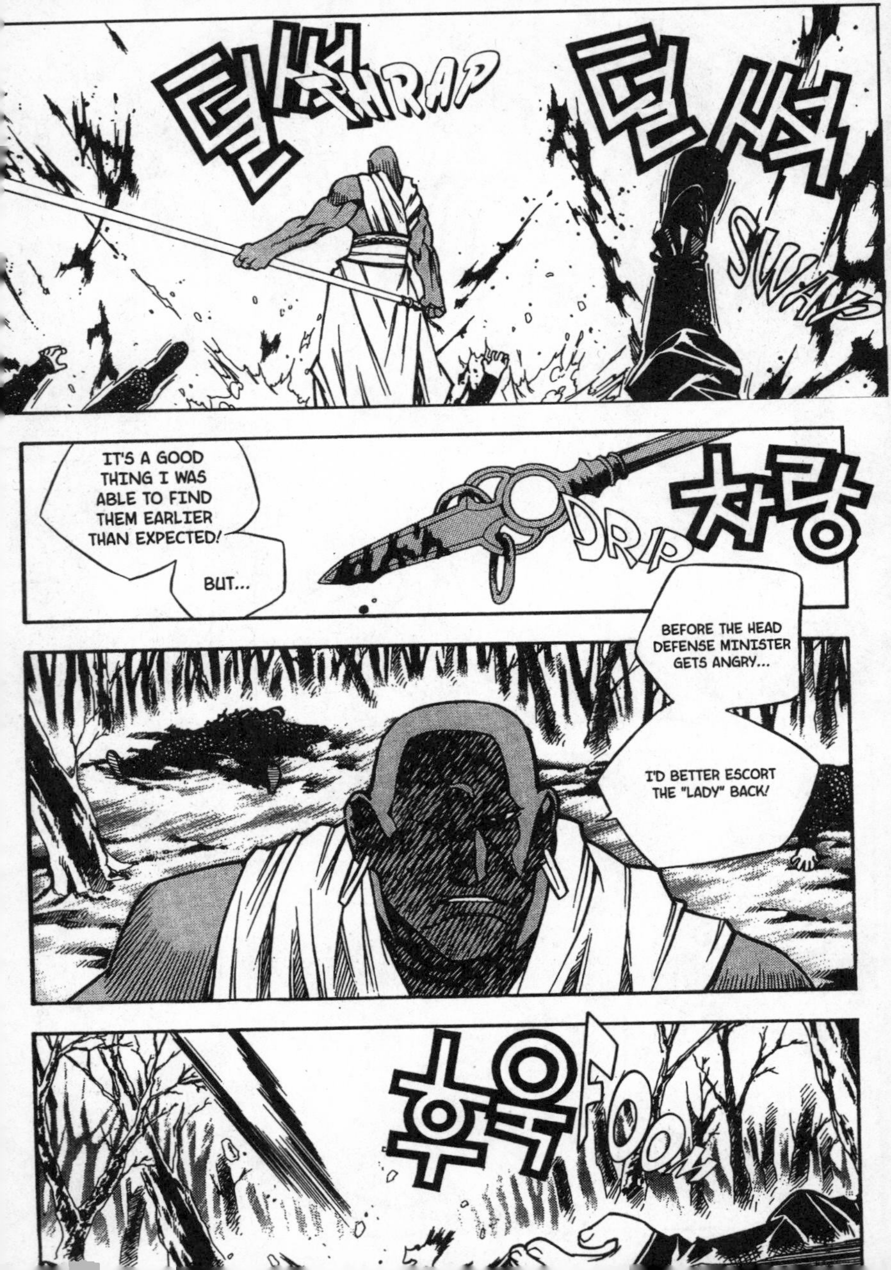
덜썩
THRAP
덜썩
SWAP
IT'S A GOOD THING I WAS ABLE TO FIND THEM EARLIER THAN EXPECTED!
BUT...
DRIP
차랑
BEFORE THE HEAD DEFENSE MINISTER GETS ANGRY...
I'D BETTER ESCORT THE "LADY" BACK!
후웅
FOOM

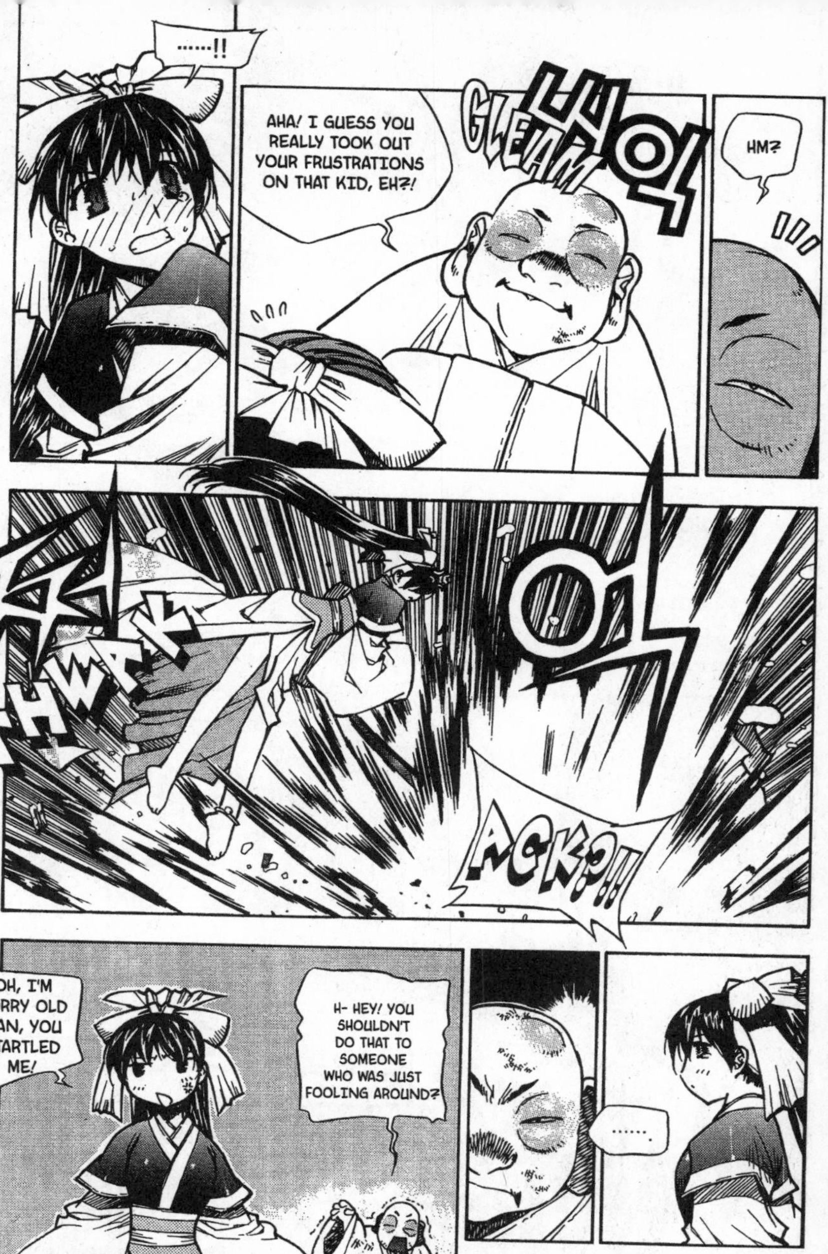
......!!
AHA! I GUESS YOU REALLY TOOK OUT YOUR FRUSTRATIONS ON THAT KID, EH?!
GLEAM
TOTOT
HM?
THWAK
ACK?!!
OH, I'M SORRY OLD MAN, YOU STARTLED ME!
H- HEY! YOU SHOULDN'T DO THAT TO SOMEONE WHO WAS JUST FOOLING AROUND?
.......

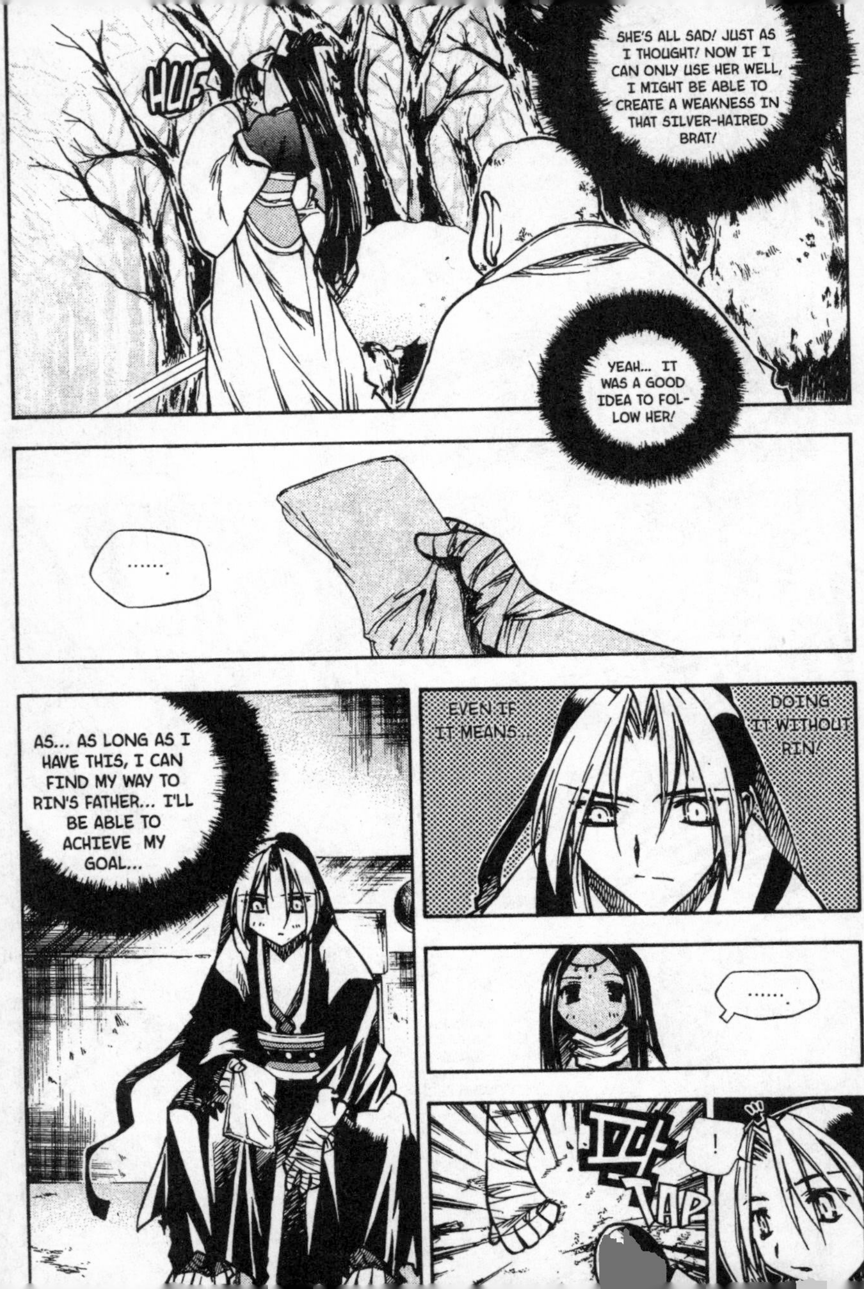

SHE'S ALL SAD! JUST AS I THOUGHT! NOW IF I CAN ONLY USE HER WELL, I MIGHT BE ABLE TO CREATE A WEAKNESS IN THAT SILVER-HAIRED BRAT!
HUF
YEAH... IT WAS A GOOD IDEA TO FOL-LOW HER!
.......
DOING IT WITHOUT RIN!
EVEN IF IT MEANS...
AS... AS LONG AS I HAVE THIS, I CAN FIND MY WAY TO RIN'S FATHER... I'LL BE ABLE TO ACHIEVE MY GOAL...
.......
!
TAP

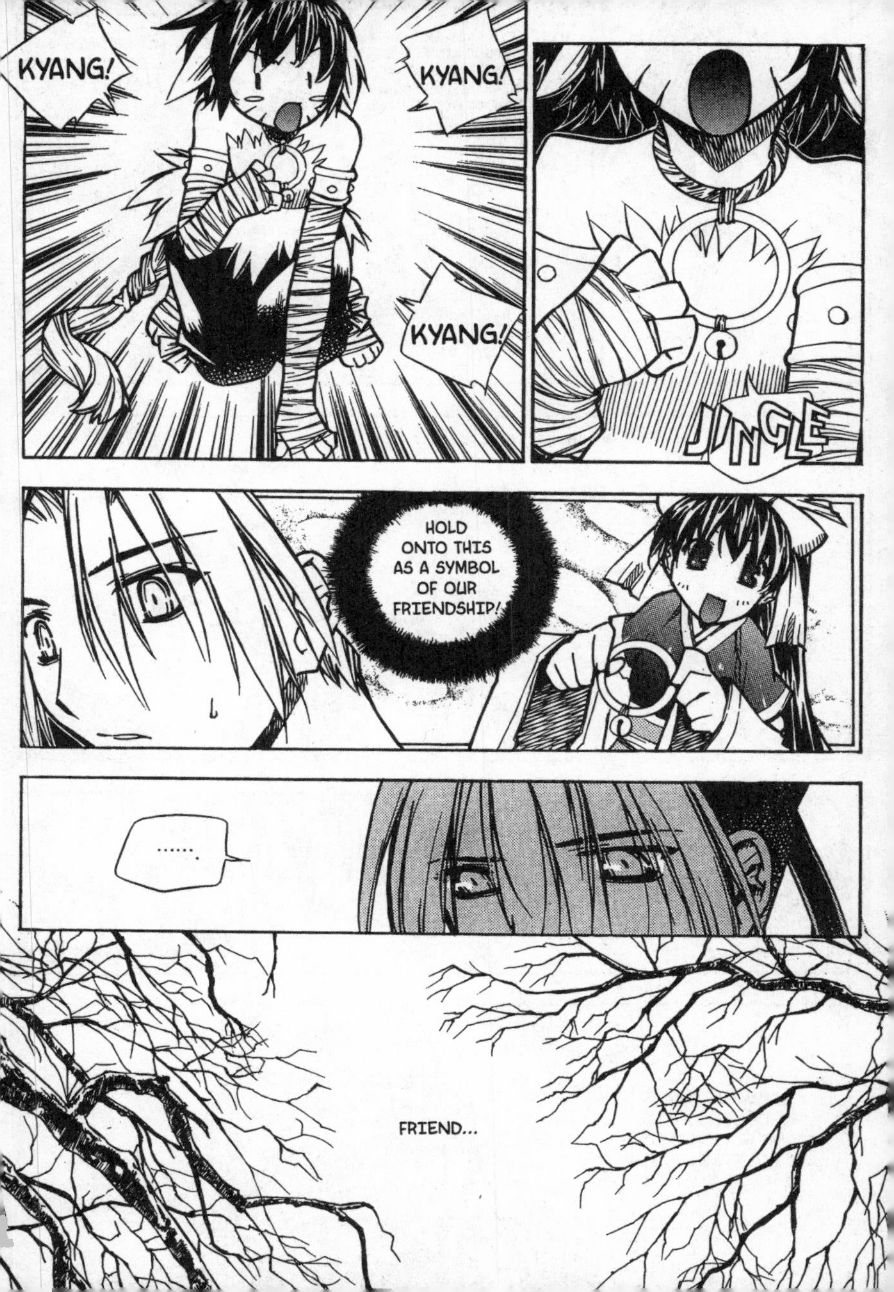
KYANG!
KYANG!
KYANG!
JINGLE
HOLD ONTO THIS AS A SYMBOL OF OUR FRIENDSHIP!
.......
FRIEND...

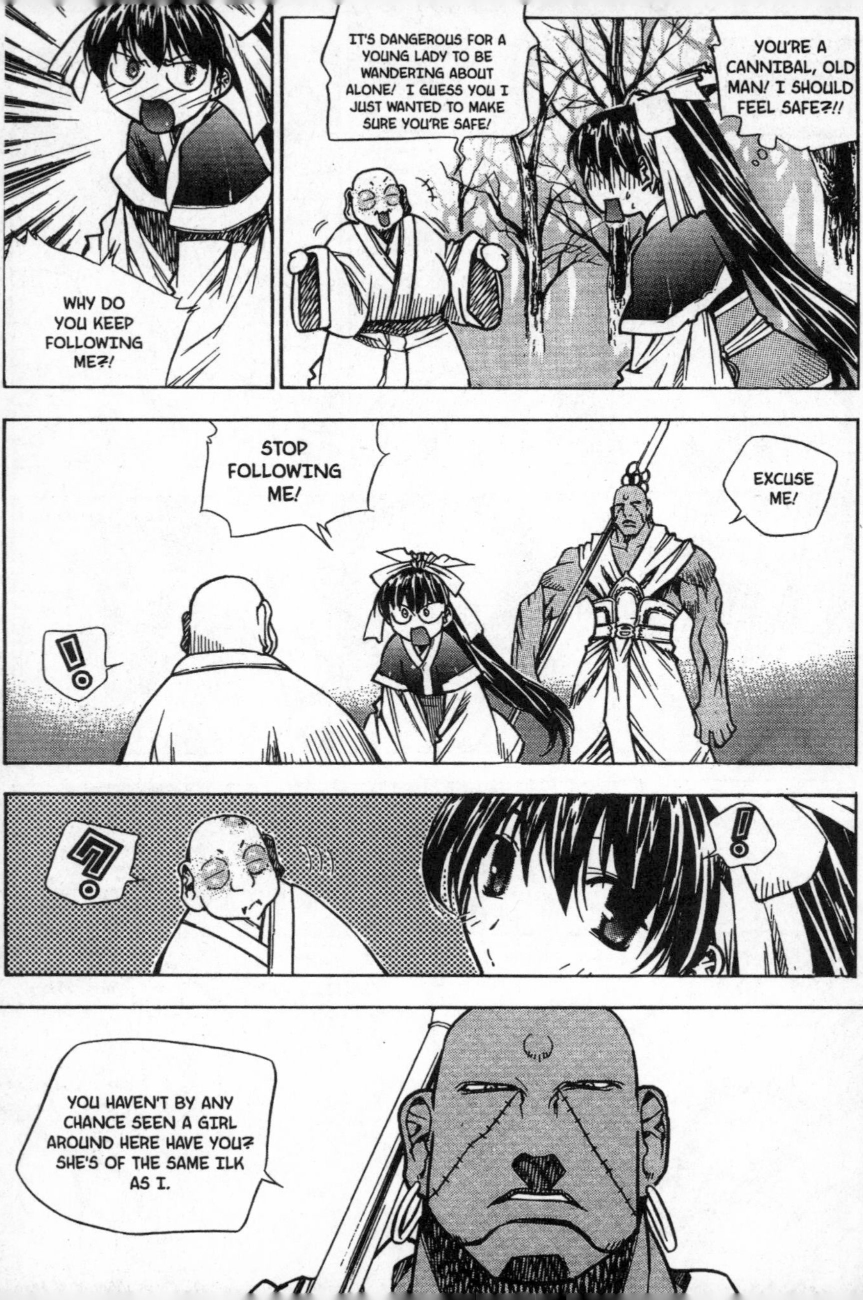

WHY DO YOU KEEP FOLLOWING ME?!
IT'S DANGEROUS FOR A YOUNG LADY TO BE WANDERING ABOUT ALONE! I GUESS YOU I JUST WANTED TO MAKE SURE YOU'RE SAFE!
YOU'RE A CANNIBAL, OLD MAN! I SHOULD FEEL SAFE?!!
STOP FOLLOWING ME!
EXCUSE ME!
!
?
!
YOU HAVEN'T BY ANY CHANCE SEEN A GIRL AROUND HERE HAVE YOU? SHE'S OF THE SAME ILK AS I.

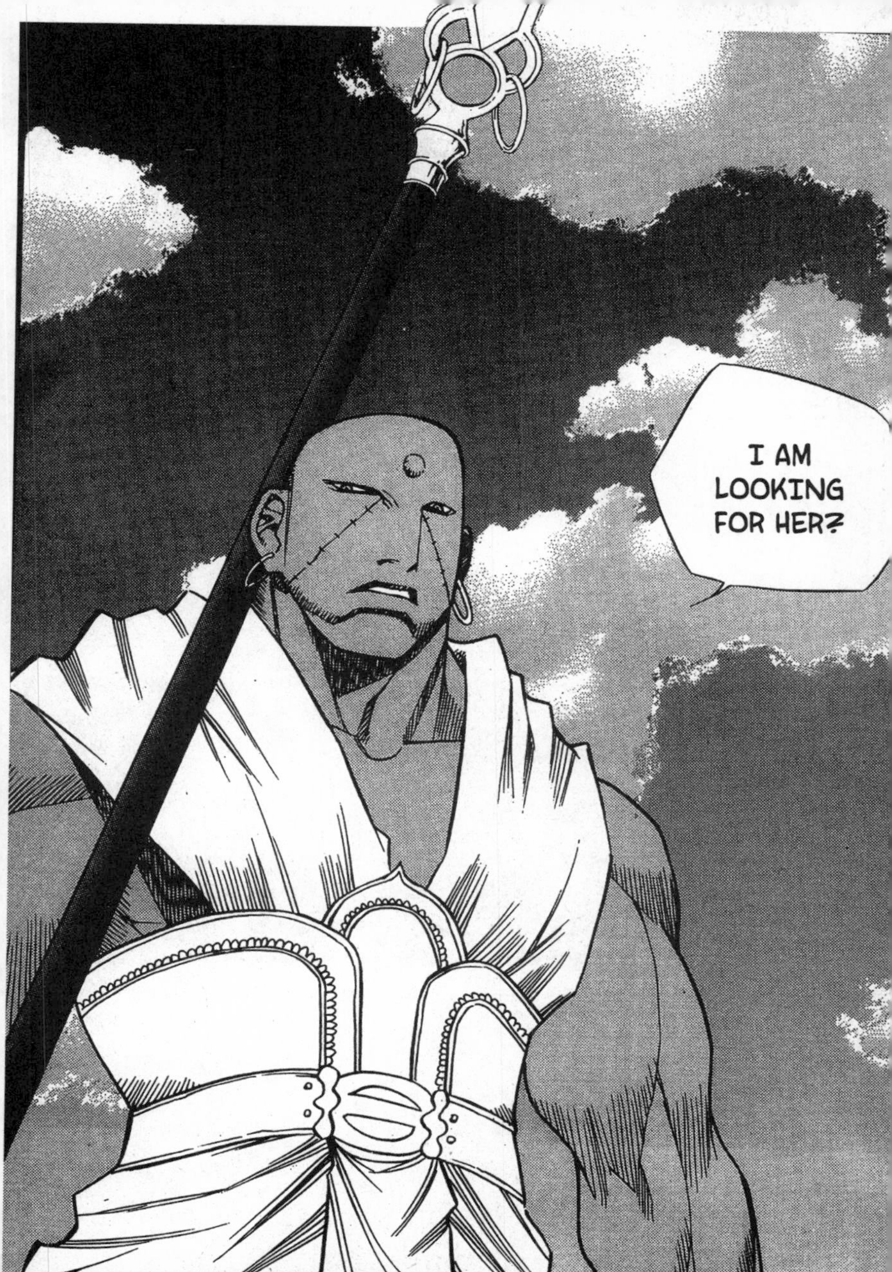
I AM LOOKING FOR HER?

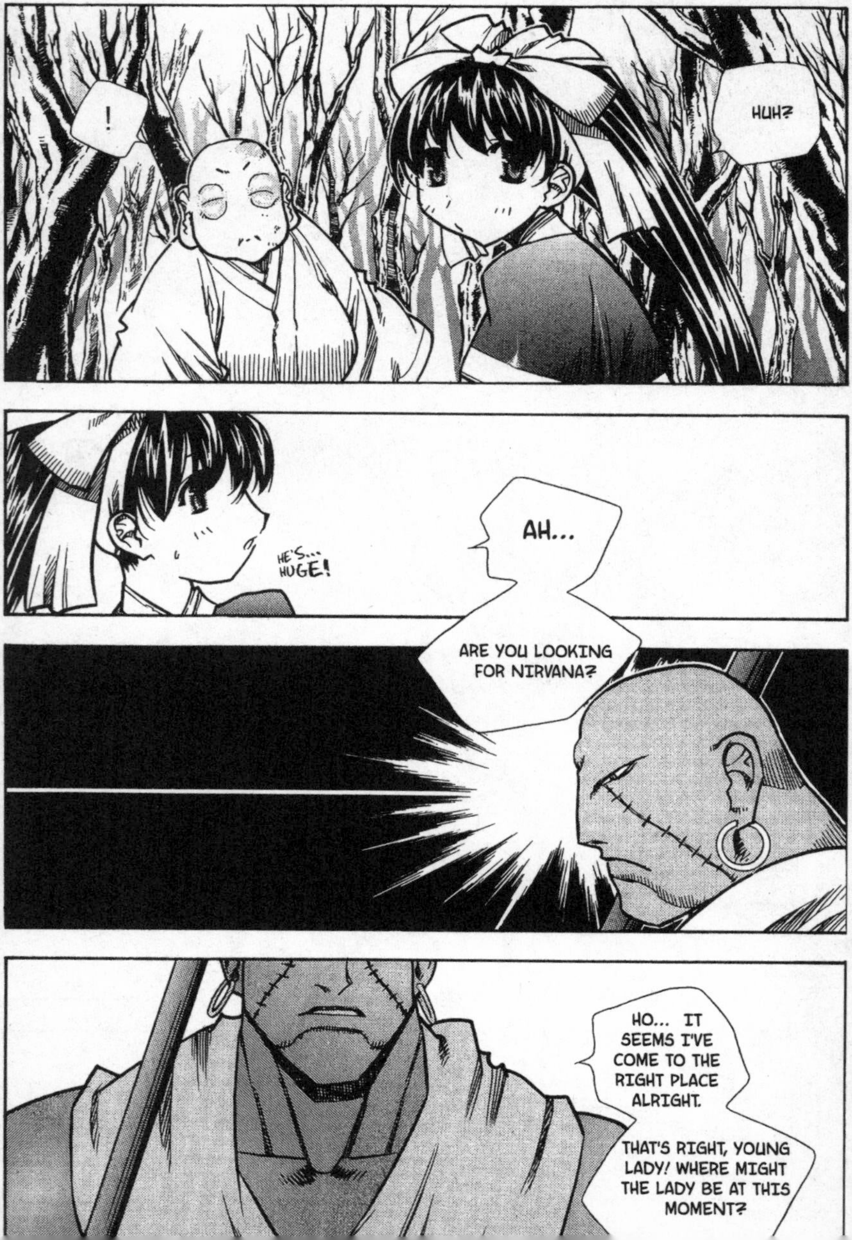

HUH?
!
AH...
HE'S... HUGE!
ARE YOU LOOKING FOR NIRVANA?
HO... IT SEEMS I'VE COME TO THE RIGHT PLACE ALRIGHT.
THAT'S RIGHT, YOUNG LADY! WHERE MIGHT THE LADY BE AT THIS MOMENT?

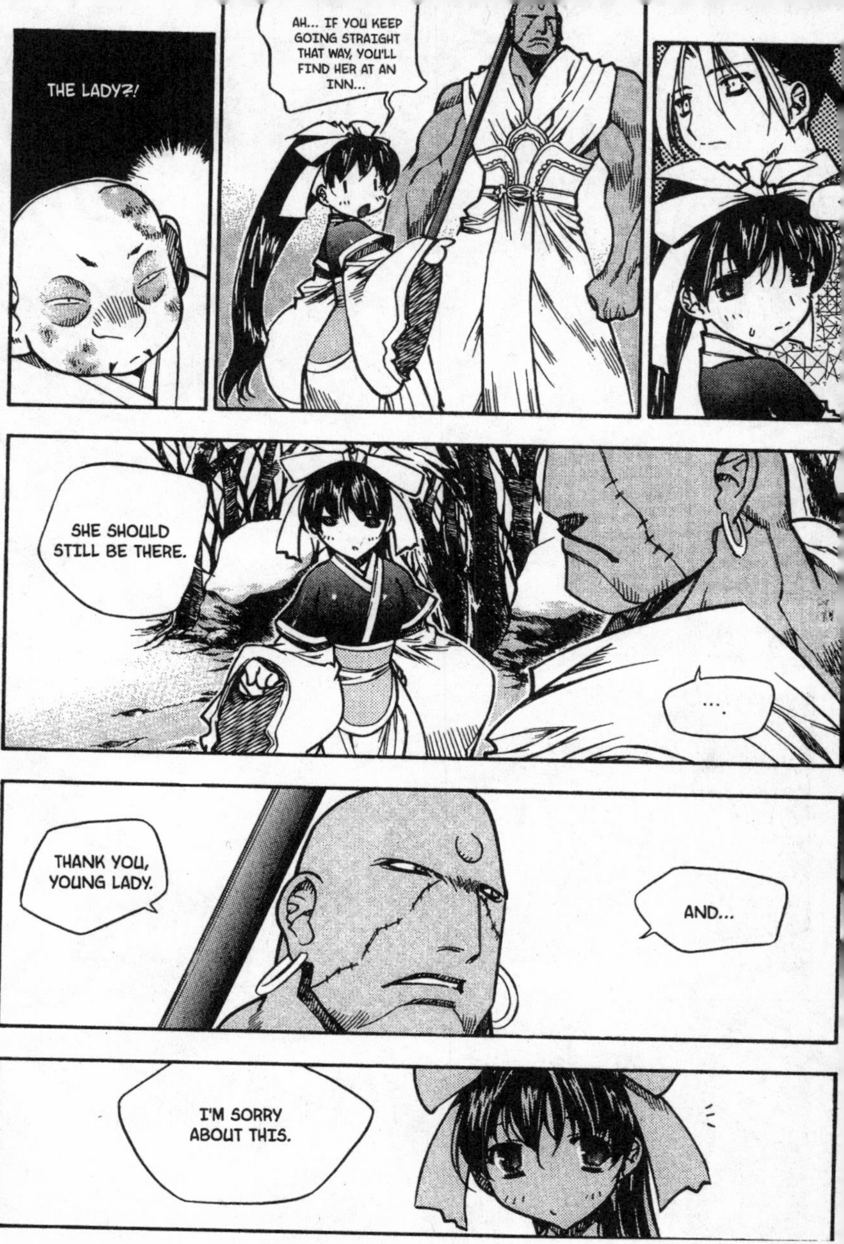
THE LADY?!
AH... IF YOU KEEP GOING STRAIGHT THAT WAY, YOU'LL FIND HER AT AN INN...
SHE SHOULD STILL BE THERE.
...
THANK YOU, YOUNG LADY.
AND...
I'M SORRY ABOUT THIS.

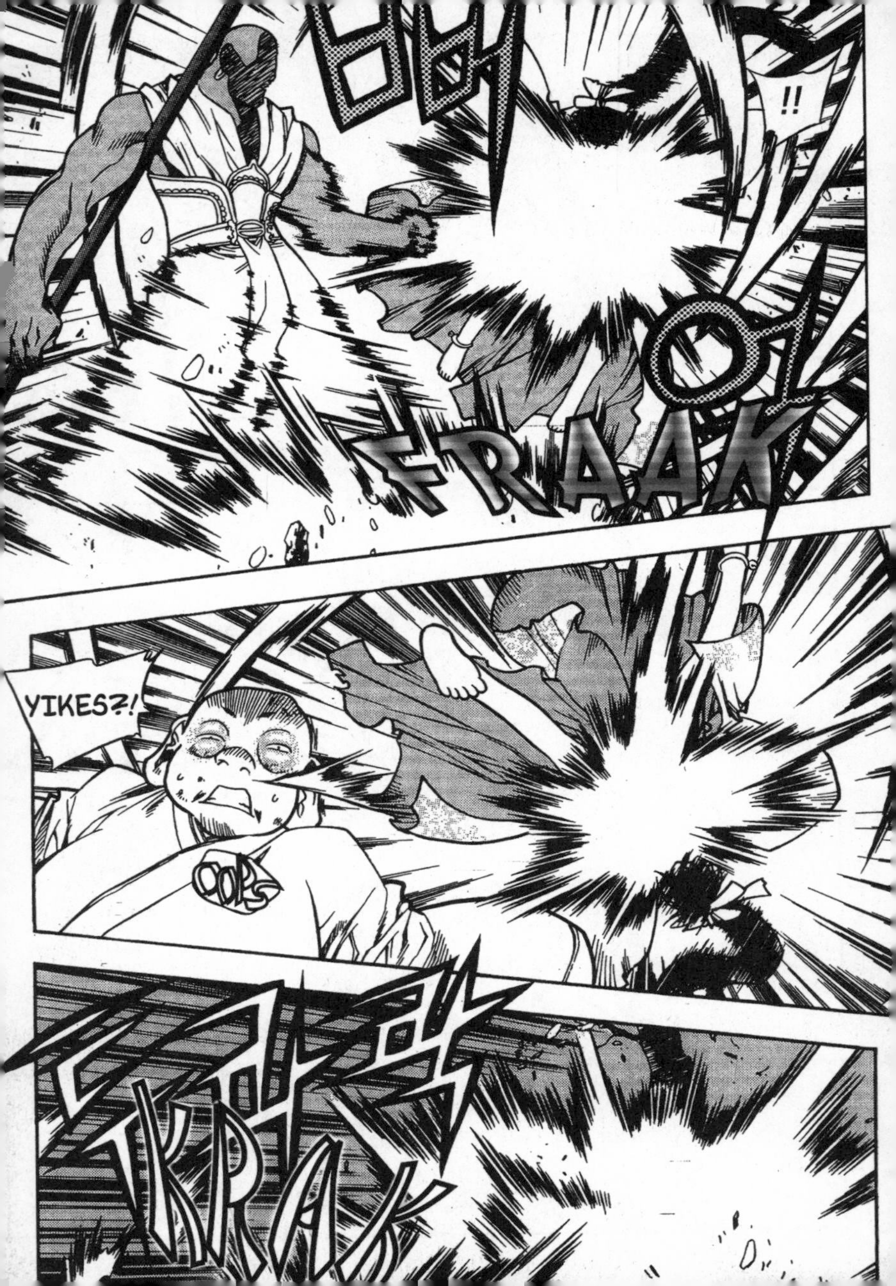
!!
FRAAK
YIKES?!
OOPS
TKRAK

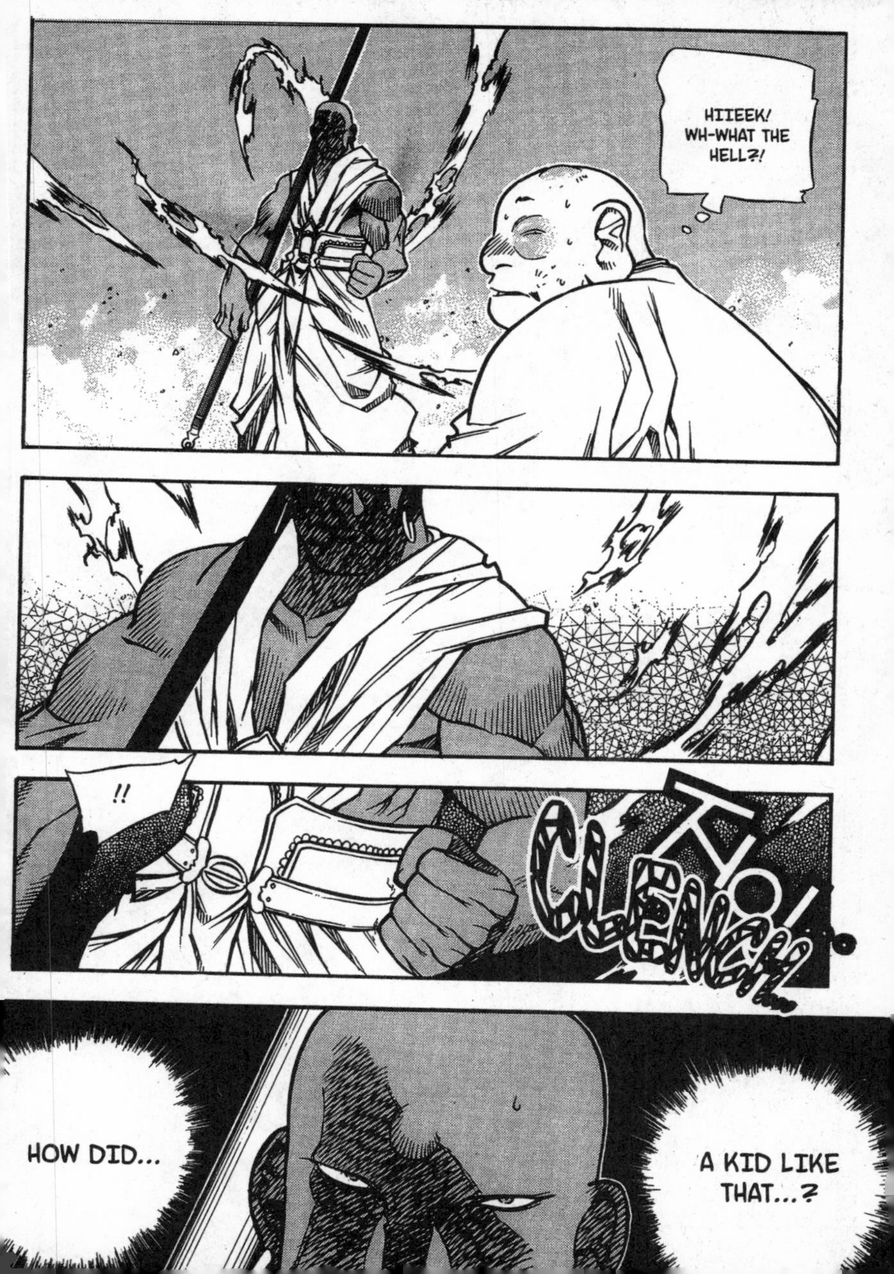
HIIEEK! WH-WHAT THE HELL?!
!!
CLENCH
HOW DID...
A KID LIKE THAT...?

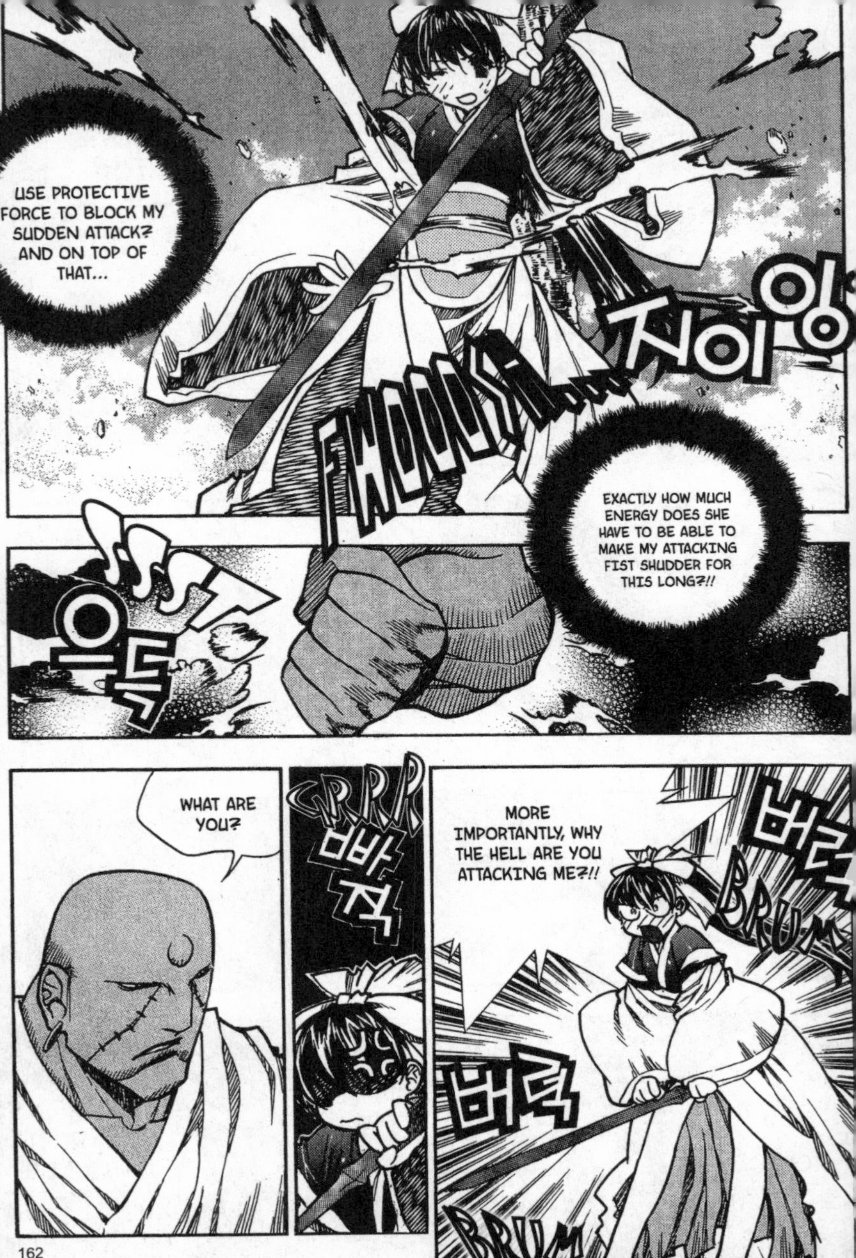
USE PROTECTIVE FORCE TO BLOCK MY SUDDEN ATTACK? AND ON TOP OF THAT...
FWOOOSH...
EXACTLY HOW MUCH ENERGY DOES SHE HAVE TO BE ABLE TO MAKE MY ATTACKING FIST SHUDDER FOR THIS LONG?!!
SSST
WHAT ARE YOU?
GRRR
MORE IMPORTANTLY, WHY THE HELL ARE YOU ATTACKING ME?!!
BRUM
버럭
BRUM
버럭

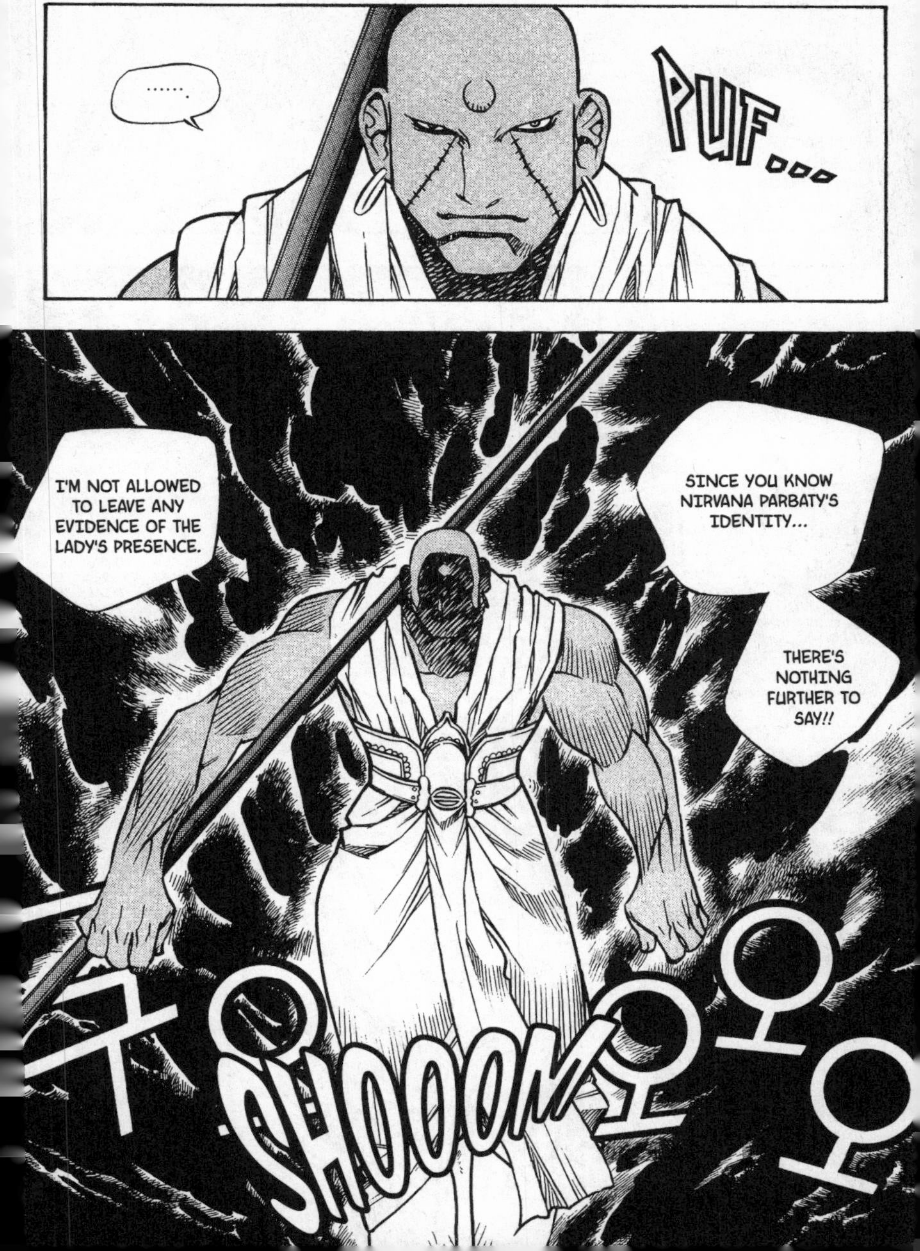
.......
PUF...
I'M NOT ALLOWED TO LEAVE ANY EVIDENCE OF THE LADY'S PRESENCE.
SINCE YOU KNOW NIRVANA PARBATY'S IDENTITY...
THERE'S NOTHING FURTHER TO SAY!!
SHOOOM

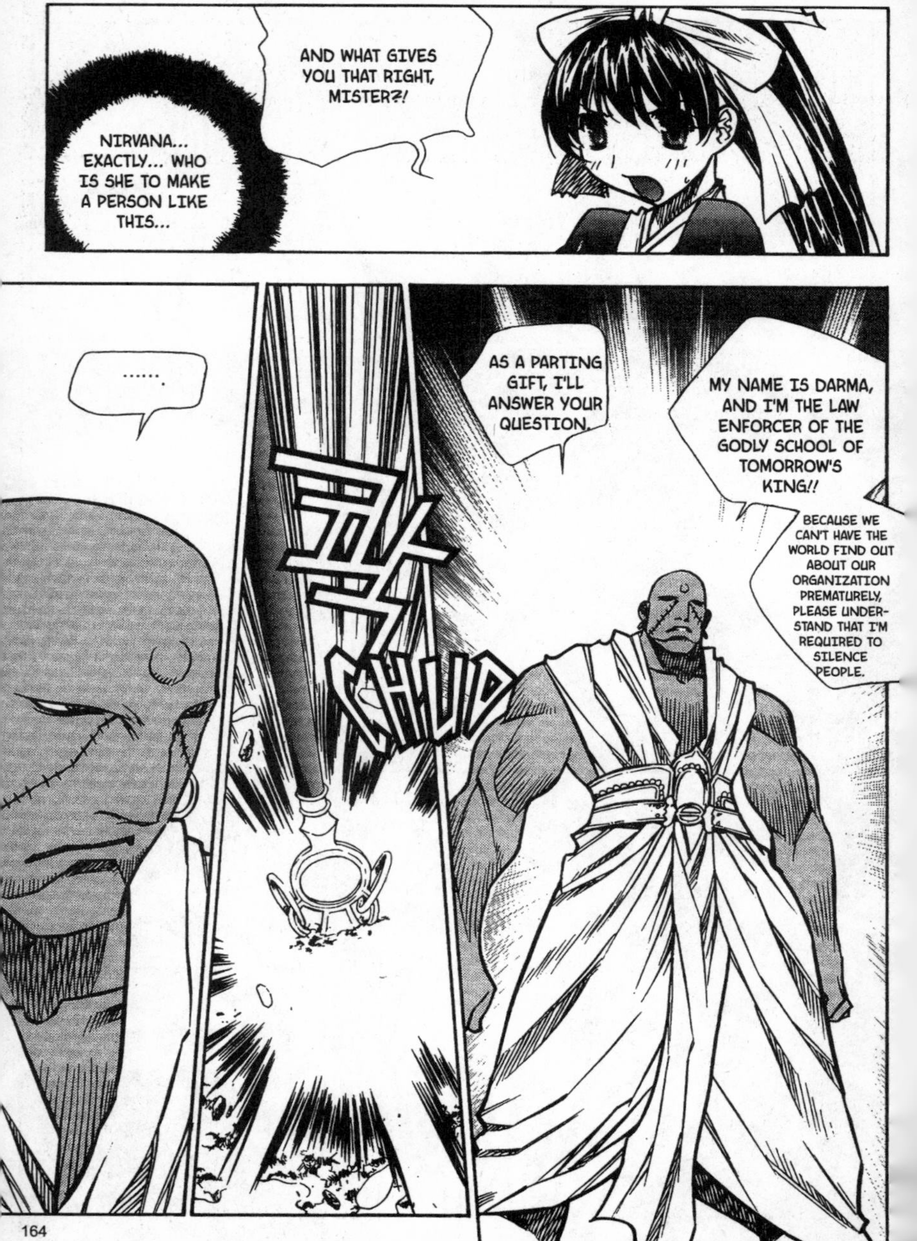
NIRVANA... EXACTLY... WHO IS SHE TO MAKE A PERSON LIKE THIS...
AND WHAT GIVES YOU THAT RIGHT, MISTER?!
.......
CHUD
AS A PARTING GIFT, I'LL ANSWER YOUR QUESTION.
MY NAME IS DARMA, AND I'M THE LAW ENFORCER OF THE GODLY SCHOOL OF TOMORROW'S KING!!
BECAUSE WE CAN'T HAVE THE WORLD FIND OUT ABOUT OUR ORGANIZATION PREMATURELY, PLEASE UNDERSTAND THAT I'M REQUIRED TO SILENCE PEOPLE.

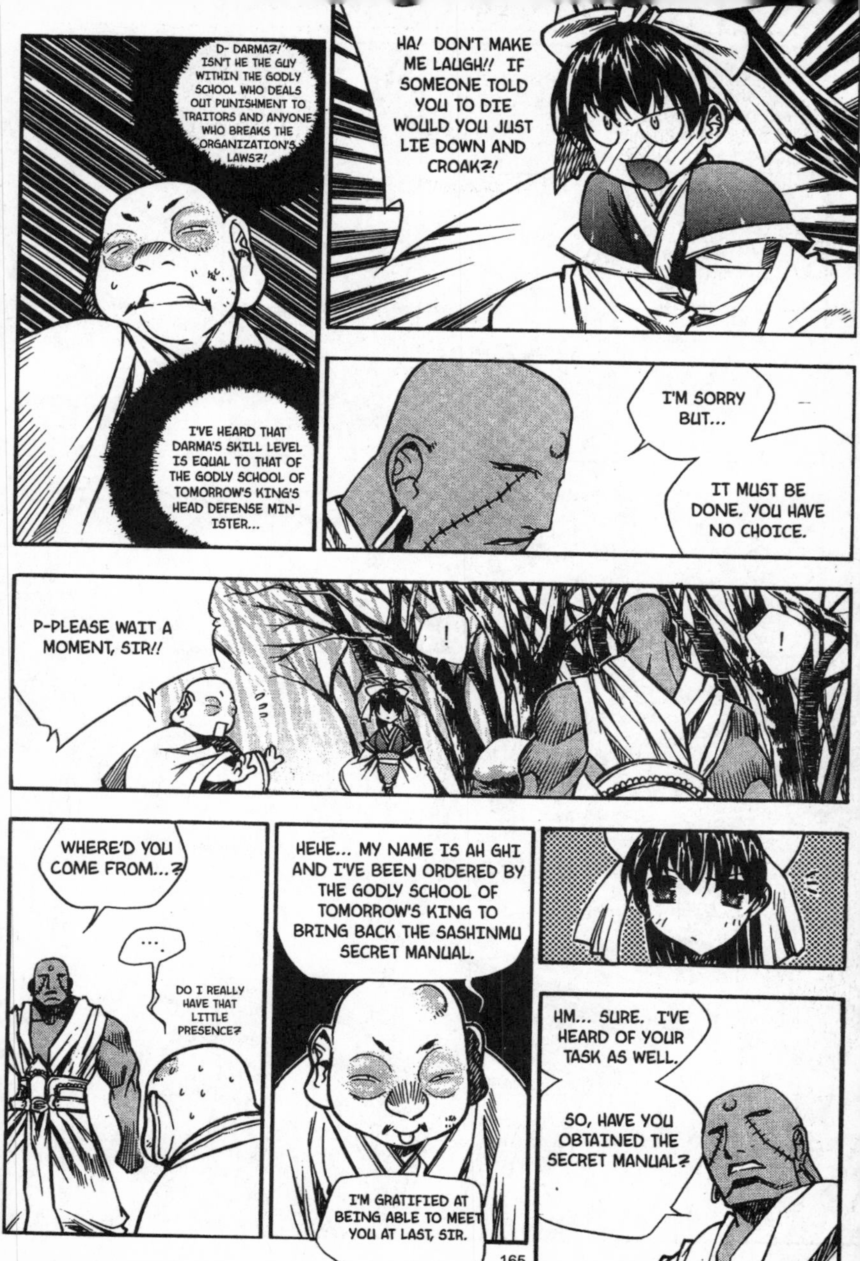
D- DARMA?! ISN'T HE THE GUY WITHIN THE GODLY SCHOOL WHO DEALS OUT PUNISHMENT TO TRAITORS AND ANYONE WHO BREAKS THE ORGANIZATION'S LAWS?!
I'VE HEARD THAT DARMA'S SKILL LEVEL IS EQUAL TO THAT OF THE GODLY SCHOOL OF TOMORROW'S KING'S HEAD DEFENSE MIN-ISTER...
HA! DON'T MAKE ME LAUGH!! IF SOMEONE TOLD YOU TO DIE WOULD YOU JUST LIE DOWN AND CROAK?!
I'M SORRY BUT...
IT MUST BE DONE. YOU HAVE NO CHOICE.
P-PLEASE WAIT A MOMENT, SIR!!
!
!
WHERE'D YOU COME FROM...?
...
DO I REALLY HAVE THAT LITTLE PRESENCE?
HEHE... MY NAME IS AH GHI AND I'VE BEEN ORDERED BY THE GODLY SCHOOL OF TOMORROW'S KING TO BRING BACK THE SASHINMU SECRET MANUAL.
I'M GRATIFIED AT BEING ABLE TO MEET YOU AT LAST, SIR.
HM... SURE. I'VE HEARD OF YOUR TASK AS WELL.
SO, HAVE YOU OBTAINED THE SECRET MANUAL?

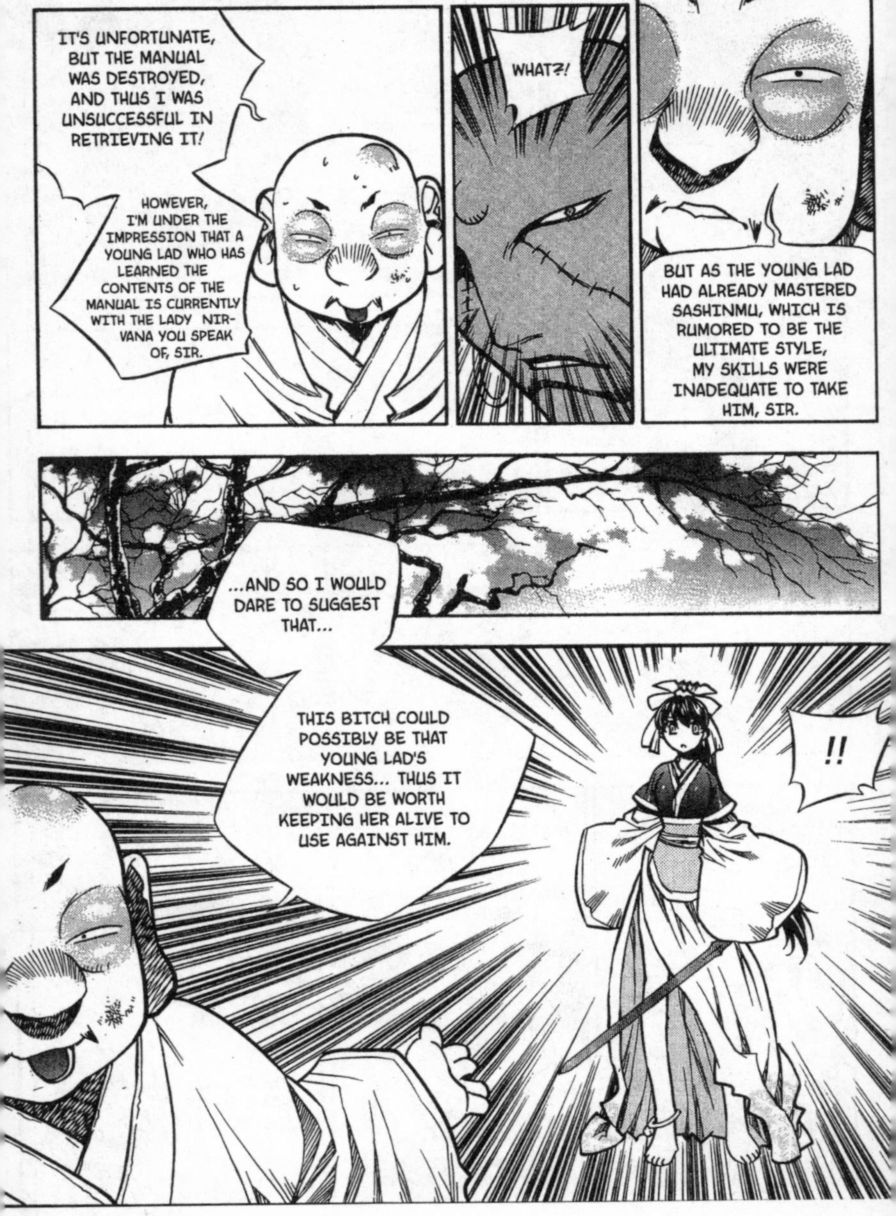
IT'S UNFORTUNATE, BUT THE MANUAL WAS DESTROYED, AND THUS I WAS UNSUCCESSFUL IN RETRIEVING IT!
HOWEVER, I'M UNDER THE IMPRESSION THAT A YOUNG LAD WHO HAS LEARNED THE CONTENTS OF THE MANUAL IS CURRENTLY WITH THE LADY NIR-VANA YOU SPEAK OF, SIR.
WHAT?!
BUT AS THE YOUNG LAD HAD ALREADY MASTERED SASHINMU, WHICH IS RUMORED TO BE THE ULTIMATE STYLE, MY SKILLS WERE INADEQUATE TO TAKE HIM, SIR.
...AND SO I WOULD DARE TO SUGGEST THAT...
THIS BITCH COULD POSSIBLY BE THAT YOUNG LAD'S WEAKNESS... THUS IT WOULD BE WORTH KEEPING HER ALIVE TO USE AGAINST HIM.
!!

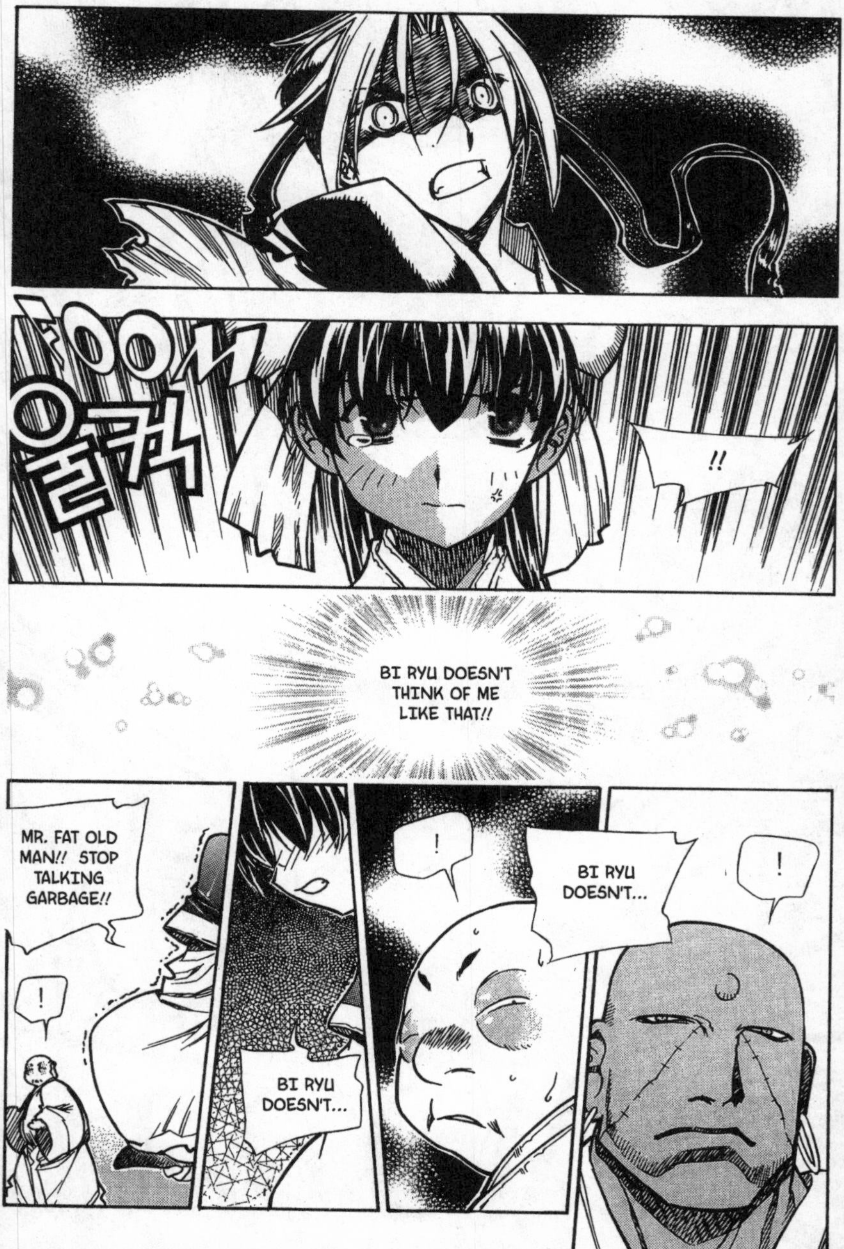
!!
BI RYU DOESN'T THINK OF ME LIKE THAT!!
MR. FAT OLD MAN!! STOP TALKING GARBAGE!!
!
BI RYU DOESN'T...
!
BI RYU DOESN'T...
!

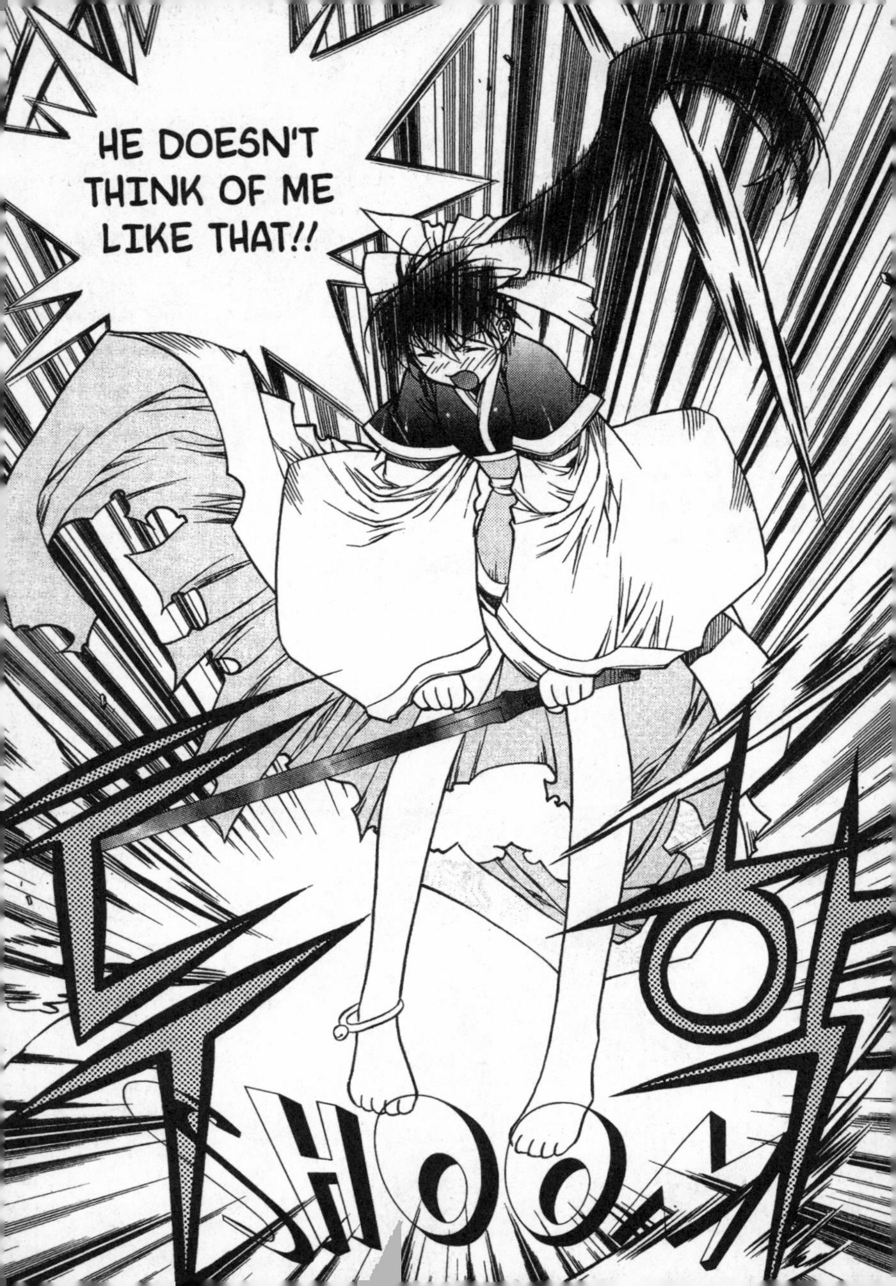
HE DOESN'T THINK OF ME LIKE THAT!!

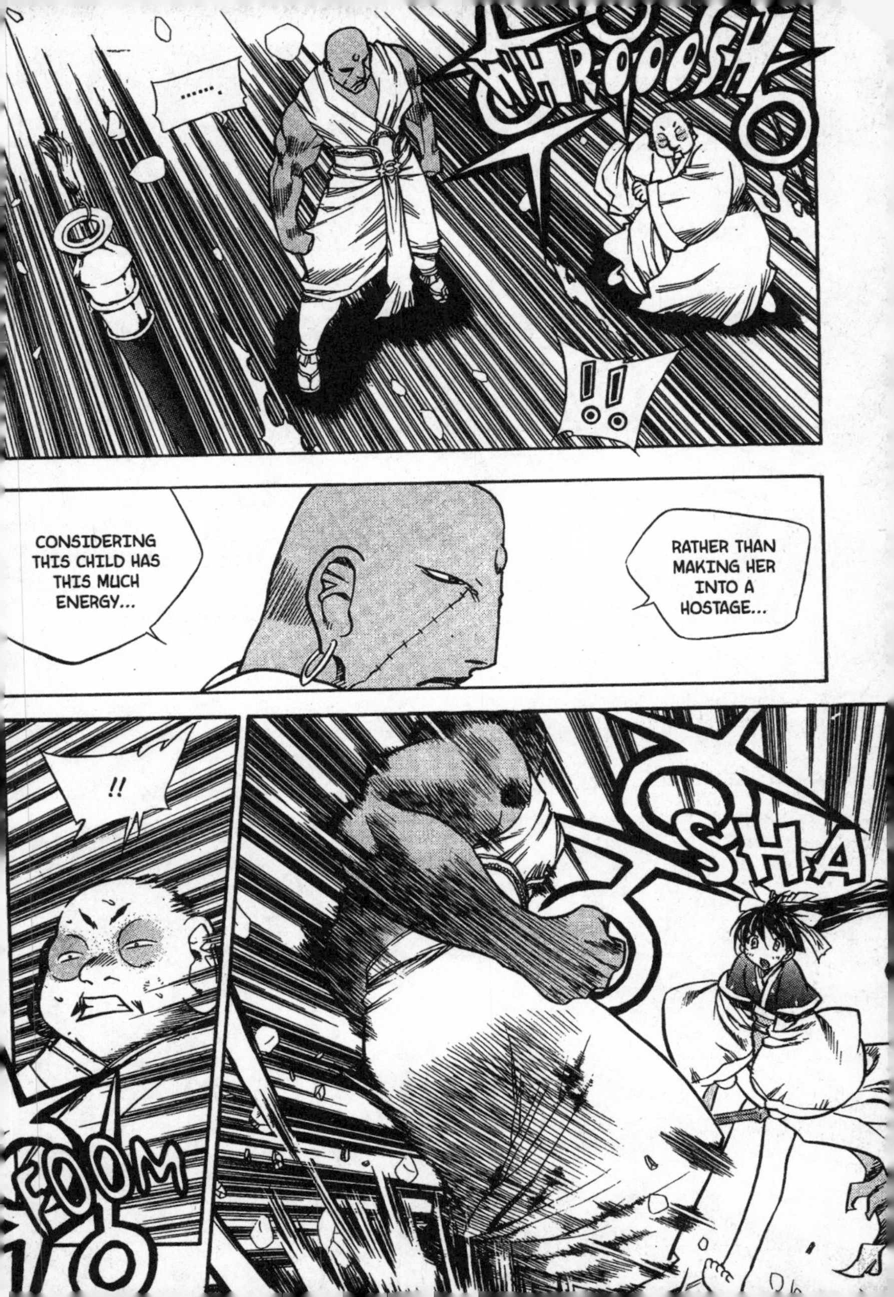
WHROOOSH
.......
!!
RATHER THAN MAKING HER INTO A HOSTAGE...
CONSIDERING THIS CHILD HAS THIS MUCH ENERGY...
SHA
!!
FOOM

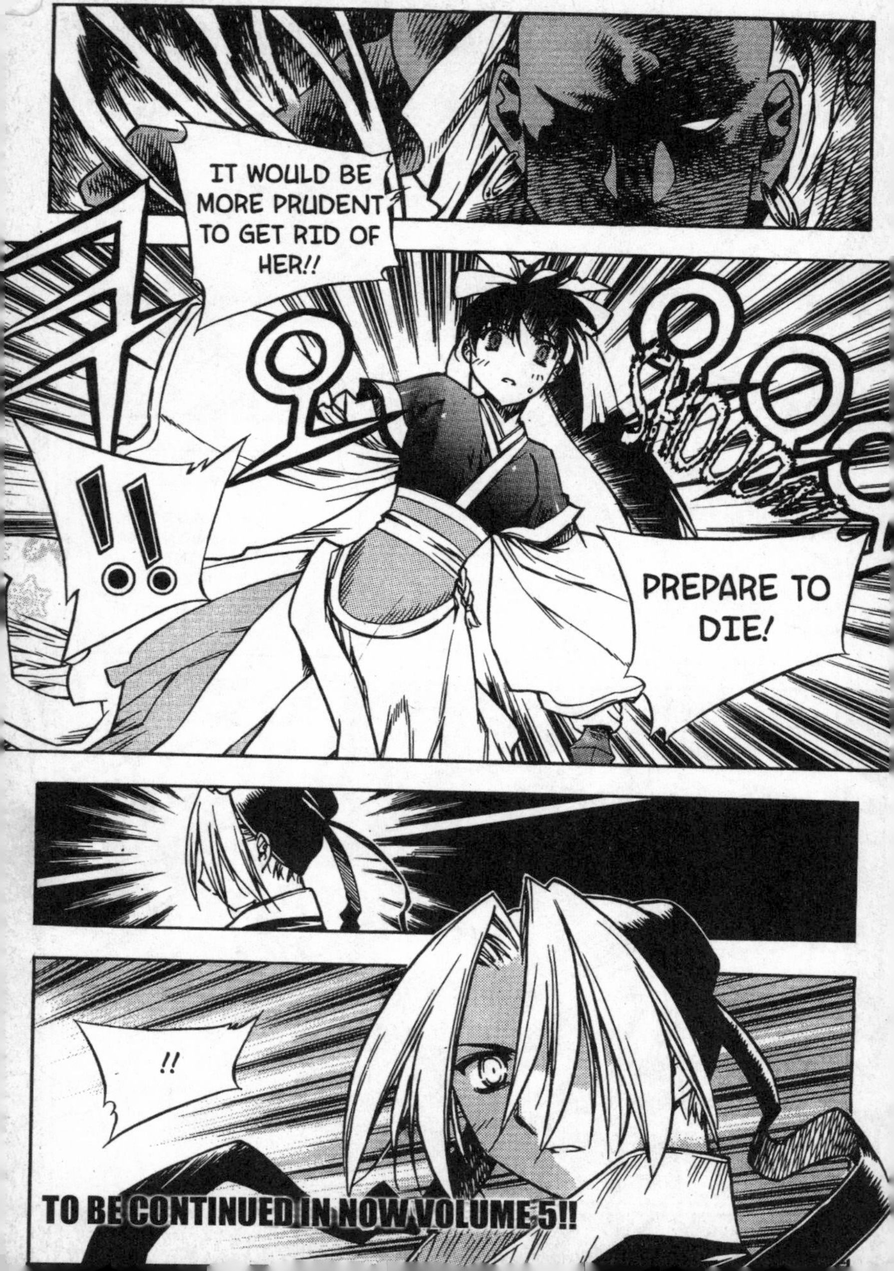

IT WOULD BE MORE PRUDENT TO GET RID OF HER!!
!!
PREPARE TO DIE!
!!
TO BE CONTINUED IN NOW VOLUME 5!!

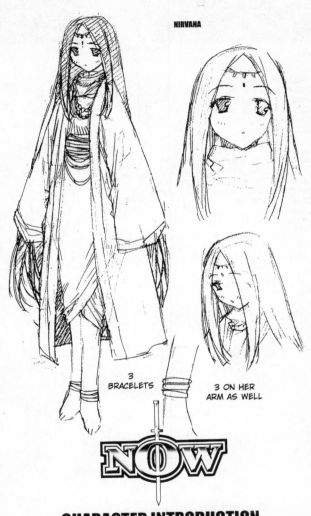

NIRVANA

3
BRACELETS

3 ON HER
ARM AS WELL

# NOW

# CHARACTER INTRODUCTION

CHIEF OF SECURITY FOR THE GODLY
SCHOOL OF TOMORROW'S KING, HE IS
THE BODYGUARD FOR THE HEAD DEFENSE
MINISTER, WHO IS IN TRUTH THE ACTUAL
LEADER OF THE GODLY SCHOOL OF
TOMORROW'S KING.

GANESHA'S RANK IS THAT OF ONE OF THE
DEFENSE MINISTERS OF THE RIGHT (OF
A RELIGION) AND IS ONE OF THE MOST
SKILLED CHARACTERS IN THE STORY. HE
IS A MYSTERIOUS MAN WHO WEARS A
MASK AND WITH THE EXCEPTION OF THE
HEAD DEFENSE MINISTER, NO ONE
KNOWS WHAT HE REALLY LOOKS LIKE.

HE IS THE GODLY SCHOOL OF TOMORROW'S KING'S LAW ENFORCER, RANKING IN POWER RIGHT BELOW THAT OF THE HEAD DEFENSE MINISTER. WHILE HE IS ALREADY CONSIDERED TO BE ONE OF THE STRONGEST, IT IS RUMORED THAT WHEN ARMED WITH HIS GODLY SPEAR NAGA, HIS SKILL IS EQUAL TO THAT OF THE DEFENSE MINISTER.

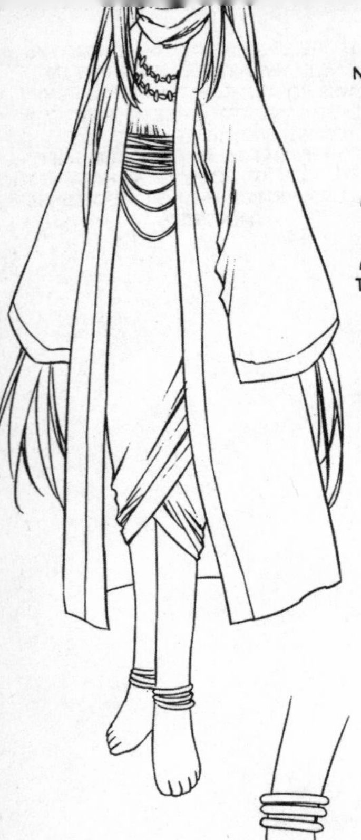

NIRVANA IS ACTUALLY A SAND SCRIPT WORD MEANING HEAVEN. I'VE ALWAYS THOUGHT THE NAME SOUNDED VERY BEAUTIFUL AND NEVER ASSOCIATED IT TO ITS ACTUAL MEANING. WITHOUT THINKING MUCH ABOUT IT, ONCE THIS CHARACTER WAS DRAWN, I HAD ALREADY NAMED HER NIRVANA.

ALTHOUGH NIRVANA ULTIMATELY DOESN'T BECOME ONE OF THE HEROINES OF NOW, SHE WILL PLAY AN IMPORTANT ROLE IN THE STORY. ORIGINALLY, NIRVANA'S ROLE WAS TO BE THAT OF AN EVIL CHARACTER. HOWEVER, I FELT THAT THAT WOULDN'T FIT THE IMAGE OF A SO NYUN MANHWA (SO NYUN MANHWA = SHON-EN MANGA \ COMICS FOR YOUNG BOYS) AS IT WOULD MEAN THE INCLUSION OF UNNECESSARY ADULT THEMES, HENCE I DECIDED TO DEPICT HER AS A SIMPLE CHARACTER INSTEAD.

BUT STILL, SHE WILL BEAR GREAT IMPORTANCE IN WHY THE TITLE OF THIS SERIES IS CALLED NOW, HENCE ALTHOUGH SHE MAY NOT BE ONE OF THE MAIN PROTAGONISTS, HER IMPORTANCE WILL BE REVEALED.

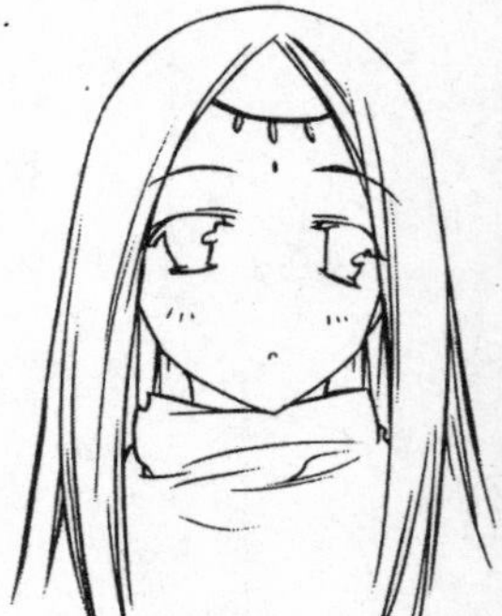

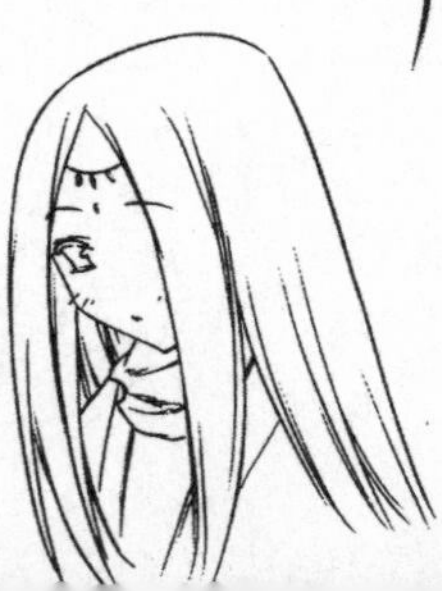

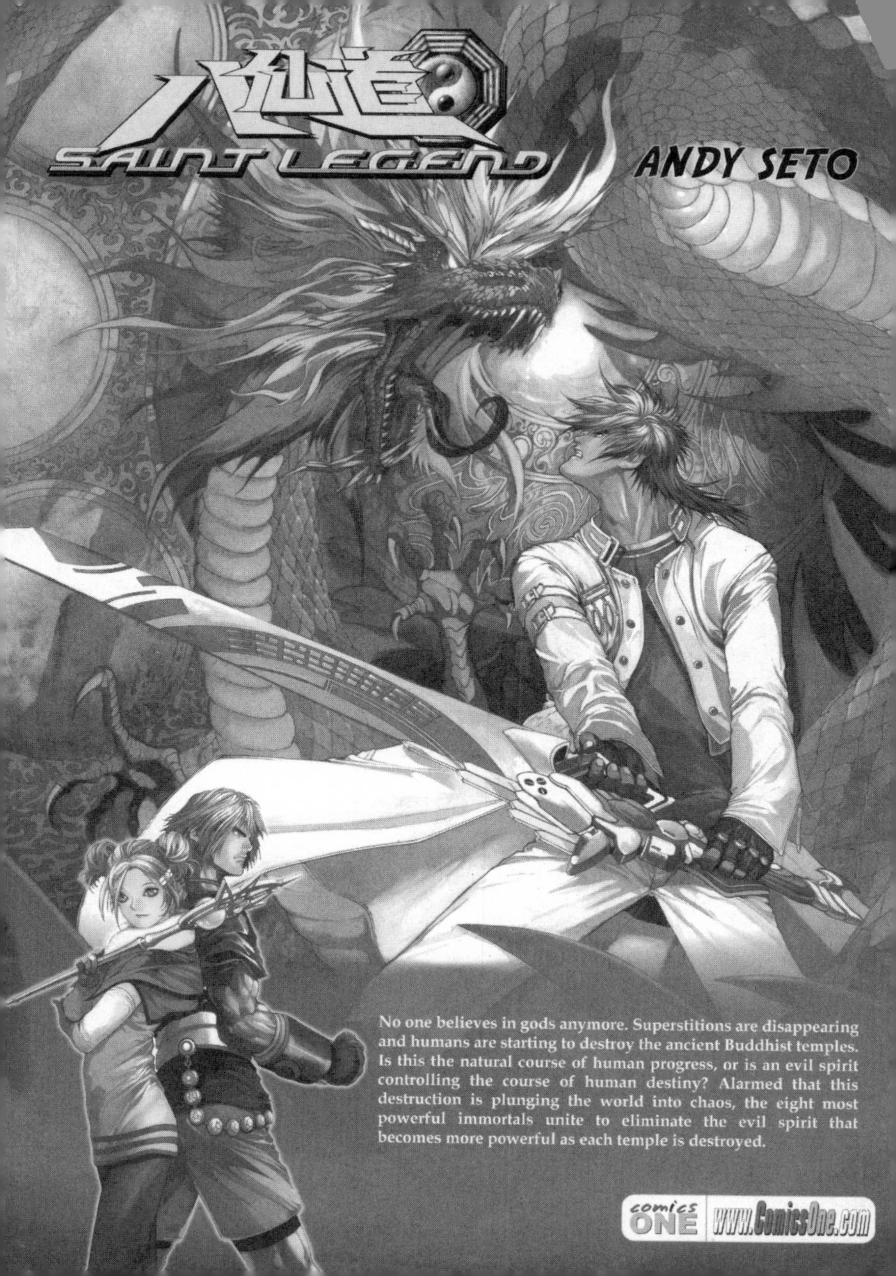
SAINT LEGEND
ANDY SETO
No one believes in gods anymore. Superstitions are disappearing and humans are starting to destroy the ancient Buddhist temples. Is this the natural course of human progress, or is an evil spirit controlling the course of human destiny? Alarmed that this destruction is plunging the world into chaos, the eight most powerful immortals unite to eliminate the evil spirit that becomes more powerful as each temple is destroyed.
comics ONE
www.ComicsOne.com